The Imperial Trace

The Imperial Trace

Recent Russian Cinema

NANCY CONDEE

OXFORD
UNIVERSITY PRESS
2009

OXFORD
UNIVERSITY PRESS

Oxford University Press, Inc., publishes works that further
Oxford University's objective of excellence
in research, scholarship, and education.

Oxford   New York
Auckland   Cape Town   Dar es Salaam   Hong Kong   Karachi
Kuala Lumpur   Madrid   Melbourne   Mexico City   Nairobi
New Delhi   Shanghai   Taipei   Toronto

With offices in
Argentina   Austria   Brazil   Chile   Czech Republic   France   Greece
Guatemala   Hungary   Italy   Japan   Poland   Portugal   Singapore
South Korea   Switzerland   Thailand   Turkey   Ukraine   Vietnam

Published by Oxford University Press, Inc.
198 Madison Avenue, New York, New York 10016

www.oup.com

Oxford is a registered trademark of Oxford University Press

Library of Congress Cataloging-in-Publication Data
Condee, Nancy.
Imperial trace : recent Russian cinema / Nancy Condee.
   p. cm.
Includes bibliographical references and index.
ISBN 978-0-19-536676-1; 978-0-19-536696-9 (pbk.)
1. Motion pictures—Russia (Federation)—History.
I. Title.
PN1993.5.R9C66 2009
791.430947'09049—dc22   2008029349

9 8 7 6 5 4 3 2 1

Printed in the United States of America
on acid-free paper

Acknowledgments

Grateful acknowledgment is due, first of all, to my home institution, the University of Pittsburgh, where the Dean's Office of the School of Arts and Sciences, the Department of Slavic Languages and Literatures, the University Center for International Studies, and the Russian and East European Studies Center are the primary units to which I am indebted for support and leave time. I would like to thank the Richard D. and Mary Jane Edwards Endowed Publication Fund for indexing support. The British Academy generously provided a visiting fellowship, sponsored by Carol Leonard, to St. Antony's College, Oxford University, during a critical stage of the manuscript. I would also like to acknowledge the National Council for Eurasian and East European Research, and Bob Huber in particular, for an introduction to the kind of broadly interdisciplinary work that developed my interest in this topic. The professional and material support, goodwill, and logistical help provided by Kinotavr (Open Russian Film Festival), in particular Mark Rudinstein, Igor' Tolstunov, Aleksandr Rodnianskii, and Sitora Alieva, were invaluable over many years in providing a working atmosphere without which this research would not have been conducted.

This volume has benefited from colleagues' responses when portions were presented at Birkbeck College (School of Advanced Studies, London University Screen Studies), Cambridge University (Trinity College), Columbia University (Harriman Institute, Center for Comparative Literature and Society), the Melbourne Conferences (University College, University of Melbourne), New York University (La Pietra), Oxford University (Magdalen College, Wolfson College), University College London (School of Slavonic and East European Studies), University of Manchester (Russian, East European, and Eurasian Studies Center), University of Nottingham (School of Modern Languages), and Yale University (Slavic Department and the University Council on European Studies).

I would like to thank in particular several of the scholars, colleagues, and friends who have read portions of the manuscript, offering counterarguments on issues about which we have disagreed. They include Peter Barta, Mark Beissinger, Birgit Beumers, Paul Bove, Joe Camp, Bill Chase, Ian Christie, Katerina Clark, Evgeny Dobrenko, Dan Field, Mario Fischetti, Ilya Goldin, Julian Graffy, Seth Graham, Jonathan Harris, Stephen Hutchings, Marcia Landy, Alena Ledeneva, all the Levines, Colin MacCabe, Alexander Motyl, Catherine Nepomnyashchy, Petre Petrov, Ilya Prizel, Greta Slobin, Terry Smith, Oleg Sul'kin, Ronald Suny, and Elayne Tobin. Among the many Russian scholars, critics, and friends who have argued with me about the ideas presented here are Liubov' Arkus, Petr Bagrov, Dmitrii Eliashev, Pavel Kuznetsov, Evgenii Margolit, Andrei and Elena Plakhov, Dmitrii Prigov, Dmitrii Savel'ev, Irina Shilova, Aleksandr Shpagin, Natal'ia Sirivlia, Elena Stishova, Vladimir Strukov, Diliara Tasbulatova, Mikhail Trofimenkov, and Neia Zorkaia. My greatest thanks for their patience, humor, and resources (in every sense) go to Vladimir Padunov, Kira, and Nikolai.

Contents

The Imperial Trace

Introduction: Custodian of the Empire

Britain had an empire, but Russia was an empire.
— Geoffrey Hosking, "The Freudian Frontier," 1995

Russian democrats destroyed the "empire"—that is, their own country.
— Aleksandr Tsipko, *Nezavisimaia gazeta,*
January 31, 1995

In this volume I anchor my argument in two overlapping fields. First, I investigate the core concerns of six major Russian directors who weathered the collapse of the USSR—and with it, the collapse of their own industry—yet managed to work from the early 1990s onward under very different professional and artistic conditions. Nikita Mikhalkov, Kira Muratova, Vadim Abdrashitov, Aleksandr Sokurov, Aleksei German, and Aleksei Balabanov are arguably Russia's lead filmmakers. Of these six, Mikhalkov and Balabanov are best known for their commercial cinema. Muratova, Abdrashitov, Sokurov, and German are widely considered the country's key art house directors, however much they have at times resisted that designation. They span a quarter-century, from Muratova's birth in 1934 to Balabanov's birth in 1959, and more than forty years of film production, from 1967 to the present.

Occupying a central place in recent Russo-Soviet film, these six directors represent a critical cultural continuum from the late Soviet to the post-Soviet years. To the extent that I am interested in capturing the directors' individual cinematic preoccupations, I do not attempt to move beyond that task to promote some unifying thesis about the state of Russian cinema today. The six directors are too diverse, sui generis not only as individual filmmakers, but also according to other markers of difference: where they studied and with whom, their generational experience, the industry demands of commercial versus auteur cinema, their political loyalties or disloyalties, and so forth. It would be difficult to argue that, individually or as a group, they are representative of some larger set: from script to postproduction, the industry conditions in which they work are highly differentiated from one another. And so, although I offer some comparisons throughout the volume (in particular in the postscript), I am not convinced that much can be gained from an ambitious effort at what I contend would be an artificial totality for its own sake. If this book succeeds in providing six individual portraits of Russia's leading directors, it will have fulfilled half its task.

The second field is the larger and more speculative issue of Russia's cultural environment and its distinct difference from the national cultures of Western Europe. It is to this second field that the weight of this long introduction is devoted so as to frame the specific theoretical issues I pursue in the directors' individual work. The research question that underlies this volume has to do with how the six directors, whatever else their concerns may be, variously figure Russia as a cultural space, and the ways their filmmaking practices, in production as well as content, articulate distinct historical patterns that we have not yet adequately explored.

If, as Hosking suggests in the epigraph, Russia was an empire, how is that relationship figured in cinema? How does the condition of being an empire (or the condition of its dismantling, as Tsipko suggests) circulate in the work of these directors? I again do not see this second task as equatable with a summary of Russian cinema today. Quite the opposite: a summary account would tie up loose ends, providing a more coherent picture of a discrete cultural field; the effort here is instead to initiate a line of inquiry, potentially cutting across all cultural fields, but left intentionally open-ended, to ask a set of research questions for which only conjectural responses at best may be attempted.

As the reader may appreciate, I have sought to balance these two tasks. There is much to be said, for example, about Nikita Mikhalkov's work beyond those features that are neatly consistent with a model for a regenerated empire. And in the work of a complex director such as Kira Muratova the ideological trace is laid out in a playful and circumspect modeling system. An easier approach would have been to select only those films with irrefutable mimetic evidence of the empire and then to "discover" its presence. Such an approach is akin to tackling the dog in Chekhov only in order to stumble upon his "Lady with a Lapdog." I am interested instead in a somewhat more fraught and speculative investigation: examining the work of Russia's lead directors as such and, within that portraiture, to ask whether a particular concept of cinema has a place in a larger investigation of their work. Subsuming what I have called the imperial trace to their cinema (rather than the other way around), each chapter functions first as an interpretive frame within which I ask how the work refracts the social and political conditions of the imperial imagination.

In my treatment of that imagination, however, I am not entirely invested in the textual domain. The remainder of this chapter, for example, lays out the social and theoretical groundwork of my argument: how I understand the terms of the debates around empire and nationhood; how I see Russian culture positioned within those debates. Moving on to the specifics of the cinema profession, chapter 2 provides an overview of the Russo-Soviet film industry from the early 1980s to the present and key information on attendance figures, production costs, and certain critical events, such as the May 1986 Fifth Union of Filmmakers Congress and its aftermath. The next six chapters are devoted to examinations of the six filmmakers, followed by a postscript in chapter 9. The portraits of the filmmakers have a common structure: each begins with a brief opening statement, followed by biographical remarks on the director's life and training. The remainder of each chapter is devoted to an elaboration of the issues mapped out in the chapter's opening paragraphs.

Discursive Schizophrenia

The year 1913 marked the three-hundredth anniversary of the Romanov dynasty. Within four years it would be destroyed, together with the dynasty's empire. But unlike much of Europe in the course of the twentieth century, Russia in 1917 did not undergo the transition from empire to nation-state. Instead, it gradually replaced its dynastic empire with a socialist one enduring three-quarters of a century, until 1991. Russia as a postcommunist polity, a project in its infancy, is the most ambitious exception to the transformations throughout Central and Eastern Eurasia, described by one scholar as the "fourth great moment in the history of nationalism" (Hall 3).[1] For Russia the 1990s belonged not so much to the twentieth century as to the twenty-first, marking Russia's emergence as a different polity. In these years after the collapse of the USSR the critical task facing Russia's political leadership was not merely the appropriation of an existing structure, but the forging of a new entity from the remains of Europe's last multinational empire, the third largest empire in human history (Lake 62; Taagepera 117) after the British and Mongol Empires, with a legacy traceable to the 1550s.

The search, therefore, to understand Russian "national identity" in contemporary culture is a project as timely as it is overly assumptive about its research results. A quasi-mythological species, national identity is spotted often as an apparently empirical, inert thing, uniquely available to us now after the fall of communism. It must be allowed, of course, that cultural analysis is a project more of argument than of verifiability, and so the invocation of the national is never without a deeply subjective element. Everywhere unable—like the undead—to afford the luxury of absence, the term loses meaning. In some variants, reminiscent of efforts in the 1920s to produce a proletarian culture, national identity is similarly primordialized, such that it had always potentially existed, awaiting its historical moment. For proletarian culture the historical moment was the arrival of socialism; for national identity, the departure of socialism.

If the positive premises of this volume have to do with the relationship of six leading filmmakers to the complex problematic called Russia, then its single negative premise is this: a discussion on Russian national cinema—and Russian national culture more broadly—might productively revisit its core terms. At stake is less the exceptionalist argument about Russia and its *Sonderweg* than a skeptical return to the originating assumptions of nation and national culture long after much ink has been spilled on that topic. This introduction provides little in the way of a guide to the *general* debates on national cinema as a conceptual category. Instead, I present the problematic usage of the term "Russian nationhood" to mark assumptions we must set aside if we are to address contemporary preoccupations in contemporary culture. Fraught with misapprehensions and internal contradictions, Russia's "national cinema" is a kind of antitopic. Its conditions of impossibility, if integrated into a larger discussion of national cinema, unwrites much of what has been written.

In that regard I have long been struck by the discrepancy between two conflicting knowledge systems concerning Russia, one lodged in cultural theory, the other in political theory. These intellectual communities, engaged in what would appear to be parallel debates about nation and empire, are thrown into productive incompatibility when compared with each other. In mapping out their discrepancies I suggest that the search for national identity as we conduct it in much contemporary, post-Soviet cultural analysis neglects the very terms on which it is constructed. If our colleagues in political theory fear a loss of empirical moorings, we in culture function as if "the national" were an occasion for improvisation.

My particular interest engages such questions as these: What are the limitations associated with "nationhood" as a model for Russian collective identity? How do we situate "the national," in whatever sense and insofar as it exists, as a conceptual category vis-à-vis the category of empire? What relation does the very act of situating bear to other acts that, for shorthand's sake, I will call postcolonial theorizing, the dominant models for which, principally the Anglo-French empires, are ill suited to and resiliently neglectful of the second world, all the more so after the latter's demise in 1991?[2]

Conversation A: Russia, the Robust Nation

Let us assume for the moment that the usual objections to the national are bracketed, objections that might be raised with respect to all fields of contemporary culture from any region: that the category of national is displaced by the global circulation of culture, diffused among diasporic communities, dispersed by hybridity, nomadism, the emerging transnational identity, and so forth. This is not my focus. These diagnostic details are of a different order for the purposes of the discussion here.

By contrast, it is to the viability of the historical category of Russian national cinema that I refer as the first knowledge system, one that is traditionally housed in film studies and, more recently, in cultural studies. In this sense of the term no less a figure than Jean-Luc Godard has placed Russian national cinema in the pantheon of premiere examples. In an extended monologue-interview at the British Film Institute, Godard claims:

> Movie-making at the beginning was related to the identity of the nation and there have been very few "national" cinemas, . . . only a handful: Italian, German, American, and Russian. This is because when countries were inventing and using motion pictures they needed an image of themselves. (Quoted in Petrie 98)

While Slavists can only rejoice that Russia figures among Godard's leading national cinemas, the unreconstructed empiricists among us may yearn for something more evidentiary. For their sake one might well argue that the narrative of Russian national cinema is a long and honorable one, from Vladimir Romashkov's historical drama *Sten'ka Razin* (*Ponizovaia vol'nitsa*; Drankov, 1908) through Eisenstein, Pudovkin, and Dovzhenko to Mikhalkov and Balabanov. It is the story of a robust production, distribution, and exhibition system that at its height in the 1960s and 1970s claimed the highest annual per capita attendance in the world (Menashe 10) at twenty visits a year (Dadamian 76). Comparable figures for the United States in these years were a mere 4.5 visits annually (Christie, "The Cinema" 43). A Soviet hit in the early 1980s could expect 80 million viewers or more; average attendance was 40 million for a steady, consistent production rate of 150 films a year over two decades (Dondurei, "Kinodelo" 127; Schmemann, "Some Soviet Films" 13). All this and more, examined in the following chapter, would seem to underscore Godard's recognition of Russia's cinema. In this knowledge system the national is alive, although it is unclear what the nation is.

Conversation B: Russia, the Absent Nation

When we turn to other knowledge systems, however, things go awry. In the realm of political theory, "nation" for Russia turns out to be a highly elusive phenomenon: historically fragile, vulnerable to mutation, slow to emerge—if indeed it has emerged at all—from the imperial legacy, traditionally dating from Ivan IV's conquest of Kazan' in the 1550s, the moment when ethnically, linguistically, and religiously distinct peoples fell under the sway of the Muscovite ruler. Here, in this knowledge realm, Russia learns to be an empire long before it learns to be a nation, if, once again, it is ever a nation that Russia strives to be. In this knowledge system Russia is often characterized as a powerful and overbearing state but a "weak, and even uncertain, national identity" (Hosking, *Empire and Nation* 9; see also Lieven, *Empire* 384; Pipes, "Introduction" 1–2; Prizel 2; Szporluk, "The Russian Question" 67).

Scholars disagree as to whether instances of the empire's weak nationhood are largely a function of size (Tolz, "Conflicting" 267) or sequence ("timing," as Parrott [10] would have it) or its status as overland empire, wherein the blurred boundaries between core and periphery affect the development of a distinct national identification. Still others would look to autocracy (and its heir, democratic centralism) in impeding autonomous, horizontal linkages that both imagined and physically constructed the loyalties of nationhood. These enduring features of Russia are, of course, neither unique, nor adequate in themselves, nor mutually exclusive explanatory models, but shifts of emphasis among interrelated parts. Size—to seize on the first explanation—is structured by the terms of historical sequence and territorial contiguity. It is beyond debate, however, that Russia's nongovernmental institutional legacy has been discontinuous, a culture with an unpredictable past, quick (at least in the twentieth century) to eradicate traces of documentary and archival evidence, as well as the custodians themselves—historians, memoirists, photographers, museum staff, teachers, librarians, and archivists, as well as writers and journalists—that might constitute autonomous national memory systems.

Karl Deutsch (143, 188) long ago suggested that at the heart of the nation-building process lies mediated communication within a community, itself formed in the process of this mediation. Deutsch's intellectual descendants, most visibly Ernest Gellner and Benedict Anderson, have favored more historically nuanced models that incorporate a range of social institutions into the construction of the imaginative sphere, however much they have disagreed on the relative importance of communicative media. Gellner has emphasized national education systems as a central instrument of consciousness formation; Anderson looks to print language, specifically in the newspaper and the national novel of imaginary, common space, as the vehicle by which both language ("the fatality of human linguistic diversity" [43]) and national experience move toward a more standardized and contained sense of itself.

Gellner and Anderson would agree, however, that nation and nationalism are modern constructs, whether invented or imagined.[3] Deriving from the Latin *nasci*, "to be born," English-language usage of the word in reference to a distinct collectivity can be traced to at least twelfth-century Bologna, and then with more specificity to fourteenth-century Paris, where Jean Charlier de Gerson, a theology student at the University of Paris, was twice (in 1383 and

1384) elected procurator of the other French-born, francophone students (the *nation*). This model of student societies was adopted around the same period at the University of Prague and subsequently (certainly by the mid-seventeenth century) at the Universities of Uppsala and Lund. As modernists Gellner and Anderson would identify the late eighteenth century as a critical moment when "nation" took on a valence very different from its medieval significance: acquiring a different register of meaning, the nation was a congeries with its own sovereign state, distinct from yet interdependent with that state, rendering the state legitimate by a range of practices, such as elections, tax collection, the draft, and the rightful monopoly on violence.[4]

As for nationalism and its relation to nation formation, in contrast to the scholarship of John Armstrong (*Nations before Nationalism*) and Anthony Smith ("The Nation: Real or Imagined?"), Gellner (*Thought and Change* 169) has compellingly argued in a much-quoted phrase that "nationalism is not the awakening of nations to self-consciousness; it invents nations where they do not exist."[5] The burgeoning array of nationalist groups in Russia today might caution us to recall that their existence does not confirm the fulfillment of their party platform in material reality any more than the "dictatorship of the proletariat" did in its era.[6] But whether one attributes the emergence of the nation to the logic of education and the factory, as do Gellner and other scholars of the industrial society school; to print literacy within an imagined community (Anderson 37–45); to the more elite structural contradictions of the society of orders (Greenfeld, *Nationalism*, 189–274; Greenfeld, "Transcending" 49); to a displacement, traceable to the French Revolution, of the subject's loyalty from king to nation (Kohn, *Idea*); or to a range of other causes (Prizel 13), a primary task of the nation emerges in these arguments as the social effort at an autonomously functioning correlation of culture and polity.

The predominance of nationhood as a key source of discourse available for the state's legitimation from roughly the mid-eighteenth century onward strengthens two unacknowledged beliefs: first, that state and nation are necessary, if imperfect, correlates of each other ("Every nation is a state, every state a nation," as Johann Kasparr Bluntschli so compellingly formulated it in his 1866 *Allgemeine Staatslehre*); and second, the belief that, even where this has not been the case (as in Russia), "lagging" institutional development culminates in the inevitable emergence of the nation-state. The nation-state, whether founded on ethnic or civic notions of nationhood, becomes thereby a singularly privileged measure and trajectory of perceived cultural maturity. In fact, as distinct, if interdependent, categories, nation and state have only under certain conditions sustained each other in a complicated effort to occupy analogous boundaries. In the ways that they variously occupy those boundaries lie some of the critical historic differences between nation and state, differences that get erased in the pedagogical frenzy to align them. Lost in any rigid formulation are at least two things: the lush variety of noncorrespondences between collectivity and state and the implications of that historical noncorrespondence for this region. As Ronald Suny ("History" 338) has remarked:

> Flowing from the discourse of the nation is a narrative of human history that claims that the nation is always present, though often concealed, to be realized fully over time in a world of states in which the highest form is a world of nation-states. . . . While in some cases national history is seen as development toward realization, in others it is imagined as decline and degeneration away from proper development. In either case an interpretation of history with a proper trajectory is implied.

To argue, as some scholars have, that the nation-state is the most natural form of organization is not only, in Chaadaevian fashion, to place Russia outside the history of nature; it is also, implicitly, to argue that a hierarchy of nation-states, some more natural than others, might guide the less natural ones in a fashion oddly reminiscent of imperial oversight by the community of nations in which Russia is endlessly enjoined to participate. Two of the most pressing issues here with regard to Russia are, first, the manner in which the congruence of nation with state has historically been resisted ("delayed," as Suny would suggest, presents too narrow an interpretive framework) and, second, the implications of a weak historical articulation of nation—and one that has proceeded almost exclusively through the lens of the empire—for issues around what has been called "national culture" generally and "national cinema" in particular.

It might have seemed at first glance that Anderson's invocation of imagination holds promise for such cultural analysis. And yet in fact his text is productive largely as a cogent articulation of its *inapplicability* to Russian historical congeries. If we were to take up the authority to claim Russia—tsarist, Soviet, post-Soviet—as an imagined community, this imagined community can nowhere consequently confirm Russia's status as nation. Instead, a certain vulnerability in Anderson's argument is revealed, namely his assumption that the category "nation" is the sole available slot for an imagined community after the advent of print capitalism, thereby occluding a potential diversity of description for other collectivities in the modern world, for which "nation" is a less productive concept.

This deployment of "nation" as the default category for collectivity may speak to the impoverishment of our vocabulary for describing modern collectivities in terms *other than* nationhood. The invocation of an imagined community—in all its material, institutional articulations[7]—might, like the contiguous empire itself, in some instances be more ragged around the edges, more vertically structured and more firmly soldered to state institutions than would suit the demands of the modern constructivist concept of nationhood. How would we describe the collective loyalties, anxieties, and fantasies of late tsarist, Soviet, and even post-Soviet identities, subject as they have been to what more than one scholar has described as extreme statism (see, for example, Martin, "Modernization" 175)? If "imagined community" and "nation" are conceived as coterminous and yoked categories they must either be unyoked or else set aside as being of little help in understanding Russia's discursive formations.

If we were to entertain the possibility that Anderson's strong, autonomous, horizontal ties of nationhood might—for Russia, even today—be ephemeral, absent, subject to dispersion, even alien to the social imagination, a more nuanced reading (i.e., one that permits the cultural text to speak back to us with a broader range of possible, available interpretations) might find a displacement of the national in favor of a diversity of strategies more suited to its imperial particularity: a narrative transcoding of its massive expanse as endless peregrination, as seascape,[8] as sacrificial mysticism; a representation of collectivities as a naturalized comity of hierarchy and difference; a compensatory preoccupation with *terra nullius* (the noble idea that inadequately used resources, such as land, might be taken over for proper use); a necessary paranoia at the center; a deferral of egalitarian commonalities in favor of a transcendent, spatialized totality, periodically utopian or apocalyptic; the transformation of imperial desire into millenarian ecstasy or messianic obligation; and myriad other projects that have captured our attention in ways we remain oddly ill equipped to articulate.

And so, for once in our recent intellectual lives, we need not cite Benedict Anderson and his concept of the national as a "deep, horizontal comradeship," an imagined community, limited and sovereign. Even without Anderson we can see a radical misalignment between familiar theorizing on nation—Gellner, Kedourie, Kohn, Hobsbawm, Deutsch—and the imperial structure of Russia, whether we are speaking of the dynastic, the socialist, or the postsocialist empire extending over four and a half centuries. If, as most contemporary theorists of the nation argue, despite their diversity, nation formation is the modern product of labor, engaging efforts of elite and masses, marked since the late eighteenth century by the forging of independent, autonomously functioning horizontal ties, simultaneously consecrating the state and yet operating as a whole, distinct from the state in its own self-confirming practices, then these markers, common to the idea of nation, are poorly compatible with the dynasty's autocracy, socialism's democratic centralism, or Putin's United Russia. Should we care to equivocate on this matter, Stalin (303–4) would gently remind us that "Austria and Russia are stable communities, but nobody calls them nations."

The Austro-Hungarian Empire followed its own history of fragmentation, but Russia as a territorial totality—and here I use "Russia" vernacularly as a catchall term for three states: the Russian Empire, the Soviet Union, and the Russian Federation—resisted nationhood in the Western, terminal sense outlined above, in ways hardly overcome either after 1991 or in the current, second modernity, the post–cold war age of terror.[9] As the largest country in the world, Russia currently stretches across eleven time zones—one-seventh of the world—from one end of just its formal, internal empire to the other, an expanse compounded by sparse population, underdeveloped infrastructure, and persistent material scarcity. Such size has militated against a sustained drive to nation formation, if by this we mean the independent, autonomously functioning horizontal ties of the modern era.[10] As Aleksandr Hertzen ruefully remarked in his "Du développement des idées révolutionnaires en Russie," Russia is "more subject to geographic than to historical authority" (Gertsen 16). "Our spaces," the poet Aleksandr Blok (*Zapisnye* 83) wrote some fifty years later, in the first decade of the new century, "are fated to play an elemental role in our history."[11] Historical attempts at theorizing Russian national identity have been confounded by this mismatch of—at the risk of hyperbole—Russia's hypertrophic empire and relative absence of nationhood.

I should add for clarity's sake that my argument here is *not* that empires cannot be nation-states or cannot sustain distinct national identities. Britain and France, with their developed autonomous institutions, are often cited as cases in point.[12] Rather, for Russia circumstances militated in favor of, on the one hand, a strong centralized state and imperial identity and, on the other—in that space where one might look for the nation to have resided—ethnic and linguistic categories *not* identical to territorial boundaries, *not* identical to each other, and *also not* identical to nation as the constructivist theorists have elaborated that concept.

These two Russias—coarsely put, the Robust Nation of cultural theory and the Absent Nation of political theory—form the puzzle at the heart of this study. Their mutual discrepancy is symptomatic of a kind of discursive schizophrenia, marking a disjuncture in our disciplinary practices. I do not promise a manifestly verifiable resolution of the sort more conservative colleagues in the social sciences would proffer; the categories of empire and nation, as Mark Beissinger ("The Persisting Ambiguity" 180; see also Kappeler, "Ambiguities") and others have argued, remain stubbornly ambiguous, subject to perception and persuasion. Instead, I suggest that a terminological step backward to re-examine the analytic claims of Russian national identity would reveal its isolation from other lines of inquiry that might contribute to a more coherent analysis.

A Limitation of Terms: Empire and Its "Nations"

Like the Habsburg Empire, Russia's empire dates to the mid-sixteenth century. It was built on the ruins of the Mongol empire, which had survived two centuries after Temujin's ascension in 1206, disintegrating in the late fifteenth century. An enormous body of literature exists on the nature of empires, of which research by Michael Doyle and Anthony Pagden plays a recurrent role in scholarly debate. I will not revisit at length the theoretical writings on that expansive topic, other than to summarize a common view of that polity as a composite structure marked by inequality, subordination, and difference, with hierarchically distinct units, such that the metropole is the center through which the peripheries largely negotiate their relations to each other.[13] These hierarchically distinct units may be signaled by a range of markers kept in place to sustain systematic relations of inequality of access and privilege. It is by this definition of empire that Ivan IV's 1552–56 conquest of Kazan' and Astrakhan, rather than Ivan III's suppression of Novgorod or Andrei Bogoliubskii's sacking of Kiev, is traditionally claimed to mark Russia's imperial turn, the moment when ethnically, linguistically, religiously distinct peoples fall under the sway of the Muscovite ruler.[14]

Already in the seventeenth century the world's largest state (Pipes, "Is Russia Still an Enemy?" 68), Russia's critical years of state building between the seventeenth and nineteenth centuries coincided with rapid imperial expansion. In the seventeenth century alone, Muscovy tripled its size; in the next two centuries, by some estimates, it continued to expand at a rate of fifty-five square miles a day (Greenfeld, *Nationalism* 205; Thompson 28). During Russia's second major period of expansion this transformation to empire was explicitly institutionalized in 1721 following the Great Northern War with Peter I's assumption of the title *imperator* and the assignation to Russia of the title *imperiia*.[15] Significantly, Peter's earliest invocations of these terms were addressed to European countries and pertained to newly conquered European lands (Greenfeld, *Nationalism* 195), a gesture of competitive prestige, asserting Russia's "place at the European table" (Thompson 26). Under Catherine II the empire grew to include modern-day Belarus, Lithuania, and much of Polish Ukraine, excluding Galicia; the reign of Aleksandr I saw the additions of Finland and the so-called Congress Kingdom to the west.

It should be added that Russia's imperial model, if we can speak of it in unitary terms, was inconsistent and improvisational in the extreme, even with respect to nearby Slavic cultures. Whereas the Ukrainian metropolitan elite tended to intermingle with the hierarchy of the Russian imperial elite, the Ukrainian rural elite and Belarus local elite more closely resembled what might be described as a French pattern of suppression in favor of the Russian metropole. If the imperial drive in the Far East was marked by the interests of financial and missionary expansion—for shorthand's sake, let us say something resembling a Spanish model—then the imperial pattern in the Baltics, at least prior to the 1917 revolution, was more recognizably British in its appropriation of an already existing German elite. Yet with all these variations the tsarist and Soviet use of Russian language and culture as key tools of state cohesion—and the administrative structure of ethnoterritorial units, paradoxically both constituting the empire and conditioning its eventual nationalist transformations

(Martin, "Affirmative" 67–90; Tuminez 271)—shaped relations of cultural difference along an axis of domination and subordination rather than putative egalitarian, diverse, or integrated access.[16]

Events around the October revolution further reconfigured the empire. While the western and northern regions (Poland, Finland, and the Baltic territories) became sovereign states, regions to the south and southwest (Ukraine, Belarus, and the Caucasian territories) remained within a newly formed USSR. In the years immediately following the revolution and during the early 1920s the nationalist impulses of these territories were understood by the Party as modern, historically conditioned responses to emergent capitalism. And while the Party leadership—Bukharin and Piatakov on the one hand, Lenin and Stalin on the other (Eighth Congress, March 18–23, 1919)—fiercely debated strategic options available to deal with nationalism's threat of a transclass alliance, these debates took for granted the modern and constructed quality of nationalist sentiment. However, partly as an unintended outcome of the bureaucratic need unambiguously to ascribe, record, classify, and archive the (now) "immutable" categories of ethnic difference, and with the introduction of internal passports in 1932, and certainly by the mid-1930s, the constructed and modern quality of ethnicity gave way to a newly primordialized concept, "depoliticized by an ostentatious demonstration of respect for the national identities of all Soviet citizens" (Martin, "Modernization" 167) and distinct from the all-union culture of the socialist state.[17]

Although some readers might object that the Soviet Union cannot be considered an empire because its leaders never declared it to be such, they might bear in mind Lieven's (*Empire* 6) salutary, caustic assessment of the criterion of self-identification:

> The laziest approach to the concept of empire is simply to accept a state's right to call itself whatever it chooses. Bokassa's polity was an empire because he chose to call it one. The Soviet Union was not an empire because its rulers vigorously rejected the term. This approach will not yield many rewards.[18]

The traditional resistance to the notion that a socialist state may itself also be an imperial structure—resistance that had grounded itself in such texts as Lenin's *Imperialism: The Highest Stage of Capitalism* and Rosa Luxemburg's *The Accumulation of Capital*—neglects or excludes the many ways Lenin's own inheritance of the tsarist, dynastic empire preserved or, more often, reinvented key structural and relational features, even as it adopted a stance of implacable opposition to imperial rule. This contradiction became more pronounced as Stalin's increasingly imperial bent required an extensive recasting of the anti-imperial rhetoric of the 1920s so as to accommodate the ambitions of the socialist empire, rescripting Russia's imperial past as a historically progressive phenomenon.[19] By the 1930s and 1940s an entrenched system of differentiated access to goods and services was intricately structured through a range of operators, most evidently the ascription of social class, or *soslovie:*[20] the denial of passports to peasants and the restriction of access to closed shops, scarce goods and services, and summer homes to identified specialists (leading scientists, cultural figures, athletes, military personnel). The final major period of Soviet expansion, during and immediately after World War II, saw the annexation of the Baltic states and eastern Poland to the Soviet Union proper and the extension of Soviet political influence over the countries of Central and Eastern Europe.

Across cultural fields, a performance of symbolic ethnicity, simultaneously permitted and mandatory, nourished in the Soviet but non-Russian ethnoterritorial units and allowing a local and limited autonomy under the sign of the imperial center, did not contradict but rather held in place a political system that structured the so-called national in a sense very different from its more familiar Western usage: the national as a subcategory within an imperial universe rather than as a terminal category, the first element in a hyphenated, Western model of the terminal and independent nation-state.[21] If this is so, we can provisionally note a working distinction between two concepts of nation. The first is the terminal nation, which strives for an isomorphic replication of sovereign state boundaries. The second, more central to this argument, is the subterminal nation, which might be traced from the Austro-Hungarian example and the revolutionary debates with Otto Bauer. The discourse of nationhood is perpetually caught between these two ideas of nation: the first nation, a set unto itself; the second nation, a subset of a larger, "supranational" (in this second sense) polity. On the one hand the terminal community strives for an ideal correspondence to the state's terminal boundaries; on the other hand, as in the Soviet instance, an ethnoterritorial unit figures the so-called national as an ethnoterritorial unit *within* the imperial.[22]

Because of the recurrent potential for confusion—not to mention the concept's historical contingency as certain ethnoterritories emerged in the 1990s as nation-states—I avoid the translation of *national'nost'* as "nationality," preferring instead "ethnicity."[23] Although this choice by no means resolves all the methodological questions, it signals an effort to hold in place a working distinction between the two concepts of nation.

It is likewise useful in the negotiation of these categories to acknowledge Doyle's distinction between the inner empire—here, the fifteen Soviet republics—and the outer empire of Eastern Europe, not only in the immediate sense of geographic proximity and the degree of political control, but also in the greater determinacy of the inner empire in Russia's identity formation.[24] Social relations linking the inner, formal empire with the center tended to be more coercive, constraining the USSR's periphery and mediating relations through the center.

The distinction between "inner" and "outer" has been subject to debate (for example, Rosecrance 53–55; T. Smith 69–84), and recent research has productively argued that the internal Soviet periphery harnessed and redefined metropolitan command to suit local interests (Martin, Suny, and others). Still, the distinction is of heuristic value both retrospectively—bracketing off Eastern Europe from the rapidly obsolescing Soviet state for the purposes of discussion here—and prospectively, anticipating the ways by which the newly emergent states of the former Soviet Union themselves subsequently sought to reconfigure their relation to post-Soviet Russia.[25]

Two Russias: The Imperial and Demotic Identities

Russian was of course the dominant ethnicity and state language of the Soviet empire. Its federation was the largest of the Union; its capital's clock was the country's state time. Beyond this, however, Soviet Russian culture experienced a curious alternation between disenfranchisement and hyperenfranchisement, inconsistently permitting its own republican institutions, depending on the historical moment and the politics of the culture industry under question.[26] A Russian Soviet Federative Socialist Republic (RSFSR) branch of the Writers' Union was permitted in the late 1950s for a specific set of political reasons;[27] an RSFSR Cinematographers' Union or RSFSR Academy of Sciences, however, was not. Similarly, the Russian Federation had no Russian Communist Party, no Russian TASS, radio or television programming, no Russian KGB or MVD (Ministry of Internal Affairs).[28] As Gellner ("Return" 4–13) and Graham Smith (48) have extensively mapped out, Russian pride was thoroughly, if inconsistently, imbricated across Soviet pride as constitutive of its superpower consciousness. "Russian" both did and did not, depending on administrative exigencies, stand in for "Soviet," allowing for strategic and highly contingent conflations of ethnicity and empire, geography and politics. Nor was this metonymic quality of "Russia" a modern phenomenon, necessarily linked to its substitution for "Soviet"; as Hosking (*Empire* 6) has argued, "Russians identified with their empire to a greater extent than any other European people."

From the mid-1960s on, distinct features of Russian culture exhibited a slow but marked process of attempting to disengage from the empire. This tendency was first evident in the literary work of the Village Prose writers, who produced the first "totally nativist intellectual body" of writings in Russia's thousand-year history (Prizel 194). The prose of such authors as Fedor Abramov, Vasilii Belov, and Valentin Rasputin sketched out a third alternative to the Soviet contradictory solution of Russia's disenfranchisement and hyperenfranchisement. The increased official russocentrism (as distinct from "russification") of the Stagnation period transformed these relative outsiders into respectable, conservative insiders to the project of state-sponsored official *narodnost'*.[29] Here, as periodically in the history of Russian culture, it was precisely the *conservative* cultural forces that precipitated reform, changes that are paradoxically led by the palladium of conservatism.[30]

By early 1990 the idea of Russia's independent status was already an explicit issue of debate in the wake of vigorous independence movements that had spread beyond the Baltic to the Caucasus (1987–88) and Ukraine (1989). The state's historical policy, perceived as "active subjugation and passive neglect" (Tuminez 31), led to claims of russophobia by major cultural figures such as the Village Prose writers Belov and Rasputin.[31] Their voices lent credibility to the notion that an independent Russia was as viable a political entity as an independent Latvia or Ukraine. The implicit logic of Mikhail Gorbachev's June 23, 1990, televised praise of the "unifying role that [the peoples of Russia] played in the formation of our enormous, multinational state" (*USSR Today*, June 24, 1990) had already become a double-edged sword for the leader of this Soviet polity. Unlike Latvia's or Ukraine's political sovereignty, however, Russia's potential sovereignty did not automatically imply its sovereignty as a nation-state.

Russia's double life, as many scholars have elaborated at length, is figured in the linguistic distinction between two Russian words for "Russian," *rossiiskii* and *russkii*, a linguistic fact that became of greater significance as the idea of sovereignty gained viability. As *rossiiskii*, Russia had been not a nation-state but a term that, among other things, gestured at the imperial state. As *russkii*, it had been not a nation-state but a dominant ethnicity—a default category and privileged metonym for the whole, at times a strategically ill-defined substitute for the imperial polity. Manifesting a weakly developed sense of independent cohesion except in times of state crisis—1613, 1812, 1941–45, when, as Hosking (*Empire* 9) has argued, a temporary and strategic cohesion, unsustainable across its geographic expanse, was evident—"Russia" has occupied a space between empire and ethnicity, the place where nation does not cohere.

The gulf between the educated, Europeanized, and largely urban elite and the rural, uneducated or illiterate, largely non-Europeanized masses has been remarked upon from at least the Slavophiles forward. It receives its most serious cultural elaboration in Michael Cherniavsky's *Tsar and People* (51), which traces this gulf from the reign of Ivan IV, an age of transition in which the early tradition of prince and saint was modified by the new conception of the state. Russia's emergent identity concerned two distinct projects, not determinate of each other but rigorously indivisible. Cast as an opposition of city to country, of educated to uneducated, of Westernized to less Westernized, Russia's dyadic identity was inconsistently these, though none is a sufficient axis.

The first identity project emerges as an effort by the elites to forge a set of lateral ties intended, in Hosking's (*Empire* 8) terminology, to "command the mechanism of the state" through civil bureaucracy, economic patronage, and other means. It largely failed to integrate the masses in any sustained, autonomous institutional forum, whether because of hypertrophy, absence of autonomous institutions, intense dynastic and state loyalties of the elites, or competing identifications of those same elites with their counterparts in Western Europe. Western culture, education and private tutors, and elite language, fashion, customs, manners, and norms confirmed a sense of belonging disconnected from a local, intimate knowledge of life in the backwater that constituted much of Russia's territory. This first project, what Hosking calls an imperial identity, further codified in the Table of Ranks, extended downward only to the professional classes. Its relation to Russia's masses, however, remained haphazard, fragmented, at least as textual as it was institutional, and imbued with a kind of strategically deployed millennialism that relied for its intense allure and credibility on the *absence* of autonomous, mediating administrative systems.

The second project, for which Western education, language, culture, and travel had little relevance, is the demotic identity. Rarely at odds with the imperial, rarely aligned with it except in times of crisis, the demos construed the empire's ragged borders as a wholly different realm. For the first, elite project they are ragged because of the strong international identification across state boundaries; for the demotic identity they are ragged because territorial boundaries are of less urgency than localized concerns.[32]

Hosking (*Empire* 9) finds evidence of this deep division in the coexistence of two fixed epithets for Russia, *Rossiiskaia Imperiia* (Russian Empire) and *Sviataia Rus'* (Holy Rus'), linguistic testimony to the coexistence of an imperial and an ethnic Russianness: "To talk of *Russkaia Imperiia* would be impossible; only *Rossiiskaia Imperiia* is permissible usage. On the other hand *Sviataia Rossiia* . . . would be equally unthinkable; only *Sviataia Rus'* is possible." Rejecting the two traditional explanatory models—the Mongol period as the superimposition of a pernicious autocracy, and Peter I's rule, which only deepened an existing split—Hosking returns to Ivan IV's rule as the originating moment.

This demotic identity finds its most evident expression in the notion of Holy Rus', whose desired relation to the "pious and gentle Tsar" (the title later rejected by Peter I in favor of emperor) is as the holy land to the sacred ruler. It is a model not easily adapted to the modern state, the loyalties of which are abstract, depersonalized, and no longer even necessarily dynastic. The breakdown in this covenant between the distant, demotic congeries and its gentle tsar is only one of the traumas militating against the constitution of a national collectivity. The imperial identity, by contrast, formed its relation to the demos at best through textual celebration and at worst through neglect and the waging of war, in collusion with the state, through state-engineered famine, purges, agricultural devastation, deportation, and exile. But as for nationhood, Hosking (*Empire* 9) cautions, "the Russian nation has never been able to develop to the full its own political, economic or cultural institutions, since these have been distorted or emasculated for the needs of the empire."

Support for the notion that contemporary Russia has retained cultural practices shot through with imperial citation may be evident not only with reference to its secular coordinates, but also with respect to its spiritual ones, principally the Russian Orthodox Church as institution. One might reasonably anticipate that this autocephalous body, in contrast to Catholic universalism, might serve as a kind of talisman of local, ethnic, even national particularity, arguably since the eleventh-century appointment of Ilarion as Russian metropolitan to the Kievan see. Here, however, a curious paradox obtains, because for all its apparent availability as a potential resource for a primordialist retrohistory strengthening the "national," whatever that would mean, Russian Orthodoxy has historically been just the opposite: an imperial structure of the first order, prone to misidentification and misassignment precisely because it underwent the same set of conceptual conflations to which other, centuries-old imperialized projects had been subjected in Russian history. An "empire-saving institution" (Dunlop, *The Rise of Russia* 158),[33] the Orthodox Church was able to broker a common ground between the imperialism of a conservative precommunist past and the imperialism of its communist successor, a "natural ally of the CPSU in the struggle for moral values," in the words of Russian communist leader Ivan Polozkov in 1990 (quoted in Dunlop, *The Rise of Russia* 158). The Church's post-Soviet elevation draws on a compelling set of imperial identifications, which it had long deployed for conversion in both a spiritual and a political sense. The Russian Orthodox Church remains an autocephalous church, but its autocephaly is that of the empire. As Patriarch Aleksei II cautioned in 1991, "The Orthodox Church, although it is called Russian, is multinational, because Orthodoxy exists both in Ukraine, and in Belorussia, and in Moldavia, and in the Baltic."[34]

Ilya Prizel has cogently argued the evidence of imperial investments of the Russian Orthodox Church, pointing to its alliances with right-wing and, to a lesser extent, communist forces so as to reduce the likelihood of fracturing the power structure of the Church and thereby inadvertently triggering other autocephalous movements associated with nationalist stirrings. Although communism and nationalism (the latter sometimes functioning as a pseudonym for precommunist imperial nostalgia) were historically opposed to one another, the key, common element of this peculiar alliance is the experience of the empire. The Church became an invaluable repository for an etiolated imperial grandeur, a virtual empire of signs that had ceased to function quite so unequivocally in military, economic, and political affairs.

The paradox, of course, is that the gulf between the metropolitan elites and the demotic periphery was unbridgeable except as state practices associated in the West with nation building, the most effective unifying mythologies of which underscored the imperial past: war at the imperial periphery, the Orthodox Church as an imperial institution, and Mongol imperial rule, whose destruction both marked the emergence of the Russian Empire and provided some of the cultural categories for its structure. These mythologies at the same time strengthened Russia's claim to exceptionalist status vis-à-vis Western Europe around its most vexing question from Chaadaev onward: How does Russia participate in the family of nations? Its solution, wherein nationhood is largely a site of *internal* differentiation (as the subterminal "nation") under the larger imperial rubric, left the Russian Empire in a position of supranationalism and prenationalism, the latter a variant of delayed grandiosity and exceptionalist deferral that has accompanied it since its early state relations with Byzantium. Unlike those societies in which a range of independent legal parties, religious denominations, or civic activists vie for power over and a claim to the narration of public conscience, Russia's culture—including its technology of textual production, the texts themselves, their guardians, and consumers—has historically served in their stead as historian and augur, cartulary and politician.

Sequence, Duration, Contiguity

Russia's eventual emergence in December 1991 was marked from the outset by contradictions that confound much familiar theorizing on both empire and nation-state. These contradictions are organized around three core features of Russia's history: the sequence of a strong imperial identity long predating the age of nations, the duration of the empire for four and a half centuries, and the contiguity of Russia's territories as an overland empire with closer resemblance to the Ottoman and Habsburg Empires than to more familiar examples of maritime empires on which much of the literature is based.

Sequence

With respect to Russia's political history, "empire" and "state" have long been connate categories. The work of empire building and state building shared a number of features: the monopoly on legalized violence, the establishment and maintenance of a civil bureaucracy, a permanent military, some legislative functions, the allocation of resources, goods, and services, and the rationalization of revenues. Thus it is a deeply interpretive move to argue which of these two processes was at work at a given historical moment. The imperial structure in Russia preserved features distinguishing it from the modern state, among them a strategic fluidity of territorial boundaries and an explicit concern for the culling of resources for a ruling elite rather than for the fulfillment of articulated national aspirations and common well-being. As one scholar has remarked with some panache, there was "no other region of the world in which empire-building and state-building have been subject to such ambivalence" (Beissinger, "The Persisting Ambiguity" 180; see also Suny, "Ambiguous Categories").

As Doyle has discussed at length, the European empires, weathering the dual onslaught of nationalism and democracy, found themselves yielding to elements of the nation-state model in ways that came to blur many of the distinctions between empire and nation-state. Increased territorial fixity, enhanced social mobility and access, and the state invocation of citizenship confirm the productive distinction between the traditional and modern empires, however much the latter category still maintains a nonintegrated set of cultures within its strategy of state building. Russia too was not immune to this shift, and it is with reference to this narrower legacy of the modern, formal empire—one that evidences the benchmarks of modernity (urbanization, secularization, industrialization, universal education, etc.) without necessarily bearing the marks of nationhood—that a discussion of the Russian cultural imagining finds its focus in this study.

The relevance of these ambiguities—between empire building and state building, between the traditional and modern empires—pertains with less urgency to the tsarist or socialist empires than to the period under discussion here, the moment when Russia finds itself in its third imperial collapse (1613, 1917, 1991) and the increasing kinship resemblance of the new Russia to its imperial forebears. "Unlike empires of modern times that fell while their former metropoles were gradually being transformed into 'normal' nations and nation-states," Szporluk ("The Russian Question" 65) has argued, "the tsarist—and then the Soviet—empire fell apart before a modern Russian nation and a Russian nation-state had emerged." It is hardly surprising, therefore, that at every turn as Russia renegotiates its relations with the "near abroad" of newly emergent nation-states—its former inner empire—its efforts to play a determining role as a regional leader are subject to wildly differing interpretations by regional neighbors. What for the Russian leadership evinces regional leadership is, for the new nation-states of the former empire, further evidence of neo-imperial ambitions.

Scholars may disagree (see Beissinger, "The Persisting Ambiguity" 163; Solchanyk 339) concerning whether this conflict is, in essence, a Russian identity crisis or a regional one.[35] To the extent that it is a crisis of *relations*, and only secondarily a crisis of identity, it is doubtful that Russia alone can resolve this issue. The sequence of the empire existing centuries before (and intimately entwined with) any nationalist advocacy is, if not wholly, then strongly determinative of the way Russia's efforts at forceful and effective state building must provoke its neighboring polities and its own domestic constituencies to interpret these moves as the coercive resurgence of neocolonial ambitions.

Duration

A second key feature pertaining to Russia's contradictory status concerns the duration of the imperial structure far longer than its Western cohort—indeed, one might argue, to the present day. In a European framework, where the logic of the nation-state had become naturalized to the point of invisibility, the maintenance of a large, multinational empire with dissimilar units having unequal access to the center's power and resources became increasingly identified as an archaic, malfunctioning polity, however ill-coordinated that perception was to issues of communism and the Soviet state. Indeed, for the duration of the cold war, and in particular the early 1980s, Soviet society as an instance of outmoded, mechanical failure was scripted into a compelling narrative about the ideological ills of communism rather than about the imperial polity's structural vulnerability, overweening land surplus, or increasingly unmanageable relations of access between center and periphery, distinct from the cold war agenda.

The most influential body of Western writing on the Soviet Union in this respect was, of course, totalitarian theorizing, the structures of which continued to shape Western thinking long after its critics, already in the 1960s, had begun to dismantle its core assumptions. Those assumptions, which cluster Russia with the other totalitarian experiments of Germany (1933–45) and Italy (1922–43), ignored the fact that the Soviet experiment demonstrated greater duration and flexibility than its "fellow experiments." In fact, Russia had a protean capacity for survival much greater than totalitarian theory itself.[36] The increasing inapplicability of the model both for intrinsic reasons—an underdeveloped theory of change, for instance—and for external shifts in Thaw and post-Thaw political culture (see Cohen; Gleason; G. Smith 21–22) led to a search for a wide variety of other, more dynamic systems of thought, such as Cook's social contract thesis or Zaslavskii's consensus thesis, to understand how the party-state apparatus might in fact contribute to Soviet stability, offering the century's most striking alternative to Western notions of modernity.

Indeed, the discrepancies between the Soviet social structure and the conventional carapace of modernity—nation-state, capitalist economy, liberal democracy—through which are advanced the social agendas of urbanization, industrialization, nationalization, mass education, communication networks, and the like, have led some scholars to the false assumption that the Soviet experiment was a rejection of modernity rather than a flawed and ultimately failed alternative, a "counterparadigm of modernity" (Szporluk, "After Empire" 23) or an "abortive form of modernization" (Minogue and Williams 241).[37] The disappearance of second-world modernity and its characteristic features—the monopolistic party-state, a central command economy with its five-year plan, mass political mobilization without Western-style democracy, and a system of explicit ideological orthodoxy—has left behind a Russia that still resists many features of first-world modernity, whether or not, at Russia's western borders, a set of local, vernacular modernities reclaim filiation to the presiding norms of the nation-state.[38] Paradoxically, these norms were invoked in the "old age of the nation-state" (Mann 115; see also Hobsbawm 181–83; Verdery 45), as the norms themselves were increasingly subject to weakening through transnational flows, both legal and illegal.[39]

In debates with the theorists of totalitarianism, Western scholarship of the past decade, drawing on the constructivist turn in political theory, stresses a competing, if not incompatible, interpretation of Soviet failure, having less to do with the evil empire's politics than the valence of its status as an empire to begin with.[40] Indeed, the very brilliance of Ronald Reagan's conjuration of the "evil empire" lay in its capacity to capture three ways—stunning examples of U.S. disavowal—in which the second world was "wrong": it was immoral, it was archaic, and it did not work.[41] Once the rhetorical link between empire and these "intrinsic" characteristics was made, the Soviet Union's rightful destiny was to succumb to a kind of moral metal fatigue: "The concept of a 'Soviet empire' implied immediately a state that had lost its legitimacy and was destined to collapse" (Suny, "Empire" 23).[42]

The lack of consensus among scholars concerning the normative implications of "empire" might thus productively be understood not only with respect to the category's structural status (Beissinger, "The Persisting Ambiguity"; Parrot) but also through these intersecting axes of immorality, archaism, and dysfunctionality. When, for example, Motyl ("Building Bridges" 264) insists that "the term *empire* is not a pejorative designation for the Soviet Union, but the source of insight into its dynamics," he addresses its mechanical functionality ostensibly independent of the cold war agenda, as a "seemingly transparent empirical category" (Suny, "Empire" 23). When Beissinger begs to differ, insisting that "the term as it is now used is inherently pejorative" ("The Persisting Ambiguity" 157 fn. 14; see also his "Demise"), he invokes the moral axis, though admittedly less as his own position than as a characterization of his colleagues' scholarly assessment.[43] Since 1991 the term implies not just a past structure unworthy of contemporary political life, but one with a dangerously nostalgic drive for a neo-expansionist future. To the extent that national self-determination through autonomous civic institutions is a less familiar disposition in Russian history than is centralized empire building, nationhood is in perpetual danger of association with a set of imported European and thus perceptually false cultural identifications for a society with a long philosophical tradition of relinquishing self-determination in the name of strong centralized state rule.

Contiguity

A third parameter shaping Russia's contradictory identity concerns its status as a land empire, wherein the boundaries between homeland and colony were more vulnerable to redefinition than those of the maritime empires. Despite the fact that the contiguous empires of Persia, China, Rome, Islam, and medieval Europe, as well as the Ottoman and Austro-Hungarian Empires, were, in many ways and over the great expanse of history, a more typical figuration than the overseas empire, contiguity has been largely left out of the discourse of empire. In more recent historical times it has occupied instead a site that is peripheral both in geography and in theory.[44] Unlike Britain or Portugal, Russia's empire did not easily divide geographically or culturally into incontestable categories of "ours" and "theirs." Foundationally hybrid, its blurring of territorial markers carried with it a blurring of ethnic identifications compared with those of the imperial thalassocracies. Stories of departure and return to the homeland, of political exile to the periphery, of finding one's place in the empire's expatriate communities or—its inverse—remaining an outsider-resident in the metropole's heartland have a different set of resonances and representations in an empire constructed such that no vast interruption signals the space between center and colony.[45] Absent an equivalent of the ocean's third space between England and India, the Russian journey to the empire's outer regions was measured in incremental expanses rather than discontinuous units of land and sea. Cultural hybridity, ambiguity, and contested boundaries are scripted into landscape and ritual from before the empire's inception, rather than solely as a modern result of, say, advances in the technology of travel, the late collapse of imperial hierarchies, or the subsequent influx of diverse immigrant populations.

Moreover, as Suny ("Empire" 24) and others have pointed out, distinctions between "metropole" and "periphery" are problematic as simple geographic coordinates, in particular with respect to contiguous empires. Those distinctions engage a broad range of issues—ethnicity, language, party affiliation, and other social operators—that mediate access to political rights, status, and goods and services across a fluidly determined, overland space. Thus, although the Soviet metropole may have been predominantly ethnic Russian, urban (or even Muscovite), Russian-speaking, and Party-affiliated, these characteristics did not define the metropole as necessary and simultaneous conditions of presence, but were unevenly sedimented upon one another, dependent in certain historical periods on the strategic disenfranchisement of precisely those metropolitan traits.[46] The Soviet Union at times strove to reconstitute imperial loyalties precisely through the early suppression of Great Russian superiority in favor of developing local networks of ethnoterritorial culture under the larger Soviet state, constituting what Terry Martin has aptly described as the "affirmative action empire." With the empire's collapse, the existence of 25 million ethnic Russians residing outside the Russian state but within the former inner empire further muddled notions of the imagined community and its entitlements (Kolstoe 276–80). Just as those 25 million ethnic Russian *pieds noirs* left behind in former Soviet territories would problematize any pull toward ethnic nation formation in the Russian Federation, so too would the domestic suppression of non-Russian minorities within Russia, now 83 percent ethnic Russians, problematize the process of civic nation formation to a greater degree than in maritime empires with a more stable history of civic nationhood.

By 1991 even the country to which many of the Russian minorities of the near abroad would return ceased to exist. Responses to 1992 and 1993 opinion polls conducted among ethnic Russian minorities abroad (in Kyrgyzstan, Lithuania, Moldova) by the Center for the Study of Inter-Ethnic Relations (Institute of Ethnology and Anthropology, Russian Academy of Sciences), as well as in

June 1995 in Ukraine by the Institute of Sociology and the Democratic Initiative (both located in Kiev) and elsewhere, consistently confirmed a homeland identification with the Soviet Union, not Russia; a much smaller percentage considered the Russian Federation to be their homeland (Tolz, "Conflicting" 292–93). Analogous polling within the Russian Federation for this period (February 1995) by the Public Opinion Foundation, headed by Igor' Kliamkin, suggests that respondents saw "Russianness" less as a matter of language, citizenship, or even ethnicity than as a passport entry (Kliamkin and Lapkin 87).[47] Taken together—that is, as if somehow inhabitants of one (nonextant) country rather than (now) several—the Russians abroad and Russian Federation citizens shared a sense of community, though surely of a very limited life span, based on a *Soviet state interpretation* of Russian imperial culture, an environment in which exit and voice bore a different relation to loyalty than in the West.[48] Thus what might seem a developed sense of national culture—a common canonical knowledge of literary classics, a high level of cultural literacy more broadly, the "most reading" people, enjoying the highest cinema attendance, and so forth—is only such if one accepts as the "national" a *state-defined and state-enforced* knowledge system, any organized deviation from which was met with a highly calibrated system of punishment. Surely at the heart of the metropolitan intelligentsia's own struggle was the attempt, both individually and collectively, to define and sustain some autonomy, however insufficient to nationhood, from precisely that extreme statism that would effectively cast doubts on such an interpretation of "the national."

If Soviet dissidence was one attempted articulation of individuation from and autonomous recollectivization of state cultural control, then emigration—at least the emigration of the educated, metropolitan elite of the First and Third Waves—was a related and, in many cases, more extreme variation on the same impulse. The most visible arena in which these debates were waged was literature, though "literature" served as shorthand for both writing (secular philosophy, theology, political theory, memoirs) and art more broadly, cinema being the least productive in these discussions for obvious reasons, both technical and technological. As Slobin (515) has argued, the émigrés' parallel universe of "schools, churches, journals, publishers, and professional associations," its own cult of Pushkin, its Days of Russian Culture, its invocations of foreign exiles from Dante to Adam Mickiewicz, its Russian Montparnasse—all constitute a move from afar to repossess culture from the state, as well as to preserve and expand key features of Russian culture perceived as incompatible with the Soviet state's agenda. This diasporic custodianship was never internally coherent, containing within itself early on, for example, both the cultural exiles of the Silver Age and a deep distrust of the Silver Age (Raeff 102–3). Yet its philosophical claims often aspired to counter the monolith of Marxism-Leninism with the monolith of Orthodoxy.[49] These two Russias—usually couched in the questions "There or here?" ("Tam ili zdes'?") and "One literature or two?" ("Odna literatura ili dve?")[50]—were first and foremost a rift *within* an elite imperial identity, dating, coincidentally or not, from the same decade that the dynasty took an imperial turn, that is, at least from Andrei Kurbskii's exilic polemics with Ivan IV. If the Soviet citizen risked becoming merely the instrument of a ventriloquizer-state, the émigré risked hallucinating the desire of a wholly imaginary—as distinct from imagined—nation. The émigré's forced deterritorialization of Russian culture was only timorously addressed during *perestroika* and then, as a longer process far from completion, was gesturally marked on November 1, 2000, when President Vladimir Putin visited Sainte-Geneviève-des-Bois to place carnations on Russian émigré graves (Slobin 528).

To return to the issue of contiguity, however, the Russian overland empire's most treasured "battlefields, holy cities, rivers, lakes" (Thompson 88) exhibited a greater capacity to "become Russia" than did the maritime empire's Bombay to "become England." "Russia" thus became a privileged metonym for the empire's totality in a fashion that "England" did not.[51] The cultural representation of World War II, wherein the suffering of the "Russian people" is a universally accepted trope, provides a case in point. Ewa Thompson (31) may be factually correct that the Germans occupied a mere 5 percent of the RSFSR for less than three years, but her conclusion, with its imputation to the titular ethnicity of a kind of inauthentic victimhood, is perhaps harsh in a number of respects. The cultural weight and center, including the linguistic center, of the war experience suggests a more extensive trauma for reasons not easily reducible to the prestidigitation of an imperial center. "Russia" was never reducible to the RSFSR any more than it was reducible to ethnic Russians; as a privileged metonym, it supported a larger set of collective identifications across ethnic and geographic differences. Such identification was "false"—rather than something more interesting—only if one ignores a cultural practice, the political implications of which (in fairness to Thompson) indeed served the ideological interests of the imperial center, according to which the RSFSR was always an inadequate synonym for Russia. If "Soviet" was a way for the Russian empire to be modern, "Russia" was a way for the Soviet empire to have a continuous past, however much its leadership would inconsistently disavow its imperial genealogy. Hence in the universe of culture rather than the logic of statistics it was the "Russian" people (as a strategically fuzzy and shape-shifting category) who suffered, just as it is the (now textual and imaginary) "Soviet Union" to which (some) ethnic Russians of the near abroad may long to return.

Contiguity likewise factors into how we must grapple with those key Western postcolonial analyses available to us as we think through the problematic of Russia and empire. There is little speculation in Said, for example, on the construction of empire and Orient for cultures beyond the British, French, and American. Along with the Spanish, Portuguese, Italians, and Swiss, "the Russians" appear only in sporadic citations. Unlike the Spanish, Portuguese, Italians, and Swiss, however, Russia's inconsistent adaptation of what Said

(*Orientalism* 3) describes as the "Western style for dominating, restructuring, and having authority over the Orient" remained precisely that: a *Western* style with attenuated and complex relevance for Russia's contiguous empire and differently inflected Orientalism. This topic deserves a more extensive treatment than it will receive here, where I will make only passing comments.

As Said suggested in his opening remarks, the Orient had historically served Europe as a "sort of surrogate and even underground self" (3). Yet that underground self for Russo-Soviet culture was something more substantial, both more material and more integrated into the daily life of the street, the marketplace, the train station, the school, the army, and elsewhere. If the modern (i.e., from the eighteenth century on) Western Orientalist's detachment in confronting the Orient's peculiarities "helped a European to know himself better" (117), then "knowing" took on a different cast for a culture that was itself liminally European. The surrogate, underground self that the Russian elite comes to know is not as easily disambiguated from himself, whether the Oriental be found at the geographical periphery of the empire, in the semiliterate, cultural heartland of an ethnic Russia (often simultaneously cast as his own roots), or whether that Oriental turns out to be the Russian elite itself, situated at the *European* periphery and bearing a striking resemblance to the Russian whom Chaadaev tendered in his First Philosophical Letter.

Writing in French to an imaginary Russian noblewoman, Chaadaev indicts Russia in terms that resemble those of a minor French Orientalist administrator omitted from Said's manuscript. The triviality of Chaadaev's remarks is rendered painful only because the reader knows its author to be Russian. In Chaadaev we can hear the voices of Said's most retrograde Orientalists: Russia exhibits "the childish frivolousness of the infant"; it is "divorced from space and time," with "no proper habits . . . no rules," "in the narrowest of presents, without past and without future," absorbing "none of mankind's traditional transmission." As "a culture based wholly on borrowing and imitation," it has a tendency to "grow, but . . . not mature," the ability to "advance, but obliquely," taking "no part in the general progress of the human spirit save by blind, superficial, and often awkward imitation of other nations," a "flightiness of a life totally lacking in experience and foresight," a "careless rashness," "incapable of depth and perseverance," "lazy boldness," borrowing only "the deceptive appearances and the useless luxuries," with "something in [the] blood which drives off all true progress," "a void in the intellectual sphere" (109–16). This is not the condescending Orientalism of the Russian noble elite toward the *narod*, but the noble elite's Orientalism toward itself, as if to shame itself out of the very practices it had newly learned to condemn from an Orientalizing West. This Orientalist task of "knowing"—in the circuitous sense of knowing the self through the Oriental other—thus arrogated to itself, alternately with pride and self-humiliation, traces of that same Orient it simultaneously sought to dominate and from which it would ostensibly separate itself.

Inversely, any number of Said's culled examples of Orientalism could easily have come from Chaadaev's hand: a "tendency to despotism . . ., its habits of inaccuracy, its backwardness" (Said, *Orientalism* 205). The Orientalist assertion that "since the Orientals were ignorant of self-government, they had better be kept that way for their own good" (228) is unavoidably evocative of attitudes from the Slavophiles onward in the construction of ideal relations between autocrat and people. When Said speaks of "up-to-date empires [that] have effectively brought [the Orientals] out of the wretchedness of their decline and turned them into rehabilitated residents of productive colonies" (35), he might be speaking of Soviet Russia as simultaneously subject and object, Orientalist and Orient, of its own reflexive project.

Russia's geographical Orient—the Caucasus, Central Asia, Siberia—was not simply, in Said's poetic sense, a "theatrical stage affixed to Europe" (63), but a continuation of the eastern empire ("a kind of appendage [*priveska*]," as Dostoevskii [27: 32] describes it in *A Writer's Diary*), inextricable from both its land mass and its domestic discourse of Russianness. Moreover, by the 1950s, to the extent that the East (variously defined) had often "signified danger and threat even as it had also meant the traditional Orient, as well as Russia" (26), the Soviet Union's political coloration further contributed to its multiply paradoxical status. The series of paradoxes goes something like this: whereas Russia had historically been imperial but not necessarily Western (and therefore Orientalist, but always incipiently Oriental), the Soviet Union had become the anti-imperialist empire, an East that supplanted the ancient threat of the Orient with the nuclear warheads of second-world modernity.

One of the most difficult Soviet fits with Said, however, must be traced back to the notion of hegemony, so productive for Plekhanov and the early Russian labor movement. Gramsci's (124) "two great 'floors' of the superstructure," civil and political society, with their corresponding functions of hegemony and direct rule, become difficult to argue in a Soviet culture in which the state historically figures directly in virtually all aspects of what would, in Gramsci's schema, be considered the private sphere. This is not to argue the absence of hegemonic rule (even in the bleakest days of 1930s Stalinism), yet the powers of the state bureaucracy, extending far beyond the army, police, and central administrative system, shape the operations of culture in ways that have never easily corresponded to Western understandings of hegemony by the cultural elite. Instead, such powers are cast as political supervision a telephone call away from the direct coercion deployed by the security police and other forms of direct state control.[52]

After 1991, with the state reduced to the territory it had occupied three centuries earlier, and now with a population of approximately 83 percent ethnic Russian, the new polity, despite its relative homogeneity, faced a daunting set of choices in sorting out the relative import of ethnic and civic priorities. The first potential, whereby "ethnic" underscores language, religion, culture, and a putative shared ancestry, takes on a different coloration for the first time since the sixteenth century in Russia's history. It imagines a newly empowered role for culture in shaping collective identity yet retains complex implications both domestically and internationally with respect to the culture's treatment of non-Russian minorities and the culture's configuration beyond the boundaries of the state. The disjuncture between state boundaries and the ethnic diaspora too constantly threatens to render unstable and unclear the legitimizing practices, filiations, and representations of belonging.

The second potential, a civic collectivity, which seems to proffer universal (i.e., ethnically neutral) practices of belonging, must contend both with a present demographics of an overwhelming Russian majority and with a past of the Soviet Union's own flawed civic legacy: the category of "civic" comes to post-Soviet Russia highly contaminated by Soviet state excesses and lacking in most of the key features of Western notions of civil society.[53] This contamination vitiates civic nationhood of the very hopes in which Western capital, figuratively and economically, had invested its interest. This memory is marked by a profound skepticism and caution about the investments of civicness, in comparison with which a primordial ethnic identification, however constructed it might be, retains a compelling allure.

Four Contradictions

Within these parameters of sequence, duration, and contiguity are structured key contradictions of Russia's struggle with its cultural identity. The "unfinished business" of 1918–21 played itself out only in 1988–92, described by Hobsbawm (165) as "an apparent explosion of separatism." The election of Yeltsin in June 1991 and the related events of that year, however much they may be enshrined as Russia's independence narrative, were less a rising up of the impassioned and visionary nationalists than a calculated effort by seasoned politicians—"opportunistic 'migrants' from Staraia Ploshchad'," as Prizel has described them (221)[54]—led by Yeltsin first in the 1990 RSFSR parliamentary elections, then again in 1991 to displace the increasingly conservative Gorbachev agenda. Far from a self-sacrificing struggle for the right to self-determination and homeland, the Russian declaration of sovereignty was a brilliant political move intended to demolish a rival's power base. Although over time it would become inevitable that the myths of collective struggle would accrue to the anniversary, the new cultural custodians of 1991 inherited a homeland as a knight's move in a game of high-stakes administrative politics.

This first contradiction, then, was the "homeland they had not fought for" (G. Smith 48), won at the costs of global status and displacing a Soviet homeland, however much the result of state construction and coercion, for which many of its older inhabitants had indeed fought and for which the less fortunate had died. The new Russia was born not from military victory but from imperial collapse, its third in modern history.

A second contradiction concerns the paradoxical place of Russia in the hierarchy of Soviet values. While Russia sloughed off the empire that had so burdened its economy, it had to forge a set of postcolonial ties with new nation-states for which it bore the status of metropolitan stand-in for that same vanished empire. Bracketed on either side by two other major events, the 1989 breach of the Berlin Wall and the failed August 1991 coup d'état, Russia's election of Yeltsin by public ballot in June 1991 occurred in conditions somewhat equivalent to those of England's blazing a trail of independence from the United Kingdom (as Aleksandr Tsipko put it, "the absurd idea of 'Russia separating from Russia'").[55]

A third contradiction concerns Russia's uneasy position as a polity the internal units of which make their own claims to sovereignty. If the relationship of the United States to Puerto Rico, of Britain to Northern Ireland, of the People's Republic of China to Tibet could be argued as cases of continued imperial coercion, it takes little effort to entertain the separatist claims of Chechnia, Tatarstan, Sakha (formerly Yakutia), and Bashkortostan. By this logic Russia is a shrunken empire vulnerable to further disintegration by "matreshka nationalism" (Hall 20) through secession efforts stretching from the Russian Caucasus to the Far East. Hosking's (*Empire* 33) comment, a year after the Soviet collapse, still commands our attention years later: "It remains to be seen," he wrote in 1992, "whether Russia . . . can ever constitute itself as a nation without an empire." Recalling Suny's ("History" 338) cautionary remarks about the "proper trajectory" of the nation-state, we might also ask why it should.[56]

The fourth and most interesting contradiction, arising from this troubling issue of how far the empire might yet shrink, concerns Russia's relationship to its own heartland and by what notion of "real" this heartland comes to be identified as the real Russia. In its most provocative formulation, the question might be asked how the relationship of the Russian metropole to the more ethnically homogeneous, rural heartland is different from the imperial relation to its far-flung ethnoterritorial peripheries. In his *Utopia and Exchange* (*Utopiia i obmen* 358) Boris Groys polemically argues a colonial relationship with Russia's own heartland and suggests that the Petrine reforms were a "unique act of self-colonization of the Russian people":

> One part [of the Russian people] pretended in some fashion to be
> foreigners in their most frightening and threatening guise, and under-
> took a consequent and radical persecution of everything Russian, graft-
> ing all that was, at that time, the most modernized and Western, which
> real foreigners, had they attempted in earnest to conquer Russia, in all
> likelihood would not have undertaken to do. As a result of that cruel
> inoculation, however, Russia actually did save itself from real coloniza-
> tion by a West superior to her both technologically and militarily.[57]

In a related line of argumentation, Aleksandr Etkind contends that the ethnic Russian *narod* itself constitutes Russia's core Other. Substituting the peasant's beard for the more familiar postcolonialist category of race as the key marker of cultural distance, Etkind (8) identifies the Russian heartland as the primary site of colonization by metropolitan exiles, foreign settler communities, and military colonies alike:

> The people were the Other. They were excluded from the public
> sphere and relations of exchange. They were subjected to surveillance
> and concern; classification and disciplinary measures. They spoke in
> Russian . . . but pronounced the very same words differently and in-
> vested in them very different meanings.[58]

Together, Groys and Etkind have mapped out a trajectory of thought unsettling to Slavic studies, with its investment in a Slavic core, and to some postcolonial theorists for whom the concept of self-colonization runs counter to an eman-cipatory project.[59]

It must be noted in passing that their thesis derives polemical strength from Iurii Lotman's earlier writings on the poetics of everyday behavior in the eighteenth century.[60] Lotman ("Poetika" 67–68) likewise suggests that the Rus-sian elite adopted norms of foreign behavior, a theatricalization of everyday life *as if* they themselves were foreigners:

> A member of the Russian gentry of the Petrine and post-Petrine
> epochs was like a foreigner in his own country: a person who, at a
> mature age by artificial methods, must learn what people usually
> acquire in early childhood by direct experience. That which is alien
> and foreign takes on the character of the norm. To conduct oneself
> correctly was to conduct oneself as a foreigner, that is, to act in a
> somewhat artificial way, according to the norms of an alien life-style.
> To bear these norms in mind was as necessary as to know the rules of
> a foreign language for its proper usage. . . . It was necessary *not to be*
> a foreigner . . ., but to behave *like* a foreigner.[61]

Though in no way directly addressing issues of colonization, Lotman's writing lays the groundwork for Groys's and Etkind's identification of Russian colonial-ism as informed by its distance from its own core ethnicity rather than from its relation to groups defined by other markers of distance, such as race or religion.

Here we might open up an intriguing contradiction in Groys's and Etkind's common argument. Unaddressed in their logic is the powerful mythology in Russian culture, most vividly articulated in Village Prose, that the journey from the metropole to the deep Russian heartland is inevitably a journey backward and homeward, an intensely symbolic ontological trip to childhood and origins, even when the traveler is not, in a literal sense, from the heartland to which he journeys.[62] In much of Village Prose, at the end of the journey, with deadening predictability, is the elderly mother, alternately requiring and resisting metropolitan help,[63] coding peasant culture as the early childhood of the (now adult) metropolitan elite. Assertively nativist in their aspirations, the Village Prose writers were at the same time nothing if not deeply Soviet in their orientation, imperial recluses who, while retaining the cultural traces of rusticity, ostentatiously shunning the trappings of empire, thereby marked in opposition all its traces and signs. The rustic village, submerged beneath the waters of the Soviet hydroelectric dam, is at best a deeply ambiguous and hybrid image, profoundly dependent for its cultural resonance on the new imperial usurper, agent of its physical destruction and symbolic preservation.

A related pattern might also be found in a range of other texts depicting the elderly, uneducated peasant nursemaid, former nanny of the metropolitan artist, as in Pushkin's treatment of Tat'iana's peasant nurse (and implicitly his own nurse) in his novel in verse *Evgenii Onegin*, or Léon Bakst's 1906 portrait of Sergei Diaghilev with his former nurse, an elderly peasant woman, positioned in the background of the canvas. In each case the nurse is more than mere individual biographical fact. She serves as an imaginative reminder of collective origins, nursemaid to the empire.[64] When the Village Prose writers later displaced the elderly maternal figure back into the deep countryside, this act was dictated in part by its polemic with urbanophile and technophile fashion of the late Thaw period. At the same time, the trope of the long geographical return afforded Village Prose writers the opportunity for an analogous symbolic return to the childhood of the empire itself.

Hence the question: how do we reconcile this nativist equation—the journey to the hinterland as the journey to home and childhood—with Etkind's assertion of the Russian folk as Other and with Groys's "unique act of self-colonization"? If Etkind and Groys are in any sense correct, what conceptual glitch transforms the homeland of Village Prose to Oriental colony? Unless we are inclined (as I am not) to discard their speculations altogether, then an answer, however incomplete here, might be that self-colonization, the symptoms of which they convincingly describe, is a second-order phenomenon, not a generative or core feature of Russian colonialism. That is to say, the Petrine era—that historical frame implicitly present in Groys's and Etkind's analyses and explicitly identified in the Lotman quotation above—was by no means the first chapter in the biography of the imperial elite, but the maturation of imperial codes put in place a century and a half earlier, tracing from the imperial overreach of Ivan IV. Having extended its claims, the dynastic empire then modernized its relations to its own heartland-childhood in a fashion consonant with historical contingency, that is to say, not the mercantile imperative of the British overseas empire but the state consolidation of the contiguous empire, organizing ("updating" perhaps is the better word) its relationship to

FIGURE I.I. Bakst. *Portrait of Sergei Pavlovich Diaghilev with His Nurse.*

the heartland, renovating it in the way most historically available to it, that is, by inscribing onto the heartland its own relations of domination and difference as a creative, local improvisation on Western imperial practices in which it aspired to participate as an equal.

The relationship of the newly westernized Shaved Man to Bearded Man, if we may contingently adopt Etkind's terminology, is thus not a primary colonial relationship but a necessary and secondary variation, an afterthought in Russia's imperially inflected experience of state formation from Ivan forward. By extension, having learned from Russian history what a colonial project was, the Village Prose writer returns to the heartland as to both homeland and unacknowledged colonial project: pristine and uncontaminated, it serves as both his symbolic birthplace and as inland *terra nullius.*

What Etkind has described as the self-Orientalizing tendency of the Russian Empire was therefore not only a late phenomenon but also one, in a sense, narrated in reverse. In Europe an existing elite sets off on the imperial journey and in so doing constructs an Oriental Other; in Etkind's terms, the Shaved Man travels overseas to find the Bearded Other. In Russia, by contrast, a different process was at work, the outcome of an already existing imperial competition, followed by a turn to internal consolidation. A century and a half after Ivan IV, the Petrine Newly Shaven, having already entered into the game of Europe, came to narrate the rural, Russian Bearded Man as if the Shaven Man himself had *always already* been beardless (an element of the theatricalization of which Lotman writes). Having encountered his difference from the Westerner, but then in turn displacing the category of difference from himself onto the Bearded Man, this newly Europeanized self—a self, not coincidentally, in increasing control of the economy of cultural representations—rendered the Bearded Man newly legible, retrospectively ascribing difference to the very social strata who lacked equivalent cultural resources to contest that ascription.[65]

If we agree with Cherniavsky (*Tsar and People*) and Hosking (most succinctly in *Empire and Nation*) that the gulf between elite and demotic collectivities long predates Peter, a condition for which Hosking (10) finds evidence already in Ivan IV's division of dominions into *oprichnina* (the realm under extraordinary rule) and *zemshchina* (the "earthly" realm), then we might speculate that the gulf produced Peter (rather than the opposite), just as it produced beardlessness. Peter was one cultural symptom of an already existing gap.[66] The journey from metropole to heartland was of course a symbolic trip home. But more important, it was a *staged* trip home, where the prestige of being *like* a European, but on no account *being* a European, could reach its fullest articulation, a theatricalization more extreme than that performance afforded by the metropolitan mise-en-scène.

The Cultural Turn

Why not translate *nationalité* as *narodnost'*?
> —Prince Petr Viazemskii to Aleksandr Turgenev
> (1819), in *Ostaf'evskii arkhiv kniazei Viazemskikh*
> (Knight, "Ethnicity" 50)

There [in Europe] *narodnost'* means some kind of separate autonomy [*samobytnost'*].
> —Nikolai Nadezhdin (1837), Pushkinskii Dom
> archives (St. Petersburg), fond 93, opis' 3, no. 881, 1

My attempt, in rudimentary terms, to mull through a different way of thinking about Russia invites questions closer to our disciplinary home, questions concerning the implications for Russian culture of the imperial habits presented in broad strokes here. In so doing we might well recall the dangers of Jean-Bédel Bokassa's claims for his Central African Empire. On the one hand, proof by assertion is not proof. On the other hand, in the highly subjective world of national discourse, no litmus test exists by which to exclude those claims we find ill conceived. The fact that, at the end of the nineteenth century, a Russian imperial elite, extraordinarily few in number with respect to its counterpart in Western Europe, appreciated and financed oil paintings, ballets, art, and music with native subject matter does not therefore suggest that this cultural circuitry, magnificent though its contribution to world culture might be, adequately fits the category called "national." Rather, in Russia the elite desire to construct a "national"—that is to say, an equivalent to the labor of a much broader, integrated set of Western European cultural associations with developed national identities—strategically conflates two sets of apparently equivalent cultural texts produced under profoundly different social conditions, forgetting that each stage of its own cultural circuitry (production, representation, regulation, consumption) is filtered instead through a system structured according to very different material institutions and cultural mythologies.[67]

At a more fundamental level a profound source of confusion resides here at the level of language. Setting aside the multiple meanings of "nation" and "nationalism" in our own language,[68] we find ourselves stymied in the misguided and futile attempt at an equivalency between "nation" and *narod*, "national" and *narodnyi*, "nationality" and *narodnost'*. We are in good company: no less an authority than the Russian lexicographer Vladimir Dal' (1284–85) lists the Russian *narod* and the foreign calque *natsiia* as synonyms, as he does the Russian coinage *narodnost'* and the foreign calque *national'nost'*. The raw presumption in questioning this apparently canonical equivalency of *narod* and *natsiia* is aimed less at a defense of an immanent correct usage than to cast light on the fact that the substitution of one potential set of meanings for another—say, the substitution of folk practices for popular sovereignty—is not an innocent act, not a neutrally chosen predilection of freely circulating definitions. It is instead a sleight of hand worthy of a tonic curiosity about the ways Dal''s formal registration of meaning thereby reveals a politics of displacement—how, for example, the serf chorus might stand in for the will of the people.[69] Here neither a formal, neutral range of meanings nor an attempt at correct substitution would be of help in understanding how this contradiction arises.

Beyond these linguistic debates, capacious as the Russian terms *narod* ("people" or "folk") and *narodnost'* ("of the people" or the heinously awkward "people-ness") may be, their limit lies in the fact that they align uneasily with the unifying, organic totality implied by the Germanic tradition of *Volksseele*, inherited and transformed from J. G. Herder (1744–1803), and they in no sense align with the Anglo-French connotation of popular sovereignty. "Both aspects of Russians' nationhood," Geoffrey Hosking (*Russia* xx) notes with reference to the German ethnic-cultural and the Anglo-French civic traditions, "have been gravely impeded by the way in which their empire evolved." Few would argue with Hans Rogger's description of a tentative search by the intelligentsia after 1812 for a meaningful Russian *equivalent of* national consciousness, producing such imperial masterpieces as Pushkin's *Eugene Onegin* (*Evgenii Onegin*), Gogol''s *Dead Souls* (*Mertvye dushi*), and Tolstoi's *War and Peace* (*Voina i mir*). Yet the search for the national remained largely the textual preoccupation of a minuscule imperial elite. The fact that a century-long state literacy campaign vastly expanded the domestic readership leaves unresolved the ill fit of, on the one hand, the organic unity of the German tradition and, on the other, the liberal-democratic state, sustained by popular sovereignty, free civic association, and the rights of individuals at the heart of the Anglo-French traditions.

Indeed, the breezy optimism with which the poet and dedicated Schellingian Prince Petr Viazemskii, originator of the abstraction *narodnost'*, writes on November 22, 1819, to his friend, the historian Aleksandr Turgenev, "Why not translate *nationalité* as *narodnost'*?,"[70] is more a function of a historically specific euphoria—post-1812 but pre-1825—than of a felicitous linguistic discovery of empirically based meaning whose time had finally come. Tellingly, by 1837 a very different and more characteristic cast to *narodnost'* was acknowledged by the embattled Nikolai Nadezhdin, editor of the journal *Telescope*, in the wake of the Chaadaev affair:

> I spoke of *narodnost'* contrasting it to a false Europeanism. . . .
> There [in Europe] *narodnost'* means some kind of separate autonomy
> [*samobytnost'*]. . . . Is it not in the name of this *narodnost'*, this
> senseless pride, this dreaming of some kind of autonomy of the
> people [*narod*] that the constant upheavals there are committed.[71]

The noncorrespondence of *narodnost'* to Western notions of nationalism and to the reactive policies of official *narodnost'*—whether its original articulation in the 1830s by Nikolai I's minister of education Count Sergei Uvarov, its later articulation by Mikhail Katkov after the Polish rebellion of 1863–64,[72] or indeed its articulation today—had (and still has) no easy resolution in the pure realm of linguistic translation; efforts by the intelligentsia to produce a national culture remained similarly resistant to cultural translation, resulting, despite its occasional conflicting claims, in the story of empire written across what might elsewhere be the story of nation. Uvarov's official *narodnost'* was tempered, as Hubertus Jahn has suggested, with disdain for Russian ethnic culture and, not insignificantly, recorded in German or French in his correspondence (S. Franklin and Widdis 60).

The persistent myth, first traced in a scholarly fashion by Cherniavsky to Holy Rus', of Russia as a God-bearing people endowed with a universal mission of salvation that transcended its official, secular boundaries, became a way of reconciling Russia's ambitions with its differences vis-à-vis the West. Now, armed with, rather than encumbered by, its mute folk, its vast expanse, and its impoverished core in comparison to even its own more developed Western periphery, the Russian imperial intelligentsia of the late nineteenth century could paradoxically resolve the status of the humble commune by rendering it a parallel (i.e., metaphysical and sacred) empire, invisibly magnificent in proportion to its earthly poverty, drawing an internally contradictory equivalency between collective suffering, potentially without content or limit, and a perpetually expanding, transcendent empire at a time when, perhaps not so coincidentally, the process of nation-formation in the West was most intense. This symbolic empire could function as a spiritual and cultural retort to the measure of the Western nation-state and to Russia's own official *narodnost'*.

The most developed articulation of this problematic was to be found in the later writings of Dostoevskii (147–48) and most intensely in his speech for the Pushkin Celebrations of 1880:

> Yes, the Russian mission is unquestionably an all-European and
> a universal one. To become a true Russian, to become completely
> Russian . . . is to become the brother of all people, a universal
> human being, if you will. . . . To become a true Russian will mean
> exactly this: to strive to bring lasting reconciliation to European
> contradictions; to indicate a way out of European languor in the
> Russian soul, all-human and all-uniting. (Translation mine)

Dostoevskii's speech engages one of a familiar series of paradoxes of Russian culture: to be Russian is to be universal. Reaching back along this philosophical trajectory are other related turns of logic: to be poor in this world is to be rich in the other world; to be humble is to be great; to suffer is to prevail; to be mute is to be eloquent; to renounce power is to gain power. This inverse logic, occupying a cultural space unclaimed by default, was completely compatible with the Great Power politics both at home and vis-à-vis the West, reproducing internationally those domestic relations of subsumption that were practiced locally within the empire.

Its philosophical trompe l'œil was evident in other grand works of the period, such as Aleksandr Ivanov's earlier masterpiece *The Appearance of Christ to the People (Iavlenie Khrista narodu)*, completed in 1858. The painting, hailed by Il'ia Repin as "close to the heart of every Russian" (quoted in Lebedev and Burova 38), was—interestingly enough, given Repin's remark—utterly devoid of specific, identifiable Russian subject matter.[73] Yet it symbolically captured key elements of the inherited myth of Holy Rus': the positioning of Christ as a small, remote figure, visually refusing the large, central position on the canvas; Christ's framing by two crowds of common people in the foreground; the meticulous attention displaced onto the slave in the right forefront (see Gray 120–21). This utter *absence of native subject matter*, in the inherited logic of Holy Rus', was its own eloquent confirmation of its universal status: absence as presence. Ivanov's canvas was an early articulation of a late nineteenth-century resurgence of interest in the cultural logic of Holy Rus', which was to acquire a particular intensity decades later, reaching a climax in Mikhail Nesterov's mystical canvases, Vladimir Solov'ev's *Russian Idea* (*Russkaia ideia*, 1888), then culminating in Nikolai Berdiaev's (1946) work of the same title.[74] This claim to cultural power through its apparent renunciation, including the renunciation of its political correlates, is the optical illusion, to use Hosking's (*Russia* xx) term, of simultaneous surplus and absence that underlies Russia's paradoxical status as both greater than and less than familiar Western categories of national culture, laying claim to the potential for supranational status through an acceptance of the radical contingency, even spiritual unsuitability, of national cohesion.

Though we might therefore be inclined to smirk at the overweening ambition of Dostoevskii's rapturous call for a renewed spiritual universalism under Russian leadership, his claim to an embodiment of the particular as universal (and its obverse) had at its core a well-founded suspicion about the compatibility for Russia of alternative paths. As the music historian Richard Taruskin notes with characteristic acerbity, to be merely national (absent Dostoevskii's universalist claims) at the European periphery foreclosed full participation in universal (i.e., European) culture. Although Taruskin's penetrating and salutary remarks concern the politics of musicology and their unacknowledged Orientalist underpinnings vis-à-vis Russian composers, his skepticism with regard to cultural expectations in other fields of artistic production merits extensive quotation:

> We begin to see why it remains the Western habit to group all
> Russian composers . . . as "nationalists" whatever their actual
> predilections; why composers of the panromanogermanic
> mainstream are rarely described as "nationalists" whatever their

FIGURE I.2. Ivanov. *The Appearance of Christ to the People.*

actual predilections; and why, for "peripheral" composers, stylistic dependency on autochthonous folklore is taken in the West as an indispensable earnest of authenticity, a virtual requirement. It is yet another manifestation of fetishized difference. . . .

In conventional "canonical" historiography Russian . . . composers are in a double bind. The group identity is at once the vehicle of their international appeal (as "naifs") and the guarantee of their secondary status vis-à-vis the unmarked "universal." Without exotic native dress such composers cannot achieve even secondary canonical rank, but with it they cannot achieve more. . . . Without an exotic group identity a Russian composer can possess no identity at all. Without a collective folkloristic or oriental mask he is "faceless." The recent British biographers who have meant to vindicate Chaikovsky against this sort of dismissal have not questioned the orientalist premises on which the dismissal has been based. Vindication on their terms has meant vindication as a "nationalist." (48–50)

The so-called national is that concept in Russian culture that always undergoes its own annulment: more than a synonym for a localized native, it strives to serve as a stand-in for something else, a repetitive impulse to incorporate into the textual practices of Russian elite culture (including for its own consumption) thematic and stylistic elements from the demotic identity, in no way therefore consonant with the autonomous, horizontal ties of nationhood. The "national" was often an inaccurate descriptor of elite efforts to produce—in contrast to the West—a distinct *imperial* style, including the training of serf artists, serf choruses, and serf musicians. If we would trace an inconstant and ephemeral national in Russian culture—that is to say, the ways its texts have served as touchstones of identification across economic, gender, spatial, ethnic, and religious divides—we might best examine the life of that putative national through the thick filter of imperial practices. That imperial lens risks being forgotten, and its cultural production becomes thereby characterized unreflectively as an unproblematic national project comfortably analogous to Western models.

The Imperial Trace: Six Examples

A number of Slavists have explicitly addressed the imperial dimension of Russian culture. The best-known critical efforts have drawn almost exclusively on literary rather than cinematic texts; although we may disagree about its extrapolation to other instances of culture, it is my position that the larger theoretical issues can be so extrapolated that the "national" is misunderstood in similar fashions across cultural production.

Some of the best-known research on imperial culture in literary texts is by Vitaly Chernetsky, Monika Greenleaf (both alone and with Stephen Moeller-Sally), Katya Hokanson, Susan Layton, Harsha Ram, and Ewa Thompson.[75] With the exception of Chernetsky's work, the framework for much of this research chooses an early historical period: in time, the explicitly imperial preoccupations of the late eighteenth century and early nineteenth; in space, the explicitly Caucasian themes as, among other things, a form of local Orientalism. The specificity inherent in much of this research (the Golden Age, the Caucasus) works to great advantage in mapping out foundational research questions, although it also leaves unasked a different set of questions leading *beyond* the time and space usefully privileged in their research. In the six brief examples that follow I move incrementally away from the early nineteenth century and the imperial periphery.

One implicit question is whether the imperial trace is adequately accounted for by content alone, by, let us say, court life and wild mountains. What would be omitted from analysis if we are driven primarily by content in understanding the ways the political and the cultural texts overlay and interdetermine each other? Let us look at a concrete example within these same confines of time and space but beyond the limits of what content alone provides:

> Farewell, unwashed Russia,
> Land of slaves, land of masters,
> And you, blue uniforms,
> And you, a people so devoted to them.
>
> Perhaps, beyond the Caucasus's wall
> I'll hide myself from your pashas,
> From their all-seeing eye,
> From their all-hearing ears.
> (Lermontov 388)[76]

At the level of content, Lermontov's binary—the land of slaves and lords, the land of blue uniforms and devoted folk—yields in the second stanza to a potential refuge "beyond Caucasus's wall," an ambiguous space neither entirely foreign nor homeland. As both poet and reader cannot fail to know, that space is produced both socially, not just as content but also as military fact outside the text, and textually, not just as content but also as its very material existence, circulating among similar texts by Pushkin, Aleksandr Bestuzhev-Marlinskii, Lermontov himself, and then later by Tolstoi and others.[77]

The welter of connections, evoked between the textual practices of Lermontov's lyric and the military practices of imperial Russia and formally united in iambic tetrameter, reveal a complexity beyond the poem's capacity to render a representation of reality. Instead—and here I apologize for the wordplay—what equally (but more elusively) matters is the reality of representation, specifically the reality of imperial representation, operating both within and through the text, that lards its content with other layers of significance, including those situated in the production of the text itself, at a level distinct from its content. The ways the text transcodes social reality, in particular the material terms and social conventions of the poem's *production*, interdeterminate with its content, are evident through a range of strategies irreducible to mimetic representation but performed as displacement, tactical silence, and other mediations as it struggles with a resolution to crises lying outside the boundaries of the artistic text.[78] Is there, therefore, something that might be described as an imperial refraction of culture, something that lies in the very operations of transcoding itself, beyond content's homologous replication of social reality? Apart from the imperial as a set of narrative and visual clues (court life and mountain ridge) what are the operational codes of Russia's imperial culture? What are its structures of representation, and how would we know them, beyond the time of the Golden Age and the space of the Caucasus?

Pushing the limits of this line of inquiry, let us move one step further to choose a second example still with a Caucasian setting, but now *beyond* the Golden Age. Fazil' Iskander's collection of stories *Sandro of Chegem* (*Sandro iz Chegema*, 1973–88, complete edition 1989) plays extensively with the conceptual category of the Soviet national subsumed beneath the imperial gaze. I choose here a brief passage from one of the best-known stories, "Balthazar's Feasts" ("Piry Valtasara"), a reference to King Balthazar, the moment foretelling the end of the Babylonian Empire, and Balthazar's death (the implicit parallel, of course, with the USSR and the death of Stalin).[79] The local Abkhasian dance troupe is summoned to Stalin's table in the center of the large banquet hall. In the passage below, the pronoun "he" (in Russian, *on*) refers to Stalin:

> Thus, twenty slim dancers were transformed into blossoming
> delegates of his national policy, exactly as the children, running
> to the Mausoleum where he would stand during holidays, were
> transformed into heralds of the future, into his rosy kisses. And
> he knew how to appreciate that like no one else, conquering those
> around him with his unheard-of expanse. (232)[80]

At the level of content, the treatment of Stalin and his "delegates of national policy" functions as a kind of literary conceptualism, situating the characters both spatially (in the banquet hall as well as on the ethnographic map) and ideologically as center and periphery on a flat—one might argue, cartographic and contiguous—space.[81] Iskander's ironization of their structural relations satisfyingly captures and literalizes something akin to Terry Martin's affirmative action empire, exacting from its subjects a performance of symbolic ethnicity, simultaneously allowed and required by Stalin's "unheard-of expanse" (*neslykhannaia shirota*), at once geographic and political.

Throughout the collection's narrative structure the figure of Stalin is both undercut and held in place by the figure of Sandro, functioning as the story's central figure and its delegate of "national"—that is to say, ethnoterritorial—policy. In the register of fantasy, Iskander's text imaginatively straddles this gulf between the delegates and Stalin in ways that the social reality can only continually aspire to do. The painful irony of Iskander's writing lies in his capacity to gesture at levels of signification beyond the boundaries set by narrative content. Does (for example) Iskander's capture of these structural relations place him beyond the operations of the very cultural machinery he describes, or is his own writing, at the moment of its production, distribution, and consumption by a metropolitan readership, another dance at the state banquet table?

Of course, the danger with this research methodology is what Berdiaev in a different context has called the imperial temptation: that this interpretation is the only way to read the passage; that all passages must be read through this lens. Instead, I am asking how culture might be read differently were we to make available to analysis a broader range of reading strategies than those that hold Iskander's text somewhat narrowly either as an immanent representation of so-called multinational literature, itself a pseudonym of empire, or as a sociological instance of Soviet liberal semidissidence in the Stagnation era. However accurate these characterizations may be, another, less explored set of interpretive possibilities examines the trace across culture of internalized imperial relations, figured thematically, but also structurally and in the material conditions of the artifact's own production and circulation almost exclusively in the imperial centers. Something different from the known readings of Iskander unavoidably extrudes, namely, how the representation of the *non-Russian* "national" within the Soviet imperial space anticipates a later, post-Soviet cultural strategy with a profoundly different sense of nation—sovereignty, destiny, self-determination—thereby laying bare the foundations of, among other things, our own existing incoherence with respect to so-called national culture.

The imperial trace might be figured equally by its occlusion of other, alien models of social organization. Moving away from both the Golden Age and the Caucasus, I choose a third example, now from the Stalin period. The Dragon of Shvarts's eponymous 1944 play is conventionally figured as a euphemism for Stalin, or (elsewhere) an amalgam of Stalin and Hitler. Let us again leave those interpretations intact but ask a different set of questions, central to the play's uneasy resolution: What exactly does Lancelot expect of the townspeople? Lancelot's oft-quoted comment, "Inside each of them, a dragon must be killed," is the closest thing to the play's moral:

LANCELOT   Inside each of them a dragon must be killed.

BOY   Will it be painful?

LANCELOT   For you—no.

FIRST CITIZEN   And us?

LANCELOT   For you it will be a struggle.

GARDENER   But be patient, Mister Lancelot. I implore you, be patient.

(Shvarts, *Drakon* 309)[82]

This passage—perhaps the most familiar passage of the play—comments on the stubborn intransigence of totalitarian discourse, its deep roots in the cultural practice and mentalities of the citizenry and their unfamiliarity with the autonomy available to them in the absence of the Dragon. Neither Stalin nor Hitler per se, but any political power organized from without, fatally intervening in the absence of direct and independent association, Shvarts's villain holds together a community that might not otherwise cohere. Its interest for us lies in the whimsical treatment of the townspeople's resistance to their own autonomy, a choice foreclosed in the wholly imaginary space of the be-dragoned village. Their cumulate reluctance to "slay the dragon within"—yes, a symbol of tyranny, but more important for us, a structure of specific and familiar political mediation—might be overcome over generations only with work, patience, and (Shvarts gloomily suggests) a magic agent. In this fanciful play, political relations structured over four centuries, but filtered here through the cultural medium of the fairy tale, address contradictions in the symbolic realm that the social conditions of the Stalinist mid-1930s could in no way broach except through this complex detour into wonderland. It is in this sense that the political unconscious—by which I mean (to borrow a leaf from Jameson) the ways cultural texts mediate imperial relations—is a richer terrain than we have explored, or have known how to explore.

A fourth example, also from the late Stalin period, in film rather than literature, is the final scene in Mikhail Chiaureli's *Fall of Berlin* (*Padenie Berlina*; Mosfil'm, 1949), one of Soviet anti-imperialism's greatest celebrations of its own imperial grandeur. In the film's final scene, French, British, Italian, and U.S. POWs, newly liberated from Nazi concentration camps, crowd around Stalin on the tarmac of the Berlin airport, a potential metaphor of the expanding empire. Their respective markers of national difference—a beret, a neck scarf, a striped shirt, a flag—and their shouts of joy, each in his respective language ("Long Live Stalin!"; "Vive Stalin!") transform these POWs from representatives of their sovereign origins to quaint ethnicities, federative and subterminal "nations," jockeying with each other on the symbolic space of the tarmac under Stalin's socialist gaze. This pattern of vying, territorial bodies choreographed to the inner monologue of the empire is finally resolved in the only way available by the film's Russian protagonists, Alesha and Natasha, Stalin's imperial monads.[83]

FIGURE I.3. Chiaureli. *Fall of Berlin*. Grateful nationalities on the tarmac.

Here again content alone does not account sufficiently for this cultural symptom. As we watch this content unfold kabuki-like on the screen, resolving in the realm of fantasy that which international geopolitics leaves awry, it is striking to recall the ways that the material circumstances of Russo-Soviet cinematic production, akin to the structures of metropolitan state time, railroads, airplane schedules, and the like, have been subject to similar forms of social organization. The inheritance after 1917 is evident in the very conditions that produced *Fall of Berlin*: the key institutions of a highly centralized film industry (largely Mosfil'm, Lenfil'm, Gor'kii Studios); the single state distribution monopoly (Goskino); the capital's film school (VGIK); and the increasingly large metropolitan cinemas, reaching an audience of eight hundred in one seating.[84] These elements constituted the imperial eye (in both senses) of the needle through which cinema would pass.

The development of republican film studios in the non-Russian republics does not undercut this argument.[85] Rather, such studios undergirded the imperial project, contributing to the logic of a composite state with unequal ethnoterritorial access to goods and privileges. As I will map out in greater detail in chapter 2, the 1990s collapse of Russian cinema meant *not so much* the collapse of a distribution network—although of course it did collapse—as the collapse of the center, without which the peripheries were not structured to sustain direct, interdependent links with each other. Without whimsical precision, the freefall of the cinema could be traced to a single time and place: the May 1986 Fifth Congress of the Soviet Filmmakers' Union on Vasiliev Street in Moscow.[86] This precision is not whimsical because it does not need to be: the strongly centripetal system of state cinema itself provided the catastrophic whimsy.

Before turning to that collapse, however, I would mention two last examples—now toward the very end of Soviet power—of what I have called the imperial trace, utterly distant in time and space from the court life and wild mountains where its symptoms were first investigated by my colleagues. The fifth example operates through temporal categories that mark the imperial culture's spectral return in an extended, key sequence from Andrei Tarkovskii's 1974 film *Mirror* (*Zerkalo*), like all Tarkovskii's films until his 1983 *Nostalghia*, a Mosfil'm production. An unknown woman from an unidentified historical past appears mysteriously in a Soviet apartment to request a passage be read aloud from an antique book. The passage, an excerpt from Pushkin's answer to Chaadaev, responds to Chaadaev's First Philosophical Letter that sparked the Westernizer-Slavophile debate. We do not need this scene to track (what passes for) the film's narrative. Tarkovskii's justification, however, is telling: he writes that his mysterious visitor was present to "unite the severed thread of time" (quoted in Synessios 61). Pushkin's letter, commenting on constitutive moments of imperial identity—Byzantium, the Mongol legacy, war, Orthodoxy— underscores their spectral relevance to the contemporary divide in the Soviet present: here a Soviet metropolitan apartment in the early 1970s, the cold war "division of churches," and so forth.[87] The film crew's highly stylized use of light and extradiegetic sound create what might be described as a metaphysics of spirits (by no means unique to *Mirror* in Tarkovskii's work) present but invisible in the cinematic space, suggestive of elusive but enduring systems of knowing, a cognitive ectoplasm haunting the material present tense.

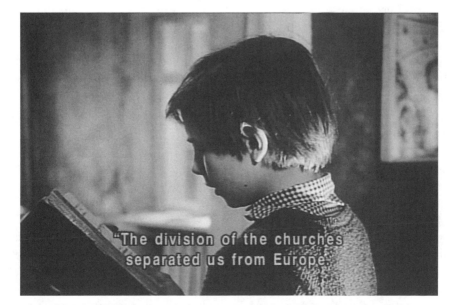

FIGURE I.4. Tarkovskii. *Mirror*. Pushkin's letter to Chaadaev.

Tarkovskii's strategic inclusion of Pushkin's final, cloying homage to Nikolai I and to Russia's history,[88] a multiple instance of Aesopian language, reminds the educated viewer that Tarkovskii, like Pushkin, like Chaadaev, occupied a precarious position vis-à-vis the ruling elite, including the cinema administration itself, without whose approval Tarkovskii's films—like Pushkin's poems, like Chaadaev's letters—would not circulate. Nineteenth-century culture's spectral return to the Soviet present tense, which officially struggled to distance itself from its imperial past, here haunts Soviet contemporaneity as a revenant that, in threatening to reconstitute itself, renders that Soviet present an unstable category.

A similar imperial haunting in an equally curious, irrelevant scene occurs in a sixth and final example, Viktor Pelevin's 1991 novella *Omon Ra*. The protagonist's friend Mitek is tortured and murdered by the Soviet authorities. In Mitek's extended and apparently superfluous monologue (77–90)—a psychotic, rambling, alien speech—we discover a curious digression that makes no sense except as the soliloquy of the empire throughout its entire human history, from the Akkadian dynastic empire of Mesopotamia (4300–4200 BC) to Queen Shubad and Meskalamdug of the Third Dynasty of the Ur Empire (2112–2004 BC), to Nimhursag, the mother earth goddess and Nanna the sun god of the Sumerian Empire (3500–2074 BC), to Nuun Ujol Chaak, twenty-third king of Mutul, part of the Mayan Empire (AD 250–900), and on to more familiar territories (the Roman Empire, the Third Reich, figured as General Erich Ludendorff, one of the first Nazi Party members in 1924), culminating in the Soviet empire. The soliloquy provides the grand historical sweep of the narrative's central project, the Soviet space mission, an extended metaphor for the endless, predatory conquest of physical space—the space of the outer cosmos and the space of the inner human psyche as analogous, available sites, the *terra nullius* of imperial socialism. The expansion of Soviet power—outward to the universe's receding edge, inward to the consciousness of the Soviet subject, a site as limitless and mysteriously unknowable as the universe—provides Pelevin with the occasion for his imaginative and grotesque refraction of the empire's predations.

These necessarily brief and associative citations are insufficient to map out an entire interpretive system, variously inflected over time, throughout the sweep of Russian culture in all fields throughout four centuries of imperial rule. Their purpose instead is to provoke a different way of thinking about Russia today, a way that suggests its imperial preoccupations are far from exhausted and that they may be found, first, beyond the imperial periphery and, second, beyond narrative content alone. It is this set of questions that I bring to a study of recent cinema, a line of inquiry at times speculative, but one intended to unsettle some of the answers concerning national identity that beg for productive disruption.

Trouble in the House of Culture

A core task of this volume is an exploration of the ways recent Russian cinema and, implicitly, other forms of contemporary culture cannot easily leave behind its imperial legacy, but rather retains patterns that reveal in and through culture its own diverse habits of articulation. We do not yet know how the imaginings of new Russian cinema will, over decades, represent, embody, and engage the new social imaginings. It is likely that Russia, caught between the stubborn persistence of its own empire and the growing global obsolescence of the nation-state, is engaged in a quest to make sense of an imperial past that is unpredictable at a time when the future of the nation-state may itself be a thing of the past (Habermas 58–112). Russia will not resolve its imperial legacy; to paraphrase Hosking, it *is* its imperial legacy. The retrospective sense that the culture makes of this legacy in its own artifacts will play a key role in the empire's prospective sense as a newly constituted project of global mediation in the region.

Imperial culture is conceived here not as a fixed set of signs and conditions but as a set of ongoing and irresolvable debates, both deploying and challenging social myths, teleologies, and traditions. As Hill ("British" 111; "Issue" 16–19) has argued in several contexts, the adequacy of a cinema to its culture's complexity is measured as much by its critique as by its confirmation of inherited notions of identity. The myth-making labor of the cultural intelligentsia includes precisely a challenge to cohesion in favor of, for example, an account of the fragmentation that the empire has undergone and the thematics of that fragmentation as paradoxically constitutive of collective identity, capturing the cultural imaginary as a field of ironic subversion, fantastic causation, a hybrid and ambiguous struggle that addresses multiple fears: the hollow core in the midst of the empire, eschatological disintegration, the evaporation of a sustaining myth, the tyranny of an exclusionary one.

There is, then, no iron necessity that recent Russian cinema transform a system previously built on hierarchy and the maintenance of regional difference into one of alleged cohesion and the putative egalitarianism of nationhood. Why should it? Indeed, both the last years of the Soviet empire and the early years of postcommunist Russia seem virtually compelled to generate many of the same contradictory marks, as if continuity were a symptom of the social conditions of upheaval.

With the collapse of the USSR in 1991, the scholarly command to write the—now real—genesis story of Russian national culture has seemed more urgent. Each cultural field seeks to identify the new national figure. In cinema Mikhalkov, we are told, or Balabanov, or someone else is where to look for national identity, the new national hero, the birth of the nation. This project is a noble one; perhaps it will be a self-fulfilling prophesy, despite the barriers of infrastructure, geography, and Russia's increasingly imperial stylistics.

Still, the very substance of the emerging culture is haunted, as if by Tarkovskii's specters, by its own imperial legacy. In cinema alone Bodrov's 1996 *Prisoner of the Mountains*, Rogozhkin's 1998 *Checkpoint*, Abdrashitov's 1998 *Time of the Dancer*, and Balabanov's 2002 *War* return to the colonial wars; Mikhalkov (*Barber of Siberia*, 1998) plays a cameo role as Aleksandr III. Lebedev's 2002 World War II film, *Star* (*Zvezda*), euphemistically displaces Russia's anti-Chechen war onto the antifascist one, as if the glory of World War II would redeem the imperial futility of war in Chechnia.

In this volume, I am not so much interested in this literalist representation; rather, as the previous comments have indicated, I ask how the empire has structured the ways Russia's filmmakers have conceived of cinema and the social collectivities in which they live and work in ways not exclusively evident in the thematics of, say, Aleksandr II and the Caucasus, the court, the mountains, the Chechen wars, and so forth. Although in each chapter I take stock of the filmmaker's work as a whole, my emphasis and interest also lies in the crisis of the early 1990s through the present moment, when the socialist empire collapses and something else—a shrunken empire?—takes its place.

In October 2002 in central Moscow Chechen nationalists, so-called terrorists, seized a drama theater. The Chechens did not seize a movie theater presumably because its potential hostages were home watching pirated videos. Two years later, in September 2004, they seized a school in Beslan, with even more dire consequences. As we rush ahead to tell the Russian "national" story, its imperial periphery, eager to gain its own national freedom at any cost, plots genocide in Russia's houses of culture. What if, in 1991 as in 1917, *an* empire had fallen but many of the structural, affective, and thematic components remained? It is precisely this stubborn contradiction, not its availability for resolution, that deserves thoughtful hesitation. This hesitation is grounded in a molecular, originating curiosity about the semantics of empire and nation. If we assume that "nation" is adequate to capture the dynamic of contemporary culture, we will have missed half the intellectual fun. "National culture" is not only a bad fit; it is a stubborn reinscription of a "daily plebiscite," to quote Renan, where there may not be one in our lifetime. How would we know Russian culture differently if we did *not* erase two enduring features of Russian cultural production: the drive for state control and imperial continuity?

2 ✴

Cine-Amnesia: How Russia Forgot to Go to the Movies

The film director's complete protection from Hollywood has come to an end.
—Daniil Dondurei, "Mestobliustiteli" (2007)

Russian filmmakers have long shared a ritual, the origins of which are forgotten. Before filming begins the director smashes a plate, and the shards are distributed among the crew. Each crew member, for good luck, keeps a shard until the film is done.

The story of cinema in Russia begins on May 4 (Old Style; May 16, New Style), 1896, in the St. Petersburg's Aquarium Theatre, where, between the second and third acts of the operetta *Alfred—A Pasha in Paris*, a ten-minute screening of several short, one-shot films of the Lumière Cinématographe was scheduled (Segida and Zemlianukhin, *Domashniaia sinemateka* 5). By 1913, 1,412 theaters had opened in Russia, with 134 in St. Petersburg alone. By then the standard running time had lengthened from ten minutes to over an hour.

To get some sense of the great parabola of Russian cinema production and its collapse in the twentieth century, it is worth noting that the 129 films released in 1913 were nearly four times as many films as were released some eighty years later, when the 1996 production figures dropped to thirty-four full-length feature films (Segida and Zemlianukhin, *Fil'my Rossii* 245).[1] In the interim, between 1913 and 1996, the viewing public grew to claim the highest per capita attendance in the world (Menashe 10) at twenty visits a year by the 1970s (Beumers, "Cinemarket" 871; Dadamian 76).[2]

Two brief periods of sharp production decline, the post–Civil War years (1921–22) and the postwar Stalin years (1948–51), saw fewer than twenty films a year completed.[3] But from the early 1960s to the early 1980s the industry maintained a consistent production rate of 120 to 150 films (Dondurei, "Kinodelo" 127; Schmemann, "Some Soviet Films" 13).[4] It seemed as if the lean years of so-called cine-anemia (*malokartin'e*) were gone for good. With an average production budget of just under $600,000 (Schmemann, "Some Soviet Films") and an average film attendance of 40 million viewers by the early 1980s, the film industry could proudly point to such hits as Boris Durov's adventure film *Pirates of the 20th Century* (*Piraty XX veka*; Gor'kii Film Studio, 1980) and Vladimir Men'shov's melodrama *Moscow Doesn't Believe in Tears* (*Moskva slezam ne verit*; Mosfil'm, 1980), which each drew 80 million viewers or more in the first year.[5]

The increasing availability of television sets and the expansion of broadcasting range contributed to a gradual decline in cinema attendance, from twenty visits in the 1970s to fifteen visits a year by 1982 (Schmemann, "Some Soviet Films"). Yet the cinema industry remained robust, with production expenditures compensated for by ticket sales as late as 1983 (Venzher et al. 17). As the director Sergei Livnev recalls nostalgically, a film of the early 1980s that attracted fewer than 15 million would have been considered a failure ("V poiskakh" 26).

Beginning in the late 1980s, Russia's third cinema crisis would be utterly unlike the previous two. Instead of cine-anemia, it was now a case of cine-amnesia: the audience forgot about the movies. Even during the three years (1989–91) that a fantastically high one thousand films were made, the audience was already in steep decline (Dondurei, "Mestobliustiteli" 5).[6] By the time the problem reached full-blown crisis the state had few resources and even less political interest in forging a new ideology for a cultural medium of radically diminished status since the early Bolshevik years celebrated it as "the most important of all the arts."[7] And unlike the late Stalin era, when state policy called for "few pictures, but many—very many—spectators" (L. Karakhan, "Cinema without Controls" 1), the new crisis that followed in 1991 was marked by few films and no spectators.

By 1995 even the most successful film barely drew 300,000; per capita attendance had fallen below once a year. In Moscow, where one might expect a higher rate, attendance had fallen to once in four years (L. Karakhan, "Cinema without Controls" 2). The Russian cinema public, the most cinema-going public in the world, had ceased going to the movies.

How did this happen?

The "Intellectualization of Society": May 1986

Perestroika is impossible without the intelligentsia because *perestroika* is also
the intellectualization of society.

—Aleksandr Iakovlev, CPSU Central
Committee secretary for ideology (quoted
in Cohen and vanden Heuvel)

They thought freedom would be announced and everyone would run to see
art. Huge lines would form for Fellini.

—Daniil Dondurei, "Mestobliustiteli" (2007)

Aleksandr Iakovlev's call for the intellectualization of society, inspiring at the
time for the Soviet liberal intelligentsia, unintentionally spelled out the very
weakness of the Gorbachev reform drive across the culture industries, and
in cinema in particular. For cinema the impulse was symptomatic of an overweening emphasis on the creative freedom of the cinema elite, unfettered from
the constraining forces of state ideology on the one hand and audience demand, about which the creative elite had always been relatively ignorant, on
the other.

All the same, *perestroika* was not solely to blame for the industry's collapse;
it was an accelerant to a process already under way. As early as 1985 signs of
trouble were evident. Attendance for that year had dropped to 14.8 visits (Markov, "Kinoperestroika"; *Variety*, July 1, 1987). Such prominent cinema figures as
the director Vladimir Motyl' had begun to express concern in the official press
about the decline in attendance (*Sovetskaia Rossiia*, December 2, 1985), which
dropped to 13.9 visits in 1986 (*Variety*, July 1, 1987). A draw of 20 million visitors
was becoming a rarity, despite a respectable 1986 production level of 142 films
(Schmemann, "Winds") and total 1986 ticket sales at nearly \$2 billion (Don-
durei, "Artistic Culture" 266).[8] While the Soviet attendance rate considerably
outstripped U.S. and British annual rates of 4.5 and 1.5 million, respectively,
for these years (Christie, "The Cinema" 43), it would continue to decline in the
next several years (1987–88) to ten to twelve visits a year.

As for the internal politics of the industry, long-suppressed stirrings of
discontent with the restrictive policies of Goskino, then under the direction
of Filipp Ermash, were evident in the official press as early as mid-1985 (Chernov), nearly a year before the historic May 1986 Fifth Congress of the Filmmakers' Union. A month before the Fifth Congress an April 1986 student revolt
at the USSR's principal film school, the All-Union State Institute of Cinema
(VGIK), demanded the removal of incompetent professors, including Rector Vitalii Zhdan, and the selection of new instructors by student vote (Viktor

Demin in Batchan, "Mad" 50).[9] Yet the student restlessness of April 1986 was less seditious than it was responsive to the spirit of greater tolerance signaled from above, first by Gorbachev at the April 1985 Central Committee Plenum, then at the February 1986 Twenty-Seventh Party Congress of the Communist Party (Harris, "The Public Politics" 19–21; Harris, *Subverting the System* 25–30). A few city blocks from where Gorbachev had delivered his Central Committee Plenum speech only a few days earlier, the VGIK student demands were symptomatic of an intricately intertwined metropolitan elite. The VGIK, after all, some affirmative action admissions to the contrary notwithstanding, was not an egalitarian institution. The very hypercentralization of the state structures in which it was embedded ensured that the unrest was a movement from below only in the sense that its elite was younger and could be expelled, not from below in other, larger (i.e., social) measures of disenfranchisement.

It was the Filmmakers' Union Congress, however, that caught the attention and admiration of the liberal intelligentsia as the first large-scale institutional response in the culture industry to undertake radical structural and administrative changes clearly linking the greater ideological openness advocated at the April 1985 Plenum and February 1986 CPSU Congress to its own industry crisis, including its declining statistics.

The irony is that the key elements in the late Soviet period, structuring and supporting the cinema industry, were also those that led to its collapse. Yet this collapse was impossible to have foreseen, for it was eclipsed by the mammoth and (apparently) indomitable bureaucracy of Goskino. Whatever the political objections to Goskino's monopoly, the system appeared to be robust (maniacally robust, the liberal intelligentsia would argue). The relative functionality of its flawed monopoly became fully evident only in its absence, when the May 1986 Fifth Congress wrested power from Goskino without any capacity, policy, professional experience, or network to provide a substitute under the changing conditions and collapsing infrastructure of the late communist period.

Goskino's inverted system, whereby the center predetermines the ticket sales in accordance with its own complex policies (including, but not exclusively, political contingency), contributed to a stubborn, reactive logic that ill served Russia's leading filmmakers in the decade that followed. A low box-office return (or none at all) was therefore often read as a mark of artistic quality, alternative moral leadership, and a religiously tinged purity of vision more suitable to the economics of lyric poetry than to the maximally expensive industry of film production.

Decades of contradictory and erratic decision-making by Goskino came to a crisis at the May 1986 Fifth Congress, when the film director Elem Klimov was put forward by Aleksandr Iakovlev, then CPSU Central Committee secretary for ideology, for election to lead the Union.[10] Although Klimov's difficulties with Goskino were by no means the most egregious instance of Goskino's whimsy, five of his six feature films had been stymied in one way or another by its political caprice, and his case serves as an interesting example less of Goskino's egregiousness than of its internally conflicting policies. Klimov's fourth film, *Agony* (*Agoniia*; Mosfil'm, completed 1974, released 1981; distributed in the United States as *Rasputin*), had been released for screening at foreign film festivals but took years to reach its (eventually) substantial domestic audience of 18.4 million viewers (Kudriavtsev, *Svoe kino* 13), an excellent number at a time when the average draw for a Mosfil'm production was 17 million (Schmemann, "Some Soviet Films"). Yet Klimov's next film, *Farewell* (*Proshchanie*; Mosfil'm 1982),[11] based on the Village Prose writer Valentin Rasputin's popular novella *Farewell to Matera* (*Proshchanie s Materoi*, 1976), encountered precisely the opposite obstacle from Goskino: released for Soviet *domestic* distribution, the film was blocked by Goskino in negotiations with Cannes as a possible Soviet entry for the 1982 festival (Schmemann, "Winds").

Klimov's case is illustrative of the insufficiency of attributing political difficulties tout court to content or—an equally convenient alternative—to the changing relations between the individual filmmaker and the film bureaucracy. The subjection of the problem to a single-lens instrument such as content, stylistics, professional alliances, or interunion rivalries and allegiances falsely clarifies a cultural process that was multiply contradictory, fluid, and ultimately unpredictable, even to its own culture police.[12]

The Fifth Congress of the Filmmakers' Union opened on May 13, 1986. Iakovlev, who was instrumental in advancing the agenda of a younger and more liberal wave in the Filmmakers' Union, positioned that faction advantageously to win the union secretariat election, bringing Klimov to power as first secretary of the Union and ending Lev Kulidzhanov's twenty-year leadership (1965–86).[13]

More than "intellectualization"—whatever that was[14]—Soviet cinema urgently needed a substitute distribution system, precisely the sort of decentralized infrastructure, one that would have more densely and directly connected periphery to periphery. Yet not one person in the Fifth Congress's new Union administration had professional experience in distribution. The utopian lure of maximal freedom and creativity fatally distracted the new leadership from difficult economic decisions, which therefore inevitably fell available to those who could most rapidly profit in the late 1980s and early 1990s. As the journalist Iurii Gladil'shchikov ("Novye vremena") comments:

> The Union saw its job as the freeing of cinema from the *diktat* of
> the bureaucrats, from the lying; as a "de-stating" of the cinema
> industry and an introduction of the market. Down with Goskino!
> Hail to independent cinema! It turned out, however, that each new
> step the Union took engendered a dozen unexpected contradictions
> that began to snowball.

By the conclusion of the Fifth Congress three-quarters of the 213 seats had turned over in what has since been referred to as the Revolt of May 1986

(Dunlop, "Soviet Film" 33; Lawton, "Soviet Cinema").[15] Goskino, though still an active participant in the cinema process, including a presence on the newly founded Conflicts Commission, was forbidden to conduct any major business without Klimov's signature. "Without the consent of the Cinema Worker's Union," Klimov was assuring the Western press by January 1987, "not a single substantive decision can be made by Goskino" (quoted in Bortin; see also *Variety*, July 1, 1987).

Yet for all Klimov's verdant enthusiasm the May 1986 revolt had clear ideological limits, even for the new Union chief himself. "Studios will be led by exemplary citizens of our country, many of them Communist Party members who follow the current line of our party," Klimov comforted the Western media. "The state leadership will remain" (quoted in *New York Times*, January 27, 1987). Moreover, the ongoing system of "state command" (*goszakaz*)—the state commissioning of films to instantiate some aspect of current Party policy, which thereby guaranteed a high-ranking distribution category and a higher pay rate than for other filmmaking projects—would remain in place, producing as much as 25 percent of total film production.[16] Skeptics, particularly those in the émigré press (cf. Markov, "Kinoperestroika" and "Zriteli"), attributed to these limits an underlying fraudulence extending through the entire reform process.

Among the first projects to be taken up by the Union after the Fifth Congress was the convening of a Conflicts Commission, chaired by *Pravda* critic Andrei Plakhov.[17] The Conflicts Commission was composed of twenty prominent film directors, scriptwriters, critics, and Goskino administrators to review the status of films in several distinct categories: films that had been shelved, films released in severely mutilated form, films assigned a minimal release (so-called underdistribution), and films blocked even before their completion.[18] In the last category was Aleksandr Sokurov's *Mournful Unconcern* (*Skorbnoe beschuvstvie*; Lenfil'm, 1983, released 1987), which had languished unfinished at Lenfil'm Studio until its "liberation" after the May Congress and its screening in 1987.

By early October 1986 the Conflicts Commission had released seventeen films. Its work continued through the end of the 1980s, to include Kira Muratova's two melodramas, *Brief Encounters* (*Korotkie vstrechi*; Dovzhenko Film Studio, completed 1967, released 1987) and *Long Farewells* (*Dolgie provody*; Dovzhenko Film Studio, completed 1971, released 1987), as well as her controversial *Asthenic Syndrome* (*Astenicheskii sindrom*; Odessa Film Studio, completed 1989, released 1990), which bore the dubious honor of being the last forbidden Soviet film.[19] Among the best known of the Commission's releases were Aleksandr Askol'dov's *Commissar* (*Komissar*; Gor'kii Film Studio, completed 1967, released 1987) and Andrei Konchalovskii's *The Story of Asia Kliachina Who Loved but Did Not Marry* (*Istoriia Asi Kliachinoi, kotoraia liubila, da ne vyshla zamuzh*; Mosfil'm, completed 1967, released 1987, also known by the censor's imposed title of the mutilated but still unreleased copy, *Asia's Happiness* [*Asino schast'e*]).[20]

By August 1987 the Commission had reviewed 120 films (*Radio Liberty* 347/87 [August 28, 1987]: 8). One of the more bitter ironies in these releases and re-releases was the appearance of yet another obstacle: the extreme short-age of raw film stock, severely limiting the distribution of several interesting films that remain virtually unknown to this day.[21]

Following the May 1986 Congress the major cinema research institute, the All-Union Research Institute for Cinema Art (VNIIK), replaced its conservative director, Vladimir Baskakov, a former deputy director of Goskino, with the liberal screenwriter Ales' Adamovich, the author of the script for Klimov's *Come and See* (*Idi i smotri*, Belarus'fil'm/Mosfil'm, 1985). The industry's two principal film periodicals, the monthly *Cinema Art* (*Iskusstvo kino*) and the bimonthly *Soviet Screen* (*Sovetskii ekran*), appointed the liberals Konstantin Shcherbakov and Iurii Rybakov, respectively, as new editors in chief (Batchan, "Mad" 49). The liberal critic Viktor Demin became the head of the Association of Soviet Film Critics.[22]

Most noteworthy, however, was the forced retirement on December 28, 1986, of Filipp Ermash, who had headed Goskino for fourteen years, and his re-placement by Aleksandr Kamshalov (*New York Times*, December 29, 1986). The magnitude of this shift can be discerned by bearing in mind that concomitant to Ermash's Goskino position were his posts in the Politburo and the Central Committee CPSU (Chernov). Significantly, Ermash's departure from Goskino was noted by TASS without the pro forma thanks routinely accompanying such departures.[23]

Freed from Goskino's micromanagement, the Soviet Union's studios could now submit two- to three-year plans limited to film subjects for the purpose of avoiding duplication, rather than for Goskino's supervision or approval. The studios gained the freedom to select their own scripts and shooting schedules and to organize their own finances and distribution plans. As of the January 1988 introduction of a self-financing system (*khozraschet*), the creative associations within the studios could keep production profits, with a longer range stipulation that they must also absorb losses from unsuccessful productions. Moreover, with production personnel no longer considered permanent employees, the creative associations could hire and fire workers, lobby the government for direct support, and supervise production without the interference of the studio (Faraday 131). Mosfil'm Studio, expanding first to eight, then by 1988 to eleven creative associations, much to the alarm of the popular press,[24] sought to keep ahead of what turned out to be a disastrous cinema boom, disastrous primarily because the sharp increase in annual production bore no coordinated relationship to distribution, the outdated conditions of theater exhibition, or audience demand.

It should be mentioned that, however much the May 1986 Fifth Congress was a revolutionary moment, a number of the changes introduced there had been anticipated on a smaller scale more than two decades earlier by Grigorii Chukhrai's Experimental Creative Studio (Eksperimental'naia Tvorcheskaia Kinostudiia), which had managed to complete thirty-four productions with an average annual attendance per film of 32 million in the period 1965–72.[25] Then, despite its evident viability as a prototype for self-sustaining film production, it was closed down by Goskino.[26] In 1986 production units would be organized according to similar principles of self-management, and now with elected unit chiefs, subcontracted production staff, and a considerable shift to freelance work. The July 1, 1988, Law on Cooperatives further accelerated the process of de-centralization by permitting the formation of independent production companies, of which Andrei Razumovskii's Fora-Fil'm is the best-known early example. Although this increased organizational freedom was greeted by the liberal creative intelligentsia with tremendous enthusiasm, it bore several serious drawbacks: "freedom," as Faraday (133) points out, meant an increasing miscoordination and lack of planning between and among studios and production companies. Moreover, the burgeoning number of production companies further deflected industry attention from the increasingly acute problem of outdated equipment and production facilities on which the production companies themselves depended but would not renovate.

Of course, for those who wished at the time to believe that the film industry was finally entering a historical period of international acclaim and artistic freedom, there was much to support that view. The three-year period from 1986 through 1988 saw an unprecedented number of major international festival prizes awarded to Soviet cinema. German's *My Friend Ivan Lapshin* (*Moi drug Ivan Lapshin*; Lenfil'm, 1984) was awarded a Bronze Leopard at Locarno in 1986; Gleb Panfilov's *Theme* (*Tema*; Mosfil'm 1979) won a Golden Bear at Berlin in 1987; Nana Djordjadze won a 1987 Golden Camera at Cannes for her debut film *My English Grandfather* (*Moi angliiskii dedushka*; Gruziia Film Studio, 1987); Tengiz Abuladze's *Repentance* (*Pokaianie*; Georgian title *Monanieba*; Gruziia Film Studio, completed 1984, released 1986) won a 1987 Cannes Special Jury Prize.[27] According to William Fisher, Soveksportfil'm left Cannes in 1987 with $2 million in foreign sales.[28] In the following year Soviet cinema received sixty major international awards (*Variety*, July 5–11, 1989). This international recognition was of a different order from that of the earlier cinematic entente of the Thaw period.[29] Now the recognition was accompanied—indeed, perhaps even determined—by a virtual dismantling, rather than a reform, of the Soviet system of administrative-aesthetic controls. The spectacle of the apparatchiks' dismantled system increased the commodity value of the Soviet films of this era.

By the May 1989 Eighth Plenum of the Administration of the Filmmakers' Union participants were already laying the groundwork for Union repudiation of the artistic credo of socialist realism and endorsing changes in the Union charter that would eliminate socialist realism as a governing principle of artistic production.[30] This resolution, which would not take effect until the upcoming Sixth Congress of the Russian Filmmakers' Union, passed by unanimous vote in June 1990 (Lawton, *Kinoglasnost* 93).

Although this new creative independence was enormously important to the morale of the film community, it was not adequate—indeed, it was fatally distracting from any serious effort—to address the growing economic crisis of the industry. By the late 1980s 95 percent of Soviet films attracted fewer than the five million spectators minimally necessary to recoup production costs through theatrical release (Beumers, "Cinemarket" 878; see also Furikov 5).

Another piece of the puzzle, well fitted to the ideology of socialist exhibition practices but ill suited to the changing economy, was the stable admission price, unchanged for half a century (*Variety*, July 1, 1987) and linked neither to a profitable return nor to societywide economic changes more broadly conceived. Ranging from roughly 70 kopeks (one dollar) in the centrally located metropolitan cinemas to 27 kopeks (42 cents) for inexpensive seats in provincial cinemas (*New York Times*, January 27, 1987; see also Christie, "The Cinema" 72 fn. 51), ticket prices were neither high enough nor reliably reported as a return of revenue by which to calculate the success or failure of the manager's selection.

Meanwhile, as falling attendance further eroded any incentive for reporting accurate ticket sales to distributors, theater managers boosted their income by leasing out their undercapitalized space—in particular the spacious, socialist-era cinema lobbies—for entrepreneurs to exhibit the commodities, such as furniture and automobiles, of New Russia or to reconstruct that space for leisure activities, such as casino gambling and discothèques, which had been largely off limits under socialism.[31]

The financial uncertainty of the industry was in part a function of the fact that theatrical release was still virtually the sole mechanism for return. Consistent with the system of state socialism in which it was embedded, Goskino in the late 1980s routinely turned over to state television a selection of feature films for broadcast six months after release in exchange for little more than free advertising. As the television industry grew increasingly powerful and the cinema industry failed to establish a reliable revenue stream, the practice of de facto free television broadcasting for free advertising of a film was enormously detrimental to cinema.

As for video sales as a source of potential revenue, legal production in the mid-1980s was in its infancy. By the mid-1980s Goskino had established the practice—very much an extension of the socialist Weltanschauung but lethal for cinema's position in the emerging market—of allowing films to be copied for rental onto video without authors' payments. By 1987 Kamshalov, celebrating the step-up in domestic production of some 400,000 Soviet Elektronika VCRs by the following year, promised the construction of a thousand new video halls over the next eighteen months,[32] while at the same time taxing the legal video market a crippling 70 percent on profits, thus providing ideal conditions for a flourishing black market (Beumers, "Cinemarket" 887).

Meanwhile, captivated by issues of artistic freedom, leading figures in the film industry could not focus on how the absence of a legal exhibition system and the concomitant flourishing of pirate video production would gut the legal industry. Again the most intelligent and outspoken warnings came from the cultural analyst and journalist Iurii Gladil'shchikov ("Priglashenie" 8):

> I share [the Union of Filmmakers'] desperation. But there's something I don't understand: Wasn't it clear from the very beginning that whoever had the theatres in his hands would also have the power? That there can be no absolute creative freedom in times of a market? That the market would pound away at art like a sledgehammer?

The critical expertise in the distribution sector of Goskino became, if not wholly criminalized, then certainly morally unavailable to the liberal directors-cum-administrators (the conceptual inverse, one might argue, of the problematic relationship of the Bolsheviks to the bourgeois experts of the 1920s), thus facilitating its actual criminalization in the late 1980s and early 1990s, when the Soviet Union and then Russia would come to lead the world in video piracy, second only to the People's Republic of China (Nicholson). Kamshalov's cheerful promises of a "video-encyclopedia in every household" (Variety, July 1, 1987) came to fruition, but not in the way he imagined.

In the meantime administrative attempts to address falling cinema attendance were enthusiastic but inadequate. As early as 1987, in an effort to woo the audience back by opening bars and cafés, a number of metropolitan theaters organized lobby exhibits of rare minerals, stamps, model cars, and postcards, providing a bizarre mix of old-style Soviet mentality and new-style entrepreneurial panache (Variety, July 1, 1987). Missing, however, were the vision and resources to address the rapidly changing viewing practices of the Soviet public on a much vaster scale. In 1986–87 only 2 percent of the Soviet Union's 5,257 permanent cinemas were multiplexes (Variety, July 1, 1987). Permanent cinemas tended to be enormous, often unheated structures; 250 of them had a seating capacity of over eight hundred (Venzher et al. 17, quoted in Beumers, "Cinemarket" 883). Beyond these 5,257 cinemas the country had a great many small, geographically isolated projection units located in workers' clubs and rural houses of culture, for a total of 84,506 projection units. As the liberalizing effects of perestroika produced a vastly more diversified consumer in all branches of cultural production, cinema in particular suffered because its viewing conditions could not easily respond to this growing audience diversity and expectation, however wildly premature, of consumer satisfaction.

Meanwhile the Conflicts Commission was completing its work. By 1990 it had examined 250 films.[33] This work, however, so critical to the creative intelligentsia in 1986 and, paradoxically, a measure of the Commission's success, had by now become a secondary concern.

Audience neglect, shifting consumer demands, and the unstable economy took their toll on the very culture with the greatest number of cinemas in the world: by 1993 the number of permanent cinemas had dropped from 5,257 in 1986–87 to 2,380, and by 1995 to 1,920, only slightly more than the 1,412 theaters of 1913. In addition to closures, cinema construction virtually ceased. In the 1980s the construction rate in the Russian Republic had averaged about fifty new cinemas a year; by 1992 only three cinemas were built, and by 1995 only two (Dondurei, "Kinodelo" 136).

Phantom Cinema: The Early 1990s

There is one integral indicator of the state of Russian cinema after 1988: its absence from the screens of its own country.

—Daniil Dondurei, "Kinodelo" (1995)

Yet another crisis was looming in the early 1990s, again the outcome of the greater openness and diversity of the *perestroika* period. Back in 1986 domestic Soviet feature films accounted for 70 percent of ticket sales in the country's 5,257 permanent cinemas (*Variety*, July 1, 1987). The few U.S. films, a mere eight of the 107 foreign films in 1986,[34] were watched by only 5.4 percent of the cinema-going audience, largely in Moscow and Leningrad. When the 1987 Law on State Enterprises broke Goskino's monopoly on international film negotiations (Lawton, *Kinoglasnost* 80), foreign films, in particular U.S. films, began to flood the domestic market. Kamshalov would acknowledge that "at the present time [mid-1987] we are living for the most part off the distribution of foreign films," a single U.S. film bringing enough profit to cover the average exhibition losses of ten Soviet films (Markov, "Zriteli").

By 1994 U.S. films would account for 73 percent of screening time in theaters; Russian-made films accounted for only 8 percent (L. Karakhan, "Cinema without Controls" 3). An increasing number of Soviet films were by necessity coproduced with foreign firms. Fluctuating currency exchange rates, the increased opportunity to conduct business in either hard or soft currencies, and the decreasing supervision of production projects provided an ideal environment not only for currency speculation by financially strapped filmmakers, but also for criminal activity by money-laundering operations having nothing otherwise to do with cinema. The provision of inexpensive production services to foreign production companies as an additional source of revenue buoyed up the domestic industry until the mid-1990s, when the going rates simply became too steep and inflation more generally rendered such services unprofitable (Faraday 137).

The confluence of these elements—the sudden influx of Western films in distribution; the absence of a regulatory structure through which production and distribution could at least be tracked, if not controlled; the unregulated opportunity for steep profit providing cheap production services; and of course the absence of attention to (or knowledge of *how* to attend to) the domestic market—contributed to an environment in which the film industry was vulnerable to money laundering. It is no surprise, therefore, that by 1990 the normally steady annual output of roughly 150 films suddenly ballooned to a seemingly utopian 300 films, a figure that would be cited ruefully in the next decade, when the industry collapsed (Segida, "Segida-info" 76).

The production of three hundred films in 1990 in no way reflected soaring demand of the domestic market. Rather, it reflected, first, the entrepreneurial response in the film industry to the 1987 Law on Enterprises and the 1988 Law on Cooperatives, spawning a large number of independent production companies, both legitimate and shady, 160 cooperative studios in the three-year period between 1988 and 1991 (Young, "The Name" 39). Second, it reflected the status of cinema as the most vulnerable of the culture industries to illegal currency practices in the early 1990s, a trend that spent itself due neither to legislation nor prosecution but because the money-laundering profession itself moved on to more profitable industries when the average cost of filmmaking rose steeply. While production costs had remained steady in the late 1980s at around $600,000 to $650,000 per film, these companies could produce a film at an increasingly unregulated, black market ruble cost of $100,000 or lower.[35] Yet by 1992, in association with the rapid price liberalization and the rampant inflation that followed, the average actual production cost had climbed to $300,000; a year later it had reached $500,000, and by 1996 it had risen to $700,000 and higher (Beumers, "Cinemarket" 879; *Moscow News*, December 3, 1993, 12).[36]

Produced according to shifting and variously functioning rates—official, unofficial, barter, and futures speculation in an unstable market—these films were typically neither distributed nor screened in a single theater. They were celluloid zombies, never intended for an actual life: the money circulated; the films did not. This phenomenon of unseen films had a paradoxical nature: on the one hand, the industry money laundering was part of a larger process of postsocialist, primitive accumulation; on the other hand, it was in many ways a continuation of the traditional socialist disconnect between supply and demand. As Dondurei ("Kinodelo" 128–29) provocatively puts it:

> The fewer the number of films watched by the public, and the less the public needs them, the greater the number of films that are produced. . . . And no revolutions—neither 1917 nor 1991—can influence the fundamental principal . . .: production here [in Russia] follows its own set of laws, while demand follows its own, different laws.

For legitimate filmmakers the irony in this state of affairs was a return to almost total dependency on Goskino—now *financial* dependency rather than political—for which the subsidies could annually finance at most fifteen feature films. And although this support, juried by a Goskino expert commission of cinema critics, scriptwriters, editors, and directors—but again with no one, as Faraday (148) points out, yet experienced in distribution—was tremendously important, it effectively subsidized the blissful market neglect in favor of yet more art films, to be shown virtually nowhere else but at foreign and domestic film festivals, which themselves proliferated at an extraordinary rate.[37]

For decades Goskino's ideological monopoly had politically made the market: determining the number of copies, the centrality (or marginality) of theatrical release, and therefore the ticket sales figures. When there was no longer a market to be made, Goskino by default made its substitute, providing the only legal domestic subsidy for films that were utterly untethered from the Russian audience. In 1990 only 6 percent of the films registered with Goskino received subsidies; by 1996 about half of the thirty-four films were "Goskino Production" (Beumers, "Cinemarket" 880).[38]

Behind all this lurked the larger questions that had plagued the creative intelligentsia for as long as it could be said to have existed: Does it even matter what the "mute folk" want? And how would the intelligentsia claim to know? The enormous geographic, educational, class, and cultural divide between the self-involved metropole and (in multiple senses) the periphery, increasingly self-aware and internally diversified, was painfully evident in the figures of 1990, when a record three hundred films were produced for an empire in free-fall as per capita attendance was eight visits a year and steadily sinking (Beumers, "Cinemarket" 878; Segida, "Segida-info" 76).

By 1990 some foreign support, such as the French government fund set up through the Centre National de la Cinématographie (CNC), provided the film industry with much-needed international subsidies, without which work by such auteur filmmakers as those examined here—Aleksei German, Kira Muratova, and Aleksandr Sokurov—would never have been shot.[39] By one estimate fully one-third of the Russian films of the early 1990s were French-financed productions (Plakhov, "Une brève histoire" 229). But support from CNC and Goskino was a mixed blessing. Although Russian cinema could not have continued without subsidies during these lean years, films made for "self-order" (*samozakaz*) were unlikely to cure the public's cine-amnesia.

Black Cinema: The Faux Culprit

A convenient scapegoat of the late 1980s and early 1990s was the broad cultural trend called *chernukha*, variously translated as Black Wave or Dark Wave.[40] This cultural strategy, by the late 1980s increasingly associated with cinema in particular, was largely driven by an inversion of Russia's most enduring cultural clichés. Soviet and pre-Soviet notions of the dignity of man, the nobility of womanhood, the integrity of the family, the redemptive function of suffering, the refuge of domestic life, the righteous purposefulness of the mission, the innocence of childhood, the transcendent wisdom of animals, the sanctity of romantic love (and its concomitant suppression of the sexual), and the hygienic potential of the body as a secular temple were all turned upside down:

> Typical settings are dirty and/or crowded apartments (often with pets depicted in proximity to exposed food), littered courtyards (populated by feral dogs or cats), urban streets at night, beer bars or liquor stores, police stations or prisons, and hospitals. . . . Alcoholism and/ or drug addiction is *de rigueur*, as is a general atmosphere of cruelty: physical violence and frequent, unpredictable shouting and arguments. Bodies are commonly deformed by injury or illness, either before the narrative begins or during it. Sex is represented most often as rape. . . . (Graham 9)

With some historical distance one can certainly agree that the worst of *chernukha* films had a deadening predictability to them: socialist realism with a minus sign.[41] As professional critics could not help but notice, many of the hack directors who had previously produced such popular but opportunistic Soviet epics as Igor' Gostev's political detective film *European History* (*Evropeiskaia istoriia*; Mosfil'm Studio, 1984), described by the merciless Iurii Gladil'shchikov ("Priglashenie" 8) as a "foreign policy hit," were the very same directors now shooting such different but equally opportunistic *chernukha* films as Gostev's *No Limits* (*Bespredel*; Mosfil'm, 1989). Likewise, it was bad enough that Mikhail Tumanishvili's odious, official action film *Solo Voyage* (*Odinochnoe plavanie*; Mosfil'm, 1985) enriched him in 1985, before the fall of Goskino.[42] Now, in 1989, his *chernukha* film *Avariia, Cop's Daughter* (*Avariia—Doch' menta*; Mosfil'm, 1989) was one of the very few Soviet films available in domestic cinemas.

Inevitably, therefore, as the cinema industry was collapsing, *chernukha* became the explanatory instrument. The contemporary press attributed to *chernukha*'s images of degraded domestic and urban existence a demonic causality, as if somehow the thematics of the screen were dictating the social collapse rather than something more interdeterminative. As the director Vladimir Dostal' warned, "There is an attempt to show the negative side of Soviet life in films, but that has meant fewer adventure films are being shot. . . . There is a high level of critical awareness, but the audience is not very interested because they have it on television and in newspapers. The people want to go to the cinema to be entertained" (quoted in *Variety*, July 5–11, 1989, 68), as if entertainment alone would have attended to the crisis. In the late 1980s and early 1990s the absence of entertainment, by which was usually meant light comedy and adventure films, was a relatively insignificant problem in the wholesale absence of a functioning distribution system. A shift in genre could not yet of itself contribute in any substantial way to the reanimation of the system while the professions of producer and distributor were still underdeveloped and un-coordinated in a viable industry.[43]

Never mind the fact that attendance had already been steadily dropping for ten years, that the distribution system had collapsed, that the cinema halls were unheated and run down, that the technology was antediluvian, that the federal economy was in ruins. *Chernukha* became ex post facto "the reason why" audiences abandoned cinema. At a time of attendance and distribution freefall *chernukha* was not figurative of but rather responsible for the absent audience, who indeed frequently cited *chernukha* as the cause of their absence.[44] Uncontested in my argument is the evidence that a drop in cinema attendance was *attributed* by cinema-goers to the phenomenon of *chernukha*. What I suggest is that this attribution made coherent the act of nonattendance, which—already happening just fine on its own—became thereby a newly ethical act.

Conveniently neglected in the anodyne condemnation of *chernukha* was the fact that one of *chernukha*'s quintessential films, Vasilii Pichul's *Little Vera* (*Malen'kaia Vera*; Gor'kii Studio, 1988)—without which a discussion of *cher-nukha* makes no sense—ranked among the top fifty Soviet films of any period.[45] The usual counterclaim—that the film's appeal lay in its sexual explicitness—conveniently misconstrues sexual explicitness as somehow separate from *cher-nukha*. Nor was *Little Vera* an exception. Another blockbuster *chernukha* film, Petr Todorovskii's melodrama *Intergirl* (*Interdevochka*; Mosfil'm/Filmstallet [Sweden], 1989), drew an audience of 44 million (Kudriavtsev, *Svoe kino* 415) for each of its two series. A third *perestroika* blockbuster, also arguably a *chernukha* film, Aleksandr Proshkin's *Cold Summer of 1953* (*Kholodnoe leto 53-go*; Mosfil'm, 1988), drew 41.8 million viewers (Beumers, "Cinemarket" 877).

In fact, a number of Russia's most outstanding filmmakers found the aesthetics of *chernukha* a richly productive source of individual experimentation, to which the audience responded more readily than to other offerings of this period. Although critics debate the terms of their inclusion as *chernukha* films, the trend resulted in such startling and original pieces as Iurii Kara's *Kings of Crime* (*Vory v zakone*; Gor'kii Film Studio, 1988), Sergei Bodrov's *Freedom Is Paradise* (*SER [Svoboda—eto rai]*; Mosfil'm, 1989), Vitalii Kanevskii's *Freeze—Die—Resurrect* (*Zamri—umri—voskresni*; Lenfil'm, 1990), Pavel Lungin's *Taxi Blues* (*Taksi-bliuz*; Lenfil'm/ASK Eurofilm/MK2 Productions, 1990), and Kira Muratova's *Asthenic Syndrome*, as well as such documentaries as Hertz Frank's *Final Verdict* (*Vysshii sud*; Latvian title *Augstaka viesa*; Riga Documentary Film Studio, 1987) and Stanislav Govorukhin's *No Way to Live* (*Tak zhit' nel'zia*; Mosfil'm/Filmverlag der Autoren, 1990).

The popularity of these films would undercut the argument that the audience, having attended *Little Vera* and other *chernukha* films en masse (in the years when attendance had otherwise been dropping), then collectively abandoned cinema altogether. A less lunar analysis might suggest that the negative discourse around *chernukha* became a way of registering anxiety about larger social and political processes existing prior to the trend's circulation. Three elements—the larger social and economic collapse, the lengthy decline in attendance figures, and the filmic codes internal to *chernukha*—so sustained each other as to provide a compelling narrative of displacement and blame directed at the cinema screen, a retroactive, improvisational attribution. As an innovative visual strategy, deeply challenging to the relatively stable codes of the permissible, *chernukha* provided an irresistible opportunity through which to narrate the accumulated anxiety about the profound cultural shifts that long predated even the earliest instances, such as Hertz Frank's 1987 gritty documentary on a young man's execution for murder.

Moreover, throughout the largely sanctimonious critical discussion of its demerits, *chernukha* was not a historically isolated phenomenon but coexisted in economic circulation with the wave of U.S. B movies that colonized Soviet cinemas in the late 1980s and early 1990s. Among the most memorable of these were Pat Townsend's *Beach Girls* (Crown International, 1982) and Emmett Alston's *Nine Deaths of the Ninja* (Crown International, 1985).[46] In the urgency of critical resistance to both the experimental brutality of much *chernukha* and the derivative banality of U.S. B movies, what got lost was the difference between the two: the incommensurability of an innovative cultural intervention by Soviet filmmakers with the largely retrograde economic intervention of U.S. filmmakers. The former was an exorcism of traditional discursive codes; the latter, the repetitive detritus of U.S. culture. The fact that many of the late 1980s and early 1990s Russian films, including the *chernukha* films cited above, were Western coproductions—with Filmverlag der Autoren and Interpromex (FRG), MK2 Productions (France), Filmstallet (Sweden), foreign companies still indistinguishable from Crown International (U.S.)—contributed to this confusion, as well as to the repeated charge that the Russian *chernukha* films were made for the West, where they as a rule barely circulated. The perceived kinship of *chernukha* films and U.S. B movies—casual sexuality, heightened violence, a disregard for traditional norms of respectability—grew out of media and audience anxieties about the Soviet Union's diminished status after 1989: the possibility that the only difference left between its second-world culture and a third-world culture was the rubble of the Berlin Wall.

Art Scholar and Horse Trader: Tagi-zade

The credit for importing and distributing *Beach Girls*, *Nine Deaths of the Ninja*, and hundreds of other gems must be awarded to Ismail Tagi-zade, an Azeri entrepreneur with a putative higher degree in art history. Tagi-zade's first venture into business was with the sale of stallion herds in the early *perestroika* period.

He moved on to the rental of the Ali Bairamov Garment Factory in Baku, then, sensibly enough, to the carnation business, where he was reputed to control the vast network of flower saleswomen at the entrance to metros throughout the country. Government-imposed restrictions of the late 1980s on commercial businesses, he recounts in a 1991 interview in *Komsomol'skaia Pravda*, led him to the realization that the "end of the competition of artists" must give rise to the "beginning of the competition of producers" (Rezanov and Khoroshilova). And produce he did, mounting what Gladil'shchikov ("Priglashenie" 8) describes as "the first attempt at a monopoly in the arts under our market conditions."

From interviews of that period, it would seem that Tagi-zade was the cinema industry's version of the emergent Red-Brown coalition—red capitalists, brown nationalists—able to tap equally into legal or illegal resources, including Communist Party USSR wealth. In a telling passage from his interview with the *Ogonek* journalist Sergei Filippov (30–31), Tagi-zade offers this intriguing self-portrait of a man for whom monopoly control is self-evidently a positive term, the common desire of both Soviet communism and robber-baron capitalism:

> Each of us should ask himself what he has done for [the Party]. . . .
> We will surrender Soviet distribution to no one and will fight for our monopoly. In the West, every corporation fights for a monopoly. For a name, for glory! The rank of monopolist must be earned by long and hard labor.

In March 1990 Tagi-zade organized the First Congress of the All-Union Association of State Film and Video Distribution Enterprises (Vsesoiuznaia assotsiatsiia gosudarstvennykh predpriatii kinovideoprokata), known as ASKIN (Rudnev; Gladil'shchikov, "Priglashenie").[47] Bringing together regional cinema and video organizations, ASKIN gained financial backing from Tiskino, a trust that allegedly included a bank, an insurance company, several factories, a foreign corporation, and a production company best known for financing Gennadii Vasil'ev's *Tsar Ivan the Terrible* (*Tsar' Ivan Groznyi*; Tiskino, 1991), based on the novella *The Silver Prince* by the Soviet author Aleksei Tolstoi.[48]

Although ASKIN was initially supported by the (still Soviet) Russian Federation Ministry of Culture and Goskino, which later withdrew sponsorship,[49] the reaction of both the Soviet Filmmakers' Union and USSR Minister of Culture Nikolai Gubenko was unequivocal.[50] The Union issued a resolution challenging ASKIN's authority, and Minister of Culture Gubenko denounced the association as the revanche of former Goskino bureaucrats. And indeed it was. Tagi-zade's colleagues included the usual suspects: the former head of Goskino Filipp Ermash, former first deputy director of Goskino Nikolai Sizov, former deputy director of Goskino Boris Pavlenok, and the former head of the Goskino Film Production Board Liudmila Ivanova.[51] Yet the opportunity for a revanche had been generously if unintentionally provided by the Union's own failure in the intervening years to develop an alternative distribution structure to that of their historical enemies.

ASKIN sought to establish itself as a government organization free from taxes, with an exclusive government license for a monopoly on the acquisition and distribution of foreign films. Moreover, its financial profile increasingly suggested access to vast reserves of hard currency, enough to fund its delegation of six hundred at the 1991 Cannes International Film Festival.[52] ASKIN's Second Congress (1991), complete with a caviar reception, was held in the Kremlin's Palace of Congresses, normally reserved for state and Party functions. There the organization claimed acquisition rights to 158 U.S. films, a figure that grew by another three hundred films (including *Beach Girls*) following an ASKIN trip to Los Angeles later that year. The impact on exhibition was palpable: of 313 films screening in Moscow's major cinemas in one week in 1991, only twenty-two of them (or 7 percent) were Soviet, a state of affairs that the media attributed directly to the dubious success of ASKIN (Rudnev).

Yet in late 1991 Tagi-zade disappeared as quickly and mysteriously as he had appeared. Faraday (226 fn. 78) attributes Tagi-zade's sudden vanishing act to the final collapse of centralized power—principally the old network to which former Goskino officials would still have access—associated more broadly with the breakup of the Soviet Union in late 1991. Although this is an incomplete explanation, it is consistent with the available information. By late 1991–92 it seemed the attempted monopoly had failed and the colorful Tagi-zade dropped from sight.

Meanwhile, by the early 1990s the Filmmakers' Union was beginning to confront the hard realities of its powerlessness. Iurii Gladil'shchikov's ("Novye vremena") mordant description of the June 1990 Sixth Congress of the Filmmakers' Union is more revelatory than any political analysis:

> On a plywood board was a slogan—"Want to be Secretary of the [Filmmakers' Union]: Be Our Guest!"—and a drawing of a man in suit and tie with a naked beauty on his knees, surrounded by computers, video dubbing machines, whiskey, computer disks, and Marlboro cigarettes. Instead of his face was a hole: stick your head in and get photographed. The public laughed. The public applauded.

By the conclusion of the Sixth Congress a relatively unknown Tadzhik cameraman, Davlat Khudonazarov, had been elected head of the Filmmakers' Union, replacing Andrei Smirnov, who had been substituting for Elem Klimov and had put forth Khudonazarov's candidacy. A 1965 graduate of VGIK and former people's deputy, Khudonazarov had the distinction of early political difficulties with local Tadzhik authorities; his diploma film, *Lullaby* (*Kolybel'naia*; VGIK, 1965), a ten-minute documentary on Tadzhik village life, had been shelved before the young filmmaker's career had even begun.[53] Although Khudonazarov had competitors in the Union election, including Viktor Merezhko and Karen Shakhnazarov, most of the other prominent figures—Vadim Abdrashitov, Pavel

Chukhrai, Stanislav Govorukhin, Emil' Lotianu, Igor' Maslennikov, Vladimir Motyl', El'dar Riazanov, and El'dar Shengelaia—had declined to run, ensuring Khudonazarov's victory by a considerable margin.

The evident reluctance on the part of these most gifted, veteran filmmakers to lead the Union speaks volumes about their difficulties over the four years since May 1986. Well equipped to contend with ethical abstractions, the post-Ermash Union administration was in no position to deal with the increasingly entrepreneurial and lawless predations of New Russia, either troglodytic ex-bureaucrats or the increasingly powerful video pirates. Instead, the post-1986 Filmmakers' Union concerned themselves more with civic issues of high-minded democracy and progressive thinking so fatally characteristic of the intelligentsia in all its historical vulnerability.

To the extent that the battleground for progressive ethics was constituted as their playing field, the Union continued to push the limits of the conceptually permissible. Anticipating the breakup of the Soviet Union (now only six months away), it was the first creative union to transform itself into a confederation of former Soviet unions now with equal status ("VI s'ezd" 3). Klimov presented a new proposal for a law on cinema, a change that would permit tax relief for production and distribution costs as well as import and export fees. Yet neither the legal system nor the Union democrats were any match for the lightning speed with which the cinema industry, now utterly distinct from the Filmmakers' Union, was changing. The cinema law was signed into force only six years later (on August 22, 1996), after some 104 amendments (Beumers, "Cinemarket" 876), when the industry had already collapsed.

Meanwhile, theater attendance continued its steady decline as distributors operated in an environment of disorientation and mistrust. A 1993 survey of film distributors concerning their methods of film selection revealed a staggering portrait: given a choice of whom to rely on as their main criterion of choice—sociologists, film critics, or festival juries—68 percent of respondents answered that their overriding instrument of choice was their own personal taste (*Moscow News* 49 [December 3, 1993]: 12).

The consequences of this ambitious self-reliance were telling: "Forty people for a screening in an 800-seat hall were viewed as the norm. An attendance of 3–5% surprised no one. One occupied seat for nine empty ones today [1993] is practically a success" (Venzher, "Vyderzhivaiut" 8). Daniil Dondurei's research firm Dubl'-D reported that, if at most one seat in ten was the general occupancy for all films screened in Russia, then the occupancy for Russian films in particular was running close to one occupied seat in a thousand (*Moscow News* 49 [December 3, 1993]: 12). Indeed, as the industry press indicates, by 1993 the Moscow theaters were at 8 percent capacity, and by 1994 were down to 3 percent (L. Karakhan, "Cinema without Controls" 2; Venzher, "Ekonomika" 19). A comparison of 1994 attendance statistics reveals them to be 10 percent of those in 1987 (Dondurei, "Kinodelo" 127).

Beyond Moscow the capacity was a dismal 1.4 percent (Beumers, "Cine-market" 884), at a time when no Russian film sold more than 500,000 tickets (Dondurei, "Posle imperii" 7); more typically the figure was 100,000 tickets, the lowest attendance rate in Europe (Larsen, "In Search" 193). Only 8 percent of screen time was devoted to Russian films (L. Karakhan, "Cinema without Controls" 3). By 1995 even Hollywood hits, such as Oliver Stone's *Natural Born Killers* (Warner Bros., 1994), attracted a mere 2 to 3 million viewers (Dondurei, "Posle imperii" 7). Steven Spielberg's *Schindler's List* (Universal Pictures, 1993)—"doomed to failure in the hands of Russian distributors and exhibitors" (L. Karakhan, "Cinema without Controls" 7)—drew an audience of only 230,000, whereas a Russian film that drew as many as 100,000 viewers was, in the words of the young director Sergei Livnev, "a rare event" (quoted in "V poiskakh" 26). As Beumers ("Cinemarket" 885) succinctly puts it, "The masses [did] not want to see *these* films in *these* cinemas."

Piracy as Usual

By the time Jack Valenti, president of the Motion Picture Association of America (MPAA) and its associated international trade organization, the Motion Picture Association (MPA),[54] announced a boycott of the 1991 Seventeenth Moscow International Film Festival, as well as a halt on the sale to Soviet distributors of U.S. films produced by the seven major studios, video piracy was already well established as the dominant mode of spectatorship in the USSR. Valenti's insistence later that year that the Soviet Union cease its "state-condoned piracy" and live up to the terms of the Bern Copyright Convention, to which the country was not even a signatory (Hift 12), was a rhetorical gesture at international legality to which the Soviet government was in no position to attend. The sheer size of the country, stretching across eleven time zones, militated against any possibility of antipiracy enforcement. If a television station in the Maritime Territory, Russia's Far East, illegally broadcast Brett Leonard's *Lawnmower Man* (Allied Vision, 1992), it was highly unlikely that its legal Moscow distributor, Krupnyi Plan Plius, would choose to travel thousands of miles and file thousands of documents, as required by what passed for law, in order to receive, in the words of its distributor, Marina Trubina, "laughable damages" (Telingater 13).

While the theaters were flooded with Tagi-zade's B movie purchases, pirated videos of U.S. A movies for consumption at home had become the norm. Prerelease copies of major U.S. blockbusters were available for sale as much as two weeks before their U.S. debut (Sutotskaia 12).[55] A full month before the Moscow theatrical premiere of Victor Fleming's classic *Gone with the Wind* (Selznick International, 1939), the video version was available for viewing and purchase not far from the Kremlin.[56] Immediately following its legal theatrical premiere the film was broadcast illegally, together with Renny Harlin's *Die-hard 2* (20th Century Fox, 1990), also not licensed for Soviet release (Hift 12). The Lenin Museum Video Salon—a semantic combination I shall pass over without comment—regularly advertised illegal showings and sales of Walt Disney videos (*Moskovskie novosti* 2 [January 13, 1991]: 2). Meanwhile U.S. earnings from official Soviet sales were paltry, running under a million dollars (Hift 12).

Thus cinema was squeezed by a trio of juggernauts—the money-laundering business, a burgeoning television industry, and the illegal video pirating industry—at a time when its own distribution system was in shambles.[57] By 1993, with the U.S. boycott of sales for legal cinema exhibition now evidently useless in effecting change, U.S. studios once again began a gradual reentry into the market, including the sale of those same films—such as Kathryn Bigelow's action thriller *Point Break* (20th Century Fox, 1991)—that had been widely available at the top of the list of video piracy hits (Fix 14).[58] Although the major studios largely stayed clear of the 1993 Eighteenth Moscow International Film Festival, except for 20th Century Fox's Marilyn Monroe retrospective, the official boycott had ended (*Moscow Times* May 29, 1993). It had become clear that the problem could not be solved through the boycott of festivals and legal exhibition, which, though in shambles, was not the principal problem.

Statues and Statutes (The Mid-1990s)

In mid-October 1993 Boris Yeltsin made a visit to Yaroslavl', 125 miles northeast of Moscow. It was his first venture outside Moscow since the armed rebellion of October 4 had pitted him against both his own vice president, Aleksandr Ruts-koi, and the chair of the dissolved Parliament, Ruslan Khasbulatov. Meetings with the fifteen administrative heads of Russia's central regions concerning the upcoming elections took up most of his agenda, but the principal publicity event and ceremonial purpose of this October journey was to dedicate a bronze statue to the eleventh-century grand prince of Kievan Rus', Iaroslav the Wise, under whose rule the first Slavic legal code was set down. Iaroslav, founder of Kiev, had ruled over areas of (modern-day) Russia, Ukraine, and Belarus, yet Yeltsin's invocation of the historical unity of this region proved to be as unconvincing as his accompanying invocation of the sanctity of the Russian legal code: the president of Ukraine, invited as a show of Russian-Ukrainian friendship, was ostentatiously absent (Bykovsky and Orlov; Whitney).

It is a long stretch from statuary to cinema, yet this comparison cites the extreme ends of the spectrum of cultural production to underscore the radical vulnerability of cinema in the culture industry. While the society as a whole collapsed, different forms of cultural production were more or less positioned for adjustment to changing conditions. Those arts in which the relationship between production, distribution, and consumption were organizationally complex—the book and cinema industries, as opposed to monument production, for example—suffered enormously and were in no position to maintain stability. At issue is not simply the expanse of the shrunken empire and radical diversity of taste and subcultures, but more intricate issues of internal organization, for which statuary serves as an extreme example, sharing with theater and live music the copresence of artist and consumer (Faraday 145).

Aside from issues of economic organization, cinema was still tainted, long after it had ceased to be a convenient haven for money laundering (roughly 1989–91), with tales of massive misspent capital and corruption, played out in the press and fueled by stories of fiscal irresponsibility by the very directors who had proffered images of a new redemptive Russia. The federal government's $18 million allocation for the 1995 Moscow International Film Festival, which had been the financial responsibility of the film director and Union head Sergei Solov'ev, was a familiar tale of woe: $8 million was spent and another $10 million, designated for much-needed theatrical reconstruction and upgrading as well as other long-term capital investment, was deposited in a bank that immediately crashed, stopping all transactions and access to the festival money, which subsequently disappeared (L. Karakhan, "Cinema without Controls" 7). As for the film director himself:

> Not long ago director Sergei Solov'ev, Secretary of the Russian Filmmakers' Union, apologizing for the inevitable cynicism, publicly admitted in front of high-ranking officials in charge of cinema that he had received funds first for a [planned] blockbuster, a screen version of *Anna Karenina*, and then for an ambitious project about Ivan Turgenev, and had spent the money without taking a single shot. (Karakhan 6)[59]

Cinema's already shoddy reputation was further blackened by conflation with other, deeply criminalized media. As the public ceased to go to the cinema, "cinema" became something shown on video and television in a culture in which "the video market and cable network is 98% criminal [activity]" (Dondurei, "Kinodelo" 133). In this fashion cinema embodied the worst elements of both eras: New Russian corruption with a de-legitimized Soviet past. Unlike fine arts, theater, monuments, literature, and architecture, its virtual absence in the tsarist past rendered it less available for imaginative rediscovery than other cultural industries in an era nostalgically invested in a redemptive return to its pre-Soviet legacy.

Enterprising directors, anticipating this trend in the mid-1990s, attempted to harness its potential, providing the public with a barrage of literary adaptations, including five in 1996 alone, the year when only thirty-four full-length feature films were produced.[60] The majority of these films chose literature from the liminal period of late tsarism to early socialism—Chekhov, Sologub, Aleksandr Amfiteatrov, Gor'kii—an associative reversal, perhaps, of the liminal era in which Russian culture now found itself, so as to contemplate from a distance the opportunities chosen and not chosen. It is not surprising that Chekhov, with his recurring motif of lost chances, would lead the list of literary adaptations. Though his work had been adapted over the decades for at least sixty Russo-Soviet films dating back to the Russian screening of Kai Hansen's silent *Romance with a Double Bass* (*Roman s kontrabasom*; Pathé, 1911), his evocative potential for the twilight years of the twentieth century was evident to even the laziest of directors.

These sentimental adaptations were competing, however, with imported Hollywood hits that could be purchased by cinema managers at prices that ranged from 33 percent to .05 percent of a new Russian feature film release.[61] And so, it turned out, literary adaptations were not the magic formula, any more than the next formula, the late 1990s wave of so-called kind cinema (*dobroe kino*),[62] could prove to be magic in an unheated, outmoded, empty cinema hall. The director Sergei Ursuliak, whose *Summer People* (*Letnie liudi*; Kovsag, 1995) was one of the more talented adaptations of the period, describes this dawning realization as he watched the six chartered microbuses of the St. Petersburg's Festival of Festivals carrying the festival's ticket holders from theater to theater: "I looked at those buses and became terrified; I realized that they contained the entire audience of my pictures today" (quoted in L. Karakhan, "Cinema without Controls" 2).

The nadir of Russian cinema, 1996 marked the most intense moment of the industry's internal contradictions. The Law on Cinema, initiated back in 1991, was finally signed by Boris Yeltsin on August 22, 1996.[63] At a time when cinema had virtually ceased to exist—a mere thirty-four films reached completion, and a dismal 28 to 30 percent of promised government production funding was actually provided in 1996–97 to the newly renamed Roskino (A. Franklin 13)—the law finally addressed tax incentives and a clear-cut definition of the responsibilities of the "new" (now decade-old) Goskino in a wildly optimistic set of tasks. Together with the Law on Authors' Rights,[64] ratified a year earlier, this law on cinema provided the first postcommunist legal framework for film production. But both laws were weakened by the fact that neither was yet supported by other corresponding legal codes to make them effective. In the case of the Law on Cinema, the tax incentives were unsupported by tax law. In the case of the Law on Authors' Rights, video piracy could be prosecuted under civil law (resulting in fines) but was still unsupported by the penal code, which would have resulted in prosecution.[65] Like the statue to Iaroslav, the eleventh-century founder of the Slavic legal code, these statutes were monuments to an absence, the empty space where, sometime in the future, legality might come to be, a cinema law in the absence of both cinema and law.

Older "Young Directors," Younger "Senior Producers"

Meanwhile a massive generational shift was occurring, evident contrastively in two arenas where the social upheaval, economic instability, and decade-long deterioration in the industry had taken its toll. In 1985 the customary age of debut for young directors was twenty-six; by 1996 it had risen to thirty-seven (Dondurei, "Rynok" 53). In studio management an opposite trend could be traced. Traditionally awarded to the Russian film industry's most senior Soviet colleagues, studio management by 1995–96 was beginning to shift to young, entrepreneurial directors: Sergei Livnev, Valerii Todorovskii, Aleksandr Khvan, and the lesser-known Iurii Moroz.[66] Most notable among these was the 1995 appointment of Sergei Livnev to Gor'kii Studio, an ambitious assignment given its thousand-plus staff and four-billion-ruble debt (Veselaia). By 1995 the independent production boom of the early 1990s had abated; only a very few serious, younger cinema figures, such as the director Sergei Sel'ianov,[67] had established production companies with a track record of stable, successful work.

There is little evidence to suggest that the two phenomena—the increasing age of "young directors" and the decreasing age of "senior" studio heads—were related, that is to say, whether through desperation or ambition that younger and midlevel cinema figures were gravitating from directing into cinema management (studios, production companies, distribution companies, and the like). What is clear is that the appearance of younger figures in cinema management coincided with an upward turn in the fortunes of the industry.

Salutary too was the appearance on the horizon of younger, Western entrepreneurs such as Raymond Markovich and Paul Heth, who began doing business in Russia, respectively, as a lawyer and a businessman in the timber industry.[68] Together they founded Golden Ring Entertainment in 1993 to provide the Moscow ex-pat community with recent U.S. films at the Americom Cinema in the Radisson Slavianskaia Hotel.[69] By October 1996, as part-owners of a distribution company with exclusive Russian rights to Walt Disney and Columbia Tri-Star pictures, Markovich and Heth ventured the opening of Kodak Kinomir, a single-screen Moscow cinema with two million dollars' worth of state-of-the-art equipment backed by Eastman Kodak, which had opened a Russian subsidiary as early as 1993 (A. Franklin 13; Kishkovsky C-4). With tickets initially going at a relatively steep five to six dollars per person, the theater, built in the former House of Culture for the government newspaper *Izvestiia*, managed by 1997 to draw a profit of $3 million in ticket sales and $1.6 million in concession sales, accounting for as much as 60 percent of Russian cinema revenues (Munroe). An attendance average at Kodak Kinomir of 50 percent capacity, with evening screenings frequently sold out, was a stark contrast to the 2 to 8 percent average capacity at most Russian cinemas, where tickets sold for about twenty-five cents (A. Franklin 13).

Although Kodak Kinomir was the most visible example, it was soon no longer an isolated one. The owners of older, well-known cinemas from the Soviet era, such as Art Cinema (Khudozhestvennyi), Pushkin, and Cinecenter (Kinotsentr), renovated their theaters, installing comfortable seats, Dolby Digital Surround Sound systems, and other new technologies. Heth, parting ways with Markovich to found Cinebridge Ventures in 1999 with Shari Redstone, president of National Amusements, took on more ambitious construction of exhibition spaces (Munroe).[70]

Of course, the building and renovation of domestic theaters did not immediately address the ever elusive prospects of Russian domestic cinema. By 1996 an estimated 80 percent of theatrical offerings were still U.S. films; a mere 10 percent were Russian, and of these, 5 percent were contemporary (Dondurei, "Rynok" 28–30). Television broadcasting displayed an equally, if differently, discouraging pattern for contemporary Russian film: because broadcasting fees for U.S. films were high, an inexpensive and popular alternative was the Soviet-era film, particularly those of the 1960s and 1970s, which came to occupy more broadcasting time in 1994 on four of the five major channels than U.S., European, or even the newly popular Latin American films.[71]

Thus contemporary Russian cinema was again squeezed from three sides: it was displaced from theaters by U.S. films; it was displaced from television by Soviet Stagnation-era films; and it was displaced from the video industry by piracy, which was, of course, in no way limited in its ambitions to the piracy of Russian films.[72] By 1997 an estimated 73 percent of the video traffic was pirated copies, at an annual estimated loss of $6 million in legal business. Because a pirated video could be purchased in 1997 for the same price as a cinema ticket, the Russian public, who by now increasingly owned VCRs,[73] might be forgiven if they preferred to own a film—that is, buy a pirated video—rather than watch it for the same price a single time in a cold, undercapitalized theater.

Jack Valenti, having earlier declared a boycott of the 1991 Seventeenth Moscow International Film Festival, weighed in at the 1997 Twentieth Festival to promote the newly founded Russian Anti-Piracy Organization and (finally) corresponding legislation to punish copyright violation with prison terms of up to five years. By the end of the 1990s, however, the illegal industry was already well established, not only in the Moscow suburb of Mitino and at what was colloquially known as Gorbushka (the major video market near Moscow's Gorbunov House of Culture), but also through a federation-wide, twenty-four-hour Internet business, with an estimated 100,000 employees in a complex cell structure (Sul'kin, "Gorbushku"). By the end of the decade the piracy industry—a daunting opponent even for the MPA/MPAA, never mind the Russian film studios—handled up to seven hundred new films a year with a turnover time (including voice-over) of forty-eight hours and a cost of up to $200 for new U.S. releases.

Default: The Late 1990s

In May 1997 Sergei Livnev, head of Gor'kii Film Studio, announced a brilliant idea: the creation of the innovative Association of Low-Budget Film Studios, designed to produce inexpensive films at an average cost of about $200,000 per film, without ideological orientation, and with the profits reinvested into the next film. Given its cautious economics and sober marketing strategies, the plan might have made a major contribution in rebuilding the industry, had it not been for one factor Livnev could not have foreseen: the massive domestic economic default less than fifteen months later, on August 17, 1998.

The impact of Russia's federal default on the cinema industry was immediate and devastating. Most film projects under production were put on immediate hold. Major cinema construction projects, such as the plan by Sergei Lisovskii's advertising and concert-promotion empire Premier SV to renovate and refit a 2,500-seat cinema as a major multiplex (and mall) at Kursk Station Square, ground to a halt as Austrian investors withdrew funding and French partners sharply raised their interest rates (Kishkovsky C4). By October 1998, having produced twelve films in the Low-Budget Project (including its most spectacular successes, Balabanov's *Brother*, coproduced with CTV), Livnev resigned from Gor'kii Studio. His $94 million project to develop one hundred new-technology cinemas throughout Russia was suspended, and he left Russia for the United States.

In the waning years of the decade only the confirmed optimist would claim reasons to be encouraged by the contemporary state of the film industry. By 1997 Mosfil'm, which in Stagnation years had routinely had forty-five to fifty films in production at any given time, could now support at best five to seven productions, its 6,000-plus staff shrunken to seven hundred permanent employees; Lenfil'm, its sister studio, fared no better, renting out space to a carwash. The chief reliable production support continued to be provided by Goskino, which was in turn allocated a mere 0.2 percent of the federal budget for the development of the film industry, about $30 million a year in 1998 and 1999—the cost, as Menashe (12) points out, of a single average Hollywood production. Of this $30 million, $10 to $15 million was budgeted for the production of feature films.[74] This figure could fully finance approximately twelve feature films, at an average cost of just under $1 million and a low-budget cost of $200,000 to $300,000 per film.

As for exhibition, 1998 ticket prices at Kodak Kinomir ranged from four dollars to thirty dollars, from one day's to one week's income for the average Russian and among the most expensive ticket prices in Europe (Dondurei, "The State" 47; Faraday 232 fn. 9). Where prices were cheaper, that is to say, beyond Kodak Kinomir and a handful of other metropolitan cinemas—the Pushkin, the Art Cinema, the Cinecenter—few theaters were technologically equipped or sufficiently comfortable to draw an audience. Indeed, of the approximately one thousand remaining functioning Russian cinemas, only forty-six were equipped with Dolby Digital sound systems even as late as 2001.

The Filmmakers' Union, to which the cinema community had looked throughout the *perestroika* and early post*perestroika* years for some sense of professional identity and guidance, had become increasingly peripheral to the cinema process. By 1997, with fewer than 2 percent of its members under thirty-five, it was becoming painfully clear that the next generation of filmmakers no longer looked to the Union as its principal resource (Beumers, "Cinemarket" 875).

As for the artistic quality of the screenplays, by 1999 the newly appointed head of Goskino, Aleksandr Golutva, the former head of Lenfil'm, was unrestrained in his comments about their deadening predictability. In an interview with the film critic Viktor Matizen, he commented:

> Always the same schema, always the same narrative moves, small
> thinking . . . for example, the hero is driven to frenzy; he grabs a
> weapon and begins to avenge himself. Or the New Russian who
> seems bad, but then turns out to be good. Or all possible kinds of
> Cinderellas à la *Moscow Doesn't Believe in Tears*,[75] but much weaker.
> *Afgantsy* [veterans of the Soviet war with Afghanistan] and *chechentsy*
> [veterans of the war with Chechnia] in enormous quantity. A whole
> stratum of [funding] applications "à la Tarantino." (Golutva 26)

And yet, despite this bleak picture, a few positive signs were evident. Film production for 1997 had risen slightly from a 1996 low of thirty-four full-length feature films to forty-one; this number would to rise to fifty-five the following year. As for television, by 1997 Russian-language films and serials, though still predominantly Soviet rather than contemporary, began to cut into the foreign market to account for 45.5 percent of total film hours on television. Yet, if there was any hope emerging for cinema at the end of the millennium, it was to be found less in specific films or in a handful of rosy statistics than in a more coherent picture of what needed to be done.

Only as the century ended, more than a decade after the tumultuous Fifth Congress of the Filmmakers' Union had dismantled its own distribution system, did some predictable pattern fall into place for the potential financial solvency of film production. In the 1998 estimation of Igor' Tolstunov, the director of NTV-Profit and one of the most successful and pragmatic of the film industry's new producers,[76] a "good film"—that is to say, a film with some chance of financial return—could reasonably be expected to garner $500,000: roughly $100,000 from theatrical distribution, $250,000 to $300,000 from video, and $70,000 to $100,000 from television (Faraday 200, 232 fn. 10). Although Tolstunov's estimates for television rights were probably optimistic,[77] the sociologist Daniil Dondurei, who would have less at stake in his citations than the producer, has given similar overall estimates for 1997: $80,000 from theatrical release, $200,000 from video sales, and a top figure of $30,000 to $50,000 for television broadcast rights, for an average return of $310,000 to $330,000 (Beumers, "Cinemarket" 873). Clearly, any film beyond a budget of $300,000 to $500,000 (in a context where "low-budget" is still, following Sergei Livnev's formula, calculated at $200,000 to $300,000) would be unlikely to recoup its expenditures.

One of the more difficult lessons for the emerging cinema business to learn was the fact that in a shaky economy the (potential) cinema-going public would not respond to the lure of inexpensive tickets, but by the opposite: the lure of an expensive and stylish night out, complete with nearby watering holes, such as Kodak Kinomir's T. G. I. Friday's, Planet Hollywood, and Chuck Norris's Beverly Hills Casino. For younger, moneyed Muscovites, even after the August 1998 default, events such as the premieres of James Cameron's *Titanic* (20th Century Fox, 1997) and Michael Bay's *Armageddon* (Jerry Bruckheimer/Touchstone, 1998) could pull official ticket prices of twenty-five dollars and scalper prices of up to two hundred dollars. Confirmation of this apparent quirk was the initial failure of tie-in products, not because the products were too costly in an unstable economy where doctors and schoolteachers had no regular income, but because the tie-ins were too cheap. As Raymond Markovich explained, "This is not a T-shirt and baseball cap market. It's more Gucci and Versace" (quoted in Kishkovsky). The cinema-going experience required more glamour than Raisinets and Snowcaps alone could provide.

Glamour, moreover, had to extend beyond the comfort of the venue and the proximity of the nightclub. To preserve their slice of the international market Russian cinema stars had to be able to deliver a glamour quotient of their own. It was, as Gladil'shchikov ("Priglashenie" 8) noted, a daunting task: "It is as if we were now in the same situation as Hollywood when it was just starting to develop. We are like Hollywood of, say, 1915, but (a small detail!) surrounded by cinematic superpowers." To be more precise, Russian cinema was like the Hollywood of, say, 1915 at a time when Hollywood itself was already a $3.5 billion industry (Dondurei, "The State" 48).

Back to the Empire

A key figure in this project of glamour construction was the film director and actor Nikita Mikhalkov, to whom the first chapter in this volume is devoted. Mikhalkov brought both tsarist and Soviet pedigrees of tremendous prominence to a successful career of film acting and later directing, producing such popular films as *Slave of Love* (*Raba liubvi*; Mosfil'm, 1976), *Unfinished Piece for Mechanical Piano* (*Neokonchennaia p'esa dlia mekhanicheskogo pianino*; Mosfil'm, 1977), and his best-known film, the 1994 Oscar-winning *Burnt by the Sun* (*Utomlennye solntsem*; TriTe [Russia]/Camera One [France], 1994). A figure engendering as much animosity as respect, Mikhalkov was widely perceived, particularly among older and provincial members of the Filmmakers' Union, as the only Russian figure of world stature able to contend with the Hollywood machine, someone who had indeed been honored by Hollywood on its own terms.

Perhaps it was no surprise, then, that Mikhalkov was overwhelmingly elected as Union chair at the 1997 Third Congress of the Russian Filmmakers' Union (December 22–23), replacing Sergei Solov'ev, who withdrew from reelection. Mikhalkov's election reflected more than a rejection of Solov'ev's tainted leadership; it pointed to a shift in how the Union positioned itself as an active lobby in the emerging political power structure rather than as a Soviet anachronism in a small and insular arts community. Mikhalkov brought to his Union candidacy a team of legal and economic specialists, as well as powerful political connections in Prime Minister Viktor Chernomyrdin's party Our Home (Nash Dom). The object of speculation concerning his own possible candidacy in the 2000 elections, Mikhalkov was the new positive hero in a number of related arenas: a universally recognized lead actor, director of an Oscar-winning film, head of the successful studio TriTe, and now administrator of the Union. It was Russia's positive hero who had been missing from Russian cinema since its rejection of socialist realism in the mid-1980s.

Mikhalkov responded to this imaginative projection as the skillful director that he was. Unlike previous chairs, who had traditionally held the Union congresses at the Cinema House, Mikhalkov moved the May 29–30, 1998, Fourth (Extraordinary) Congress of the Russian Filmmakers' Union to the Kremlin's Palace of Congresses, imbuing its bureaucratic proceedings with an imperial state grandeur and symbolically reassociating cinema with governmental power, generously negotiated by the filmmaker for cinema's own mise-en-scène.[78] True to the internal logic of this shift, all 4,399 members of the Russian Filmmakers' Union, rather than only the Union delegates, were invited to attend the Kremlin proceedings, a grand gesture later to cause serious financial difficulties when the August 1998 financial crash, only three months away, left the Union unable to repay its loan.

And yet, apart from these mundane pragmatics, the professional imagination was stimulated. In the organizational semantics of the event, the Fourth Congress was promised an end to the modern-day Time of Troubles, an event akin to the boyar elite gathering to elect the first Romanov, the postcrisis rallying of *narod* (people) to *vlast'* (power), of demotic to imperial identities.

An extensive account of the Congress, including excerpted transcripts of Mikhalkov's speech, is available elsewhere.[79] Most noteworthy in Mikhalkov's Congress performance for our purposes here are two things. First, Mikhalkov called for extensive governmental support not in the form of greater subsidies—"To demand state privileges for cinema means to draw on funds needed by the health services, education, the army, and even the miners"

(Mikhalkov, "The Function" 51–52)—but in the form of extensive state restrictions and centralized controls, such as licenses for video reproduction and aerial, cable, and satellite television broadcast, to regulate the cinema industry and generate funds for the renovation and construction of its theaters.

Here one must pause briefly to savor the irony. In the twelve years from the 1986 Fifth Congress of the *Soviet* Filmmakers' Union to the 1998 Fourth Congress of the *Russian* Filmmakers' Union cinema had come nearly full circle: from the Union's rejection of state control to the Union's insistence on state control, a process within which Mikhalkov himself had moved from the defeated *arrière-garde* to triumphant trailblazer. In the grand tradition of Russia's unpredictable past—leaps forward into the past—this narrative required that previous trailblazers of May 1986 be exposed as having brought about the wholesale destruction of a viable state industry, whether through design or simple naïveté and self-indulgence. Yet, as the director Rolan Bykov dryly noted by way of comparison, "The miners didn't have any Fifth Congress; the collapse of the film industry is not the result of the Congress" (quoted in Menashe 13). Still, the bitter truth remained—most bitter, of course, for the very directors who had steered Soviet cinema toward greater freedom and creativity—that, without a chain of compliance, reaching from the smallest video vendor, through the Russian government, and ending at the threshold of Jack Valenti's office door in distant Los Angeles, the chances of recuperation were nil.

Second, and more entertaining, Mikhalkov had thoughtfully produced for the Fourth Congress his own montage film, consisting of clips from works by his colleagues and competitors, edited to demonstrate their overweening appetite for unmotivated violence and their neglect of positive role models. Mikhalkov's cinematic provocation, as his colleagues were quick to point out, conveniently overlooked the extended scenes of physical violence in his own work, including the tiresomely protracted beating toward the end of *Burnt by the Sun*. Publicly targeted for criticism in Mikhalkov's programmatic montage film was footage by the young and talented Nikolai Lebedev, whose *Snake Source* (*Zmeinyi istochnik*; Gor'kii Film Studio, 1997) was an outstanding, low-budget genre film, precisely the kind of work that deserved attention and support from a senior administrator of Mikhalkov's stature.

The stakes, however, were about power, not logic or mentoring. Mikhalkov's antiviolence montage was his filmic brawl with colleagues over control of Russian cinema. As head of the Union he would edit their films to his own administrative advantage, attributing failures of the industry to their alleged shortcomings. He would set the agenda to correct those shortcomings, and the lead item on that agenda was the coordination of cinema more closely with state desire, a promised return to imperial grandeur, interlarded with regulation, license, and control. Given the conditions of the past decade, only a fool would argue that greater control was unnecessary.

Mikhalkov's montage film was also in some sense a dress rehearsal for the February 20, 1999, premiere screening, also in the Kremlin State Palace, of his next full-length feature film, the epic melodrama *Barber of Siberia* (*Sibirskii tsiriul'nik*; Barrandov Biografia [Czech Republic]/Caméra One [France]/ TriTe [Russia], 1998). Shot in the Czech Republic, Portugal, and Russia with a production budget of $45 million, *Barber of Siberia* was that year's most expensive film outside Hollywood.[80] The 1999 premiere was itself an example of over-the-top reflexivity. The State Kremlin Palace had been specially equipped with Dolby sound and an enormous screen so that the invited guests could adequately appreciate, among other moments, Mikhalkov's screen performance as Aleksandr III, mounted on horseback to inspect the cadets on the Kremlin grounds. In honor of the premiere, the real-life Kremlin Palace hosted a period costume exhibit, "Clothing of the Imperial Family," and guests were gifted with appropriate accessories, including a specially designed Hermès scarf with an image of the Aleksandrian coronation, as well as day and evening versions of Junker eau-de-cologne, produced to Mikhalkov's specifications by the New Dawn Perfume Factory. As was the Fourth Congress, the premiere was a schizoid melding of socialism with imperial grandeur.[81]

For all the artifice of this hysterical fandango, Mikhalkov's premiere provided a highly visible example of how cinema might negotiate the key recombinatory elements: imperial elegance with authoritarian Soviet centralism; film society glitter with the state's strong hand. The melding of these elements required a Union leadership ready to attend to state policy. Although Mikhalkov, as head of the Filmmakers' Union, would at first vigorously criticize governmental attempts in 1998 to absorb Goskino under the larger umbrella of the Ministry of Culture—a move that threatened to eliminate its separate budget allocation—he soon realized that the centralizing tendencies of Yeltsin's

FIGURE 2.1. Mikhalkov. *Barber of Siberia*. Nikita Mikhalkov as Aleksandr III.

successor required a different tack, and by 2000 Goskino was subordinated to the Ministry as the State Division of Cinematography.

Such subordination, as it turned out, had positive effects. Contrary to expectations, in the following several years Minister of Culture Mikhail Shvydkoi allocated considerable money, tripling available support to approximately $53 million over the two-year period of 2002–4 (Walsh; www.gazeta.ru, July 14, 2002), of which 50 percent was earmarked for blockbuster films, 20 percent for art house cinema, and 10 percent for debut films.[82]

The Early Twenty-first Century

Piracy is very profitable, but the profits are realized by only a very rich few, at the expense of many, many others.

—U.S. Ambassador to Russia Alexander Vershbow
(www.usinfo.state.gov, November 25, 2003)

One might well imagine that this appeal for economic equality, coming from U.S. Ambassador to Russia Alexander Vershbow, might be met with some bemusement by the readers of his op-ed piece in *Vedomosti*, the *Moscow Times*, and other media outlets. With excellent, pirated DVDs of U.S. blockbusters available for two to five dollars *before* local theatrical release, compared to an official price of twenty to thirty dollars,[83] consumers in a ravaged economy had little incentive to abide by the declared ethics of Hollywood and the U.S. State Department. Despite Russia's April 30, 2001, inclusion on the U.S. Trade Representative Special 301 Priority Watch List of countries either barring U.S. films or tolerating piracy, Russia continued to vie with China for global leadership in video as well as optical disc piracy (CDs, DVDs, and CD-ROM), accounting for an annual U.S. film industry loss of $250 million in 2000–2002 (www.mpaa.org/anti-piracy, April 30, 2001).[84]

Although the Motion Picture Association of America has widely publicized its successes through the Russian Anti-Piracy Organization, seizing 655,000 illegal videos and 171,000 illegal CD-ROMs in 2000, these figures are less impressive when considered in tandem, for example, with the fact that an estimated 100,000 pirated copies of a single film, Andy and Larry Wachowski's *Matrix Reloaded* (Warner Bros., 2003), changed hands in 2003, according to Aleksandr Ageev, retail manager of Soiuz-Video, Russia's largest chain of video and DVD stores.[85]

In Moscow itself video piracy sales have been estimated at a "mere" 40 percent of the market;[86] beyond Moscow the federal rate was pegged at 80 percent in 1999 ("Putin Urges") and was higher in St. Petersburg, where DVD piracy was particularly entrenched. Piracy is widely perceived to be a victimless crime, a federal pastime benefiting both Russian entrepreneurs and their economy-minded clientele, while hurting only the U.S. film studios and re-cording industries, which had refused consideration of such short-term strat-egies as radical price reduction to undercut the illegal market (Holdsworth). And although video and optical disc piracy (together with the counterfeit pharmaceutical industry) jeopardized Russia's long-anticipated entry into the World Trade Organization, damaging trade relations with the United States and inviting increased tariffs, little could be done in an environment where the local law enforcement agencies themselves are said to account for a substantial sector of the illegal business, including bribes, sales of pirated materials, and even the raiding and confiscation of legal videos from legitimate video busi-nesses only to shut down the competition (Holdsworth). Testimony by Deputy Interior Minister Rashid Nurgaliev to a late 2003 Cabinet session was telling: of the 70,000 enterprises submitting to police inspection in January through September 2003, only 482 resulted in the discovery of illegal activity ("Putin Urges").

The Cinema Hall: Half Empty or Half Full?

By 2001 the longer term ministerial development plan had been to increase the annual production from approximately fifty-five feature films (Dondureyi and Venger 6), of which forty, or 70 percent, received substantial ministerial sup-port, to around one hundred feature films, of which 33 percent would be largely state-financed, by 2006. The projected annual goal of one hundred Russian films would seek to raise exhibition figures in an annual step-by-step process from 15 percent of screenings in 2002 to 25 percent by 2006 (www.gazeta.ru, July 14, 2002), a target figure consistent with international standards of the optimal ratio for a profitable domestic film industry (Rosbalt News, July 16, 2003).

How did they do?

Production climbed in 2003 to sixty-seven full-length feature films, and by 2005 the Russian film industry was producing at or near the hundred-film ministerial goal set for 2006, with 99 full-length feature films for 2007.[87] By 2004 state support at 46.8 percent had been surpassed by nonstate film pro-duction investments, and by 2005 it had dropped to 42 percent (Dondureyi and Venger 29), considerably short of the 33 percent goal but an improvement nevertheless.

As for cinema construction in the dawning years of the century, the Kursk Station Square project, which had been hard hit by the economic crisis of Au-gust 1998, finally opened Russia's first real multiplex, Formula Kino, a nine-screen theater in the Atrium mall, in May 2002 (Maternovsky, "U.S. Giant").[88] In September 2003 the newly formed Rising Star Media, a new joint venture of Paul Heth's Soquel Ventures with Shari Redstone of National Amusements, opened the eleven-screen Kinostar Deluxe at Moscow's Mega Mall, with plans to open a fourteen-screen theater in late 2004 at Mega-2 (both IKEA ventures) in Khimki, northwest of Moscow,[89] with additional multiplexes in a number of other cities. Gone were the days of single-screen, 800-seat capacities, and yet the route to that mere architectural subdivision had led the industry through its near extinction while it struggled to define why one would even go to the cinema, who that "one" will be, and how choice, individuation, subculture community, and the proxemics of viewing had become no small matter in the decision to attend.

Revenue figures supported the increasing viability of the industry as a whole: box-office gross in 1997 had been a mere $7 million; by 2000 it was estimated at $34.5 million, with a substantial increase in 2002 to $99.4 million (Holson and Meyers; Maternovsky, "U.S. Giant"), a figure that accounts for 90 percent of the industry's profit for all members of the Commonwealth of Independent States.[90]

Analysts who would like to see the glass as half empty point to the fact that this $99.4 million figure is merely the average budget of a single Hollywood blockbuster[91] and that $84 million of this is box-office revenue captured by U.S. studios. It is true that, compared with the French 2002 box office of $915 million or the German 2002 box office of $977 million, this $99.4 million remains insubstantial (Maternovsky, "U.S. Giant"). Moreover, stubborn problems remain in other spheres, of which the most evident are piracy and the decaying, state-owned cinemas, where Russian film is still often screened (Dondureyi and Venger 29).

By contrast, those analysts who would see the glass as half full point out that the box-office gross increased from $7 million in 1997 to $190.7 million in 2003, a 27-fold growth (Dondureyi and Venger 9). By 2006 the total cinema box-office release was $.5 billion, the target intended to be reached only by 2008–10 (53), and already higher than the $400 million by 2007 cited by the U.K. independent exhibition analysis firm Dodona Research (Kemp), putting Russia in sixth place for the European market.[92] A leader in this revival is Mosfil'm, which is estimated to contribute $4 million to the federal budget while receiving no subsidies.

This growth rate would inevitably require a stabilization of ticket prices, which, in renovated and new Moscow theaters in 2002–3, routinely ran at eleven dollars and as high as twenty-three dollars, compared with a U.S. average of $2.60 (Johnson's List 7300, August 26, 2003).[93] The Ministry of Culture target plan, according to Minister Shvydkoi, in federal blueprint for the development of domestic film production, would entail the screening of Russian films in a government-subsidized network of 230 cinema halls, which, if operated at an average 30 percent capacity and a modest ticket price of two dollars, would return approximately 50 percent of cost, a tremendous improvement over the return of the previous decade (www.gazeta.ru, July 5, 2002). By 2005 ticket prices had stabilized at an average of $3.96, only a slight rise from a 2003 average of $3.02 (Dondureyi and Venger 10).

The Russian box office—some 15 percent of the titles in 2002 (www.gazeta. ru, July 14, 2002)—did not meet the 25 percent goal set for 2006, coming in instead at just above 18 percent (Dondureyi and Venger 114). Russian cinema nevertheless sold considerably more tickets than its U.S. competitor, bringing in just under $60 million in theatrical release as opposed to just under $35 million for U.S.-produced and U.S.-coproduced films (115).

Other indicators also suggested that by 2003–4 the cinema crisis was over. Sony Pictures, Disney Production have begun building film factories outside Moscow and St. Petersburg designed to produce cinema for the Russian market (Dondureyi and Venger 53). The country boasted twenty-eight stable international and federal film festivals in 2006 and forty-seven private distribution companies (88, 53). Among the top twenty films for 2005 were seven Russian films, including first and second place, respectively, for Fedor Bondarchuk's war film *9th Company* (*9 rota*; Channel 1+1, 2005), which brought in $25.6 million, and Dzhanik Faiziev's action thriller *Turkish Gambit* (*Turetskii gambit*; Channel One, 2005), which brought in $19.2 million, competing favorably with *War of the Worlds*, *Star Wars: Episode III*, and *King Kong* (62). By 2006 Russian cinema held the top three slots in the top ten films for the year: Timur Bekmambetov's fantasy thriller *Day Watch* (*Dnevnoi dozor*; Channel One, 2006) at $33.9 million, Aleksandr Atanesian's war film *Bastards* (*Svolochi*; Paradiz, 2006) at $10.5 million, and Petr Buslov's crime film *Heaven on Earth* (*Bumer: Fil'm vtoroi*; CTV and Pygmalion, 2006) at $8.9 million. Their competition was such U.S. blockbusters as *The Chronicles of Narnia* and *Harry Potter and the Goblet of Fire* in fourth and fifth place (115–16).

As for international prizes, from 2002 onward several Russian films took major awards and others garnered extensive U.S. distribution and international press (Fishman), including Andrei Konchalovskii's *House of Fools* (*Dom durakov*; Bac [France]/Persona [Russia], 2002), which won the Grand (Special) Jury Prize at the Venice International Film Festival in 2002; Pavel Lungin's *Tycoon* (*Oligarkh*; CTV, 2002); Aleksandr Rogozhkin's *Cuckoo* (*Kukushka*; CTV, 2002); Aleksandr Sokurov's *Russian Ark* (*Russkii kovcheg*; Egoli Tossell Film AG [Germany]/Fora Fil'm [Russia], 2002); Timur Bekmambetov's fantasy thriller *Night Watch* (*Nochnoi dozor*; Channel One, 2004) with its sequel *Day Watch*; and Andrei Zviagintsev's *Return* (*Vozvrashchenie*; Ren Fil'm, 2003), which won the Golden Lion at Venice in 2003.[94]

If there is one key symbolic indicator that contemporary cinema is being gradually reintegrated into everyday experience, it belongs to the year 2005, in connection with the seventieth anniversary of the Moscow Metro. In celebration, the Red Line (Sokol'nicheskaia) replaced the customary anonymous recording with the voices of cinema stars from the past and present, including the present-day diva Renata Litvinova (Maternovsky, "Movie Stars"), gently reminding passengers not to forget their belongings as they leave the car. It would seem that Russian citizens had recovered from their bout of cine-amnesia: whether or not they remembered their belongings, they had begun to remember what it was like to go to the cinema again.

Nikita Mikhalkov: European but Not Western?

Introduction: The Imperial Reclamation Project

Nikita Mikhalkov's films constitute Russian cinema's most ambitious reclamation project. Although several of his films, including the recent *12*, address contemporary subjects, Mikhalkov's work more typically crafts an elegiac and turbulent Russia of 1877–1937, providing a spectacle simultaneously distinct from the West yet recognizably European in its cultural environment, retaining certain archaic ways of being, such as a leisured pastoral enchantment, that the West has putatively lost. The prerevolutionary country estate, offering a locus of elite cohesion, comes to be barely distinguishable from the dacha of the Soviet period; the intensely charged enactments of one era come to stand in for those of the other, as if they were eternal, recurrent, or exchangeable for each other. His films seek to draw audiences into a world in which the faded, morally ineffectual landowning class blurs into the Soviet morally ineffectual *nomenklatura*, lending old wealth, economic decline, and moral anomie an aura of nostalgic, aristocratic allure. Property's seizure, forced sale, or forfeiture becomes scripted as a recurrent, shared—and therefore, paradoxically, reassuring—disruption for both estate and dacha life.

Though often indebted to Chekhov, Mikhalkov's adaptations bear only an attenuated relation to that writer, using his work to invite the viewer's participation in a consensual fiction, to recall Wendy S. Jones's useful term, in which contradictory things happen: class distinctions are sharpened, yet gentility as a lifestyle is available with the purchase of a cinema ticket; historical rupture is reimagined as a newly coherent continuum; devastating social dispersal is rescripted as endearing melodramatic excess. Indeed, after Mikhalkov's debut film, melodrama, to which a substantial portion of the argument here is devoted, provides Mikhalkov with an invaluable convention by means of which to evoke a nostalgic pastoral unity.

Mikhalkov is uninhibited in his vision of a textual Russia explicitly traditionalist in its political orientation, Orthodox in its belief system, and patriarchal in its sexual order. It is an enlightened conservatism that lays claim to true progress by dint of its ostensive distinctions from Western practices, including its categories of justice and collectivity. Mikhalkov's stock images of Russian ethnicity—white tunics, samovars, vodka and its attendant excesses, the landscape of birch trees and sloping pastures—are less nationalist or Slavophile in a narrow sense than they are identifiers of an imperial past, a self-assignment of responsibility in which the Russians as a flawed elite are fated to bridge those turbulent years from Chekhov to Gor'kii that by chance and hard work also mark the passage of the director's family from the cultural and political power of one ideological system to that of its apparent antipode.

In 1934 the art historian Erwin Panofsky (152) famously claimed, "Whether we like it or not, it is movies that mold, more than any other single force, the opinions, the taste, the language, the dress, the behavior, and even the physical appearance of a public comprising more than sixty per cent of the population of the earth." One might be skeptical about the certainty of Panofsky's percentage but agree with his assessment of cinema's potential to marshal the imaginative power of its audience. A longer text would address all of Mikhalkov's work, but I am particularly interested in this chapter in the ways that such evocative films as *At Home*, *"Slave of Love"*, *Mechanical Piano*, *Oblomov*, *Dark Eyes*, *Burnt by the Sun*, and *Barber of Siberia* stage a story about Russia as a place of leisured, traditionalist continuity (see original titles and production information at the end of each chapter).[1]

Given the larger argument of this book, it would be simple enough (and dull beyond measure) to focus, for example, on Mikhalkov's *Barber of Siberia*, his most explicitly imperial text, with its cameo appearance of Emperor Aleksandr III, the private chitchat of the imperial family, the royal military institute, its balls and noble amateur theatrics. This focus on so-called irrefutable evidence, the bric-a-brac of the empire, misses the more elusive and conjectural ways that collective identifications organize his cinema according to patterns distinctly alien to the imaginary of the nation and the national.[2] The argument that follows is instead rooted in a kind of conjectural knowledge, to use Carlo Ginzburg's term, rather than a fixed thing that would foreclose some of the strategic contradictions of Mikhalkov's Russia. Counterposed to an effete and profligate Western Europe, his Russia is assertively different in its healthy barbarity. Counterposed to the United States, Mikhalkov's Russia is assertively European in its exquisite conservation of high culture.

Biographical Remarks: A Stranger at Home

Nikita Mikhalkov brings to filmmaking a distinguished family lineage. He is the great-grandson of the painter Vasilii Surikov (1848–1916) and the son of the children's writer Sergei Mikhalkov (1913–), who is also the author (with Gabriel' El'-Registan) of the lyrics to the Soviet anthem. Nikita Mikhalkov's brother is the filmmaker Andrei Konchalovskii.[3]

Mikhalkov's own biography is marked by good fortune and privilege constructed retrospectively by Mikhalkov himself in virtually mystical terms.[4] Even his first name, from the Greek, means "victory." Born in 1945, the Soviet Union's "victory year," Nikita Sergeevich Mikhalkov was given a first name and inherited a patronymic coincidentally identical to those of Nikita Sergeevich Khrushchev, the Soviet leader of Mikhalkov's youth. Not surprisingly, given these marks of fortune, Mikhalkov is regarded with ambivalence by the liberal intelligentsia for a variety of reasons, some more explicitly enunciated than others.[5] Among these reasons is his family's providential continuum and privilege, its claims to both tsarist and Soviet preeminence. This continuum largely contrasts with both the experience of his peers and the core narratives of Russia's traumas. His cinematic Russia is a fraught reminder that the years from Chekhov through Bunin to Gor'kii could (for very few) be ones of cultural continuity rather than rupture. This continuity coincides with the ascendancy of Mikhalkov's family to cultural and political power.

Mikhalkov first appeared in cinema at the age of fourteen, when he played minor roles in Konstantin Voinov's romance *The Sun Shines for Everybody* (*Solntse svetit vsem*; Mosfil'm, 1959) and Vasilii Ordynskii's drama *Clouds over Borsk* (*Tuchi nad Borskom*; Mosfil'm, 1960). But it was as the major character of Kolia in Georgii Daneliia's romantic comedy *I Stroll through Moscow* (*Ia shagaiu po Moskve*; Mosfil'm, 1963) that the young Mikhalkov garnered box-office attention. First enrolled in 1963 at Shchukin Theatrical Institute, affiliated with Moscow's famed Vakhtangov Theatre, Mikhalkov was expelled in 1966 for having violated the Institute's prohibition on student cinema acting, which, it was believed, contaminated stage acting methods. Mikhalkov transferred to the All-Union State Institute of Cinema (VGIK) as a second-year student in Mikhail Romm's workshop, the same workshop in which Vadim Abdrashitov was soon to study and where Mikhalkov's brother had earlier studied, together with Andrei Tarkovskii. Graduating from VGIK in 1971 with the diploma film *Quiet Day at War's End*, Mikhalkov entered the military, serving two years on an atomic submarine off Kamchatka before returning to cinema to shoot his debut film, *At Home among Strangers, a Stranger at Home* in 1974. Unintentionally perhaps, that film's title came to express Mikhalkov's own condition: widely recognized by foreign film industries while occupying an odd duck status among his fellow filmmakers.[6]

Over twenty feature films and documentaries were to follow in the next thirty years. Six films in particular remain Mikhalkov's best-known work: *"Slave of Love"* (1975), *Unfinished Piece for Mechanical Piano* (1976), *Several Days from the Life of Oblomov* (1979), *Urga* (1991), *Burnt by the Sun* (1994), and *Barber of Siberia* (1998).[7]

Unlike the other filmmakers examined here, however, Mikhalkov's professional activity is by no means limited to his directorial work. His acting career has been equally prolific, comprising some forty roles, including regular appearances in his own films.[8] In 1987 he founded TriTe, a production studio with substantial international partnerships.[9] TriTe's subsidiary publishing company, Russian Archive (Rossiiskii arkhiv), specializes in publications of documents, memoirs, and other archival material of Russia's domestic and diasporic history, including its religious heritage.[10] In addition to producing several of his own works, Mikhalkov's TriTe is responsible for such major films as Sergei Solov'ev's *Tender Age* (*Nezhnyi vozrast*; Trite, 2001), Filipp Iankovskii's *State Counselor* (*Statskii sovetnik*; TriTe, 2005), and Vladimir Khotinenko's *1612* (TriTe, 2007). From 2003 on Mikhalkov has been interested in political documentary, producing the documentary serial *Nikita Mikhalkov: A Russian Choice* on the history of early twentieth-century Russian emigration, and the documentary short *General Kozhugetych*, a fiftieth-birthday tribute to Emergency Situations Minister Sergei Shoigu.

Mikhalkov's newer work turns again to a contemporary theme, the updated courtroom drama *12*, a remake of Sidney Lumet's film *Twelve Angry Men* (Orion-Nova, 1957). *Burnt by the Sun 2*, which includes his now-grown daughter, Nadia Mikhalkova, continues the narrative of *Burnt by the Sun* into World War II.

The director's prizes and awards are sufficiently numerous to render their full catalogue a substantial task; his international film prizes include a Golden Lion at the Venice Film Festival (1991) for *Urga*, which likewise received an Oscar nomination for Best Foreign Film. He received an Oscar for Best Foreign Film for *Burnt by the Sun* (1994), which also shared the Grand Jury Prize at Cannes with Yimou Zhang's *Huozhe* (ERA International, 1994).[11] His *12* won a 2007 Special Lion at Venice.

Apart from his work as a director and an actor, Mikhalkov has taken the initiative in civil and political life to seek out a number of prominent positions, including election in 1992 to president of the Russian Culture Foundation (a UNESCO-affiliated organization), election in 1995 (later declined) to a seat in Parliament, and election in 1997 to head the Filmmakers' Union, to which he was reelected in 2005.

Mikhalkov's TriTe Studio has come to play a central role in Russia's cultural life inseparable from Kremlin politics. In 2005 the Kremlin's Patriotic

Education of Russian Federation Citizens was founded to promote such "State-friendly films" (Richardson 7) as Dzhanik Faiziev's war thriller *Turkish Gambit* (*Turetskii gambit*; Channel One, 2005) and Fedor Bondarchuk's war film *9th Company* (*9 rota*; Art Pictures Group, 2005). A five-year plan (2006–10) of support for patriotic themes across the major cultural fields (including television), the Patriotic Education program provides state funding for the "development of the creative potential of journalists, writers, and filmmakers in patriotic education," to quote from the program's mission statement (Richardson 7), and has met a willing partner in Mikhalkov's professional empire at a time when the film industry itself is undergoing both an economic boom and a certain ideological calcification.

In close cooperation with the state-owned television network Channel One, TriTe Studio has mounted Vladimir Khotinenko's historical film *1612*, a $10 million project that premiered for the November 4 Day of Unity in 2007. As Khotinenko's title suggests, seventeenth-century Mikhail Romanov's reestablishment of social order following his election (and the founding of the new imperial dynasty) might be aligned with Putin's reestablishment of social order following Yeltsin's "Time of Troubles." In this fashion the ruptures of 1612 and the 1990s are rescripted as mere turbulent episodes in four and a half centuries of continuous imperial rule. As the cultural model implies, a rule of enlightened conservatism and tradition-driven, centralized governance sustains only the slightest regard for the peripheral, come-lately tinkerings that an eighteenth-century nation-state model might provide.

Liberté, egalité, fraternité: Problems All Around

Fraternity? Of course! Liberty? Yes, but within the framework of the law. Equality? It is not achievable. . . . Equality cannot and must not exist.
—Nikita Mikhalkov, "Tak konchaiutsia smutnye vremena" (1998)

Mikhalkov cites the rallying cry of the French Revolution,[12] closely identified with the forging of modernity, nationhood, and secularity, with extreme ambivalence. In the epigraph above it is to equality that he takes exception; elsewhere, it is the other nouns in this tripartite slogan that he dismisses or pointedly leaves out. As early as his debut film, *At Home among Strangers, a Stranger at Home*, the young CheKa happily shout out *egalité* and *fraternité*, but keep leaving out the more problematic *liberté*. In *12* a banner bearing the French slogan is supplanted by a Russian banner bearing his proposed ideological substitute: Peace, Labor, Happiness (*Mir, Trud, Schast'e*).

Between these early and late films one example after another suggests Mikhalkov's ambivalence toward the French slogan of nationhood. *Liberté* is singled out in *Mechanical Piano*, when the wealthy creditor Shcherbuk, kissing the hand of Sergei Voinitsev's liberal bride, offends her feminist *liberté*. Shcherbuk's ensuing denunciation of *Liberté, egalité, fraternité* positions him as a feisty conservative to the pseudo-populist Sergei and his bride, anxious to donate their fine clothing to the peasantry but incapable of conducting their lives with moral consistency.[13] Shcherbuk is not Mikhalkov's stand-in, yet Mikhalkov ("Mne khotelos'" 1, 4) voices similar views in a much later interview:

> The words "liberty, equality, and fraternity" . . . are absolutely inapplicable for Russia. For a Russian, liberty is nothing like what it is for, let's say, a Frenchman. . . . The Russian doesn't need liberty; he needs the absence of bondage [*nevolia*]. They are similar terms, but the essence is different. Just as with the definition of equality and equal rights.

Mikhalkov's mechanical piano, a reference taken from a single enigmatic entry in Chekhov's notebooks (Sandler 46), is the film's key symbol of this conceptual difference and captures the director's ambivalence toward *egalité*. Anyone, even the house servant—its first and only musician—can play the mechanical piano; only the traditional piano can be mastered by those investing work and possessing talent. Implicit are two autobiographical moments: Mikhalkov's great-grandfather, Vasilii Surikov, emerged from a provincial Cossack family to become one of Russia's leading nineteenth-century oil painters, and Mikhalkov, together with his filmmaker brother, attended a special music school affiliated with the Moscow Conservatory. In each instance, the mastery of technique and long hours of practice are what the socially ambitious must endure.

A few years later Mikhalkov ("Tak konchaiutsia" 24) again returns to the slogan of nationhood:

> Equality is when I earn money and live in a house, while you bum around under a bridge. Then you sober up, come to me with an axe, and say, "How is it that you have everything, and I have nothing?" Equal rights—yes! Everyone has a chance. And from then on— everything depends on you.

And what about *fraternité*, the relation that, in Anderson's theorizing and elsewhere, forges the language of nationhood? What is understood by Mikhalkov's easy "of course" in the epigraph above ("Fraternity? Of course!")? For the most part, his films manifest little concern one way or the other for sibling language. *Slave of Love, Mechanical Piano, Barber of Siberia*—even *Oblomov*, for all its brotherhood—are largely preoccupied with other things; they circle around the failure of ineffectual elites, for example, to bring their romantic and civic houses into order. Siblings in any sense that one may link to Anderson's "language of brothers and sisters" figure little in this process.

An exception worthy of closer examination is the intense, symbolic fraternalism of Mikhalkov's debut film, *At Home among Strangers, a Stranger at*

Home. What can it tell us about the collective subjectivities in the filmmaker's work? Its title refers to the paradoxical status of Chekist security officers living among strangers on the exotic periphery of the newly constituted Soviet Union at the end of the Civil War (1918–21). The film is a hybrid genre, at once a buddy film and, like Vladimir Motyl''s *White Sun of the Desert* (*Beloe solntse pustyni*; Lenfil'm, 1969) of five years earlier, a western, or rather an "eastern," rendering cowboy motifs in the language of the Soviet frontier.[14] Intended diegetically as Chita in southeastern Siberia on the Chinese and Mongolian borders, the film's location supports Mikhalkov's choice of western genre and offers the Russian Civil War as analogous to U.S. frontier history: the clean slate, a *terra nullius* at the imperial periphery, an unlimited moral expanse where socialism could be inscribed.

The film's buddies, friends and former Red Cavalry officers but now CheKa security officers, strain under the task of coordinating local politics with the metropolitan center in building the new state. The Chekists' immediate assignment is to safeguard the train passage of confiscated gold through to the center. As the screenplay's title, *Red Gold* (*Krasnoe zoloto*) unambiguously suggests, the CheKa's expropriation from the landowners requires no rigorous moral scrutiny. The Reds' commitment to this assignment—in the name of the starving people—marks them as different from the film's other two cohorts, the Whites and the Greens.[15] These three color groups—the Red emergent state (personalized dominantly as Shilov), the White declining state (personalized as Lemke), and the Green nonstate (personalized as Brylov)—vie for the gold as the substance that marks them as good or bad, state-worthy actors or atavistic throwbacks driven by primal acquisitive instincts. Disciplined and uniquely capable of disciplining others, the Chekist cohort alone transcends rank and acquisitive individualism. The film's programmatic song, with lyrics by Mikhalkov's mother, the poet Natal'ia Konchalovskaia, reminds us of the director's multigenerational investments: a ship, imperfect and unfinished, is handed down from great-grandfather to grandfather to father to son, so that the next generation may sail ("Be worthy, my son, of accepting our banner in fond memory").[16]

Like the programmatic song, which rushes from ancestor worship to lost stanzas from the "International," the film suggests a certain evolutionary determinism, moving from primordial bonds—fraught with distrust and disagreements, masculine hysterics and tests of faith—to a higher stage of political development that the CheKa alone can embody. *At Home* charts the Reds' prelapsarian camaraderie to a point at which, by the film's end, they have been tempered by the uniquely compatible conditions of the emergent Marxist state. No longer simply friends or military comrades (as in the opening frame), they are monads in a larger myth of state sovereignty and governability. Mikhalkov's love of the military as a key producer of collective subjectivity will manifest in several future films, including *Burnt by the Sun, Kinfolk,* in which it is military deployment that reunites the broken family, and *Barber of Siberia*, dedicated to "Russian officers, the pride of our Fatherland." At the same time it is significant that the military in Mikhalkov's cinema engages less in combat than in domestic and social activities: they steam themselves (*Burnt by the Sun*); they wax floors, dance, and perform opera (*Barber of Siberia*). In periodic rehearsals they engage in performative fighting, trampling the harvest with tanks (*Burnt by the Sun*) or settling disputes with a virtuosic épée display (*Barber of Siberia*).

Hence the framing device of *At Home*—the young military comrades enthusiastically destroying a landowner's carriage, a symbol of the old regime—fulfills a deeply contradictory function. On the one hand, the carriage's destruction confirms the early military friendship as a foundational reference point for the rest of the film. On the other hand, the carriage's destruction leaves a space perfectly suited by the film's end for its replacement, the CheKa's sleek and modern limousine—doors flung open, motor running, a state machine now driven by the very lads who had earlier vandalized the carriage. The recurrent interlude of frolicking Red brothers is not, therefore, merely a flashback to a simpler 1917, when the Revolution was won and future Chekists could invest leisure hours vandalizing other people's property. The sequence is the early state's hallucination of itself at play, projected simultaneously backward as memory and forward as a dream state in which, welcoming the return of the wrongly suspected brother, the inevitability of statehood is reconfirmed and the modern vehicle stands as its material embodiment.

As we watch this framing sequence at the film's beginning and end, are we looking at revolt or continuity? I would argue the latter. Given the ways the Mikhalkov family dynasty managed to find its ideological bearings with each successive political change—from great-grandfather Surikov's bold political canvases of Russia's historical crises to father Sergei Mikhalkov's Soviet anthem lyrics[17]—one might see in the substitution of one vehicle for another, a normal historical seriality, a dynamic metaphor enacting the family's own political Darwinism.

And what about the invisible, starving *narod*, for whose sake the gold was confiscated? Though Mikhalkov's film might well have indulged here in populist excess, we see neither emaciated children nor righteous, struggling mothers nor aged grandparents in need of civic protection. Instead, cattle herders, random train passengers, a wedding party, and alarmed neighbors, inhabiting spheres irrelevant to one another, exist in no sustained narrative or visual contact with each other or the central characters. The embryonic state stands alone, an isolated group of overworked and febrile security functionaries, bent on fulfilling a metropolitan injunction for a people whose presence is discernible only in the bureaucratic language of their profession. The only distinct folk figure is Kaium, the film's half-wit of unspecified Asian ethnicity, a thief of the imperial periphery, childlike but available for transformation.

FIGURE 3.1. Mikhalkov. *At Home among Strangers, A Stranger at Home.*
Kaium's Marxist education.

Amid the tropes transposed from the American western—guns and
horses, campfires, fight scenes, a rigid moral coding of good and bad, the shoot-
outs, the cavalry, the train robbery—Kaium belongs to the dyad of friendly In-
dian to Shilov's U.S. marshal. Shilov—first saving Kaium's life, then affording
him the illiterate's version of Marxist dialectics—brings the tinted comrade
into the imperial fold as the state's first colonial subject, who, donating the
gold, accords Shilov a change in status from "jackal" to "brother."

And so fraternity would indeed seem to organize the film's logic. Shilov's
natural brother, Fedor (who efficiently never appears in the film), is a bandit,
a brother only by happenstance of blood. Kaium, his new Soviet brother, is a
brother in a more evolved, historical sense than mere blood ties.

But Kaium is a different kind of brother from the one figured, most memo-
rably, in Benedict Anderson's egalitarian musings of nationhood. Instead, having fulfilled his function as citizen-pupil and citizen-soldier, Kaium is finally
permitted to become a citizen-corpse in the battle for the gold that he himself had earlier possessed. Significantly Mikhalkov makes no effort to return
to Kaium's corpse for burial, mourning, or ceremonial commemoration. The
film's final word, Shilov's hoarse cry "Brothers!" as he recognizes his CheKa
comrades, underscores a kinship system whose only true symbolic siblings are
the security organs, the new state's necessary substitution for nation building,
as relevant today as it was to Mikhalkov's Soviet Union of 1974.

Indeed, Mikhalkov will return to the security organs as his personal "imagined community" more than thirty years later in *12*, in key respects very different from Sidney Lumet's 1957 film *Twelve Angry Men*. Mikhalkov's version
engages twelve jurors from a range of professions—among them, taxi driver,
academic dean, and cemetery director—but reserves the place of pride for

the cinema director himself, who acts in his own film in four capacities: as jury foreman, amateur artist, a retired FSB (formerly KGB) investigator who knows about the case in question, and, by implication, God himself.[18] In this late work the filmmaker's logic is taken to its ultimate conclusion: the state, omniscient in ways available only to God and the FSB, is made flesh here as artist-director, leading the very legal process that governs the viewer's civil life. By retrospective comparison, Mikhalkov's early *At Home* is a thoughtful and nuanced work.

And yet the most intense irony of Mikhalkov's *At Home*, one of his most explicitly colonialist efforts, is its shooting location just outside Groznyi, the capital of Chechnia in the Russian Caucasus, still the site of the center's contentious hold on the frontier, where Shilov's grandsons still alternate between killing and explaining civilization to the likes of Kaium. If *At Home among Strangers, a Stranger at Home* is concerned at all with brotherhood, it is constructed as the story of closely knit *state* brotherhood, how a fraternity of local CheKa officers managed to fulfill the capital's demand; how the proto-state marshaled its own in distant Chita to deliver wealth, and how anyone else who tries this stunt is a bandit and a scoundrel.

Following *At Home*, Mikhalkov's next film, *"Slave of Love,"* belongs to a realm completely different from that of its predecessor: a strong female lead replaces the male band; a resort in the Crimea replaces the eastern imperial periphery; the early film industry replaces the frontier CheKa; a melodrama replaces the western. Still, certain continuities slip in: again, a story in the shadow of the Civil War; again, the security forces, the Reds and the Whites, the menacing horsemen in hot pursuit. Again, the fledgling Soviet government nationalizes a scarce commodity—here, invaluable film stock—which is again stolen and smuggled away by train from the metropolitan center. And at a technical level, fast-paced editing again alternates with drawn-out lyrical moments; again, extradiegetic music regularly overwhelms the verbal register; black-and-white footage alternates with color; a strong commitment to genre conventions is larded with strong ideological elements.

For all these differences and similarities, one aspect in particular of *"Slave of Love"* marks a critical turning point for Mikhalkov, a change of lasting value and eventually a trademark feature: his shift to melodrama. One might argue that Mikhalkov's selection of melodrama is simply a penchant for one genre over another, or a constraint dictated by the circumstances in which he inherited this next project from Rustam Khamdamov.[19] All this may indeed be the case, yet on a larger playing field Mikhalkov's choice of melodrama—always in hybrid form—allowed the filmmaker to stage a kind of filmmaking increasingly attuned to his vision of a Russia united not only across the historical divide of 1917, but also across the cultural divide of citizen and émigré, as well as the spatial divide of Europe and Asia, to capture Russia as a totality, unabashedly magnificent in its continuity across time and sovereign borders.

Melodrama

The formula of human existence: impossibility, irrevocability, inevitability.
—"Nikita Mikhalkov: Dela semeinye" (1995)

Mikhalkov's formula of human existence, repeated in many of his interviews, has no apparent link to the French revolutionary slogan *liberté, egalité, fraternité*. Their recurrent citation in his work and interviews proves no necessary conceptual connection between the two, and their shared tripartite structure may indeed be a coincidence.

As Peter Brooks (15–16) has persuasively argued, melodrama as a historically specific formation burst forth as a particularly rich cultural practice precisely in the decades following the French Revolution, as a response to a world in which the sacred meanings had lost their compelling dynamism:

> The [French] Revolution can be seen as the convulsive last act in a process of desacralization that was set in motion at the Renaissance, passed through the momentary compromise of Christian humanism, and gathered momentum during the Enlightenment—a process in which the explanatory and cohesive force of sacred myth lost its power, and its political and social representations lost their legitimacy.[20]

Melodrama's efflorescence in the wake of the events of 1789–99 must be seen, however, not only as a reaction *against* the ruptures of rationalism and secularism, though it certainly also was this, but also as a related and *deeply compatible* cultural hysteria expressing, as McReynolds and Neuberger (introduction 13) argue, the "long history of affinities between melodramatic and revolutionary modes of thought, despite their differences."

This affinity of revolutionary fervor and melodramatic excess holds true no less for the Soviet period than for its French precursor. If postrevolutionary Europe had been constrained to come forth with a new ethics in a secular world, then the postrevolutionary struggle in Russia—with none of the preceding, salutary stages of the Renaissance or the "compromise of Christian humanism"—was arguably staged anew in the postrevolutionary, twentieth-century USSR in the search for a new ethics in conditions of mandatory scientific atheism.

By the Soviet revolutionary period melodrama was already well known to Russian cinema. Melodrama had been a rich source of cinematic renewal from the earliest days of Russian filmmaking. Bagrov ("Soviet Melodrama") comments most categorically on the contradictory status of melodrama:

> As far as Russian pre-Revolutionary cinema is concerned, the only genre that existed was melodrama. . . . In Russia, melodrama and

filmmaking were virtually synonymous. . . . In this way, melodrama served as a distinctive jumping off point for Soviet filmmaking. The picture that emerged was more or less clear: rejecting melodrama as an out-dated and bourgeois genre, filmmakers began to construct new models [of melodrama].

As Bagrov goes on to argue, despite melodrama's precarious status, such leading governmental figures as People's Commissar of Enlightenment Anatolii Lunacharskii underwrote "red melodrama" as a key mode of cultural appeal for the new Soviet citizens, now no longer because of their petit-bourgeois contaminations, but rather, in Lunacharskii's words, "because of their health, their romanticism, their fearlessness in the face of melodrama's stark expressivity."[21] Indeed, if we were to take Brooks's (20) thesis seriously, that "melodrama starts from and expresses the anxiety brought by a frightening new world in which the traditional patterns of moral order no longer provide the necessary social glue," it is perhaps hardly surprising that one might find a set of textual symptoms in the decades after 1917 comparable to those that surfaced after the French Revolution.

Yet melodrama's status, as popularly appealing and formally adaptive as it might be, remained ideologically complex. As Margolit ("Melodrama" 227) suggests:

> If the adventure genre without any particular effort could adapt itself to plots of class, historical battles; if the detective story turned out to be a viable medium for exposing society's enemy . . . if the classical pastorale with unexpected ease could be laid upon the folkloric-ritualistic games of kolkhoz comedies, then to melodrama the relationship was and remained ideationally irreconcilable.[22]

Melodrama continued to carry the taint of its bourgeois prehistory, yet at the same time this taint was also its paradoxical allure: "The lower the chances of [the genre's] embodiment on native soil [of the Soviet Union]," Margolit (227) continues, "the more keenly one could sense its presence. As an unembodied (or 'unembodiable') ghost, melodrama wandered through Soviet cinema from decade to decade."[23]

The affinity of Soviet revolutionary and melodramatic modes of expression extends beyond their common emotional pitch to include a compulsion to extrapolate from the *realia* of life to the "higher," yet emphatically secular, values they might be assigned to represent. Both the revolutionary and the melodramatic modes are inspired to use, as Brooks (9) would put it, "the things and gestures of the real world, of social life, as kinds of metaphors that refer us to the realm of . . . latent moral meanings. Things cease to be merely themselves. . . . They become the vehicles of metaphors *whose tenor suggests another kind of reality*" (emphasis mine). Compatible with the sublated pathos of high socialist realism, melodrama was able to accomplish something that Soviet Grand Style could under no circumstances do: gesture at a space beyond Marxism-Leninism while at the same time in no sense opposing or negating it. Indulging instead in a self-identified excess of utopian impossibility, melodrama might, "by surprise," in the end, reconcile its viewer to the ideological status quo.[24]

One period particularly compatible with the preoccupations of melodrama was the Thaw (1953–68), with its recurrent emphasis, in the aftermath of the Great Fatherland War, on intimacy, the interior world, and domesticity.[25] Vulnerable to charges of philistinism and triviality even in this relatively sympathetic period, those directors who would work in this mode often sought ways to present it in hybrid or disguised fashion, intermixing melodrama with another, less ideologically loaded genre or else misidentifying it with such vague genre pseudonyms as "film novella." By the late 1960s such Thaw melodramas as Iosif Kheifits's *Big Family* (*Bol'shaia sem'ia*; Lenfil'm, 1953), Fridrikh Ermler's *Unfinished Story* (*Neokonchennaia povest'*; Lenfil'm, 1955), Mikhail Kalatozov's *The Cranes Are Flying* (*Letiat zhuravli*; Mosfil'm, 1957), Lev Kulidzhanov and Iakov Segel's *The House I Live In* (*Dom, v kotorom ia zhivu*; Gor'kii Film Studio, 1957), and Grigorii Chukhrai's *Clear Sky* (*Chistoe nebo*; Mosfil'm, 1961) had already well prepared directors, censors, critics, and viewers alike for melodramas that were to emerge in the 1970s, including Mikhail Kalik's *To Love* (*Liubit'*; Moldova Film Studio, 1970), Andrei Smirnov's *Autumn* (*Osen'*; Mosfil'm, 1974), Georgii Daneliia's *Autumn Marathon* (*Osennii marafon*; Lenfil'm, 1978), and Vladimir Men'shov's *Moscow Doesn't Believe in Tears* (*Moskva slezam ne verit*; Mosfil'm, 1979). By the mid-1970s, as Mikhalkov was turning his attention from the Soviet western to melodrama, the latter had become much less vulnerable to ideological attack, less prone to condescension or dismissal, and indeed, oddly compatible with the self-indulgent value system of the Stagnation period (1968–85).

It is thus perhaps after all no coincidence that Mikhalkov's fatalistic "impossibility, irrevocability, inevitability" conjures up a distinct melodramatic sensibility in dialogue with the emancipatory slogan of *liberté, egalité, fraternité*. Things excluded, things that cannot be undone, and things fated to happen preoccupy such films as *"Slave of Love," Mechanical Piano*, and in fact every film that is to follow until the courtroom drama *12*. Cumulatively Mikhalkov's work comes to express a pathos that, in counterpoint to the French slogan, and just as fervently, looks backward instead of forward, invokes nostalgia rather than anticipation, and sees human powerlessness and frailty in place of voluntarism and strength. In her key essay on melodrama, "The Melodramatic Field," Gledhill (32) could have been writing about Mikhalkov's melodrama when she comments, "If realism's relentless search for renewed truth and authentication pushes it towards . . . the future, melodrama's search for something lost, inadmissible, repressed, ties it to an atavistic past."

This is the context in which Mikhalkov produced *"Slave of Love,"* a hybrid described by one critic as a "thriller, grown to maturity in the womb of melodrama" (Shepotinnik 20). Its subplot, a Bolshevik thriller about the transport of underground documentary footage, provided the film with an ideological dimension while at the same time permitting its dominant plot to operate in melodramatic mode, underscoring the continuum to Russo-Soviet cinematic history in a fashion maximally flexible in its ideology.

"Slave of Love" stages the romance between the actress Ol'ga Voznesenskaia, loosely modeled on the prerevolutionary actress Vera Kholodnaia (1893–1919),[26] and the activist Viktor Pototskii as an affair of cameras, Voznesenskaia's melodramatic camera with Pototskii's Bolshevik documentary camera. The two are exquisitely matched: in the real world of the Civil War the Bolsheviks will prevail, and the 1920s will turn out to be the halcyon days of Soviet melodrama.[27] Reflexively, Mikhalkov's own film, in its depiction of melodrama's affair with Bolshevik cadre activism, is the descendent of these two cameras, the "generator of dreams and . . . their exposer," as one critic astutely put it (Sandler 144). The natural descendent of a melodramatic great-grandmother and a documentalist great-grandfather, Mikhalkov's film creates a diorama of how Russian cinema's past might be imagined, and is itself an example of the hybridity it represents on the screen.

In a fashion compatible with both Russia's social history and the specific professional history of the cinema industry, Mikhalkov's film stages melodrama *as content*, but also as the genre-fate of Russia's sturdiest and most adaptable mode. Like a fallen woman, notwithstanding its censured status, melodrama would not go away, but rather lived its own marked and (appropriately) melodramatic existence. More than comedy and adventure—the other two contenders for mass popularity from Russian cinema's earliest beginnings—melodrama effected the illusion of continuity across time, space, and (most fecund) ideological incompatibilities.

Beyond the specific example of *"Slave of Love,"* four features of melodrama's common profile more broadly dominate Mikhalkov's work. They are given somewhat abbreviated treatment here because the larger question to which I would link them is their fungibility in the Russia we have come to associate with Mikhalkov's cinematic vision. The first of these is the tendency for the melodramatic mode to tell the story of the political and social body through the instance of personal experience. *"Slave of Love,"* for example, narrated the 1918 Bolshevik seizure of the Crimea through the private love story and Bolshevik conversion of Voznesenskaia; *Burnt by the Sun* personalizes the purges of the mid- to late 1930s as the destruction of Red Army Commander Sergei Kotov's family in the summer of 1936 at their family dacha near Moscow and the dispersal of that family through the gulag. A hyperemotional engagement of the individual personality thereby becomes the instrument by which abstract social theory is made ideologically visible in a fashion that would have pleased

Lunacharskii. As Elsaesser (354–55) suggests with reference to the Western context, but with perhaps unintended relevance to Soviet melodrama:

> The persistence of melodrama might indicate the ways in which popular culture . . . has also resolutely refused to understand social change in other than private contexts and emotional terms. In this, there is obviously a healthy distrust of intellectualization and abstract social theory—insisting that other structures of experience (those of suffering, for instance) are more in keeping with reality.

As a symptomatic response to the dominant ideology, while opposing none of its operative assumptions, the figures of Voznesenskaia (*"Slave of Love"*) and Kotov, and for that matter his nemesis, Mitia (*Burnt by the Sun*), extrude ideological meaning—a meaning of collective affect, not reason—as the result of their individual suffering. The larger social peripeteia of modern Russian history is enacted on the screen as if it were the sudden reversals of unique individuals who stand in, through the very intensity and contradictions of their inner lives, for a collective that can absolutely no longer be summoned in sacred terms and can not be summoned *in this fashion* by the explicit dictates of the dominant ideological canon.

In this manner Voznesenskaia, the lead actress in *"Slave of Love,"* had been called upon to stand in for those cultural figures who both did and did not emigrate to Paris, who both did and did not switch to the side of the Revolution. The scriptwriter of the very melodrama in which she acted does indeed emigrate at the story's end, as if in intimation of the viability of emigration as minority choice. In a heightened fashion the same could be said of the NKVD officer-cum-émigré Mitia in *Burnt by the Sun*: his complex backstory, his masked identities as White Army officer in the Civil War (1918), as OGPU double agent (1923–34), as NKVD officer (from 1934 on), and as the agent who arrives to arrest his romantic rival, Kotov, strategically enable this intensely individual figure to stand in for multiple and otherwise incompatible instances of Soviet ideology.[28] With Mitia, as earlier with Voznesenskaia, there is an exquisite quality to these characters—a trivial celebrity who "goes Red," a young intellectual caught between the OGPU/NKVD and White émigrés—that suggests their status as vessels to contain a rich ideological brew, a composite of otherwise distinct political positions, the implications of which were played out in the Soviet film industry, both in the story line of the film and in film history itself.

"I do not give the viewer the right to pity [Mitia]," insists Mikhalkov ("Rezhisser ne dolzhen" 11). While the filmmaker is surely motivated by an ideological concern for keeping the viewer properly oriented toward the eventual poignancy of Kotov's fate, his foreclosure of pity also points at Mitia's chiefly instrumental function: we must not pity him because he stands in for too many contradictory ideological positions simultaneously. (Who exactly would we be in danger of pitying?) He is intended to signal those whose fate, through cowardice or ill luck, deviated in a wide variety of ways from official Soviet history.

Mikhalkov reserves our attention instead for Kotov, the film's first character, figured in the opening bathhouse scene as in edenic origins. A military man from humble beginnings with a well-to-do wife in a peasant-style bathhouse, Kotov is offered to us as a happy totality of signs, everything the *deserving* elite need be about, a naturalized baseline in comparison with which we must account for Mitia's deviation and disruption. In a culture where Stalin had found time, in Bazin's ("The Stalin Myth" 26) merciless formulation, "not only to decide the outcome of a battle, but also to locate a bad spark plug in a broken tractor," the protagonists of Mikhalkov's melodramas performed the inverse operation. Moving from the tiny, the trivial and personal, to an intimation of a larger political drama, the magnitude of which remained inaccessible to them but not to us, such characters as Voznesenskaia (*"Slave"*), Platonov (*Mechanical Piano*), and Kotov and Mitia (*Burnt by the Sun*) function as the devices by which the intensity of their personal frenzy stands in for larger political dynamics.

A second common feature of melodrama pronounced in Mikhalkov's work is a love of the richly appointed interior, the cluttered, ornamented domestic space: the crystal decanters, walls of old photographs, brass beds, warped gramophones, parasols, oversized vases of wildflowers.[29] The claustrophobic space solicits us on two levels. On one level it invites identification, as if we too were the owners of a prerevolutionary life whose leisure hours might be spent noticing the tasks that neither we nor the household help had inclination to do. But this domestic tourism for less privileged readers, as Roger Sales has mordantly described it, is supported by another, textual level: the richly decorated interior conjures up screen memories of Russia's own prerevolutionary melodrama, Evgenii Bauer's "cult of the object, his romance with things, . . . more

FIGURE 3.2. Mikhalkov. *Burnt by the Sun*. Red Army Commander Kotov with Stalin.

than a Victorian cliché of accomplishment and acquisition" (McReynolds and Neuberger, introduction 1). In both social history and film history the objects propose a continuity unimpeded by expropriation, social rupture, and violent intervention, uniting the viewer across the revolutionary divide and erasing class differences in the darkened space of the cinema hall.

This identification, as we see in *Burnt by the Sun*, is not without its dark side. As Elsaesser (372) remarks (with particular resonance for this film):

> The banality of the objects, combined with the repressed anxieties and emotions, forces a contrast that makes the scene almost epitomize the relation of décor to characters in the melodrama: the more the setting is filled with objects to which the plot gives symbolic significance, the more the characters are enclosed in a seemingly ineluctable situation.

A third feature of Mikhalkov's melodrama, and one highly compatible with late Soviet anomie, is its preoccupation with moral and emotional compromise. Whether it is Platonov (*Mechanical Piano*), crippled by an awareness of middle-aged descent into mediocrity and compromise, or Oblomov, or Mitia (*Burnt by the Sun*), broken by a security system in which he himself was complicit and cowardly, these melodramas unsparingly show "the way self-pity and self-hatred alternate with a violent urge toward some form of liberating action, which inevitably fails to resolve the conflict" (Elsaesser 376). As Anna Petrovna (*Mechanical Piano*) darkly reassures us, "Everything remains the same" ("Vse ostaetsia po-prezhnemu").

Melodrama's characteristically lurid exploration of "the aggressive, erotic, and fetishistic" (Lang 16) is well suited to Mikhalkov's cinematic signature, an interbreeding of machismo with masochism. On the one hand, the unashamed aggression of Mikhalkov's appealing predators, on the other, the complex, self-punitive world of his victims produce what Elsaesser (374) has described as the "typical masochism of melodrama, with its incessant acts of inner violation, its mechanisms of frustration and overcompensation." A trivialized and effete liberal intelligentsia, the bearers of empty solutions, lead shabby personal lives that shadow their shabby civic lives: the doctor Nikolai Triletskii (played by Mikhalkov himself) who fears cholera and cannot bear the ill (*Mechanical Piano*); the ineffective scriptwriter ("*Slave of Love*") who despises his own work and emigrates; and of course Mitia (*Burnt by the Sun*), "a dissembler, a man without deep emotions and ties; in a word, an *intelligent*" (Broude 39). In *Barber of Siberia* the positive hero André Tolstoi is rescued from this fate only by his salubrious exile to Siberia.

In this respect Mikhalkov's work is a distinctly late variety of melodrama, one for whom the victim is often a campy figure, with only himself to blame, lacking the self-awareness to see, as the audience is invited to do, that he is the author of his own suffering. By this stage of late Soviet history and well-worn melodrama the earlier critics have now become wrong: "Melodrama always sides with the powerless" (Vicinus 130) or "melodrama as echo of the historically voiceless" (Grimstead 80). Instead, Mikhalkov's victims, privileged in ways they cannot acknowledge, usually have exactly themselves to blame.

Melodrama's moral compromise is thereby also our own compromise, what Gledhill ("The Melodramatic Field" 38) aptly captures as melodrama's "double acknowledgement" of excess and mediocrity: the morally flawed universe, vitiated of a capacity for change; the sweet allure of fatalism; complicity at every turn; unsustainable transgression that reverts to oblivion and amnesia; a personal torment "uncomplicated by self-awareness" (Lang 20) of its greater insignificance; the inkling of personal mediocrity without the capacity or will to rise above it.

A fourth and final element of melodrama recurrent in Mikhalkov's work is the self-conscious localizing of time and place, ostentatiously signaled by props in a fashion specific enough to encourage the viewer, newly aware of belonging to a different time and place, to notice the period's ruling ideational modes. As McReynolds and Neuberger (introduction 5) suggest:

> Melodrama exaggerates the circumstances of time and place in which
> it is produced, and as a result it offers a uniquely accessible mode
> of analysis for audiences to perceive the interaction among politics,
> art, and everyday life. Because melodrama is self-consciously about
> its own present, it offers . . . a new perspective on the dominant
> ideologies—political, cultural, social—in which the story is set.

Mikhalkov further heightens the local atmosphere by using two temporal slices: a past, often a lost or bungled opportunity, haunts the present's diegetic frame. In *Mechanical Piano* seven years separates the love affair between the protagonist Platonov and Sofiia. Eighteen years in *Five Evenings* divide the hero's affair with Tamara from his return to her Moscow apartment. The heroine narrator of *Without Witnesses* frames the story with the six years measured by the birth of her daughter. Romano (*Dark Eyes*) recounts his lost Russian love of eight years earlier, ostentatiously marked as 1903 in the resort's flower bed. *Urga*, narrated (it turns out) by Gombo's as yet unborn fourth child, tells of his conception two decades earlier: how his father went to town for a television and some condoms, returning home with the former but not the latter. *Burnt by the Sun* is structured around Mitia's ten-year absence from the Soviet Union. The 1905 heroine narrator of *Barber* recounts to her twenty-year-old son the story of his conception two decades earlier, the result of her 1885 affair with the cadet André Tolstoi. In *Oblomov* and *Burnt by the Sun* the omniscient narrator intervenes at the story's conclusion to account for the fates of the surviving protagonists. The tension between two slices of time lends Mikhalkov's films their nostalgic feel, as if the viewer were leafing through archival records—or, in *Oblomov*'s case, a novel—that intensify the sensation of displacement and retrospection.[30]

The film titles too engage in this technique of framing things as if they referred to a textual past: citational quality from silent cinema (the quotation marks in *"Slave of Love"*), music (*Unfinished Piece for Mechanical Piano*), opera (*Barber of Siberia*, modeled on Rossini's *Barber of Seville*), and the torch song *The Wearied Sun* (*Utomlennoe solntse*), which produces Mikhalkov's distortion as "wearied by the sun" (*utomlennye solntsem*), evocative as well in Russian of Margaret Mitchell's 1936 novel *Gone With the Wind* (in Russian *Unesennye vetrom*).

This retrospective frame is often symbolically marked by a viewing object or observatory space, such as the telescope of *Mechanical Piano*, the "two-way" television of *Urga*, and the raised camera platform in *"Slave of Love."* These objects invite the viewer to contemplate the temporal distance in the unfolding narrative. They function as a reminder that although we watch the characters, they cannot watch us. The double acknowledgment—an intensely local time, but revelatory of larger time—is ours alone; the characters lack self-awareness, a seasoned knowledge outside the frame of the transience or eternity of events in their own time and place.

An astute scholar of Chekhov's work has characterized a common shift in the writer's stories from "it seemed" (at the story's beginning) to "it turned out" (at the story's end)—more delicately in Russian, from *kazalos'* to *okazalos'* (Kataev 268). In Mikhalkov's work this shift takes on an exaggerated poignancy, as cinema's grand illusion reveals more sharply the grand illusions of its protagonists.

Chekhov's "drama of the ordinary" (Brooks 13), his world of small deeds, and the pathetic revolt of the "'small deeds' liberal" (Figes 257) in the face of powerlessness and compromise had a tremendous appeal in the subdued times of the late Soviet period. Of all prerevolutionary writers, it is Chekhov who most intensely informs Mikhalkov's work. Though Chekhov preferred to describe the genre of his major plays as comedies, they shared with melodrama a quality, as Elsaesser (376) describes it, of "tragedy that doesn't quite come off: either because the characters think of themselves too self-consciously as tragic or because the predicament is too evidently fabricated on the level of plot and dramaturgy to carry the kind of conviction normally termed 'inner necessity.'" The compatibility of Chekhov with Mikhalkov's melodrama recurrently revealed high tragedy as banal and quiet mediocrity as imbued with exquisitely painful, unrealized aspiration.

Impending Seizure: Appropriating Chekhov

From *"Slave of Love"* onward Mikhalkov's melodramas were often inflected with a "Chekhovian intonation" (Sandler 211), an odd undertaking, given the dissimilarity of their artistic personalities.[31] Even when Mikhalkov turned to Ivan Goncharov's novel *Oblomov*, the result gradually mutated toward Chekhov in its ironic and melancholic introspection. Elsewhere, when he would appear at first to move away from Chekhov toward the grotesque, as in *Dark Eyes*, the result was Chekhov à la Gogol', as the director himself has described it (Sandler 238).[32] *Burnt by the Sun* (1994), while drawing on elements from Arkadii Gaidar's 1935 story *The Sky-Blue Cup* and Ivan Bunin's 1925 *Sunstroke*, nevertheless remains firmly within the symbolic universe of Chekhov's work in its mise-en-scène, characters, and pacing, interweaving the Grand Style of high Stalinism into the "lace gentleness of Chekhov's intonation" (Rtishcheva 108). It would be difficult to insist on a distinction between Mikhalkov's explicitly Chekhovian films, such as *Mechanical Piano* and *Dark Eyes*, and those, such as *"Slave," Oblomov, Burnt by the Sun*, or even *Anna: From 6 to 18* for which Chekhov appears to have been an artistic consultant. As Mikhalkov puts it, he often looks "with today's eyes *through Chekhov* at the world" (quoted in Lipkov, *Nikita Mikhalkov*).

Mikhalkov had strong practical reasons to be interested in Chekhov. Chekhov and the chrestomathic tradition more generally in Russian literature helped retain a script on the right side of ideological scrutiny. It was a common strategy for a Soviet director, whether of melodrama or other vulnerable modes, genres, or topics, to use an already existing work of literature, either a socialist realist classic or an established nineteenth-century masterpiece. After all, the great works had passed the censors; in the case of nineteenth-century fiction, they had passed through multiple regimes of censorship. Until the 1960s the most frequent choice for film adaptations had been Gor'kii's writings, but by the more reflective and melancholic late Thaw Chekhov's texts supplanted Gor'kii's as first choice, outstripping Ostrovskii and even Pushkin (Segida, "72 Lenina").[33] To shoot Chekhov, therefore, was to join the swelling ranks of filmmakers from 1911 forward who, for a range of reasons, ideological and artistic, found in Chekhov a compatible scriptwriter, analogous in some respects to Jane Austen, whose cinematic life was likewise tenuously tied to her literary works.[34]

And so from *"Slave of Love"* on Mikhalkov appropriates Chekhov again and again as one might appropriate any property left unattended—that is, because it is possible to do so. Chekhov's writing provided the pre-Soviet cultural credentials by which Mikhalkov could narrate the story of usurped property, a major theme long after *At Home* and *"Slave of Love,"* as we see in *Burnt by the Sun* and *Barber of Siberia*, and a theme that figures in Chekhov's short stories.[35] In *"Slave"* the film-set villa for the crew's final scene could itself be the stage backdrop for a Chekhov play and anticipates the authentic estates of Mikhalkov's later Chekhov films, such as *Mechanical Piano*. The film company's life between takes as they await the arrival of film stock is led as if the rest of the estate or the dacha were just beyond camera range, off set and (as with us) temporarily unavailable.

Mikhalkov's next idiosyncratic Chekhov, *Unfinished Piece for Mechanical Piano* (1976), relies largely on material from the writer's 1877 unpublished play, "Fatherlessness" ("Bezotsovshchina"), rewritten and often produced as *Platonov* or *Play without a Title*.[36] Here, Anna Petrovna, like the more familiar Liubov' Ranevskaia (*Cherry Orchard*), lives in perpetual danger of losing her estate. Elderly creditors, arriving alternately to court her or to repossess her property, force a choice between "my estate or my honor" ("imenie ili chest'"). Anna Petrovna's invocation of honor, meanwhile, obscures a prior act of usurpation: as stepmother to Sergei Voinitsev, she had in fact taken over his hereditary family estate. The house indexes a more complicated chain of usurpations in which only predators and victims—stock characters in Mikhalkov's melodrama—drive the terms of exchange.

In this process the mansion and its lands are ontologies separate from one another: for the elite guests and house servants (as well as for the cinema viewers, who are never taken beyond the mansion's nearby pond), the peasant dwellings are, in the words of a house servant, a "Polar expedition," marginally part of the realm but a distant and unfamiliar space. When a worker stumbles in on Anna Petrovna's dinner party it quickly becomes clear that no one, not even the doctor at a time of urgent medical need, would undertake the unfamiliar journey to that periphery. Life off the estate is—in a strictly demographic sense—an unfathomable region with ragged borders that those in the mansion can neither imagine nor navigate.

I would hesitate, however, to extend this argument, claiming that Mikhalkov's country estate is a symbol tout court of the Russian Empire. The list of correspondences is perhaps obvious: hypertrophic, costly to maintain, complex and archaic, lacking in adequate direction to ensure proper management. The cause for hesitation is the presence of a larger symbolic investment than a homology between the mansion and the empire in which it is embedded. That dominant investment is precisely one of temporal continuity. The lifestyle of the estate in the 1870s and 1880s is imbricated across Mikhalkov's visual system of the late 1970s and early 1980s in ways that had come into cultural crisis: the holding of power in one, late feudal system suggests the holding of power within the other, late socialist system as mutually validating ways of life, mutually coherent through their web of visual associations that we are invited to witness. In a fashion comparable in some respects to the English heritage films, we are encouraged to observe how we might fit in. As Ruth Barton (136) argues with respect to English heritage films, "The stately homes of the English films and the society that inhabits them are structured on a naturalized hierarchical system that encompasses both the aristocracy and their servants," potentially extending outward to include the cinema public.

In Mikhalkov's next, explicitly Chekhovian effort, *Dark Eyes* (1986), one cannot help but notice that his Italy maintains strong compatibilities with his own, already established Russia. The diegesis requests that we believe this is

Italy, and therefore in an opposition of cultured Italy to provincial Russia. And yet a different dyad is already prepared for us from previous films, in which Italian opera often accompanied Russian estate life. *Mechanical Piano* incorporates extensive passages from Nemorino's romance in Donizetti's *L'Elisir d'amore* (indeed, the final ten minutes is shot entirely as if it were a filmed Italian opera); *Oblomov* repeatedly returns to *Casta diva* from Bellini's *Norma*; even the working-class *Kinfolk* includes extended passages from Verdi.[37] The familiar material culture of Mikhalkov's "Italy"—the veiled haberdashery, lace gloves, and parasols—the comic interludes, magic tricks, and concerts all suggest this is still his Russia, a privileged Russia strongly derivative of Italian operetta but staged in Russian, by Russians, for those Russians well enough connected to invite foreign guests. Once again Lotman ("Poetika" 68), describing this critical detour, reminds us that, for the Russian imperial elite, it is more important *to be like* a foreigner than *to be* a foreigner. The Italian estate is what the Russian estate might have been had the overburdened caretaker attended to its broken statues, last summer's hammock, the forgotten goblets, the *natures meurantes* on the abandoned outdoor table.

The ostensible opposition Italy/Russia suggests a second, background opposition of imperial center to provincial culture, of metropole to fringe, of a Europeanized elite to its provincial country heartland, eternally gullible, verdant, and available to exploitation. The knowledge that wealthy Russia *could be* Italy (though we know it is not) and that we ourselves *could be* Chekhov's estate owners (though we know we are not) accounts for the fetishistic quality of Mikhalkov's nostalgia (as Manonni [125] would say, "Je sais bien, mais quand-même . . ."). The Italian overlay allows Mikhalkov to explore through a set of transcodings a Russia that (like Italy) is European but not English, French, or, God forbid, German.

In this newly coded dyad of center and periphery we are provided an already familiar pattern: a male protagonist adrift between old and new loves; elegant, impoverished women (in *Dark Eyes*, one newly impoverished, another born into impoverished circumstances); trivial guests; the mercantile pragmatism of entrepreneurial wealth. The financial crisis of Romano's wealthy wife, Elisa, forces her to sell the mansion to avoid impending seizure. Romano sets out to usurp another man's wife (the Russian "lady with the lapdog") but is incapable of carrying through with his passion. In *Mechanical Piano* the female protagonist ran off; in *Dark Eyes*, as in *Burnt by the Sun*, the male protagonist disappears, but the result is the same: a gradual transition to a compromised existence. Romano's beloved woman, like Sofiia of *Mechanical Piano* and Marusia of *Burnt by the Sun*, goes on to marry another man, the chance listener to Romano's rambling confession. The three male characters—Platonov (*Mechanical Piano*), Romano (*Dark Eyes*), and Mitia (*Burnt by the Sun*)—having failed in their great love, are finally inadequate either as predators or partners. Platonov's farcical suicide attempt, Romano's flight, and Mitia's attempted suicide are acknowledgments that a victory over their rivals does not eliminate the inevitability of their own failures.

In his fourth Chekhov adaptation, *Burnt by the Sun*, Mikhalkov underscores the familiar patterns of displacement, usurpation, and victims as predators. Mitia is displaced by Kotov, "the master in another family's house" (Moskvina, "La Grand Illusion" 97), from both his adopted home and the woman he loved. The walls of the home Mitia knew as a young adult are hung with his usurper's photographs; Mitia's own image, as he himself remarks, has been erased. He plays with dolls to recount a fairy tale of love lost; his story, apparently for little Nadia, is in fact directed at his lost Marusia. It is a scene intended to underscore the similarities with Platonov (*Mechanical Piano*), who played the guitar to accompany his story of love lost; the story, apparently for everyone, is in fact directed at his lost Sofiia. So, in the larger frame of the cinema screen, Mikhalkov plays with actors and cameras to recount—apparently to the viewer, but in fact more broadly—the melodrama of Russia's impossibilities, irrevocabilities, and inevitabilities.

Narrated as a crisis *through* Chekhov, the anxiety is one of first principles: What would be the *conditions of possibility* for rightful ownership? It is hardly surprising that Mikhalkov stages this question on the historical platform of the late imperial and early Soviet periods, when terms of rightful ownership became impossible to formulate, blessedly delivering an exhausted elite from the travails of maintaining unmanageable claims.

Indeed, Said's comments in *Culture and Imperialism* on the English novel of the country estate might be read here in reverse. "What assures the domestic tranquility and attractive harmony of one," Said (104) suggests of the British elite and their imperial holdings, "is the productivity and regulated discipline of the other." By contrast, in a narrative of forfeiture rather than of mastery, Mikhalkov's Chekhovian melodrama suggests that what disturbs the domestic tranquility of one is the deteriorated productivity of the other. Leaving its "ghostly notations," as Said (151) has called them, historical time is reinscribed by Mikhalkov to suggest that somehow in cinema all things might, in the midst of extreme upheaval remain the same.

For all the Chekhovian intonation, therefore, it is nevertheless an inaccurate claim that Mikhalkov's great love is the world *before* 1917. His love is rather the buckle of history, the sixty-year period from 1877 to 1937. That most disrupted period of Russia's recent history is in Mikhalkov's work one of continuity, in which "children are born, rivers flow, autumn follows summer" (Tirdatova 4). Six of his major films are clustered within these sixty years. Two (*Mechanical Piano*, and *Barber*) are set in the last quarter of the nineteenth century. Four (*Dark Eyes, At Home, "Slave of Love,"* and *Burnt by the Sun*) belong to the first third of the twentieth century. Five lesser-known works—the Khrushchev-era setting of *Five Evenings*, the Stagnation-era setting of *Kinfolk*, the *perestroika*-era *Hitchhike*, the late *perestroika* setting of *Urga*, and the contemporary *12*—situate themselves in relation to this corpus.

Within this sixty-year bridge Mikhalkov's continuity-amid-rupture offers the illusion of an ongoing, unified text. As critics and the filmmaker himself have noted, *Burnt by the Sun* might be read on several levels as the *Platonov* of 1936 (Kulish 109; Rtisheva 109); the elderly dacha residents of *Burnt* could earlier have been Anna Petrovna's guests (*Mechanical Piano*) who had survived into the 1930s (Arkhangel'skii 5). This sense of historical continuity inheres as well in the mise-en-scène, the architectural and design details, costumes, and props that weather and fade: the parquet floors, glassed verandas, leggy house-plants, tatty wicker furniture, ill-tuned seven-string guitars, ceramic pitchers with chipped washbasins, steamer trunks, and lace curtains that billow out into the ill-tended garden of both estate and dacha. The distinction between them is gently but strategically smudged, using real estate to facilitate the further smudging of class and lifestyle and the encroachments of urban life so necessary for an updated maintenance of the elites.

The characteristic piquancy of Mikhalkov's cinema is predicated on this curious oxymoron: things outlive people.[38] The home is the site of *human* impermanence, and the instability of its property title articulates larger instabilities of class. This hazy period between the last hours of feudalism and the high noon of socialism is inhabited by figures attired in white suits, suspenders, and straw boaters for the one and white dresses, broad-brimmed hats, and shawls for the other, blending the cultural codes of tsarist and Soviet Russias. The simpering, homicidal cuckolds and long-suffering heroines, the infantile excesses, lost loves, and botched suicides all overtax the logistical resources of the few remaining members of the household staff. They have "wept their lives away, missed their opportunities, learnt nothing" (Arkhangel'skii 5). Meanwhile, property, like pieces in a board game, change hands around them in a social regulation shot through with impromptu and indiscernible patterns of confiscation and reclamation. At stake in this frenzy are the contending property agendas of feudal Russia and socialist Russia, unable to resolve ownership.

"Russia as I Imagine and See Her"

And I very much wanted, comparing these two childhoods—the little girl in the Soviet empire and the little boy [Iliusha Oblomov] in the long-gone empire of Russia—to understand that point where these childhoods diverged from each other, and whether they might again converge.

—Narrator, *Anna: From 6 to 18*

Some would see in Mikhalkov's cinema a contemporary political blueprint for Russia.[39] The filmmaker's own performance as Aleksandr III in *Barber of Siberia* set off in the liberal intelligentsia a ripple of anxiety about monarchist pretensions, a fear fueled by Mikhalkov's own political ambitions. That he has had political ambitions is indisputable (for a discussion, see Beumers, *Burnt* 2–3), but this biographical fact does not easily permit us to read his films, with the exception of *12*, backward as a platform.

In this last case the director recasts Lumet's courtroom drama such that only formal similarities remain. Where Lumet would frame civic duty as the individual man's conscience regarding guilt or innocence, Mikhalkov would put on trial the Western-style jury system itself. The film's conventions already inform us of the accused boy's innocence. At issue instead appear to be the relative merits of two forms of justice, ethnic and civic, both of which fall short. By the norms of ethnic justice the boy is likely to be a murderer because he is a Chechen; by the norms of Western-style civic justice the boy is innocent but marked for criminal execution by the very gangsters who killed his father. What Mikhalkov proposes as Russia's special path is a higher force beyond the law: the jury foreman, a retired FSB agent, it is strongly suggested, played by Mikhalkov himself, takes the boy into his family, embodying an extraterrestrial compassion that transcends Western categories of justice.

A recurrent reading, relevant here, of Mikhalkov's work sees him as a nationalist in search of an authentic Russia, stripped of European influences and enhanced to a kind of magnified ethnicity. Yet such an account has difficulty making sense of Mikhalkov's evident love of European culture, his extensive use of bel canto, for example, as uniquely expressive of intense emotion, rather than Russian peasant song, surely a more appropriate choice for a nationalist director. And so one might well hesitate before assigning him to the ranks of nationalism without some reflection on what the term might mean.[40] Mikhalkov's Russia, a European empire, is also a Russia that is not Western. In Mikhalkov's cinema, this political condition presents no necessary contradiction, as if Russia will bring into being a Europe of the future.

Mikhalkov's uninhibited statist indulgences—from the Chekists (*At Home*), through Kotov (*Burnt by the Sun*), to Aleksandr III (*Barber of Siberia*), to the retired security officer (*12*)—generously share the stage with his folk extravaganzas, of which the most memorable (and artistically weakest) are the bread-and-salt welcoming scene at Sysoev (*Dark Eyes*) and the caricatured Shrovetide feast (*Barber of Siberia*). These displays of ethnicity are the staged enactments of official *narodnost'*, where the state, in the presence of *narod* and the absence of nation, has full rein. In this demotic kabuki the Russian folk are a tradition-minded, state-bearing people, a linkage of the organic peasant, bread-and-salt practices to the aristocratic patrimony of the empire, defended by a military that is held to strict standards of loyalty and honor. Hardly a nationalism with the usual associations of newly empowered egalitarian agency, liberationist collective expression, or the independent civic life of nationhood, it is instead the divine state, an official *narodnost'* whose anointed, titular ethnicity nobly sustains strong imperial and military traditions on the basis of enduring moral authority.

Mikhalkov is committed to the robust construction of a cultural continuum, trimmed with folk habits and uniquely restorative of (putatively) endangered values. Against the clamor of modernity, figured most evidently in the disco cacophony of *Kinfolk* and the insistent telephone in the final shot of *Urga*, a few thoughtful folk, linked to the land and already mournful over irreparable loss, hold fast against heedless modernizers. Konstantin (*Dark Eyes*), a secondary and stilted figure, could well stand in for any number of such thoughtful figures, from *At Home* to *Barber of Siberia*, in his advocacy of a pastoral collective ownership: "I am not against factories," Konstantin explains to Romano at the film's conclusion, "but it wouldn't work here. If we burn the trees for machines and if the river dries up, we'll be finished. . . . A home isn't just a bit of land surrounded by a fence. It's everywhere—the river, the forest, the stream, everywhere." Mikhalkov's cinema divides into those films in which this irreparable loss has just begun (*Dark Eyes*), those films in which it is happening (*Barber of Siberia*), and those in which it has been long completed (*Kinfolk*).[41]

This orientation toward the past gives an unusual valence to the children who litter Mikhalkov's films. They function not as signs of the future but as judgments on the past, on how the protagonists have lived their lives. They function as the instruments through which the past becomes morally intelligible. In *Without Witnesses* the son Dima never appears in the film but functions as the measure of adult capacity for sacrifice. The adopted Slava (*Five Evenings*) refers us back in time to the heroine's compassionate interior and mediates the reunion of the lovers, parted eighteen years earlier through war. In *Kinfolk* the baby passed from hand to hand at the film's end is not a promise of future family happiness but a reminder of an earlier fragmentation, briefly and temporarily overcome as the older children are deployed for war. And *Anna* is in many respects the story of Mikhalkov's moral accountability, for which the daughter is the sign.

As engaging as the children may be (little Bouin in *Urga*, for example) they are inert. With the exception of Nadia (*Burnt by the Sun*), they are necessary as an umbrella is necessary, or a wheelchair, or the hammock; they could equally be household pets or bent bicycles. In *Mechanical Piano* the unmotivated Petia, a motherless boy brought along to the Voinitsev estate, is allowed neither to cross over into the main story line nor to dream the entire film, despite what the final shot might suggest. This dreaming child is the measure of the adults' intentions. Another such sleeping child is Ol'ga (*Dark Eyes*), daughter of the veterinarian Konstantin, who carries her across his chest as a sash of honor, a dormant testimony to his political integrity. The pointed comparison of this daughter, in the arms of her civic-minded father, with Romano's distant daughter underscores the difference between these two male characters, lending moral authority to Konstantin's political philosophy of a pristine, exceptionalist Russia. As Susan Larsen ("National Identity" 494) cogently suggests, in this "heroic genealogy of Russian filmmaking" "patrimony, paternity, and patriotism merge and reinforce one another."

Against a context of Westernizing, false solutions, Mikhalkov again and again constructs a space in which such positive heroes as André Tolstoi (*Barber of Siberia*) gather up an amalgamated social identity: born into modest circumstances, educated according to elite military codes of honor, sympathetic to the radical intelligentsia (as we learn from the film's early terrorist scene), wedded to a woman of peasant stock, well suited for the taiga, yet speaking French. A certain homegrown hybridity can be mapped extensively in the earlier films as well: the tsarist and Bolshevik interbreeding in *"Slave of Love"* and *Burnt by the Sun*; the Oblomovian warmth and Stoltzian discipline in *Oblomov*;[42] the mating of rural Mongol with urban Chinese in *Urga*. The same hybridity surfaces in Mikhalkov himself, progeny of prerevolutionary aristocracy and Stalin's court poet. "How much [Mikhalkov] . . . would like to join socialist Russia with the non-socialist Russia of the future," the critic Iurii Bogomolov ("Kontsy" 18) writes, "almost in the way that Mikhalkov's once distinguished parents (and not only they) had hoped to combine Bolshevik reality with the pre-Revolutionary education level of the nobility."

And what about the Russian American son, Andrew McCracken (*Barber of Siberia*)? The film's tagline—"He's Russian; that explains a lot"—offers us a slogan without content. What is that "lot" that has been explained? The U.S. Army sergeant detects in McCracken's genes a stubborn but noble resistance, an immunity to the virus of mindless U.S. culture, something high-minded and unpredictable, now fortuitously interbred into American genetics. Above all, Andrew is blessed to have inherited his Russian father's stubborn honor, his elite cultural values ("Mozart is a great composer"), and his imperial demeanor. Andrew manages to remain European to the U.S. Army sergeant without therefore becoming in any sense a Westerner in his cultural orientation.

Mikhalkov's core political vision concerns itself with how a multiethnic community sustains coherence under strong state leadership; how, for Russia, Western alignments of state to nation have been prone to failure; how its geographic size and the politics of elite contestation have militated against a Western emancipatory imaginary of *liberté, egalité, fraternité*, where "Peace, Labor, Happiness" would better serve the plural self. The recurrent trope of the foreigner's visit, precipitating failure or destruction—the foreign Romano's failed visit to Anna's provincial city (*Dark Eyes*); the émigré Mitia's visit to what is now Kotov's house (*Burnt by the Sun*); the American woman Jane's visit to André Tolstoi in Siberia—all suggest a larger, doomed encounter of incompatible cultural sets. Mikhalkov's Russia suffers from their alien modernizing, registered most starkly in the debased Western gadgets of *Kinfolk* and the closing episode of *Urga*.

More than screening a political philosophy, Mikhalkov's cinema is a response to a Western, universalist model for Russia. His work counterposes a

Russia salvaged from indenture to Western models of statehood and its false presumption of a national corollary. Merciless about how liberal solutions have proven consistently inadequate, Mikhalkov insists that his cinema matters both in the construction of representations and as the prize of that struggle, the way political representations inhere in artistic representations, how one set comes to stand in for the other. This is, perhaps, one reason the liberal intelligentsia reacts with such unease to Mikhalkov's cinema. He interpolates them into a social identity—elite yet state-populist, European but not Western—that they would still resist, sensing perhaps its constructed quality and preferring instead to inhabit a different Russia, still unformulated, but in which they would have, in both senses, different representation.

FILMOGRAPHY

A Girl and Some Things (*Devochka i veshchi*). 1967.
. . . And I Go Home (*. . . A ia uezzhaiu domoi*). 1968.
Quiet Day at War's End (*Spokoinyi den' v kontse voiny*). Diploma film. 1971.
At Home among Strangers, a Stranger at Home (*Svoi sredi chuzhikh, chuzoi sredi svoikh*). 1974.
"Slave of Love" (*"Raba liubvi"*). 1975.
Unfinished Piece for Mechanical Piano (*Neokonchennaia p'esa dlia mekhanicheskogo pianino*). 1976.
Five Evenings (*Piat' vecherov*). 1978.
Several Days from the Life of Oblomov (English release title) (*Neskol'ko dnei iz zhizni I. I. Oblomova*). 1979.
Kinfolk (*Rodnia*). 1981.
Without Witnesses (*Bez svidetelei*). 1983.
Dark Eyes (*Ochi chernye*). 1987.
Illusion (*Illiuziia*). Television. 1989.
Hitchhiking (*Avtostop*). Short. 1990.
Russian Elegy (*Russkaia elegiia*). 1990.
Close to Eden (English release title) (*Urga, Territoriia liubvi*). 1991.
Remembering Chekhov (*Vspominaia Chekhova*). 1993.
Anna: From 6 to 18 (*Anna: Ot 6 do 18*). Documentary. 1993.
Burnt by the Sun (*Utomlennye solntsem*). 1994.
Nikita Mikhalkov. A Sentimental Trip to My Homeland. Music of Russian Painting (*Nikita Mikhalkov. Sentimental'noe puteshestvie na moiu rodinu. Muzyka russkoi zhivopisi*). Television documentary serial. 1995.
Requiem for the Great Victory (*Rekviem Velikoi Pobedy*). Documentary. Codirected with Sergei Miroshnichenko. 1995.
Barber of Siberia (*Sibirskii tsiriul'nik*). 1998.
Father (*Otets*). Documentary. 2003.
Mother (*Mama*). Documentary. 2003.

Nikita Mikhalkov. A Russian Choice (*Nikita Mikhalkov. Russkii Vybor*).
   Documentary serial. 2003.
General Kozhugetych (*General Kozhugetych*). Documentary. 2005.
12. 2007.
Burnt by the Sun 2 (*Utomlennye solntsem 2*). 2010.

4 ✳

Kira Muratova: The Zoological Imperium

Introduction: Tsar of Nature, Crown of Creation

I always hear the same thing, the same human self-advancement: I am the tsar of nature, the crown of creation, more important than anything. It is despicable.

> —Kira Muratova, quoted in Tsyrkun, "Kira Muratova: 'A mne naplevat', chto vam naplevat', chto mne naplevat'" (2002)

Egoism is the essence of my métier.

> —Kira Muratova, quoted in Frodon, "Kira Muratova: L'oeuvre mutilée" (1988)

The line of inquiry proposed here examines Muratova's enduring skepticism toward an imaginary of belonging. Her resistance sets the stakes very high, disallowing not only the higher-order collectivity of a social imagining, but by extension the commanding heights of the human, dismantling boundaries distinguishing humans from animals, the living from the nonliving, the organic from the inorganic such that the only meaningful boundary is that of the film itself, capacious enough to accommodate the filmmaker's playful and capricious rule. Any effort, Soviet or later, to galvanize anything from without, to marshal a set of "lofty utterances," as the cinema bureaucrats would say, is doomed to failure. Her fiendish subversion of aspirations is symptomatic of a larger refusal to be bound by imposed loyalties, countering them with mock schemas of collectivity that mirror a coercive civilization of iron restraint and demonic optimism.

The strategies of Muratova's cinema are composed of two related refusals: the lofty ennoblement of humankind, and collective loyalty as such, a refusal to set apart one subset from another to confirm a special status. Her radical egalitarianism, coupled with her refusal of imposed collectivity, allows her to set the only functioning limits to behavior as the formal limits of cinema as a play space. In this sense Muratova's work functions as a kind of preserve within which her diverse characters roam freely, innocent of any knowledge that they belong together.

Biographical Remarks: The Rare Talents of a Disqualified Filmmaker

Kira Muratova (born 1934) has had a complex life. Its details, which have been discussed at length elsewhere,[1] are summarized here only briefly. A student of Sergei Gerasimov at VGIK, she graduated in 1959 and went to work at the Odessa Film Studio in 1961. She has directed over a dozen full-length feature films and several shorts, including *Letter to America, The Information,* and *The Dummy* (original titles and production information provided at the end of the chapter). Her first two films—the diploma film *By the Steep Ravine,* based on Gavriil Troepol'skii's short story, and *Our Honest Bread*—were codirected with her (then) husband, Aleksandr Muratov.[2]

During the Soviet period Muratova encountered severe criticism for the unconventional work of her first individual feature film, *Brief Encounters* (1967), based on Leonid Zhukhovitskii's short story "House on the Steppe" ("Dom v stepi").[3] The film was assigned a low-distribution release category and was screened in a total of six prints at film clubs rather than larger, more prestigious venues (Bozhovich, "Rentgenoskopiia" 58; Galichenko 93). Her second individual feature film, *Long Farewells* (1971, released 1987), encountered a worse fate: the film was banned entirely. The filmmaker herself was downgraded ("disqualified" in Soviet parlance) in her professional status and required to take on a different profession, earning money as a scriptwriter while working in a film studio museum.[4] These two early films are often referred to by Muratova and Russian film critics as her "provincial melodramas"; together they mark the first stage of her work. They are both shot in black-and-white film, and they share a strong narrative line, though the first film, *Brief Encounters*, was highly experimental in the Soviet context for its complex use of flashback.[5]

A second stage is marked by another pair of films dating from the late Stagnation period: *Getting to Know the Wide World* (1978) and *Among Grey Stones* (1983), based on Vladimir Korolenko's short story "In Bad Company" ("V durnom obshchestve"). It is during this period that several shifts in her work take place. The move from black-and-white footage to a vivid, mannered color scheme is complemented by associative camera work that Taubman has linked in part to Muratova's friendship with the Armenian artist and director Sergei Paradzhanov, who then had only recently been released from four years of his first prison sentence (1973–77).[6] Dubbed by the film critic Andrei Plakhov ("Kira Muratova" 208) "the first specimen of socialist postmodernism," Muratova's *Getting to Know the Wide World* was strongly contrapuntal to the plot line of its screenplay, Grigorii Baklanov's traditional novella, "The Birch Trees Whisper in the Wind" ("Shelestiat na vetru berezy"). Marked by a high degree of ornamentalism, consonant with Paradzhanov's own style, Muratova's film encountered bureaucratic criticism for its "excessively metaphoric quality" (*Kadr*, October 13, 1978). The second film of this pair, *Among Grey Stones*, filmed at the very end of the Stagnation era, was so severely cut by the censors that Muratova removed her name from the credits entirely, substituting instead the generic moniker "Ivan Sidorov."[7] *Among Grey Stones* occupies a contradictory status in her work: as the negatives were destroyed, the director's version can no longer be restored, and yet, despite the pseudonym, Muratova does not reject the film as her work (Bozhovich, "Rentgenoskopiia" 70).

A significant breakthrough for Muratova came in July 1986, the time described in chapter 2 when the Conflicts Commission, led by Andrei Plakhov, finally reviewed her provincial melodramas and released them in 1987 for circulation. This breakthrough marked a new stage in Muratova's cinema. A third pairing, new work dating from this period, is Muratova's two films from the *perestroika* era, *A Change of Fate* (1987) and *Asthenic Syndrome* (1989, released 1990). The former, based on Somerset Maugham's short story "The Letter," continued Muratova's love of contrapuntal narrative, playing against a strong story line with an apparently improvisational rendition of the plot; the latter returned to an embedded plot structure, signaled here by an internal shift from black-and-white to color. The embedded narrative recalled Muratova's early *Brief Encounters* and anticipated her later *Two in One* in its narrative complexity. Now, however, it was the film's spectacularly obscene language rather than its narrative complexity that delayed its release.

Muratova's fourth stage, in the early 1990s, after the fall of communism, marks a gentler period in her work. The pair *Sentimental Policeman* (1992) and *Enthusiasms* (1994) continue her mannered style but without the narrative and verbal provocations of *Asthenic Syndrome*. *Enthusiasms* is loosely based on memoirs by the horseman Boris Dediukhin. Filmed in the Askania-Nova game preserve, it is the least plotted of her work and the most unstructured in its camera work and character development. The mannered intonation, verbal pacing, stylized speech, and ritual repetition that initially surfaced in *Getting to Know the Wide World* continues, but the verbal and visual violence has given way to a neoprimitivist naïveté and stylized romanticism that only occasionally shifts into an ironic register.

Three Stories (1997) and *Minor People* (2001) continue this interest in color films. *Three Stories* is strongly plotted, each of its three brief narratives having a clear structure and story line. *Minor People* exhibits a kind of exhaustion of the devices for which Muratova is best known: the mannered speech, the endless repetitions, the random plot digressions, and so forth.

Muratova's *Chekhovian Motifs* (2002) and *Tuner* (2004) mark a return to the black-and-white footage of her early work. They seek a balance between the subdued surface of the black-and-white screen, on the one hand, and the ornamentalist mise-en-scène and verbal play, on the other. The latter film shows uncharacteristic restraint in its range of ornaments and a reduction of theatricalization, downplaying a number of trademark devices, such as ritual repetition that had long characterized her work.

Two in One (2007) is a color feature film with an embedded narrative: the first part, the play "Stage Hands" ("Montirovshchiki") by Muratova's long-term partner and collaborator, Evgenii Golubenko, sets the stage literally and figuratively for the second part, the short screenplay "A Woman Who Has Seen Life" ("Zhenshchina zhizni") by the actress and writer Renata Litvinova. In this two-part film Muratova's light hand effortlessly combines trivial humor with incest, life's superficiality with suicide, absurd laughter with theft from a corpse.

It is hardly surprising that critical reactions to Muratova's cinema have been diverse in the extreme. Some critics see her as "the greatest talent in Russian cinema in the last thirty years" (Bossart 81); others react to her work with extreme discomfort. Her work has won considerable recognition at home and abroad, including two Nika Awards for Best Director a decade apart, in 1995 for *Enthusiasms* and in 2005 for *Tuner*; a 2007 Nika for Best Film of CIS and the Baltics for *Two in One*; and the Silver Bear at the Berlin Film Festival for *Asthenic Syndrome* (1989).

Monad A: Human as Feral Mammal

Their neighbor is for them not only a potential helper or sexual object, but also someone who tempts them to satisfy their aggressiveness on him, to exploit his capacity for work without compensation, to use him sexually without his consent, to seize his possessions, to humiliate him, to cause him pain, to torture and to kill him. *Homo homini lupus.* Who, in the face of all his experience of life and of history, will have the courage to dispute this assertion?

—Sigmund Freud, *Civilization and Its Discontents* (1930)

Muratova's work overall is less accessible through its narrative plots than through its recurrent patterns. Although this latter term imposes a somewhat studied fixity on her work I will use it for the time being. A common theme in these patterns is the psyche's opposition to the social machine that would conventionalize it, tyrannically herding it into normative patterns.

Until the mid-1990s it would have been simple enough to cast this loosely conceived preoccupation in Muratova's work as a self-restorative and anticommunist project, though this focus is both too narrow and too partisan. Its appeal is that her own biography inadvertently contributed to such a reading. As Galichenko (92) has pointed out, as late as 1986 S. I. Iutkevich's film encyclopedia *Cinema* (*Kino*) cites only half her actual work,[8] the result of two decades (1967–87) of professional struggles with the state cinema monopoly. As for her gradual rehabilitation from the mid-1980s onward, Muratova is characteristically caustic:

> I became a figure for speculation along the lines: "see how bad it
> was for Muratova." It was like a kind of poster: don't anyone dare
> complain it is bad for you. Because once it had been bad for her, and
> now, since it has become good for her, that means you all are lying; it
> is fine for everyone. (Quoted in Gersova 167)

After the fall of communism it has been tempting to see in her work a broader humanist message, let us say, the artist's utopian lament for the fettered soul in search of a gentler environment. This too is a partisan distortion, now by the humanist rather than by the cold warrior. Instead, the fettered soul of Muratova's cinema is fettered for good reason; it more closely resembles the rabid ferret than the thwarted soul. Her filmic environment is hostile as a very condition of possibility, the mise-en-scène for a civilizing process both uncivilized and inescapable.[9] Typically its ambient soundtrack of invisible things—the howling canines in the opening of *A Change of Fate*, the exploding mines in *Enthusiasms*, the car alarm and overhead helicopter in "Ophelia" (the second panel of *Three Stories*), the buzzing fly in many of her films (*Long Farewells*; *Enthusiasms*; "Little Girl and Death," the third panel of *Three Stories*; *Tuner*)—only heightens the sense that something nasty lurks off-screen at the film's periphery.

The encounter of the psyche with the disciplining institution does not require, however, that the psyche be a human one in any conventional sense. Muratova's settings—the schoolroom, the hospital ward, the police office, the sanatorium, the children's home, the Orthodox church, the courtroom, even the metro with its signage of the mandatory and forbidden—constitute arenas of discipline no more or less constricting than the hippodrome, the zoo, the birdcage, the pound, and the circus ring, given equal prominence in her work. In this sense animals are not exalted substitutes for *Homo sapiens* but exist on a continuum with human life, enduring similar torments in similar disciplining environments. And if Muratova's humans torment animals more than the reverse, this fact is less a moral difference than a taxonomic distinction, a testimony to the humans' more developed fine-motor skills and greater dexterity for tormenting.

When Muratova's animals draw an empathetic contrast to humans—the horses in *Enthusiasms* and *A Change of Fate*, the dogs in *Asthenic Syndrome*—it is not inherent goodness that marks them but a reassuring if incidental *absence* of human reason. The kitten plays with the hanged man's dangling shoelaces (*A Change of Fate*) because living things cannot resist play. And so, by extension, Muratova too is a living thing: her cinema's assaults on human hypocrisy, always in danger of mutating into moralism, are rescued from ethics by their own perverse recreation, "games for adults," as she has described her work (quoted in Gersova 162).

The eccentric photographer of centaurs (*Enthusiasms*) most materially enacts Muratova's childlike curiosity about this physiological juncture of animals and humans. Proffering images of the animal-man centaur, this photographer is one of Muratova's symbolic appearances,[10] a portrait of the director herself. He figures her enduring fascination with, as Nikolai in *Asthenic Syndrome* puts it, "the point at which I become an animal." The reverse process, the moment the animal's uninhibited aggression sickens and festers into "moral reasoning," is cast in Muratova's work as repellent humanism with a capital H, about which Viktor Erofeev ("Krushenie") has also written so disparagingly.[11] These

FIGURE 4.1. Muratova. *Enthusiasms.* Half man, half beast.

latent links between humans and other species, subverting humanist aspirations to a higher purpose, figure Muratova's counter-Darwinism, an evolution of the sickest. To the implied question provoked by *Three Stories*, "How could a lovely little girl poison her elderly babysitter?," Muratova provides an irrefutable answer: "Rat poison." The babysitter's similarity to the rat, in Muratova's interpretive system, is not characterological but mammalian.

Muratova's ethical minimalism,[12] historically disorienting to her critics, began with her reserved contemplation of the love triangle (Valentina-Maksim-Nadia) in *Brief Encounters* and extended to her equally calm contemplation of the matricidal triangle (Ofa-newborn-Tania) in *Three Stories* and the incest triangle (father-daughter-friend) in *Two in One*. Soviet and Russian criticism's insistence over three decades on a conventional moral compass for Muratova's work is eloquent testimony only to the filmmaker's success at provocation, subjecting the humanist's moral compass to continual dismantling.

No surprise, then, that the recurring scenes in which *Homo ludens* torments animals tend to be innocent and childlike, as in *Asthenic Syndrome*, which intercuts a boy blowing bubbles with grown men tormenting a cat, while classical music lyricizes and aurally unites their unreflective play.[13] For the educated Russian viewer this intercut references the legendary staircase scene from Grigorii Chukhrai's *Ballad of a Soldier* (*Ballada o soldate*; Mosfil'm, 1959), which contrasts an anonymous boy innocently blowing bubbles down a stairwell with an adultery scene in a nearby apartment. By contrast, Muratova's intercut of the innocent boy with amoral adult play is one of analogy rather than contrast. In their leisurely torment of the cat her human mammals are neither aberrant nor immoral, but, as the soundtrack suggests, on a biological continuum with the cat and the boy.

The latent family resemblance of Muratova's pan-mammalian menagerie is displayed for the viewer in her shots of the tiger in *A Change of Fate*, the horse ballet of *Enthusiasms*, the abandoned dogs of *Asthenic Syndrome*, and the zoo animals of *Sentimental Policeman*, the elephant, the bear, the yawning lion. In *Three Stories* the unnamed hero (played by Sergei Makovetskii) of "Boiler Room No. 6" (the first panel of *Three Stories*) exchanges behavioral twitches and grimaces with the zoo's peacock not out of a human desire to commune with nature, but in an interspecies face-off, a mutual display of aggression.[14] One of many functions of phatic repetition in Muratova's work has to do with human speech as a cacophony of encoded noises, once learned in the jungle, but now, after civilization, rehearsed compulsively in the zoo that is their social reality.[15] That humans can claim no position of privilege does not even imply pantheism, since theism too is subject to cancellation. Hers is the radical egalitarianism of the nonbeliever, an atheist not just in declared belief (Dolin, "Kira Muratova"; Gersova 162; Getmanchuk; Morozova 4) but in creative orientation. This pragmatism informs the tenor of both major and minor scenes throughout her work: Nikolai (*Asthenic Syndrome*) gorges himself on caviar stolen from the refrigerator not because he is rude or uncivilized, but because certain mammals feed on the eggs of other species.

It is therefore one of the great ironies in the reception of Muratova's work that among the most consistently insightful critical comments were those of Soviet bureaucrats and Communist Party committee members who most impeded her work. Read as neutral description rather than censure, remarks by the Lenfil'm Party Committee on *Getting to Know the Wide World*, for example, were at least as thoughtful as those by some of her greatest admirers. The committee noted a "deliberately complicated style"; "absorption with formal experiments" that "eclipsed the content of an essentially simple story"; the "poetic episodes . . . lacking in realism and motivation"; the "conjunction of humdrum and the poetic" (*Kadr*, October 13, 1978). There is surely little to disagree with here.

But it is the committee's gravest reproach—"An artist cannot forget that lofty poetry presupposes lofty citizenship and lofty ideological-artistic resonance"—that most brilliantly if inadvertently captures key preoccupations that Muratova indeed "cannot forget." They remain among the targets of her caustic laughter long after the criticisms of 1978. Addressing human subjectivity at a much more molecular level than her colleagues—with the possible exception of Aleksei Balabanov—Muratova replaces the humanist query (What does it mean to be human?) with her own: What use, in the first place, is this distinction?

From this vantage point "lofty citizenship," vitiated of its disciplinary authority, is more akin to human despotism, an unjust tyranny by *Homo sapiens*. The social is reduced to biological struggle without moral exemption for the human. Predatory human consciousness is pitched in a losing battle with its own predatory rule of law. Insofar as no moral difference exists between discipliners and disciplined,[16] all legal and civic projects inevitably turn to brawling.

FIGURE 4.2. Muratova. *The Sentimental Policeman*. Two institutions: orphanage and militiaman.

Aesthenic Syndrome provides a cascade of examples: the school principal Irina Pavlovna attacks her colleague, Nikolai, who in turn attacks his student, Sitnikov, who in turn brawls with passersby. This scene is witnessed by a father who returns home to his own martial hierarchy: the pet bird is chased by the pet cat, chased by the father, chased by his daughter. The film returns to Nikolai, eventually hospitalized in a psychiatric institution where the staff pummel each other in the exercise yard. The school, the street, the family home, and the psychiatric hospital are linked in a visual continuum as common sites for an ongoing discharge of aggression.

Muratova's unfolding social panorama of rebellion against genteel conventions has a broad reach, traceable throughout her work: teachers' meetings, funeral rituals, state law, bureaucratic procedure, social chitchat—all are presented to the spectator on a flattened narrative plane, without nuance, hierarchy, or moral urgency. More radical still, her human mammals resist literacy, numeracy, name and address. Indeed, the underlying charm of *Three Stories* and *Two in One* is the enthusiastic narration of crime without punishment, action without consequences.[17] To sustain the cheerful lunacy that murder is a reasonable response to life's vexations—never mind the purer gratification, as Freud reminds us, of inflicting pain on others for its own sake—all three sections of *Three Stories* are structured so as to end before the government vexingly intervenes.

FIGURE 4.3. Muratova. *Getting to Know the Wide World.* Komsomol collective wedding.

How, then, as early as 1978, could Muratova *not* but distort Grigorii Baklanov's script, in particular the mass Komsomol wedding rituals in *Getting to Know the Wide World*? Ways of belonging, categories of commonality, kinship, and community are held together not by high-minded loyalty but by mindless participation in the same rituals, maniacal passions that Muratova extends to her own filmmaking: "I am engrossed in cinema, just as the horsemen are engrossed in their world" (quoted in D. Bykov, "Kira Muratova: Ia ne koshka" 48). The jockeys and circus people in *Enthusiasms* in this respect resemble the hypothetical tribes in Maksim's monologue in *Brief Encounters*, whose differences lie in eating other humans either fried or boiled, beginning with either the head or the feet. The characters' ritual treatment of other mammals is an unreflective reiteration of their own domestication: selecting, adopting, breeding, feeding, raising, neglecting, and abandoning random animals. And if the site of domestication is a brutal manège with no reliable trainer on duty, then transience and homelessness have an odd attraction, whether for the construction workers in *Getting to Know the Wide World* or the paupers in *Among Grey Stones*.[18] Their contingent existence recalls a lost feral state, imbued with atavistic regret that the instilling of social inhibitions is an inevitable and deeply unsatisfactory process.

These thematics of domestication had appeared in a muted fashion in Muratova's early works, such as the doomed project of "taming" Maksim (*Brief Encounters*), whether by the rural Nadia or the urban, professional Valentina Ivanovna ("my little boss," as he calls her). We see a similar theme assert itself in *Long Farewells*, as the adolescent Sasha bridles under his mother's predatory, genteel gaze. These early films focused on a single, intimate figure, the female enforcer of the social order whose rigid expectations precipitate crisis. In later films Muratova plays for higher stakes: the domestication machine is depersonalized, no longer embedded in the psychologically complex, professional woman, but in human civilization as such, deployed most evidently by the state, but most often masquerading as a conspiracy of the civic-minded. Muratova is most eloquent on state education as the prime machine for processing ready-made consciousness:

> The first mandatory horror—mandatory for everyone, since
> education is mandatory—is school. And of course it is the least
> appropriate place to find someone who knows any answer . . . some
> kind of hypnotic posing, mutual posing, conventionalized questions
> and answers, toadying. It is the first barracks of posing, the most
> widely prevalent, vile hell that can exist. (Quoted in Gersova 163)[19]

If Muratova's radical egalitarianism can be traced with considerable consistency through her narrative structure, we might productively look further at her most typical space: the genteel, well-appointed apartment. With its lacquered wardrobes, matching crockery, vases, grand piano, framed pictures, and houseplants, this setting figures as the mise-en-scène from Valentina's apartment in *Brief Encounters* through to the 2004 *Tuner* and 2007 *Two in One*, a higher order variant of the zoo and the pound, a site of confinement, sexual predation, and incipient violence.[20]

The desecration of the well-appointed apartment, therefore, is weighted with particular significance: in *Asthenic Syndrome*, Natasha's eccentric "wake" for her husband—bread, water, goblets knocked off the grand piano, clothes ripped from the wardrobe—savages, in multiple senses of that verb, this well-bred propriety as a core function of more than the character's mourning process. This shot had been anticipated early in Muratova's work in *Brief Encounters*: the close-up of cascading glasses that shatter on the floor as the rural waitress Nadia mourns Maksim's departure. This shot is inversely linked to the final scene of the same film as a reverse sequence: Nadia's setting of an elegant dinner table, with all the trappings of domesticated life, for her rival and their shared love interest. The carefully set table is *not*, as critics have suggested, romantic closure, or the rural competitor's "noble retreat" in the face of her city competitor's triumph. Instead, the well-set table is the well-set trap, bait for the doomed couple to repeat the endless cycle, hastening Maksim's return to the countryside.

Muratova's fascination with how the maverick psyche might be broken thus bears a certain pathos in the early films that it loses once it turns into a victimless crime. By *Three Stories*, Muratova's ("Mne vsegda" 59) acknowledged return from stream of consciousness to plot, we are not dealing with the transient Maksim (*Brief Encounters*), a self-described "free bird" ("vol'naia ptitsa"), or the restless, maturing Sasha, would-be lyric hero of Lermontov's poem "Sail." Instead, the maverick psyche is the homicidal neighbor, the serial murderess, and cinema's most endearing little sociopath, Lilia Murlykina.[21] The hedonistic pleasures of the kitchen knife, the stocking, the deep blue sea, and the rat poison are completely within the range of reasonable human gratification. It comes as no surprise that Muratova, dismissing comparisons of her work to that of Ingmar Bergman, finds his cinema overly gentle.[22]

After the late *perestroika* indulgences of *Asthenic Syndrome*, however, Muratova's renegade consciousness undergoes a kind of rehab in *Sentimental Policeman* that comments, by gentle contrast, on the brutality of domestication.[23] The camera lingers fetishistically on the domesticated spousal routine—bathing, dressing—that resembles instructional footage on intergalactic hygiene. The routine's obedient repetition, in some ways a companion piece to *Asthenic Syndrome*'s metro profanities, has the quality of a primer, a child's version of what human mammals do in the morning. Its erasure of primitive drives—the drive to copulate, to kill—will be only temporary, erupting again in *Three Stories*. Yet for this short interlude in *Sentimental Policeman* the premise of the film is structured around the insistence that the major characters—Tolia as a puppet Adam, Klara as a puppet Eve—do not copulate as mammals do: he finds a baby in the cabbage patch; she becomes pregnant, apparently through immaculate conception, once called upon to do so by the judge. The fairy tale, woodcarving (*lubochnoe*) quality of their lives omits all trace of the erotic, as well as aggression more generally, in favor of an infantilized romanticism.

Ultimately Muratova's interest—without any particular moral engagement—is subjectivity in its most extreme form, narcissism without the minus sign, as a morally indifferent life force, stripped of any redemption that early critics struggled hard to ascribe to her work ("Egoism is the essence of my métier," as she remarks to Frodon [72]). The ensuing impossibility of mutual comprehension—Chekhov squared—is underscored by the instances of the verbal construction "to *not* understand" ("ne ponimat'") in her repertoire of compulsive repetitions.[24] Muratova makes no such commitment to any particular mammal, especially the human, which she finds to be of "doubtful ethical stature" (quoted in Gersova 158). Hers is not a moral yardstick—"I don't know what the norm is" (quoted in Gersova 163)—but a litmus test for moral discrepancy. To be human in Muratova's world is to be continually tripped up by the disjuncture between declared collective values and uncensored impulses. She rejects moral correctives to human error for the simple reason that her sympathies are on the side of the error, not the corrective.

Monad B: Twin Mammals

There is a very ancient curiosity around doubling in nature.
—Kira Muratova, quoted in Kriukova,
"Davali by snimat' fil'my" (1994)

But how is the predicate of being "instinctual" related to the compulsion to repeat?
—Sigmund Freud, "Beyond the Pleasure
Principle" (1920)

The instances of the feral mammal elaborated above are a single operation in Muratova's cheerfully demonic project of debasing voluntary linkages of loyalty and filiation. It is a class of debasements related to another, apparently incidental set that operates in a similar fashion: the recurrent use of female doubles or twins.

We encounter female twins in a number of different forms, some more accessible than others. In *Getting to Know the Wide World* they are Vera and Zoia, one of whom speaks, while the other echoes her. In *Sentimental Policeman* they appear as the two nurses in the Children's Home. In "Ophelia" (*Three Stories*) they appear as the two elderly women archivists, El'vira and Al'bina; in *Tuner* they are anonymous, silent twins in a single shot at the film's conclusion. A variant of the female twins is the mother-daughter dyad, such as the ancient mother and elderly daughter in "Ophelia" who call uncomprehendingly to each other "Why don't you pick up the phone?" and "Why don't you ever call?" This pair functions in the same film as a foil to the eponymous Ophelia ("Ofa") and her mother. When Ophelia (a young, thin blonde in a scarlet dress, an eccentric devotee of the Shakespearian Ophelia) drowns her own mother (a fat blonde in a scarlet dress, an eccentric devotee of the Shakespearian Ophelia) that murder becomes an act of protracted, postmodernist suicide that completes Ofa's literary destiny.[25]

A variation of Muratova's twins is her insistent use of inseparable buddies with similar functions: the nameless girls in *Asthenic Syndrome* who torment the retarded Misha; the two gay cruisers in "Boiler Room No. 6" of *Three Stories*, a male variant of this species; the two blind men at the concluding shot of "Ophelia"; and the two Father Frosts who appear twice in *Two in One*. Elsewhere the buddies are opposites: Nikolai's schoolgirls in *Asthenic Syndrome*, one plump and plain, the other thin and pretty, referred to collectively as "Masha"; the blond Liliia and the dark Violetta in *Enthusiasms*, whose status as twin opposites is visually underscored by their light and dark clothing; and the First and Second Girls (Natal'ia Buz'ko and Renata Litvinova) in *Two in One*, one dark, the other blond, identically dressed. Periodically at the audition stage Muratova transformed a single character to a female pair (Litvinova, "Boites'" 10; Muratova, "Iskusstvo rodilos'" 94; Taubman, "Cinema" 380); at other times, she assigned two roles to the same actress, as with Aleksandra Svenskaia, who plays both the school administrator and the mother in *Asthenic Syndrome*.[26]

If we work backward, then, to Muratova's earliest work, before this feature achieves its freak show quality, we can see tentative efforts in this direction as early as *Brief Encounters*. Its two heroines coexist in an asymmetrical opposition, like unequal halves of the broken plate in its opening scene: Nadia cooks and mends clothes; Valentina Ivanovna does not wash dishes and does not mend broken crockery. The film's "stereoscopic quality" (Bozhovich, "Rentgenoskopiia" 54) shuttles back and forth between two women's memories, intensified by the film's structural asymmetry: first Muratova introduces Valentina before Nadia; then Nadia is granted the first flashback memory of Maksim before Valentina's flashback. This supposed inconsistency, consistent with Muratova's love of unpredictability and asymmetry, lends the film a random quality, rendering the women substitutable yet opposed, as indeed they are in Maksim's narrative line. One might argue that a similar pattern is evident in Muratova's heterosexual pairs, such as the matched matrimonial pairs in *Getting to Know the Wide World* or Tolia and Klara in *Sentimental Policeman*, a Punch and Judy with a penis and breasts affixed as props in order to pair and distinguish them, not as humans but as objects.

These pairs can be seen as relating to a larger concern in Muratova's larger, dehumanizing project: What if, as in the freak show, the unique, stable self were doubled, inverted, so as to deface it and expose it as a "stereotype of thinking"

(Gersova 159)? In this fashion Muratova's human pairs become figures of speech: tautology (identical twins); synonym (interchangeable buddies); antonym (visual opposites); oxymoron (the mother-daughter pairs who give birth to and murder each other, who "never call" and "never answer the phone"). They are visual counterparts to Muratova's aural repetition and variation, doubled in space rather than repeated over time. Played out at times over the entire film—as when two separate nameless women, at the conclusion of each segment of *Asthenic Syndrome*, murmur identical clichés to their men[27]—these repetitions construct a universe of cyclical time and human objects distinguishable from one another only in manifest traces, their repetition constantly threatening to transform any utterance into rehearsal, autism, dementia, dictation, nonsense poetry, citation, language lesson, hypnosis, somnambulism, puppet theater, and idiocy. It aestheticizes and frames all speech, defamiliarizing it in a tradition with which Muratova's formalist forebears would find a deep affinity.[28]

Monad C: Discourse on Legs

What this repetition requires is a different notion of character, one that thwarts the temptation to treat Muratova's characters as dynamic, celluloid representations of people with psychological depth or narrative development, an unproductive approach to this director's ark. Her characters are not so much people as fragments left behind from the world's conversations, fragments clustered temporarily into a disturbed but functioning microcosm. Not disconnected identities but disconnected utterances: "my characteristics," Muratova ("Iskusstvo rodilos'" 94) once called them.

In Muratova's early work the disjuncture between character and characteristic—the dislocation of utterance from conventional notions of character—takes the form of alien, exemplar, or framed speech: Valentina Ivanovna's halting rehearsal of her speech ("Dear comrades . . .") at the outset of *Brief Encounters*; Liuba's stilted speech in *Getting to Know the Wide World*. As Muratova's work matures, however, the alien quality of speech is foregrounded, marked by repetition—described by Muratova as her trademark device (Kudriavtsev, "Ukroitel'nitsa" 294), "my mania" (quoted in Taubman, *Kira Muratova* 107)—that stresses its artificial status, bereft of diegetic motivation that would soften its effect. Though not all human utterance in her late work bears this alien, mannered tone, its frequency contaminates all speech, lending it a framed quality analogous to the visual, literal frames—picture frames, window frames, door frames—throughout her work.

This overwhelming preference for characteristics over characters, contingent parts over organic totality, first appears unambiguously in *A Change of Fate*, both in characters and in setting. Her Singapore, the site of Somerset Maugham's short story, becomes abstracted, a fragment without regard to authenticity, what Muratova herself describes as "some undefined Eastern country . . . a sign" (quoted in Taubman, "Cinema" 377).[29] Following this pattern her later characters likewise tend toward sign-ness, discursive display, verbal templates of consciousness, species of language, haphazardly housed in biological membranes only because the membrane is necessary for the performance of utterance.

Critics have occasionally noted in the work of Muratova's major cameraman, Gennadii Kariuk (*Brief Encounters, Long Farewells, Sentimental Policeman, Enthusiasms*), the tendency to cut off characters, presenting them as disconnected body parts or off-center talking heads. Indeed, the lower right-hand corner is often the beloved section of Muratova's and Kariuk's screen. This fragmenting tendency has been seen as an isolated, formal device rather than one aspect of a larger skepticism toward human consciousness (Bozhovich, "Rentgenoskopiia" 63, 67). In *Brief Encounters* its most explicit, early manifestation—the shot of Nadia and Valentina Ivanovna, the film's two narrative trajectories, staring at Maksim's tape recorder, which itself fragments Valentina's rehearsed speech—suggests that Muratova's fragmented utterances and fragmented bodies are related processes, detachable aspects of human consciousness over which no sovereignty, other than that of the film itself as artifact, can be claimed.

With respect to Muratova's later characters, therefore, we can no longer speak of the monad Natasha (*Asthenic Syndrome*) in the same terms as we spoke of women such as Valentina Ivanovna (*Brief Encounters*) or Evgeniia Vasil'evna (*Long Farewells*). Nor can we contrast Nikolai's passivity in *Asthenic Syndrome* to Natasha's aggression, as if these were traits inherent in individuals rather than polarities embedded in the structure of the film itself and passing through the device of these matched characters. In this later period (from *A Change of Fate* onward) Muratova no longer permits us to move from concrete characters to their philosophical abstraction. Rather, the characters are abstractions from the outset.

This very different notion of character—for which we have no word, but which might be best conceived as a kind of discourse on legs—is most evident in the performance of the actress and writer Renata Litvinova, who appears first in *Enthusiasms* and then again in *Three Stories* and *Tuner*. Litvinova's monologues explore a notion of character akin to Muratova's own. "My character in the novella 'Ophelia,' which I wrote," Litvinova comments, "is not really a person, but an abstract personage, similar to the figure of Fate or Vengeance in Greek tragedy" (quoted in Sul'kin, "Renata" 17). A pale, humped figure with claw hands, vaguely resembling an albino mink, Litvinova's characters are utterly devoid of motivation beyond the most basic drives, simultaneously unreflective and plotting, exuding an obsessional quality of erotic compulsivity around hygiene and death.[30]

In the earlier *Enthusiasms* Litvinova's "Monologue on the Height of Beauty" ("Monolog o pike krasoty"), a literary variant of which appears in *Iskusstvo kino*

("Boites'"),[31] mindlessly ventriloquizes Warhol's fifteen minutes of fame and Marilyn Monroe's refrain—"And that song," Liliia murmurs, "a girl's best friends are diamonds! Diamonds . . ." ("Boites'" 13)—lending her construction a pasted-together, recycled quality of pure language. By *Three Stories* Litvinova's figure becomes lethal, stalking and executing those—including her own mother—who had abandoned their babies. Neither good nor evil but some exquisite, predatory interspecies, the ideal device of transition, occupying some space between mammal and reptile, she soothes her victims ("It doesn't hurt, it doesn't hurt"; "a beautiful death") only to facilitate the strangulation and drowning. This is no "realist" Freud (i.e., a credible portrait of a troubled murderess, seeking to undo the early trauma of abandonment) but rather Freud's ritual abstraction, a celebration of the death instinct in all its erotic lubrication. What this game shares with her renditions of human subjectivity as the feral mammal is its goal of dethroning the Human as "tsar of nature, crown of creation," not in order to establish a more righteous model of human agency, but to reveal its explicit predatory ambitions to rule.

Monads D and E: Dolls and Corpses

Beyond Muratova's feral humans, her doubles, and shards of consciousness is another set that again unceremoniously serves to dethrone the human as an agent of higher collective claims. Akin to the shift from human to mammal, from unique self to replicate, from character to sign, this new set of operations involves the integration of dolls and corpses into her mise-en-scène. Were we dealing with a more conventional filmmaker, we might perhaps hesitate at the contrast between these two props, one inanimate, the other dead; one an object of youth, the other an object of death; one an object of pleasant distraction, the other an object of grief or horror; one an object of improvisational play, the other an object of ritual and taboo. With Muratova, however, we can safely say that these differences are immaterial compared to the common allure of dolls and corpses as nonhuman.

The dolls first appear in Muratova's 1971 *Long Farewells*. As with many of her other eccentric attractions, they are at first motivated: Evgeniia Vasil'evna (*Long Farewells*) retains her childhood doll; a doll is given to little Marusia (*Among Grey Stones*), played by the dwarf actress Oksana Shlapak, who lends her role an artificial, doll-like quality, equating the child and the object. By the later films—*Asthenic Syndrome, Sentimental Policeman,* "Ophelia" (*Three Stories*), *Letter to America, Two in One*—dolls have more intensely entered the economy of signs, circulating among other objects marked as the nonhuman.[32] Gennadii Kariuk (105), Muratova's cameraman, recounts how Muratova arranges the film set with dolls and other exotic objects to "enrich the shot, giving it a kind of 'alienation.'" Among these nonhumans, then, must be counted Muratova's own actors, "happy and restless marionettes," as one critic has called them (Mantsov 9).[33]

In the looser Soviet censorship culture of the late 1980s the corpse entered Muratova's repertoire of the nonhuman. The corpse had been implicitly present in the lengthy cemetery scene of *Long Farewells*; by *Asthenic Syndrome* it had already been ritualized, not in the opening burial scene but in a later close-up shot in which Natasha's hand compulsively uncovers and covers the face of a hospital corpse. The camera work is virtually identical to that in which an unidentified hand uncovers and covers a corpse's face in "Boiler Room No. 6" (*Three Stories*) and in a similar sequence, hands covering and uncovering the suicide's corpse, acting out conflicting standards of gentility, in the first story of *Two in One*.

This visual syntax of these oppositions—living/dead, animate/inanimate, human/animal—reaches greater coherence as we watch Muratova link them to the photographic portrait and implicitly, therefore, to her own film as the medium for dolls, actors, and corpses. The connection between the photograph and the once-living corpse is most clearly articulated at the beginning of *Asthenic Syndrome*, with sequential shots of photographs on the gravestones, followed by a shot of the shop window of the photographer's store and a sequence of Natasha, the new widow, sifting through old photographs of her now-dead husband after the burial. Dolls, actors, corpses, and photographic portraits circulate through Muratova's work to remind the viewer that things resembling human bodies are by no means necessarily alive.[34] They allow Muratova to blur the distinction even between organic and inorganic, playfully subverting any loyalty to living things by inserting examples of the nonliving—the doll, the corpse, the film image—around which emotional affect might otherwise be marshaled.

Mistress of *Steb*

It must be noted in passing that many of these devices—the fragmented characters, the doubling, the recycled utterances, and so forth—can be enumerated without any intellectual belaboring as among the familiar practices of postmodernism, in Russia and elsewhere. Rather than move to a level of analysis that needs no rehearsing here, I would like briefly to venture a more nuanced description of where in that larger cultural movement Muratova's work can be most comfortably situated.

A generational misfit born in 1934, one year after the poets Evgenii Evtushenko and Andrei Voznesenskii, Muratova is chronologically a member of the Soviet Sixties generation (*shestidesiatniki*), yet her individual work is in no way redolent of that generation's cultural orientation, with its concern for sincerity and authenticity, its verdant dream of a humanized socialism, its optimistic neomodernism and neo-Leninism, its infantilized belief in the reformability of the state.[35]

Instead, her cultural orientation is precisely a later aesthetic, belonging to the Seventies generation. This younger generation, born between 1940 and 1953, is diverse after its own fashion. What its members largely shared, however, was a fascination with the stereotypes of consciousness, and a rejection of the self-absorbed lyricism of their Thaw forebears. The Seventies generation was rightly viewed with distaste and alarm by its predecessor, which saw in its "other prose" (a mid-*perestroika* euphemism for postmodernism) the deterioration of art's moral mission.[36] In this the *shestidesiatniki* were absolutely correct, and Muratova's work very much participates in that putative deterioration, as the cinema bureaucrats and censor appreciated best of all. Despite her year of birth, therefore, she shares the consciousness of the Seventies generation, the "stokers, janitors, and lift operators" (Kheifets quoted in Anninskii, "The Sixties Generation" 22), with its parallel culture, sots-art painting, paper architecture, conceptualist happenings, necrorealism, and *steb*.

This last, untranslatable word refers to a style of parody and self-mockery that pushes mannerism to its extreme limits while preserving a veneer of deadly serious faux belief in its self-presentation (Guseinov; Matizen, "Steb"). It often is, but need not be, a kind of Soviet eccentric style (as in much conceptualist art and sots-art in particular), deploying the sign system of second-world Marxism-Leninism. More broadly than Marxism-Leninism per se, however, the target of its mirth centers on genteel rituals of civilized society, particularly around death, courtship, holidays, and education, as (variously) in Evgenii Popov's short stories, Vladimir Sorokin's "excremental poetics," Liudmila Petrushevskaia's plays and "incidents," and the necrorealist films of the directors Igor' and Gleb Aleinikov. Elsewhere still it manifests as a series of parodic remakes of mass consciousness (in the tradition of Andy Warhol), inflected in the poetry and art objects of Dmitrii Aleksandrovich Prigov, the paintings of Komar and Melamid, the installations of Il'ia Kabakov, the work of the Mit'ki, or the acting style of Ivan Okhlobystin.

Although it is largely associated with the work of a generational profile—the 1970s and 1980s—*steb* is not a movement or a group; it is a style, an angle that can be imposed on any subject matter. It is a deviation from the very norm that it nevertheless staunchly upholds in mock solemnity. Hence *steb* has no interest in dissidence, which could only neuter its all-encompassing irony. Central to *steb* is its insistence on a constructed, two-dimensional image, a sign such as Prigov's militiaman, animated by language that confirms the discursive vacuity of all human speech.

Without closely resembling any of these cultural figures Muratova participates in this same trend, with its love of distortion, fraudulence, superficiality, and indifference to redemption. Her obsession with death (as in *Three Stories*) rivals the best of Petrushevskaia, Sorokin, and the necrorealists. Occasionally in her work we see explicit sots-art (mock socialist realist) props, such as the enormous red K, presumably a fragment from KPSS (in Russian, Communist Party of the Soviet Union), abandoned in an apartment stairwell, or the political poster "Our Strength Is in the Declaration of Truth," in front of which two anonymous girls torment a retarded boy (*Asthenic Syndrome*). Her transgressive humor, lacking any promise of salvation, is particularly striking because (like Petrushevskaia) she is both the wrong generation and the wrong gender to engage in this kind of play.[37]

This generational disconnect may in part explain Muratova's complete invisibility from the brilliant analysis offered by Viktor Matizen, himself one of Russia's consummate "*steb* masters," as he passes over cinema's two spectacular women *stebshchitsy*, Muratova and Litvinova.[38] Yet it is within this particular subset of postmodernism that Muratova most comfortably operates, within a set of aesthetic codes that supports her love of transgression, repetition, provocational superficiality, ornamentation, and two-dimensionality, where human communication is rendered as an undifferentiated broadcast at a generic recipient.

It is in this respect that Muratova was able to make the transition from the gentle ideological tyrannies of late Soviet culture to the tyrannical gentilities of post-Soviet life. At each stage the target of her scorn was the intelligentsia, whose logic she would apparently accept, then, in the customary gesture of *steb*, take to its breaking point.

The Dog Pound and the Metro Car

An instinct is an urge inherent in organic life to restore an earlier state of things, which the living entity has been obliged to abandon under the pressure of external disturbing forces.

—Sigmund Freud, *Beyond the Pleasure Principle* (1920)

Asthenic Syndrome is often cited as Muratova's watershed. Filmed at the historical moment of the Soviet Union's demise, it bears the dubious honor of being the last film shelved in Soviet history, largely because of its famous cursing scene, which delayed its release for six months.[39] Muratova herself refers to *Asthenic Syndrome* as her "dead-end film" ("tupikovaia"; quoted in Gersova 161), and she underscores this point with a framing device that functions as a visual echo similar to her aural repetitions. By the closing scene of *Asthenic Syndrome* the male protagonist sleeps in a metro car at its end station, thus bringing the film around, rebus-fashion, to its start, when the female protagonist, escaping the oppressive burial rites for her husband, pummels her way onto a tram at its end station.

The film's first segment is revealed to be a cinema screening within the second segment; here Muratova rejects simple continuity in favor of a reflexive solution. In the opening scene of the second segment the cinema manager introduces the actress who played Natasha—using the real-life actress's actual name, Ol'ga Antonova—and initiates a moviegoers' discussion by mindlessly enumerating Russia's leading auteurs ("Real cinema! German, Sokurov, Muratova . . .") as the diegetic audience scrambles for the exits, leaving only the sleeping Nikolai. The first, black-and-white segment is thereby not simply linked to the second segment, but is embedded as an episode into the larger, second segment involving Nikolai, indifferent to the grieving, celluloid Natasha.

So, one might speculate, this second segment is implicitly embedded into a third part, our lives as we sit in our cinema watching Muratova (or German, or Sokurov . . .). Muratova's deployment of the real-life actress's name confirms this speculation.[40] An episode in our larger, lived experience, the reflexive, two-part film implies that we, like Nikolai, are sleeping spectators. Abandoning linear narrative, the plot structure reproduces itself as mise en abyme, a series of nested revelations about resistance to knowledge, our somnolent status as living corpses. Circularity, conceptualist mise en abyme, and other forms of embedded self-referencing have marked Muratova's films from her early work. In *Brief Encounters* Nadia replaces Maksim's guitar with another instrument that some passerby had left it behind at the café, thus recapitulating Maksim's earlier passing by with his own guitar. In *Long Farewells* Sasha opens a door serving as a makeshift viewing screen and interrupts his mother's covert viewing of slides of Sasha with his father, thus appropriating the audience into a triple abyme.[41] In *Sentimental Policeman* Tolia brings home an orphan baby girl to his wife, Klara, who had also been an orphaned baby girl. A similar strategy is deployed in *Chekhovian Motifs* to goad the cinema audience to behave as badly out of boredom as the wedding guests in the church behave on the screen and to underscore the analogical position of the two.

In *Asthenic Syndrome* Muratova extends her use of abyme as a structural or narrative device to a more explicit manifesto about the workings of consciousness. We see this most clearly in two key scenes. The first is the visit to the dog pound by four women who go ostensibly to search for a lost dog.[42] Vladimir Pankov's extended camera work depicts the appalling conditions at excruciating length—its brutality lyricized, as so often in Muratova's work, with classical music—then interrupts this visual and aural musing with the only intertitle in her work:

> People don't want to look at this.
> People don't want to think about this.
> This should have nothing to do with
> conversations about good and evil.

This unique and hybrid intertitle, somewhere between haiku and slogan, spares no one in its incriminating impersonality ("ne khotiat . . ."), neither the women nor the viewer (Muratova's implicit target) nor the director herself, who had been profoundly affected by her own visit to the pound years earlier (Gersova 158; Muratova, "Iskusstvo rodilos'" 96). Instead, Muratova prefers discomfort without resolution. "I wanted to turn all of us—me, you—around and poke us, that is, to hold our eyes open," she comments in her most extensive interview. "I don't like it either; that's why I am showing it to you" (quoted in Gersova 158).

A different kind of "holding our eyes open" occurs in a second key scene in *Asthenic Syndrome*, in which a string of obscenities is spoken by an anonymous woman in the metro. This cursing scene has been characterized with mock solemnity by Muratova as "strongly underplayed," "straight realism . . . like the singing of birds, like the rustling of leaves" (quoted in Gersova 157). An expected (i.e., plot-driven) actress for this monologue would have been Natasha, whose erratic grieving already motivates the aggressive variety of asthenic syndrome. Instead, an anonymous woman, cursing into the camera as if thinking aloud, robs the scene of contextual logic and continuity. Here Muratova performs multiple assaults on the spectator: the impropriety of a middle-aged woman's profanities and the viewer's position as recipient (rather than eavesdropper) of the obscenities. The profanity itself is patently unmotivated; it is not necessary (as it would have been in the development of Natasha's character) or relevant (if, for example, soliciting a response from the sluggish Nikolai). Instead, it is pure spectacle, a verbal orgy of misbehavior concocted by a woman director reveling in the violation of deep cultural inhibitions about the discursive behavior of the sexes, in particular the tattered hypocrisy that women are the preservers of culture.

These key scenes in the pound and the metro, a studied pairing (Gersova 158), are set off against each other so as to raise questions about what we take for granted and what shocks us. The "director's culmination," Muratova has argued, is the dog pound; the "false culmination" is the woman's profanities (quoted in Gersova 158). Taken together they share several features: incidental female figures; a deliberate disregard for plot; a claustrophobic setting (dog cage and metro car); visual manifestos or "broadcasts," one written as intertitle, one spoken *en face*. Lacking identifiable characters, these two scenes become emblematic rather than specific, abstract rather than grounded in a familiar character's movements through plotted space. Performed by an anonymous Everywomen, the scenes are performed implicitly also by the director herself.[43] This is not feminism, despite valiant efforts at arguing that intellectual sleight of hand.[44] Muratova as woman director is no more a feminist than Muratova as Russian director is a patriot. Instead, hers is a portrait of humans barely capable of recognizing others as alive, much less subdividing them into such fussy categories as mammal and fowl, male and female.

The Zoological Imperium

The morgues are overflowing, but in the zoo, the animals are starving!
                        —Gennadii, in "Boiler Room No. 6" (*Three Stories*)

The preoccupations sketched out above, as distinct as they may be from each other, are interrelated as a sustained project of creative dismantling, the breaking down of distinctions between human and animal; the myth of the unique self; the conflation of character and characteristic, person and utterance, living and dead, organic and inorganic, humankind and its lifeless but lifelike playthings. Muratova's dozen or so films, their variety notwithstanding, constitute an enormous, negative edifice, her private zoo, as formidable and uncompromising as it is entertaining, decorative, and brutal.

Those critics who would search for the human in her work would do well to remember her insistence that "living people are a very dangerous thing" ("zhivye liudi—eto ochen' opasno"; quoted in Shiverskaia), prone in equal measure to destroy each other and to offer themselves for destruction: "People want to give themselves up; they want to be robbed, to be used and to be useful to someone in that way. They're ready to give up their soul, their body, their money. It is a touching quality" (quoted in Khokhriakova, "Moshenniki").

To cast Muratova as a pessimistic filmmaker, however, would be a misrepresentation. As she herself remarks about her cinematic style, "The gloomiest thing, if it is done well, leaves an impression of joy. It is creativity. It does not mean that I do not love life or that I love death. It is a different matter that death interests me" (quoted in D. Bykov, "Kira Muratova nauchila"). With her characteristic disregard for the human, she describes herself as "biologically . . . a healthy organism with an optimistic temperament" (quoted in Khokhriakova, "Kira Muratova"). The negative edifice is rather a kind of creative reduction, carried out according to its own aesthetic system—"You must destroy something symmetrically . . . it's only then that things grab you"[45]—severing links that ennoble human filiation.

To what end is this cheerful, negative opus constructed across more than a dozen films over the expanse of nearly forty years of filmmaking? We will not, of course, find a literal answer either in Muratova's work or in her interviews or her biography. Any effort to venture speculative remarks must reckon with the certainty that Muratova's own Negative Imperative processes all interpretation through its familiar operations. Moreover, for those who would insist on verifiability, this chapter has already come to an end, and its conclusion must be idle speculation.

Nevertheless, several things relevant to the larger conceptual thesis of this volume might be said about Muratova's destructive aspirations. At their most magnificently intolerant, their target is the very project of redemption historically situated at the center of Russo-Soviet culture. Muratova's distaste for art's *mission civilatrice* is more than a personal preference; it is her counterassault on a culture she has judged to be terminally "ambitious and tendentious" (Muratova, "Iskusstvo rodilos'" 97), an antidote to a deep cultural tradition that would "adorn itself in the mantle of 'prophet,' 'life's teacher'" (Morozova 4).[46]

Here again *Asthenic Syndrome* is a key text, one in which her wholesale dismissal of the intelligentsia's self-assigned mission is captured in the film's opening shot as three elderly female characters chant, "In my childhood, in my early youth, I thought people had only to read Lev Nikolaevich Tolstoi carefully and everyone would become kind and intelligent" (Popov 40). This is no mature awakening on Muratova's part: this ironic chorus dates back to her earliest filmmaking days, a screenplay from her diploma work, testifying to its centrality as a recurrent preoccupation in her work (D. Bykov, "Kira Muratova nauchila"), a mocking dismissal of the Russo-Soviet cult of high culture, promoting itself as the fraudulent category called civic conscience.[47]

In a later, incidental scene of the film's color section, a Soviet *intelligent* and an African exchange student repetitively debate the comparative merits of two forms of social control over the wayward individual. The Soviet intellectual would "nurture his soul"; the African would "cut off his hands." The camera, framing the actors to equalize the idiocy of their logics, allows the repetitive soundtrack ("'nurture his soul' . . . 'cut off his hands'") to dominate this scene long after the camera has turned its lens elsewhere.

FIGURE 4.4. Muratova. *Asthenic Syndrome.* "Cut off his hands!" "Nurture his soul!"

Extensively substantiated in interviews (e.g., Gersova 162), Muratova's disdain for the intelligentsia undercuts the very institutions—the school, the church, the courtroom—through which the intelligentsia might lay claim to moral leadership, to the redemptive mission of nurturing souls, or to the same "lofty citizenship" her cinema bureaucrats had long badgered her to perform. "If I were to believe (unfortunately, I do not) that art is capable of re-educating or changing the world," Muratova has remarked, "then perhaps I would abandon my position. . . . I take on the task of representing. And to represent, since I am entrusted with that, let me do it completely, in the full measure and dimension that I perceive" (quoted in Gersova 158).

Yet for Muratova the intelligentsia's *mission civilisatrice*, with its pretentious litany of spiritual superiority, is not a "national tradition, but a geographical peculiarity," the behavior of naked aggrandizement: "There [in the West] the skeleton is simply not so obvious" (quoted in Gersova 160). Far from a "collective hero" (Horton and Brashinsky 107), Muratova's characters are neither collective nor heroic, but contending, parallel beings, carbon-based life forms, periodically requiring a warm body to discharge accumulated energy. Her regressive logic captures a consciousness charming in its raw exchange of impulses that sustain biological existence. The metropolitan intelligentsia epitomizes the overweening arrogance of the human as "tsar of nature, the crown of creation, more important than anything" (Muratova, quoted in Tsyrkun 22).

It is not coincidental that the zoo, a familiar setting that figures in many of her films, provides a recurring, alternative model for collective life, a kind of mock utopia that both mirrors and ironizes state-enforced collectivity. Instances of this mock utopia are scattered throughout her work, each character permitted to be individually maniacal in a fashion reminiscent of the very lines from *A Change of Fate* to which Muratova has repeatedly acknowledged her philosophical affinity:

> A plethora of complementary and mutually excluding things
> marvelously co-exist in the universe. The world is large and I like its
> variety. It resembles a zoo. Some have scales; others—needles; a third
> type is naked or breathes underwater. Some eat each other; others eat
> grass; a fourth kind isn't even visible to our eyes, it is so little. There
> isn't one single kind of animal, one that would be the correct animal—
> the standard (*etalonnyi*) animal. It's that way with people, with things,
> with ideas, with the whole of everything. (Quoted in Gersova 163)

The closest analogue here is the Soviet nature preserve Askania-Nova, her film location for *Enthusiasms* (and putative site of the centaurs). A Ukrainian nature preserve, dendrarium, botanical garden, and virgin steppe area, it is home to bison, ostriches, zebra, llama, the largest collection of Przewalski horses in captivity, and hundreds of species of plant life.

Muratova's preserve functions as a similar imperial spectacle of diversity, a topsy-turvy, ecological imperium akin to the Friendship of the Peoples, wherein "each has his own mania" ("manakial'nost' est' u kazhdogo"; Muratova, "Iskusstvo rodilos'" 96). Her cinematic world bears no relation to the nation, ethnic or, god forbid, civic; instead, it is her sovereign territory within which her actors, dolls, and corpses may roam free of "the global drama of total assault . . . by civilization" (Shilova, "V poiskakh" 186–87). Her compartmentalized eccentrics inhabit a zany All-Union Agricultural Exhibition, revealing social reality as a kind of Soviet zoo-state. Parodic of that zoo-state, and watched over by the director with a similar demonic grimace, Muratova's cinema exists in order to provide institutional shelter for individual mania. Her curatorial desire informs the cameo appearances and miniature scenes throughout her work, in which a single, irrelevant character—some of them eccentric on a scale that would make Gogol' proud—appears briefly, only to disappear forever.[48]

Within this preserve, her most beloved eccentrics are those who, as she does, produce their own, private art—most characteristically, bad art with no value other than its psychotropic effect (art as opium, she has described it in screening discussions; see Muratova, "Iskusstvo—eto utekha" 13),[49] offering contrast and relief from the fraudulent demands of social norms. Muratova's aesthetics are radically egalitarian in this regard; her most beloved characters engage in amateur artistic play, a psychotic Moiseev dance company, producing gaudy displays filmed with enormous affection by her cameramen. The spontaneous outbreaks of dancing in *A Change of Fate* and *Enthusiasms*; the pathetic, nude "living sculptures," Nikolai's novel, and the psychiatric patients' rambling stories in *Asthenic Syndrome*; Gena's outmoded 1970s declamatory poetry and Venichka's arias in "Boiler Room No. 6" (*Three Stories*); the paintings in "Ophelia" (*Three Stories*); the chansons, performing eccentrics, and retarded "art" collector Misha in *Minor People*; the girl singer-songwriter who rides public transport in *Tuner*; and Natal'ia Buz'ko's spontaneous puppet dance in *Two in One* are a consistent source of warmth and humor in her work.[50] Her cinema, which gathers these gentle eccentrics together, is in its own fashion a wayward and heedless break dance, nude sculpture, and boiler room cri de coeur. It does not gather them together as members of a community, since that would be to reproduce the terms of the problem. It gathers them instead innocent of those delusional and corruptive ties.

The most eloquent celebration of amateur human creativity in Muratova's work is the trumpet solo by the memorable Aleksandra Svenskaia in *Asthenic Syndrome*. During the transformation from Svenskaia's intimate, off-key play-along with recorded music to the flawless, prerecorded performance of "Strangers in the Night" we are permitted to glimpse the hallucinatory, inner world of the human spirit, with its capacity to transform its own flawed efforts into a magnificent, private grandeur. Here we can begin to understand what Muratova describes, in reference to *Asthenic Syndrome,* as "a film about my worldview" (quoted in Gersova 162). This worldview answers to no collective loyalties; it forgives the sectarian and schismatic. Its extreme individualism refuses all expectations, whether embedded in collective identification or the more conventional requirements of mainstream cinema.

As diverse as the specimens of Muratova's multi-eccentric menagerie may be, sharing only hysterical, self-absorbed impulses—to mate, to smoke, to eat, to urinate, and to consume and destroy those nearby—they undercut all high-minded speculation about ethics, loyalty, and filiation. These abstractions, including the "ideological-poetic resonance" so treasured by Muratova's own erstwhile zookeepers, are resubmitted through a cinematic lens that records these categories as mere species behavior. This extreme leveling has been seen by her detractors over the years as tasteless, even immoral; by her admirers, it is by turns brutal and hilarious. Her interpretive lens, trained to function as a relentless examination of the skeleton, drastically refuses conventional distinctions that, taken together, would otherwise threaten to constitute the civic community.

FILMOGRAPHY

By the Steep Ravine (*U krutogo iara*). Short. Codirected with Aleksandr Muratov. VGIK diploma film. 1961.

Our Honest Bread (*Nash chestnyi khleb*). Codirected with Aleksandr Muratov. 1964.

Brief Encounters (*Korotkie vstrechi*). 1967.

Long Farewells (*Dolgie provody*). 1971, released 1987.

Russia. Codirected with Theodore Holcomb. 1972.

Getting to Know the Wide World (*Poznavaia belyi svet*). 1978.

Among the Grey Stones (*Sredi serykh kamnei*). Released under the name Ivan Sidorov. 1983.

A Change of Fate (*Peremena uchasti*). 1987.

Asthenic Syndrome (*Astenicheskii sindrom*). 1989, released 1990.

Sentimental Policeman (*Chuvstvitel'nyi militsioner*). 1992.

Enthusiasms (*Uvlecheniia*). 1994.

Three Stories (*Tri istorii*). 1997.

Letter to America (*Pis'mo v Ameriku*). Short. 1999.

Minor People (*Vtorostepennye liudi*). 2001.

Chekhovian Motifs (*Chekhovskie motivy*). 2002.

Tuner (*Nastroishchik*). 2004.

The Information (*Spravka*). Short. 2005.

Two in One (*Dva v odnom*). 2007.

The Dummy (*Kukla*). Short. 2007.

5 ✳

Vadim Abdrashitov-Aleksandr Mindadze: A Community of Somnambulants

Introduction: The Pliable Subject

It would be difficult to find a starker contrast than that between Muratova and Abdrashitov. One might (perversely) claim that the two directors share a concern for redemption and community: Muratova's concern is their coercive functions; Abdrashitov's concern is their elusive nature.

The collaborative work of Vadim Abdrashitov and his longtime scriptwriter, Aleksandr Mindadze, resulted in eleven films. Of these, three—*The Armavir* (1991), *Play for a Passenger* (1995), and *Time of the Dancer* (1997)—are set at the colonial periphery, and the last of these directly addresses the independence wars in the Caucasus. At a superficial level these three films would be the ideal focus for content-driven analysis of the colonial scene, a modern-day snapshot of how Russia's empire looks at its edges.

As I argued in chapter 1, however, my interest extends beyond the colonial vista and the mimetic panorama at Russia's empirical borders. It takes as evident that the imperial imagination does not spring up like a sentry at the state's edge or intensify as the border approaches, but rather is engaged through the cinematic work at levels limited neither to the visual periphery nor to narrative content. The film's formal features, its stylistic register, narrative structure, and conditions of production are candidates for curiosity, however much they may constitute a kind of speculative knowledge, in considering the issue of whether the empire has its own reality of representation not limited to content alone.

With respect to Abdrashitov-Mindadze's work in particular, it is not at the level of social topicality that the filmmakers choose to engage the audience, and the Chechen wars as such, for example, are not in fact a core concern. The conflicts of the 1990s and Russia's political conduct at the border are assigned by Abdrashitov-Mindadze to the status of epiphenomena. Their preoccupations function at a different level, attempting to construct a set of constitutive metaphors about the absence of cultural practices that would confirm collective value and differentiate it from the bureaucratic interventions of the state. Abdrashitov-Mindadze turn to the lability of the human psyche, its eternal availability for habitation by state desire, the pliable, bureaucratized subject, oblivious both to its institutional appropriation and to alternative cohesiveness, however unavailable or archaic those ways may be.

Biographical Remarks: Railroads and Courtrooms

Vadim Abdrashitov (1945–) and Aleksandr Mindadze (1949–) have been Russia's most prominent and lasting director-scriptwriter team for a quarter-century. They have worked together closely not only in the initial stages of a film project, but at all stages of the production process. Though each has done some work independent of the other, their names have been linked to such an extent that until recently it has been possible to write of their major work only as a joint effort.[1] In 2007, however, Mindadze directed his first solo film, Soar (Otryv; Central Partnership 007), mentioned in passing here. Whether the partnership has ended remains to be seen.

Born into a military family, Abdrashitov studied at the Alma-Ata Railway Technical School (1959–61). One could suppose that the recurrent train imagery in their subsequent work is Abdrashitov's autobiographical trace in much the same way as the court, Mindadze's first profession, is a trace from the scriptwriter's earlier work. In any event, Abdrashitov then studied nuclear physics at Moscow Physico-Technical Institute in 1961–64 and at Moscow Institute of Chemical Technology, also known as the Mendeleev Institute, from which he graduated in 1967 to work as an engineer. He then entered the Directing Department of Moscow's All-Union State Institute for Cinematography (VGIK) to study in the workshops of the directors Mikhail Romm and Lev Kulidzhanov.[2]

Romm's early recognition of Abdrashitov can be traced in the incorporation of his pupil's six-minute "documentary etude," the silent student film Report from the Asphalt (1973), into Romm's own late The World Today (Mir segodnia, 1968–71), left unfinished at Romm's death (original titles and production information provided at the end of the chapter).[3] Even in Abdrashitov's brief student work two later preoccupations might be discerned: the burden of social demands and a formal symbol of collective life, as later figured in the ship (*The Armavir*, 1991) and the factory (*Magnetic Storms*, 2002), to choose two chronologically distant examples. Having completed his diploma film, *Stop Potapov* (1974), Abdrashitov graduated from VGIK in 1974, three years after Mikhalkov, to accept Iurii Raizman's invitation to work at Mosfil'm (Abdrashitov, "A chto" 82). His work with Aleksandr Mindadze began with his next film, their 1976 psychological drama *Speech for the Defense*.

Mindadze first worked in a Moscow district court, then studied at Katerina Vinogradskaia's Workshop in the VGIK Scriptwriting Department, from which he graduated in 1971. His full-length screenplays, independent of Abdrashitov's contribution, include three early scripts: *Spring Call-Up* (*Vesenii prizyv*, dir. Pavel Liubimov; Gor'kii Studio, 1976), *Limit of Desires* (*Predel zhelanii*, dir. Pavel Liubimov; Gor'kii Studio, 1982), and *Quiet Investigation* (*Tikhoe sledstvie*, dir. Aleksandr Pashovkin; Lenfil'm Studio, 1986). Of Abdrashitov-Mindadze's eleven feature films, ten are original scripts; the psychological drama *The Turn* (1978) is Mindadze's screen adaptation, based on the novel of the same title by Veniamin Kaverin.

Abdrashitov-Mindadze's work has always been uneasily positioned as a hybrid, art film for a mass audience, consistently drawing substantial attendance through the late Soviet period. Although their viewership rates cannot be compared with that of the blockbusters of the late 1970s and early 1980s—such as Boris Durov's adventure *Pirates of the 20th Century* (1980; 87.6 million viewers) or Vladimir Men'shov's two-part melodrama *Moscow Doesn't Believe in Tears* (1980; 84.4 million viewers for each part)—their films enjoyed a substantial attendance of between 10 and 20 million in the decade from their 1976 *Speech for the Defense* (20.5 million) to their 1986 *Pliumbum* (17.6 million).[4] From late *perestroika* on, as cinema attendance began to decline and the distribution system collapsed, such films as *The Servant* (1988) and *The Armavir* (1991) were not immune to this process, following the trajectory described in chapter 2. Unlike many films of this period, however, Abdrashitov-Mindadze's work continued to circulate in theaters and on the festival circuit, to garner prizes and awards in major competitions domestically and internationally, and to attract critical attention in major cinema periodicals, such as *Cinema Art* (*Iskusstvo kino*) and *Séance* (*Seans*).

Abdrashitov's international awards and prizes include a Gold Medal at Venice in 1986 for *Pliumbum*, the 1994 Silver Bear at the Berlin Film Festival for *Play for a Passenger*, and the 1998 Locarno Special Jury Award for *Time of the Dancer*. Russo-Soviet prizes and honors include a USSR State Prize (with Mindadze) in 1982 for *The Train Stopped* and in 1991 for *The Servant*; recognition as a People's Artist of Russia (1992); the Golden Ram Award (with Mindadze) in 1994; the 1998 Kinotavr Grand Prix (with Mindadze) at the Open Russian Film Festival at Sochi for *Time of the Dancer*; the 2003 Kinotavr Special Jury Prize for

Magnetic Storms (with Mindadze), and a 2004 Nika Award for Best Director for the same film. Mindadze's screenplays for *The Servant* and *Time of the Dancer* won the Nika Script Prize in 1989 and 1998, respectively. Both director and scriptwriter were awarded the Golden Ram for the latter film in 1997.

What Bench? Two Stylistic Modes

Investigator:　What are you telling me here? When you were sitting on the
　　　　　　　bench, you were saying something very different.
Gubkin:　What bench?

—*The Train Stopped* (1982)

Abdrashitov-Mindadze's cinema operates in two apparently incompatible stylistic modes. The disjuncture between these two modes lends a marked conventionality to their work, as if a glitch in the universe keeps disrupting a simple story about two things: a mishap and the effort to set things right.

The first and most accessible of these two stylistic modes, aptly described as hyperrealism by the film critic Elena Stishova ("Konets" 84), is its "simple story." It is typically a tale of everyday life, social themes in "message films" (L. Karakhan, "Jobless Prophets" 34) that set out to make recursive sense of empirical happenstance, everyday life gone awry. This mode often takes as its starting point an accident, legal case, or catastrophe that requires a legal response. A woman defendant is charged in an attempted suicide-murder (*Speech for the Defense*); a promising young intellectual is tried for a traffic fatality (*The Turn*); a man is mugged and his young assailant is sent to a delinquent colony (*Fox Hunting*, 1980); a train wreck kills the locomotive driver (*The Train Stopped*, 1982); a father is arrested for poaching (*Pliumbum, or A Dangerous Game*, 1986); the wreck of a cruise ship leaves its passengers stranded (*The Armavir*). In *Play for a Passenger* an ex-convict's personal catastrophe is long past, his life broken by a seven-year imprisonment and its toll on his family and health. In *Time of the Dancer* the most recent Chechen war is officially over, but veterans on both sides struggle with its aftermath.

At the level of empirical legalities, the justice system adequately sorts out the guilty from the innocent: defendant Valentina Kostina (*Speech*) is technically guilty of attempted murder-suicide; Viktor Vedeneev (*Turn*) is technically innocent in the traffic death; the delinquent Vova Belikov (*Fox Hunting*) is guilty of assault. Aksiusha (*Armavir*) is not technically responsible for the shipwreck ("Where's the crime? It wasn't an order—it was a request!"). The myopic former judge Oleg (*Play*) had performed his legal duties with no thought of corruption. The state institutions—the court, the navy, the army—and their agents are oblivious to issues of accountability beyond legalistic guilt or innocence.

It is customary to view the early films in particular, those completed prior to 1984, as Abdrashitov-Mindadze's "legal chronicles" (Baskakov et al. 328), court dramas with a narrow thematic range but considerable psychological depth. The legal chronicles are in some sense the equivalent of Muratova's "provincial melodramas," an ongoing contemplation for which similar elements were brought into play from one film to the next. By the films of the late Soviet period, from 1984 to 1989 (*Parade of the Planets, Pliumbum,* and *The Servant*), and the postsocialist films (*Armavir, Play, Time of the Dancer, Magnetic Storms*), a shift of emphasis moved the films beyond legal intervention to explore topical social ills associated with the collapse of the Soviet state: political cronyism (*Servant*), the black and gray economies (*Pliumbum, Armavir*), criminal cartels (*Play*), Russia's wars at the southern periphery (*Time of the Dancer*), and factory violence (*Magnetic Storms*). Throughout these stages the filmmakers remained preoccupied with interrogating *institutionally* constituted norms of right and wrong, responsibility and blame, in a manner that might adequately be described as journalistic were it not for the second aspect of their cinematic style.

This second mode engages knowledges, ways of knowing more than things to be known, that bind the characters together in a shared, transcendent space. This space is neither a redemptive nor a spiritual one in any explicit sense. Its promise of common but transcendent information remains unfulfilled; intuition and memory in this realm gain inadequate access. First clearly evident in *Parade of the Planets*, this mode has been described by critics as metaphoric, encoded, cosmological, futurological, suspending the laws of space and time, and intensifying a mysterious dimension to the plot.[5] The "city of women" in *Parade of the Planets*, for example, may have an empirical explanation—the all-female textile settlements, such as those around the Ivanovo-Voznesensk factories—but here and elsewhere becomes "dissolved in a mysterious, metaphorical irrationalism" (Taroshchina).

Characters thus appear and disappear without motivation; they recall events to which they were not witness but do not recall events at which they were recently present. They read each other's unspoken thoughts but fail to articulate their own. The characters seem destined perpetually to negotiate nocturnal alleyways, spying on the covert actions of other characters, whose fates are obscurely linked with their own. Their temporal universe is cyclical rather than linear. The cyclicity undercuts social justice, replacing it with cosmic justice as an occasional and unpredictable substitute. In play is no explicit religion or philosophy but a set of questions about human agency, its unacknowledged motivations, and its limited capacity to bring about change.

This abstracted dimension, which contrasts the metaphysical to a legalistic knowledge system, undercuts its own diegetic reality, throwing into doubt the claims of the narrative in favor of varying memory systems, the mind's imperfect access to an alternative, symbolic reality. In some films, such as

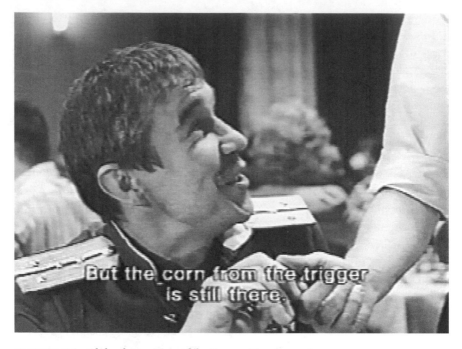

FIGURE 5.1. Abdrashitov. *Time of the Dancer*. Temporary truce.

Parade of the Planets, this ineffable dimension may lean toward Eastern phi-losophy or science fiction, elsewhere (*Armavir*) toward the psychological. None of these systems, however, adequately captures the stubborn indeterminacy of the second register and its capacity, as Stishova ("Konets" 84) has remarked, to resist catharsis. Driven by recurrent shots of narrow paths, circling Ferris wheels, endless railroad tracks that support both the quotidian and the sym-bolic registers, the films proffer a dreamscape of repetition and disappearance into nowhere.

This second mode, which is metaphysical without any claim to a specific religious basis, knows a different order of justice, incompatible with that re-quired by law and social norms. It exists as a contingent set of instincts, unre-solved contradictions, and moral alternatives that play against institutionalized adjudication. This opposition, organized around issues of justice, is presented most starkly in Abdrashitov-Mindadze's 1986 film *Pliumbum,* in which the eponymous adolescent entraps his own father. Pliumbum takes his nickname from the Latin for "lead," "a heavy metal, soft, used to make bullets and brass knuckles, a very malleable [*podatlivyi*], poisonous metal," explains Abdrashitov ("Pliumbum," n.p.). As in the story of the Soviet boy hero Pavlik Morozov, on whom the story is modeled, the letter of the law may be on the boy's side, but the spirit of Russian culture, the director suggests, is not.[6]

Between these two stylistic modes—one contemporary, epiphenomenal, pseudonymous; the other ahistorical, latent, anonymous—is located Abdrashitov-Mindadze's most productive space, into which they continually draw the viewer, a place where the material world is perpetually thrown into magnified significance by implied parables: one character carries another on his back, a scene that recurs in *The Servant*, *The Armavir*, and *Time of the Dancer*; a character discards all possessions to walk off into the woods (*Fox Hunting*, *Time of the Dancer*); men swim across a wide river to find their lives have changed (*Parade of the Planets*); a man arranges for his ship to be steered off course (*Armavir*).

The common view, therefore, of Abdrashitov-Mindadze as representing a *"rationalist* trend in Soviet cinema," as civic, journalistic filmmakers, "specializing in pictures that provoke viewers by exposing public and social problems" (Galichenko 57) is an incomplete perception of their work. Their project is precisely the sabotaging of the very rationalist trend that constitutes the surface of their cinema, creating instead what one critic has described with oxymoronic accuracy as "metaphoric rationalism" (Dondurei in "Kritiki," *Seans* 16: 99). The crisis, wherein the legalistic resolution fails to address larger speculation, is often compositionally set up using an internal frame such as a window that both contains the mishap and signals the limitations of available solutions.[7]

It has been a habit for critics to assign Abdrashitov-Mindadze's early work to the first mode of social commentary, and work from *Parade of the Planets* onward to this second, metaphysical mode. A shift in their work is incontestable,[8] yet the two modes have always vied with each other. Only after the stylistic shift in *Parade of the Planets* was it possible retrospectively to recognize more clearly beneath the social message of *Fox Hunting* in 1981, for example, that its philosophical tone questions the adequacy of institutional solutions, except as a chaperone for more complex issues. Here the film's protagonist-victim, Viktor Belov, must continually visit his young attacker to learn about his own restlessness and global discontent. His repeated visits to the delinquent colony have less to do with saving the fatherless thug, a task at which he fails, than with restaging the conditions through which a larger stock-taking—of the crime, of his own life, of the relation between the two—can be fathomed.

In this, more global project, the state is a false instrument, having provided only formal and punitive justice. In a similar vein *Speech for the Defense* was never about a young woman's juridical guilt or innocence, except as it framed the defense attorney's reconsideration of the broader ethical contours of her own life, the core trial of the film. A similar trial-within-a-trial can be discerned with respect to the newly self-reflective Viktor Vedeneev in *Turn*. In *Train* Investigator Ermakov's interrogation of the townsfolk, his legal judgments about their complicity and guilt, and his attempts to execute justice—a task at which he too fails—construct a parable about the broader collective constitution of the self in the twilight years of the late Soviet state.

I always followed the law.
I was an honest judge - one of a kind.

FIGURE 5.2. Abdrashitov. *Play for a Passenger.* "I always followed the law."

The misalignment of state justice and higher justice is among the most familiar and recurrent preoccupations in Russian culture, for centuries among its most productive themes. The incompatibility between the letter of the law and higher (i.e., noninstitutionalized) justice underlies Holy Rus' from the fifteenth century onward, and its reworking is apparent in the Slavophile project of differentiating Russia from the West, as well as the related cultural tradition, described by Vladimir Solov'ev, Nikolai Berdiaev, and others as the Russian Idea.[9] Rather than legalistic and rationalistic categories often assigned to the West, "true" justice in this cultural tradition remains uncodified and uncodifiable. That such metaphysical justice works autonomously from state law will be attested to by any Russian schoolchild citing Porfirii Petrovich in *Crime and Punishment*, who provided Raskolnikov only the barest juridical preconditions for his eventual, and more critical, spiritual salvation.

It is in relation to this unlegislatible tradition that the two filmmakers critically portray contemporary Russia as a malingering culture, dependent on the state's inadequate rituals of justice. In this project they repeatedly underscore their indebtedness to the nineteenth-century and early twentieth-century novel as a touchstone of cultural memory, a tendency that reaches its apogee in their 1997 *Time of the Dancer.* "All our pictures are filmed in the traditions of Russian literature," Abdrashitov replies to the film critic Oleg Sul'kin's question on this film. "The trajectory of a bullet that kills a human will inevitably return to the killer. That is a completely Russian tradition. This is the source of the associations with Russian literature, first and foremost with Dostoevskii" (quoted in Sul'kin "*Vremia tantsora*" 20; see also Abdrashitov, "Mesto neuznavaemo" 144; Hardy).[10]

Dostoevskian motifs, the subject of scholarly and journalistic commentary from Abdrashitov-Mindadze's early work forward (Galichenko 25; Horton and Brashinsky 87), expand in *Time of the Dancer* into a frenzy of broader literary citations. The high literary figure of Ol'ga Petrovna is a noble Turgenevian heroine manquée, whose wordless abandonment of the expropriated house after her husband's execution constitutes the film's only act of moral stature. Her Georgian analogue, Tamara, is a teacher of Russian literature, a Caucasian refugee, and the true owner of Ol'ga's house. Tamara herself is mockingly referred to as "Bela," the tribal heroine of Lermontov's eponymous story in the novel *Hero of Our Time*; her Russian "captor-lover" (though he fails at both) is referred to as "Pechorin," the hero of Lermontov's novel. Moreover the compositional pairing of Ol'ga Petrovna with Tamara expands beyond their common diegetic interests (the disputed house, the civil war) to suggest a reflexive commentary on the colonialist underpinnings of nineteenth-century Russian culture. More globally, the film's narrative structure is a jumbled *Doctor Zhivago*, with all the elements present but in a different order: civil war, a brooding doctor caught up in military conflict, illicit liaisons, and moral disorientation.

Yet however much Abdrashitov-Mindadze's work may be filmed in the traditions of Russian literature, the vitality of those traditions is drained. Largely inaccessible to the characters, cultural memory functions here as ironic contrast: the educated Caucasian Tamara (*Dancer*) is *not* the tribal, unlettered Caucasian Bela; the investigator Ermakov (*Train*) is *not* Dostoevskii's Porfirii Petrovich: his investigation redeems no one. Instead, the nineteenth-century canonical novels serve as the mark of failure by which their characters and their pallid communities are measured. The salutary resources of the high tradition provide little for their solutions, and the opposition of state justice/higher justice, central to such canonical signposts as *Crime and Punishment*, reaches a crisis in Abdrashitov-Mindadze's work. The lucid dream of higher justice fails to cohere.

The overlapping zone of these two styles, wherein disoriented characters are stranded and from which they cannot extricate themselves, is marked by their misalignment and mutual unintelligibility, the ways "we have lost each other" (Abdrashitov quoted in Stishova, "Konets" 84). State justice is inadequate, and collective memory is elusive. The legal dimension remains ineffectual in providing closure; the metaphysical in turn functions only as a disruptive force, an exhausted diagnostics.

The Most Common Name There Is: Petrov

What joy is there in remembering? It isn't as if you love your past. Yet the past
created your present, do not forget.

—Gudionov to Kliuev, *The Servant* (1988)

In the work of a different director or scriptwriter it might be of little significance
that the mise-en-scène is rarely arranged in the historical past.[11] In Abdrashitov-
Mindadze's work the contexts and props are relentlessly contemporary, yet
their present tense is fettered to a forgotten chronology and a disassembled tradition. The paradoxical status of memory—urgent, yet elusive—is marked by
the recurrence of props that would serve as memory's fetishes: the out-of-date
photograph of the elusive Marina (*Armavir*), a snapped gold necklace (*Play for a
Passenger*), a hoof print once set in the street's wet asphalt (*Time of the Dancer*).
Each image appears twice, underscoring the passage of time. That time elapsed
between the first and second shot measures the distance between matter and
recall, between the physical world and its psychic significance.

Given this instability it is no surprise that Abdrashitov-Mindadze's favorite
settings are precisely transient locales where forgotten names, false identities,
white lies, and improvisational alibis are spun: the dance floor, the waiting
room, the resort, the open-air restaurant, the cruise ship, the beach, the amuse-
ment park. The more recent films, set in unnamed or imaginary southern resort towns on the Black Sea at the periphery of the decaying empire, provide an
ideal venue for the interplay of anonymous leisure and violence.[12]

Hence the atmosphere in which time runs in two directions. If the
filmmakers' pacing is typically slow, its strategy is to force the viewer to move
simultaneously forward through the story and in reverse through the backstory.
For all the apparent diversity of characters—ranging, for example, from teacher-
cum-prostitute (*Play for a Passenger*) to pediatrician-cum-separatist (*Time of the
Dancer*)—they share a fluidity in their external coordinates, collapsing social
distinctions, introducing a radical instability to intention and self-definition,
leaving them adrift in a void where no stable entity, from state institution to
individual subject, can negotiate constancy. Instead, they seem to decompose
into surface units of narrative, to borrow Jameson's ("Of Islands and Trenches"
88) terminology, none reliable because none excludes other units of narrative.
The characters' fluidity and mutual nonrecognition are symptomatic of a larger
psychic dispersal, a nonrecognition that fails to be anchored in the self as a
stable unit.

Indirect evidence may be adduced from a curious aspect of Abdrashitov-
Mindadze's work, namely the very limited set of characters' names. "Ruslan"
appears in *Speech, Pliumbum*, and *Time of the Dancer*; their "Viktors" are major
characters in *Turn, Fox Hunting*, and *The Armavir*. "German" finds namesakes

as lead characters in *The Train Stopped, Parade of the Planets,* and *The Armavir.* As with Germann in Pushkin's *Queen of Spades,* "German" is an unusual name, distancing the character from his cohort. Unlike Pushkin, who debunks the supernatural in favor of earthly explanations, Abdrashitov-Mindadze render the earthly solution unsatisfactory. How, for example, did *their* German Ermakov (*Train*) know Malinin's telephone number by heart?[13] How is *their* German Kostin (*Parade of Planets*) transformed from a stranger into the intuitive son of a woman he does not know? At issue is not any similarity among the multiple Germans but the underlying interpretive question about the adequacy of empirical reality to account for experience. This repetitive or stalled quality of names might likewise be traced in their female characters: Marina (*Fox Hunting, Armavir, Play for a Passenger, Magnetic Storms*), Ol'ga (*Play for a Passenger, Time of the Dancer*), and Valentina (*Speech, Play for a Passenger*). Far from calling attention to common features, these repetitions signal the emptiness of the information, the arbitrariness of names—and, by extension, other socially assigned attributes—as adequate indices of identity. Closer to pronominal slots than to names, they proffer a patently false predictability, signaling something below that surface.

But whereas the films contain few names, the major characters have multiple identities, alternative names and aliases, forged as a set of temporary documents, part-time jobs, marriages of convenience, strategic alliances, temporary addresses, and parallel professions, often illegal. Characters' backgrounds are replete with cover stories, false leads, secret plans, nicknames, and alibis. Semin (*Armavir*) hides an incident of staged self-mutilation; his daughter, Marina, who is also Larisa, passes as a stowaway on a cruise ship. In *Play for a Passenger* the ex-con Nikolai's surname is a secret never revealed, though he dubiously claims it is "the most common name there is: Petrov."[14] Tamara (*Time of the Dancer*) passes herself off as a stranger in her own home, taken over both by Fedor ("Fidel") and by Andrei, a civilian in a military uniform, who presents himself as Tamara's fiancé, although she is married to Temur, who is in hiding.[15]

This nonrecognition, the failure of memory, and deception are motivated at the level of plot in a range of fashions. In *Armavir* it is cast as amnesia and other forms of psychological trauma. In *Play for a Passenger* it is criminal reinvention, narcolepsy, and neurological damage. In *Time of the Dancer* it is progressive blindness, disguises, and geographic dislocation. In *Speech* the defending attorney watches old home movies and barely recognizes herself.[16] In *Parade of the Planets* the reason for the characters' initial misrecognition of each other is ostensibly the passage of two years since the last military exercise. Senior reservist German Kostin is misrecognized by an elderly woman as her son Fedia; it seems to be senile dementia until their extended dialogue recasts their relationship as something resembling the reincarnation of a generic human dyad, reduced to its most abstract traces. Here the cameraman Vladimir Shevtsik's soft focus and eerie, noctilucent camera work and composer Viacheslav Ganelin's aural foregrounding of unintelligible murmuring in the haunting score comment on the film's narrative duality. The Allegretto from Beethoven's Seventh Symphony is overlaid with the radio broadcast of trivial popular music; Shostakovich's Toccata from the Eighth Symphony competes with the ambient, quotidian soundtrack. Throughout these directorial choices runs an inner spirit, itself kaleidoscopic, that keeps failing to align itself to socially constituted details of external life. The syzegy of the planets—which, the characters claim, occurs once in a thousand years—suggests the rarity of an ordered universe of the self.[17]

The elaborate informational surplus, the glut of facts consistently subject to change or disavowal, turns the viewer toward the emergent parable. That parable, in its most abstract coordinates, has to do with the way the memory, fractured by happenstance and frustrated strategy, is rendered incapable of holding shared interests, common values, or stable coordinates.

The train, a staple of Abdrashitov-Mindadze's filmic landscape, is thus the quintessential symbol of this transience, the vehicle by which characters move from one identity to the next, performing a radical peregrination of the self, shedding the old identity and improvising a new one.[18] The train structures the plot around a recurrent, visual oxymoron: the films begin with the end of one trip; they end with the beginning of a new trip. Framed on either side by these empirical journeys, the central narrative concerns the journey to an interior space, often signaled in the camera work by close-up head shots or elevated crane shots. The train wreck that interrupts the physical journey in the opening scene of *The Train Stopped* marks the beginning of an investigative journey into the complicity of the townspeople. In the opening scene of *Time of the Dancer* the train journey's end at a location that is itself deliberately ill-defined—Abkhazia? Chechnia?—marks the beginning of an interior journey, as the Russian military families attempt to start life anew in the confiscated houses of the defeated rebels. Here, as in Abdrashitov-Mindadze's other two Caucasus films (*Armavir* and *Play for a Passenger*), the balmy southern resort is in marked contrast to the characters' inner state: the psychological trauma of the stranded passengers (*Armavir*); the broken psyche of the ex-con (*Play*); the trigger-happy paranoia of the veterans (*Time of the Dancer*).

If Kira Muratova's work expresses a profound skepticism about the possibility of human comprehension, here the object of skepticism is recollection, the flawed instrument in a struggle to establish constancy. If Muratova's characters fail to understand each other, Abdrashitov-Mindadze's characters fail to recognize each other—or even, given the fuguist incapacities of the mind, themselves. The key fault line in this process is the failure of male relationships.

Masculinity without the Plus Sign

Abdrashitov-Mindadze's work is aptly described by Horton and Brashinsky (62) as the "male universe." Indeed, with the exception of two early films, *Speech for the Defense* and *The Turn*, the mise-en-scène—props, costumes, setting—is principally constructed as a male-governed institution—the army, the navy, the sports competition, the judicial system, the reservist militia—wherein issues of honor, integrity, and loyalty are the key foundational values. Where the profession is not exclusively male—the railway enterprise in *Train*, the paramilitary pelengation games in *Fox Hunting*,[19] the local political elite in *The Servant*—the film foregrounds the male bond, underscoring its importance through prior histories of masculine, even military prowess. Both the civil servant Gudionov and his protégé, Kliuev (*Servant*), for example, are former air force parachutists; after Gudionov's promotion, his next chauffeur is also a military parachutist. The institutionalized masculinity, particularly in the later films—*Pliumbum, The Servant, The Armavir,* and *Play for a Passenger*—foreground a disjuncture between the profession's idealized standards and its own demimonde. The films' apparently respectable men—clean-shaven, washed, and uniformed—are often criminal, on the lam, under threat, running from debts, crippled by past histories. Their financial survival depends on blackmail, pimping, rigged cards, extortion, petty thievery, and fencing.

Where characters celebrate male camaraderie, most notably the sequences in *Parade of the Planets* and *Time of the Duncer,* their celebration is stilted and short-lived, their avowals undercut by social difference and ulterior motives. Prior histories and economic status render solidarity a temporary and fragile project. In *Parade of the Planets*, perhaps the gentlest in its treatment of male bonding, the reservists come from radically diverse walks of life: an astronomer (who, not surprisingly, given the filmmakers' cosmological preoccupations, is also the senior reserve officer), a butcher, an architect, a worker, a city councilman, a stevedore, and (a late addition to their group) an organic chemist. This group, suggesting a male microcosm of urban Soviet life, has disconnected moments of friendship and loyalty, ruptured throughout by their jockeying for status, brutal one-upmanship, and unreflective abandonment of each other. Returning to the city, they unceremoniously break apart without farewells.

In a similar fashion, in *Time of the Dancer* the visual citation of Dumas's *The Three Musketeers* evokes disparity with rather than resemblance to the literary text. These Russian "Musketeers" are not loyal to each other and do not fight injustice. Nor are they even a threesome, but rather two soldiers and a civilian performer in a Cossack costume, who pays his fellow dancers in vodka to test the loyalties of the other two "Musketeers" in a staged brawl.

Time of the Dancer's non-Musketeers exist in a long lineage of false male friends, fathers, and sons enacting betrayal, antipathy, and mutual indifference. Ruslan Chutko (*Pliumbum*) betrays his father. The paternalistic Gudionov (*The Servant*) abandons his adopted son, Kliuev, whose life he had radically reshaped. Viktor Belov's fatherly overtures are rejected by the adolescent Vova Belikov (*Fox Hunting*) once the adolescent is released from the delinquent colony. Nikolai (*Play for a Passenger*) betrays his criminal "father" to the militia and befriends Oleg solely for revenge. Ermakov and Malinin (*The Train Stopped*), at first "fraternal investigators," quickly become antagonists, each advocating his own version of the train wreck. Vania and Taras (*Armavir*) befriend Semin, whom they intentionally misidentify, hailing him as "Lekha" long enough to steal his wallet.

The filmmakers' concern with a latent and potential collectivity is evident in their continual return to plural protagonists: the six reservists (*Parade of the Planets*), the three non-Musketeers (*Time of the Dancer*), the victim and his attacker (*Fox Hunting*), the journalist and the investigator (*Train*), the politician and the protégé (*Servant*), the father and the son-in-law (*Armavir*), the judge and the ex-con (*Play for a Passenger*), the two workers, Valera and Stepan (*Magnetic Storms*), and so forth. That this plurality is not merely a structural preference might be confirmed by the use of plurals in titles at the earliest stages of script production: the original working title of *The Train Stopped*, for example, was *Dialogues* (*Dialogi*); *Parade of the Planets* was *Muster* (*Sbory*, in the sense of military assemblage). Plurality is also evident in the insistent echoes of paired names both *among* films (their repeated Germans) and *within* films (Belov and Belikov in *Fox Hunting*; Oleg Petrovich and Nikolai Petrov in *The Train Stopped*).

Within these fragile masculine clusters, however, the language is impaired in two radically distinct fashions. The characters' speech is cryptically monosyllabic, inviting misinterpretation and false assumption. Alternatively, it is lexiphanic and rambling, fraught with contradictions and misrepresentations. Their attempts to operate through a series of paramilitary passwords, slogans, mottoes, and rallying cries—"Karabin! Kustanai!" (*Parade of the Planets*); "Armavir!" (*Armavir*); "Kachkanar!" (*Time of the Dancer*)—conjure up a temporary community, unsustainable beyond the moment of the slogan's utterance. They are stranded, refugee partisans from their own ill-functioning reserves; their passwords still serve to identify each other, but the entity to which they imagined belonging does not operate.

Emblematic of the fractured relationships is the condition of the male body itself, the impairment of which is a recurrent feature of their work: Ermakov (*Train*) displays a gunshot wound from his years in state investigation; Semin (*Armavir*) is crippled from a staged accident to gain military exemption; Nikolai's (*Play for a Passenger*) internal organs are failing from years of incarceration; both Valera and Temur (*Time of the Dancer*) suffer severe wounds dating from the state's southern wars. By the filming of *Magnetic Storms*, which turns its attention to factory violence at a state enterprise in the Soviet Urals, the strikebreakers' brawl of all against all resembles, in Stishova's ("Vyshli my") words, a bloody, male ballet.[20]

In this respect Abdrashitov-Mindadze's protagonists join a long line of familiar Soviet heroes whose physical impairment is a kind of "scoring"—with the double connotation of mutilation and orchestration—of the protagonist's relationship to the state. The implied seminal texts of the socialist realist canon include Nikolai Ostrovskii's novel *How Steel Was Tempered* (*Kak zakalialas' stal'*,

1932–34) and Boris Polevoi's novel *Story of a Real Man* (*Povest' o nastoiashchem cheloveke*, 1946), as well as the many renditions of the real-life Pavlik Morozov. Ostrovskii's Pavka Korchagin, like his paralyzed and blind author, sustains a series of injuries but overcomes the urge to end his life, committing himself instead to writing the novel that is his life; Polevoi's protagonist Aleksei Meres'ev, whose lost limbs are the result of a wartime air battle, overcomes similar despair to serve as inspiration to the people.[21]

In Abdrashitov-Mindadze's work the casualties, wounds, and scars, like state identity papers, are proof of participation in the degraded order. Their characters' impairments document service to the state, its tax on the body. Mutilation marks the physical encounter with the state, for which belonging cannot be constituted except as bodily impairment, a wounding that marks the state's irrefutable claim in the line of duty.

How We Have Lost Each Other

Anonymous passenger: But just one question . . . are we worth it—you, me,
           them—are we worth today's casualty?
Military man: I don't understand.

—*The Train Stopped* (1982)

"Individual versus society" has long been a critical platitude describing Abdrashitov-Mindadze's films.[22] The euphemistic function of this analytic cliché in the Soviet context, where the deployment of "society" sidesteps any speculative distinction between the state and a collective civic life, relegates dissidence—opposition to the state—in contradictory fashion to antisocial rather than to social behavior.

Abdrashitov-Mindadze were never dissidents in any conventional sense of that term, and even in such publicistic films as *The Train Stopped* a critique of the state was never their preoccupation. Instead, anemic collectivity has been the recurrent focus of their cinema. This emphasis on what might be described as a defective collectivity rather than a defective state worked to their detriment during the *perestroika* (1985–91) period, when the dissident heritage in the various constructions of that term (thematic, formal, textological, biographical, etc.) provided both Soviet cultural producers and their Western scholars more intense international interest. Their films—with the exception of *Fox Hunting*, the ending of which was edited against the director's and scriptwriter's wishes—had not been thwarted or suppressed as had the work of some colleagues (Tarkovskii, Muratova, German, Askol'dov, and Sokurov, among the most prominent names). While receiving considerable *domestic* attention from critics and scholars, Abdrashitov-Mindadze's work played a muted role in international cultural politics. They did not fit the list of available roles in

Western scholarship and journalism without extensive discursive shifts. Their deviations, particularly the mystical elements in *Parade of the Planets* and the indictment of the community in *The Train Stopped*,[23] did not end disastrously. Their work was often received by Western festival directors with either benign incomprehension or worry that this heterosexual, male universe might harbor patriarchal bacilli. After the collapse of 1991 unsympathetic Russian critics, misreading such scenes as the Palace of Culture "Cossack" performances (*Time of the Dancer*) or the cruise ship performance (*Armavir*) as innocently "Soviet"—that is, passé, outmoded, unworthy of sustained analysis—neglected to see the insistently mannered quality of such sequences, their marked theatricality and attendant commentary on the scripted quality of collective life.

In this fashion the juridical theater of *Speech for the Defense* and *The Turn* is an element that reaches greater emphasis in the later films. The interrogation chamber and courtroom (*Speech, Turn, Fox Hunting, The Train Stopped*) bear a kinship relation to the performance hall (*Speech, The Servant, Time of the Dancer*), the dance floor (*Turn, Parade of the Planets, Armavir, Time of the Dancer*), the shipboard Neptune performance (*Turn, Armavir*), and the sports exercises (*Fox Hunting, The Servant*). *Time of the Dancer*, with its theatrical costumes, fake gun, staged fights, saber dances, military parades, and public ceremonies, is a post-Soviet iteration of *The Servant*, with its tap dancing and staged bureaucratic celebrations.

The most evident staging is undoubtedly the opening credits to *Play for a Passenger*, for which the original working title, *A Grand Performance of Life*, had explicitly articulated Abdrashitov-Mindadze's interest in a two-tiered reality system. The characters, introduced to us in the tradition of dramatis personae ("Nikolai, a passenger, 43 years old"; "Oleg, a conductor, 44 years old"), are theatricalized even before their appearance on the screen. This stylistic distance signals a gap, an as yet unnegotiated, empty space, between social documentary content and its insistent conventionality, to be filled with a key question that drives the plot: Why was the callow Nikolai of 1979 convicted as a villain criminal, yet a decade later was lauded as a hero entrepreneur "to whom gold monuments are erected"? The legal system and its compliant citizenry had at each historical moment staged, as its original title suggested, an opportunistic "performance of life." The cinema audience, itself implicitly a conspirator in Nikolai's ascension from student ("racketeer") to criminal ("businessman"), is invited by the filmmakers to examine its complicity in the legitimization.[24]

The extensive camera footage given over to group enactments—the adult play on Ferris wheels, carousels, and huge mechanical swings—retains a stubbornly stilted quality, a scripted rendition of semi-somnabulance.[25] While the manifest critique of the compliant community in *Train* is figured by the investigator, who finds blame in the railroad community as a whole—their shoddy work, absenteeism, alcoholism, toleration of endemic equipment shortages—the investigator himself is a provider of retrograde, false solutions: the letter of the law, the Stalinist rhetoric, and juridical extremes. Abdrashitov-Mindadze's characteristic even-handedness—evident in their stubborn indeterminacy, for example, of *who* is the judge (*Play*) or *who* is the servant (*Servant*)—sets aside both indictments as false solutions, to point at the gap where an engaged common space might be figured, distinct from the malignant state and the malingering and obedient collectivity.

Unconcerned with individualistic solutions, Abdrashitov-Mindadze point to the failure of the aggregate, its impaired independence from state intervention. The passive congeries—its preference for formulaic, juridical rigidity; its zombie leisure; its alarming malleability; its ventriloquized desire—is rejected by this filmmaker team as a fateful and wasting unity of inaction, a falsely constituted notion of society, marked by acquiescence to institutional interests. Between the state-sponsored paramilitary games of *Fox Hunting*—eventually an extended metaphor for inculcated norms of obedience—and the recidivist's antisocial gang lies Abdrashitov-Mindadze's search for alternative ways in which communality might be imagined. Their protagonist throws off his gear and walks alone into the woods less as a triumphant individualist than as a casualty to compliance. The most extreme figuration of this condition (*Parade of the* Planets) appears in the brief and puzzling airline interior shot, intercut into the campfire scene: the dim interior shot of anonymous men asleep in the airline cabin as it flies over the reservists, visually commenting on their own unconscious state.

FIGURE 5.3. Abdrashitov. *Parade of the Planets*. Sleeping citizens.

It is this kind of collective somnambulism that stands at the center of Abdrashitov-Mindadze's critique, a suspicion that memory itself may be left solely to the tender ministrations of the state. The filmmakers posit an elusive consciousness, with its cyclical time and recurrent crises, temporarily and contingently negotiated through a set of cultural codes largely illegible to citizens of its dissolving empire. Their films' many retrospective elements, their recursions and love of archaism—the characters' complex prehistory, the faltering masculine universe, the empire's decaying southern periphery, the deteriorating state institutions, the ill-fitting prerevolutionary literary citations, the impaired, amnesiac heroes—suggest that a stalled recollection of cultural texts is the only available solace for the appropriated subject, caught between twin registers of the legalistic and the cosmological.

ABDRASHITOV'S FILMS BEFORE COLLABORATION WITH MINDADZE

A Report from the Asphalt (*Reportazh s asfal'ta*). Course project, 1973.
Stop Potapov (*Ostanovite Potapova*). Diploma film, 1973.

MINDADZE'S FILMS WITHOUT ABDRASHITOV

Soaring (*Otryv*). 2007.

ABDRASHITOV'S FILMS IN COLLABORATION WITH MINDADZE

Speech for the Defense (*Slovo dlia zashchity*). 1976.
The Turn (*Povorot*). 1978.
Fox Hunting (*Okhota na lis*). 1980.
The Train Stopped (*Ostanovilsia poezd*). 1982.
Parade of the Planets (*Parad planet*). 1984.
Pliumbum, or A Dangerous Game (*Pliumbum, ili Opasnaia igra*). 1986.
The Servant (*Sluga*). 1988.
The Armavir (*Armavir*). 1991.
Play for a Passenger (*P'esa dlia passazhira*). 1995.
Time of the Dancer (*Vremia tantsora*). 1997.
Magnetic Storms (*Magnitnye buri*). 2002.

Aleksandr Sokurov: Shuffling Off the Imperial Coil

Introduction: Serving the State

For me, there is enormous significance when a citizen serves the state. . . .
This is, by the way, our Russian tradition, very important and deeply rooted. . . .
We need a strong state.
— Aleksandr Sokurov, "Teni zvuka" (1994)

Sokurov was the first in our cinema to formulate the idea of imperial collapse
and the idea of the Other, but also the apocalyptical mood that took hold of the
large part of the intelligentsia in those years.
— Mikhail Trofimenkov, "Nigde i vsegda" (1994)

Aleksandr Sokurov is widely considered to be among the most difficult Russo-
Soviet directors, in Brashinsky and Horton's (121, 122) words "an *auteur's auteur*," "the last true Soviet *auteur*." His impressive oeuvre includes sixteen feature films and at least thirty-two documentaries, with undoubtedly more to
appear before this volume's appearance in print. One chapter cannot do justice
to the expanse of his work, nor is it meant to do so. My focus is primarily his
later feature films and their relation to the overarching thesis of the volume,
namely that, for all his differences with the other filmmakers included here,

FIGURE 6.1. Sokurov. *Aleksandra*. "Who's 'we'?"

Sokurov is concerned with a collectivity held together by linkages of cultural value and political power for which the figure of the empire—for Sokurov, late Soviet, dynastic Russian, British, even Japanese—serves as a recurrent interpretive frame. Disconnected from categories of a shared social community, from myths of inclusivity or horizontality, Sokurov's universe is chaotically diverse, inhabited by an internally stratified cultural elite and a distant, even Orientalized mass.

Thus Sokurov's cinematic ark, if I may draw upon a later metaphor, is hardly an inclusive congeries of all earthly animals, two by two. Instead, it is a gathering of imperial gentility adrift in a social catastrophe largely of its own making, dancing to the exquisite music of its isolated culture, oblivious to the impending historical accident that is in fact its own inevitable death. And while *Russian Ark* is neither typical nor representative of Sokurov's work, such distant films as *Days of the Eclipse* and *Second Circle* are, I would argue, contrastive features of a shared, imaginative topography (original titles and production information provided at the end of the chapter).

It is not, however, in a literal and geographic sense that, say, the Turkmenistan of *Days of the Eclipse* or the frozen north of *Second Circle*—or, for that matter, the Tadzhik border of *Spiritual Voices*—belong to the same cinematic empire as the St. Petersburg of *Russian Ark*. Whether or not this literal truth holds, it does not adequately capture the strategic eclecticism at work in Sokurov's imaginative realm, an inconsistency that anchors its symbolic system more surely in a larger ideological structure than empiricism alone might accomplish. Instead, Sokurov's work appropriates material from a larger and more enduring imaginative system, not exhausted by his own artistic domain: that appropriation gathers strength from the inclusion of fantasies distant, even apparently ill-suited, to Russia's dynastic or socialist experience. The African colonialist documentary footage, for example, interspliced into *Mournful Unconcern* or the seafaring preoccupations that run through Sokurov's work from *Confession* to *Russian Ark* are hardly the historical residue of the contiguous, overland imperium. Yet, as I argued in chapter 1, they are common loan fantasies from its thalassocratic kin. In this respect I elaborate a concept first suggested by Edward Said. "We need not decide here," he writes, "whether . . . imaginative knowledge infuses history and geography, or whether in some way it overrides them. Let us just say for the time being that it is there as something *more* than what appears to be merely positive knowledge" (*Orientalism* 55).[1]

Though it may be argued in reply that Sokurov's rendition of G. B. Shaw in *Mournful Unconcern* is simply "about" England, or that Sokurov's shipboard representations are a matter of personal taste,[2] such truisms do not therefore exhaust the range of potential interpretation, including the thesis proposed here: in brief, that the imperial imagination, for Sokurov, is a robust, sensemaking instrument. Across this space, tropes that might be speculatively associated with the culture of empire—an elite, insular center and inscrutable periphery; a mythology of seafaring conquest; hubristic political overreach; life as an ethical struggle over a perpetually imperiled sovereignty; a preference for grand, oracular eschatology—provide a productive analytic environment.

Biographical Remarks: "Non-Procedural Passion"

I, of course, cannot mute in myself an attraction to the military. I am after all a Russian.

—Aleksandr Sokurov, "Teni zvuka" (1994)

When an intonation of trust emerges, all else remains insignificant, all the more so if everyone speaks in a single language—in Russian. . . . Those who negate the value of a situation in which people of various confessions, of various ethnicities and customs have a medium of social contact and approach— the language—deny a great historical and God-given gift. . . . After all, in Russian it is possible to say anything at all: military men as well as bandits speak in this language. But, above all else, it is the language of unification.

—Aleksandr Sokurov, *Island of Sokurov*

Born into a military family in Podorvikha (Irkutsk district) in 1951, Sokurov moved with his family from place to place before graduating in 1968 from secondary school in Krasnovodsk, Turkmenistan, an area to which he would eventually return to film *Days of the Eclipse*. Settling in Gor'kii (as Nizhnii Novgorod was known from 1932 to 1990), Sokurov worked for six years as the producer's technical assistant and then assistant at Gor'kii City Television, producing television shows in 1970 at age nineteen; his television documentary *The Summer of Mariia Voinova*, later incorporated as the first of two chapters in his film *Mariia*, dates from this early period. He completed his university education with evening courses in history and graduated from Gor'kii University in 1974.[3] Enrolling in the Production Department of Moscow's All-Union State Institute of Filmmaking (VGIK) in 1975, he joined Aleksandr Zguridi's Documentary Film Studio, where he was supported by an Eisenstein scholarship.

From his early years at VGIK Sokurov could be a difficult colleague. In her foreword to *Sokurov*, Liubov' Arkus writes with ironic affection of his reputation at the film school, where he was known for his "iron discipline and a heightened 'social activism' ": "a non-procedural [*neprotokol'nuiu*] passion in the struggle for fairness, an unmeasured seriousness in the pronouncement of the words 'justice' [and] 'society' were attributed to the excess fervor of a neophyte" (Arkus and Savel'ev, *Sokurov* 21). Sokurov's intended diploma film (and what would have been his first Lenfil'm production) was *Lonely Human Voice*, an unconventional rendition of Andrei Platonov's stories "Potudan' River" ("Reka Potudan'," 1937) and "Origin of a Master" ("Proiskhozhdenie mastera," 1929). Objections by VGIK (in particular VGIK Rector Vitalii Zhdan) and Goskino officials led not only to the film's proscription, but also to an order for the destruction of both the negative and the print itself.[4] Both negative and print were initially hidden by Sokurov's scriptwriter Iurii Arabov and cameraman Sergei Iurizditskii,[5] then the print circulated unofficially in cinema clubs for nearly a decade (1978–87), in the words of the film scholar and director Oleg Kovalov ("My v odinokom golose" 13), as an "unseen film, a film-phantom, a film-legend, a film-rumor." *Lonely Human Voice* saw the light of day only in 1987, when it was released in the wake of the Conflicts Commission rulings described in chapter 2.

In an effort to salvage Sokurov's diploma defense, sympathetic VGIK colleagues attempted to substitute a version of his earlier television color documentary *The Summer of Mariia Voinova*.[6] Eventually a further reedited and developed version, subsequently entitled *Mariia*, would also be delayed for a decade, released only in 1988, again thanks to the Conflicts Commission.[7] The result of these conflicts with VGIK and Goskino administrators was that Sokurov did not graduate with his class; he finished as an external student, but with highest marks.[8] Finding work at Lenfil'm in 1980, he continued much of his early work at Leningrad Documentary Studio.[9]

As a result of these conflicts Sokurov's Lenfil'm debut inadvertently turned out to be *Demoted*, filmed with the cooperation of both Lenfil'm and Mosfil'm. Its lead character, a state traffic inspector demoted to taxi driver, acts out Sokurov's imaginary demotion of a different state employee—a VGIK or Goskino administrator, one can only assume—to a lowly position. In a delicious settling of scores, Sokurov wrote a small, reflexive moment into the film: the demoted state official sits in a cinema hall that is screening Sokurov's still-banned *Lonely Human Voice*.

Unsurprisingly, Sokurov's creative difficulties continued beyond his VGIK years. His 1982 documentary *And Nothing More*, commissioned by Central Television for the fortieth anniversary of victory over Nazi Germany, was deemed too brooding and politically ambiguous; the work was shelved until 1987. His 1986 *Moscow Elegy*, initially begun as a tribute to mark the director Andrei Tarkovskii's birthday, encountered difficulties with the Union of Filmmakers, and work on the film was suspended until 1988. As the filmography starkly shows, Sokurov's work enjoyed no surety of production until the mid-1980s.

There is a certain perverse comfort, a satisfying homology of life and work, in the fact that Sokurov's biography, so rife with face-offs, pugilistics, and misunderstandings, is matched by an oeuvre similarly operating from a principle of combat, a calling-out of either the viewer or of established film tradition to engage in a new form of provocation each time. It would be a mistake to assume that the duel is a friendly one: Sokurov has often repeated that he is unconcerned whether his films find an audience.[10] If this assertion by a thin-skinned director is hardly to be taken at face value, it might nevertheless be viewed as another aspect of Sokurov's hopology, his military stagecraft requiring that new terms of engagement be invented for each film.

Russian Ark, Sokurov's most celebrated provocation, for example, was filmed on the shortest day of the St. Petersburg winter, with a mere four hours of daylight. Filmed in a single shot between noon and 1:30 p.m. on December 23, 2001, it was, among other things, a virtuosic retort to the Russo-Soviet montage tradition, most notably in Eisenstein's *October* (*Oktiabr'*, 1928).[11] But a taste for provocation is discernable much earlier than *Russian Ark* and often takes the preemptive form of denying the viewer that key piece of information central to the film. In *Mariia*, for example, documenting the life of a simple woman who died at forty-seven, the emphasis on death and on the cemetery where Mariia is buried stubbornly withholds any mention of how or why she died.[12] One might consider this omission incidental, yet a similar strategy of omission is evident in *Petersburg Elegy*, Sokurov's documentary on Fedor Chaliapin's family and legacy that does not concern itself with the singer's musical contribution. This practice of omission in *Whispering Pages*, which evokes *Crime and Punishment* while never identifying the key figures or events, is described by Aleksandra Tuchinskaia as Sokurov's "inverse perspective," the act of withholding precisely the information most likely to be sought.[13] In a similar spirit *Soviet Elegy*, the documentary on Boris Yeltsin at the height of his 1989 battles, provides no political context. The few words spoken by this normally voluble political figure are irrelevant in contrast to the film's protracted silences.[14]

Further, why, at the height of the *perestroika* period, when the "real documentary truth" could finally be chronicled, would Sokurov make a film about Leningrad (*Leningrad Retrospective*) perversely composed entirely of *official* newsreels, lasting more than thirteen hours?[15] Or *dolce . . .* , a sixty-minute film with twenty-two minutes shot in silence, the camera principally focused on a single, immobile character?[16] Or *Sun*, a film shot in such virtual darkness (sun, indeed) that the premiere's audience assumed the projector was defective? To watch Sokurov is to accept in advance one's own voluntary condition of exasperation, disorientation, and frustrated expectation. His "excess fervor of a neophyte," as Arkus (Arkus and Savel'ev, *Sokurov* 21) has described it, would turn out to be his most enduring, regenerative quality.

Sokurov's cinematic production reached greater stability in the late 1980s. As his films finally left the shelves he gained international recognition. At the height of the *perestroika* period *The Lonely Human Voice* won the Bronze Leopard at Locarno in 1987. *Eastern Elegy* won the Grand Prize at the Oberhausen documentary festival in 1996, and *Hubert Robert: A Fortunate Life* won the Main Prize, again at Oberhausen, the following year. Sokurov was now regularly invited to conduct film seminars at Lenfil'm Studio and was awarded a State Prize in 1997. His television program, *Island of Sokurov* (*Ostrov Sokurova*), was broadcast from 1998 to 1999.[17] His frequent scriptwriter, Iurii Arabov, was given the 1999 award at Cannes for Best Screenplay for *Moloch*. Sokurov's *Taurus* received the award for Best Director, the Golden Aries, from the Russian Guild of Cinema Scholars and Critics in 2001; that film garnered three Nikas, for Best Director, Best Film, and Best Cinematography, in 2002. In 2004 Sokurov was recognized as a People's Artist of the Russian Federation. Among his projects are the development of a noncommercial studio, Shore (Bereg), affiliated with Lenfil'm.

An Attempt at Taxonomy

If for no other reason than the sheer quantity of Sokurov's films, I attempt here a brief description of the larger thematic clusters in his work. An obvious working division would distinguish between Sokurov's feature films and documentaries. Although I have observed this convention in the filmography at the end of the chapter, where documentaries are marked by asterisks, scholars will agree that his cinema is hardly sympathetic to such a division. His feature films routinely incorporate documentary footage into the artistic material, and his documentaries have no primary regard for empirical truth, but are something closer to what André Bazin ("Bazin on Marker" 44) has called an "essay documented by film."[18] As the film scholar Maia Turovskaia ("Na korable") puts it, "Aleksandr Sokurov de-documentalizes old newsreels."

Moreover, Sokurov himself groups his films in ways that are by no means self-evident or helpful as an introduction to his work. The most confounding cluster is the trilogy *Days of the Eclipse* (a quasi-science fiction film set in Turkmenistan), *Second Circle* (a naturalistic film set in the late Soviet period in the provincial North, about a father's burial), and *Stone* (a film about Chekhov's ghost set in the writer's former house), three films that on the surface would seem to have little in common.[19] Elsewhere Sokurov undertakes massive, long-term projects, such as his unfinished tetralogy *Moloch*, *Taurus*, *Sun*, and a planned fourth film on Mephistopheles, based on Thomas Mann's *Doctor Faustus*, or his unfinished family trilogy *Mother and Son*, *Father and Son*, *Two Brothers and a Sister*, the last of which has not yet been shot, for which ongoing production has extended over a decade.[20]

In the face of these complexities I nevertheless offer a working taxonomy that identifies seven recurring preoccupations that surface routinely in Sokurov's work. Though not exclusive of each other (and often overlapping), they serve as a contingent account of Sokurov's recognizable concerns. The earliest of these is his focus (in both documentary and feature films) on the humble life: *The Summer of Mariia Voinova*, *Mariia: Peasant Elegy*, his three Japanese stories (*Eastern Elegy*, *A Humble Life*, and *dolce . . .*), *Mother and Son*, and *Father and Son*. A second, related impulse in Sokurov's work is his documentary cycle of elegies, which currently comprises eleven explicitly named works.[21] A third strain explores the lives and works of elderly or deceased artists: the composer Dmitrii Shostakovich (*Viola Sonata*), the singer Fedor Chaliapin's family (*Elegy* and *Petersburg Elegy*), the filmmaker Andrei Tarkovskii (*Moscow Elegy*), the ghost of playwright Anton Chekhov (*Stone*), the French painter Hubert Robert (*Hubert Robert*), the three Petersburg diaries (on the novelist Fedor Dostoevskii's legacy, the director Grigorii Kozintsev's cultural contribution, and Mozart's *Requiem*), the writer Aleksandr Solzhenitsyn (*Conversations with Solzhenitsyn*), the family of the Japanese writer Tosio Simao (*dolce . . .*), and the cellist Mstislav Rostropovich and the singer Galina Vishnevskaia (*Elegy of Life*). Except for *Stone*, his feature film on Chekhov's shade, these films are stylized documentaries.[22]

A fourth, related cluster comprises Sokurov's highly subjective adaptations of literature: *The Lonely Human Voice*, based on Platonov's writing; *Mournful Unconcern*, from George Bernard Shaw's play *Heartbreak House*; *Days of the Eclipse*, based on the Strugatsky brothers' novella *Definitely Maybe* (its Russian original title is *One Billion Years before the End of the World* [*Za milliard let do kontsa sveta*]); *Save and Protect*, based on Gustave Flaubert's *Madame Bovary*; and *Whispering Pages*, loosely organized around nineteenth-century Russian literature, in particular Dostoevskii's novel *Crime and Punishment*.

Military life could be counted as a fifth recurring concern: the World War II allies in *And Nothing More*, the Russian soldiers at the Tadzhik-Afghan border in *Spiritual Voices* and *Soldier's Dream* (a twelve-minute excerpted version of the former five-and-a-half-hour television documentary), and the Arctic navy border patrol in *Confession*.[23] A sixth theme is the cultural life of St. Petersburg, the subject not only of several films already mentioned—*Petersburg Elegy* and two of the Petersburg diaries (on the Dostoevskii monument and Kozintsev's apartment)—but also of *Leningrad Retrospective* and *Russian Ark*, with its celebration of Petersburg's crown jewel, the Hermitage Museum.

Finally, a seventh thematic preoccupation has to do with political life. Sokurov's earliest effort in this regard is his compilation documentary *Sonata for Hitler*. His interest soon turned to contemporary Soviet politics: May Day preparations (*Evening Sacrifice*), the two Yeltsin films (*Soviet Elegy* and *An Example of Intonation*), his portrait of Lithuanian president Vytautas Landsbergis (*Simple Elegy*), and the political responses to the Chechen wars (*To the Events in Transcaucasia* on the Krasnodar demonstrations and, arguably, *Aleksandra*, with its encounter between the military and civilians). By 1999 Sokurov's films on political life took on another dimension. He directed his attention to larger and more distant historical subjects, including—now as a feature film rather than a compilation documentary—the figure of Adolf Hitler (*Moloch*), as well as Lenin (*Taurus*) and Emperor Hirohito (*Sun*).

These clusters are, of course, fluid, as the example of *Aleksandra* demonstrates, given its compatibility with the family cluster as well as the military or political films. For those uncomfortable with this fluidity, I mention one other, more brutal taxonomy. In conversation with Sokurov, the British film scholar Edwin Carels proposed a useful working opposition in Sokurov's work: between those films that are mannered, deliberately cluttered, eclectic, ornamentalist, fussy (in Carels's words "baroque, kaleidoscopic") and those that are severe, minimalist, ascetic, elegiac, and stern (Sokurov, "The Solitary Voice" 73). The operative working decision is this: Saturate the mise-en-scène or strip it altogether? Uncharacteristically, Sokurov has acknowledged in principle the legitimacy of such a distinction.[24]

If this is indeed a functional distinction, then to the first category might belong *Russian Ark*, as well as *Mournful Unconcern* and *Save and Protect*. To the second category, with its minute, even vivisectional preoccupations, belong *Stone*, *Mother and Son*, *Father and Son*, and *Aleksandra*, but also, by Carels's reckoning, *Lonely Human Voice* and *Second Circle*. Ardent admirers of Sokurov's earlier work would add to this category the Japanese stories (*Oriental Elegy*, *A Humble Life*, and *dolce . . .*). The fragile, moment-by-moment dissection of an intimate family relationship or of the invisible emotional life of an elderly Japanese woman in a remote corner of an outlying island posits the sharpest possible contrast to the elite distractions of the first category.

We might already see the way this imperfect opposition teases out important differences between the more theatricalized *Moloch* and the more minimalist *Taurus* and *Sun*. But more accurately than this we may see that the unfinished tetralogy attempts variously to graft the simple life onto the great, imperiled and isolated edifices of political power, to observe, as in an experiment, how it cannot be done. The gulf between these two aspects of Sokurov's cinema—the effete ornament and the ascetic icon—is striking in the extreme; it speaks of the stubborn absence of mediations in his textual world between the pinnacle of elite culture and the human in its most spiritual attenuation, as Kovalov ("My v odinokom golose" 11) describes it, "the magma of historical existence [held] directly in his palm."

Sokurov's ascetic films, as painstaking reconstitutions of ideal human relations, are in no sense portraits of the folk, the *narod*, or any other such easy opposition. Rather, they are abstracted and rarified moving icons, in Sokurov's ("An Interview" 26) words, "a fairy-tale-like discourse . . . a narrative that's both universal and extremely rare and strange." Laconic and monologic, they are "a mythological text,"[25] made for contemplation, not dialogue.

Indeed, since the late 1970s Sokurov's work has shown little interest in the folk, whether rural or urban, contemporary or historical. His earliest television work at Gor'kii produced several documentaries on demotic and agricultural life, including *The Most Earthly Cares*, *The Summer of Mariia Voinova*, and later *Mariia: Peasant Elegy*, but it is not a topic that held a sustained interest for him. As for the urban working class, his portraiture in *Demoted* is in no sense concerned with, let us say, the taxi driver as a populist portrait, but is concerned instead with the clash between mundane and transcendent justice, suggested by the rundown car's radio that happens to broadcast the philosopher Merab Mamardashvili discoursing on Goodness and Justice.[26]

Sokurov's cinema, as Jameson (*Geopolitical* 89) puts it, "can never 'share the destiny of the popular masses,'" but instead enacts the rift between two types: those who have an inner world and those whose inner world—the African dancers of *Mournful Unconcern*, the Turkmen in *Days of the Eclipse*—remains inaccessible, its unrepresentability marked as a permanent mystery.

Death, Empire, Culture: *Mournful Unconcern*

This theme [of death] . . . expresses the essence and value of Russian art. It is that which, I think, distinguishes Russian art in its most honorable examples from all of world art, from Western culture.

—Aleksandr Sokurov, "Glavnym" (1994)

I show in detail how things work and invite the viewer to join in the [death] ritual, as if it were a rehearsal.

—Aleksandr Sokurov, "The Solitary Voice" (1999)

Death, Sokurov's most life-affirming preoccupation, has been remarked upon by many critics. It figures prominently in his early works, such as the *Mariia* couplet, as well as in the later films of humble life, including the Japanese stories and *Mother and Son*. In *Empire Style* it is figured as murder (and, musically, as Violetta's death from consumption); it is extensively developed in the elegies, as well as in the artists' portraits. Death figures at the center of *Mournful Unconcern*, with its autopsy scene; *Days of the Eclipse*, in which the protagonist communicates with a corpse; *Save and Protect*, with its lengthy funeral ceremony; *Second Circle*, with its central theme of the father's burial rites; and *Stone*, set in the museum-home that Chekhov owned just before his death, then visited in the film by his shade (Sokurov, "Glavnym" 69).[27] Death is the impending event of *Taurus* and a dialogic feature of *Moloch*. It is encoded in the very soundtracks, such as Mahler's *Kindertotenlieder* in *Whispering Pages* and passages from Wagner's *Götterdämmerung* in *Sun*. Even in the films that were never produced, such as *Tiutchev* from the late 1970s, it was "mandatory" in the director's diaries of that period that the poet's death must figure prominently.[28]

Sokurov's preoccupation with death cannot be reduced in its complexity to a singular function; nevertheless, a dominant pattern in the visual necrophilia of his later work is its persistent association with a perpetually vulnerable political power—the Third Reich, the fragile Russo-Soviet Empire, the Japanese imperial court—and the empire's unholy accumulation of elite cultural value. This nexus (death-empire-culture) holds together with particular force in Sokurov's recent work: the incomplete tetralogy *Moloch* (1999) on Hitler in 1942, *Taurus* (2001) on Lenin in 1922, and *Sun* (2005) on Hirohito in 1945, as well as in the better known *Russian Ark*. These three elements, death-empire-culture, form a conundrum. With many variations, the conundrum is this: the political leader has been powerful but not immortal; art, by contrast, powerless in the politics that produced it, may reasonably aspire to immortality.

Sokurov ("Nastoiashchee iskusstvo" 97) has repeatedly stressed that his unfinished political tetralogy (*Moloch, Taurus, Sun*) must be seen as an entire whole rather than as individual films.[29] Moreover, because their production order was heavily reliant on funding and location availability they must be thought of as related instances rather than as a single linear episode: *Moloch* focuses on Hitler at a moment of splendor, at the height of his success and adoration; *Taurus* treats Lenin at the onset of physical extinction;[30] *Sun* figures Hirohito in a moment of transfiguration. Their paradigmatic display of possibilities unites them as a set: acme, decline, transformation.[31]

This principle of paradigmatic display is evident in multiple registers. The color palette, like paint samples of some mineral oxide, is displayed across the trilogy: manganese brown, ocherous green, sepia.[32] Each film recycles familiar elements—the servants, the female partner, the bedroom and the ritual of assisted dressing, the dining-room table talk, the extended outing—but in no particular narrative order.[33] Exhibition, rather than narrative resolution, dominates the films' stubborn, variant stagings of the inevitability of death, the fragile psyche at the apex of a fragile empire, the value of human life despite its debased features, and the foundational complicity of elite culture in a compromised political life.

In this regard the ark has been a productive figure for Sokurov as the image of a fatally imperiled vessel for the cultural elite. In *Russian Ark*, its eventual and most explicit articulation, to which we turn shortly, Sokurov invites comparison of the imperial palace to Noah's gathering of animals in the face of impending catastrophe. The "flood" of 1917 sets Russia adrift for some seventy-four years. Like the passengers of the biblical ark, the Hermitage aristocracy is visually united two by two in the culminating ballroom scene; unlike the biblical passengers, they are oblivious to the impending catastrophe as they exit into the maw of the flood.

Yet this film is not Sokurov's first imperial ark, endangered on all sides. Already in 1983 his *Mournful Unconcern*, based on Shaw's *Heartbreak House*, took a ship as its model of the imperiled household.[34] Leading cinema critics were quick to ascribe biblical associations: as Dobrotvorskaia ("Pliaska smerti" 103) describes *Mournful Unconcern*, years before *Russian Ark*, "The inhabitants of the House-Ark are provocatively indifferent to history and it [history] in revenge wipes them from the face of the earth."[35]

Shaw's play, written in 1913–16 as a pitiless portrait of "cultured, leisured Europe before the [First World] War" (Sokurov, "The Solitary Voice" 76), featured inhabitants whose vapid airiness is enhanced by Sokurov's casting of the ballet dancers Dmitrii Briantsev and Alla Osipenko,[36] with stylized movements and arch manner that underscore the frivolity of the company. Shaw's "Fantasia in the Russian Manner on English Themes" (the play's subtitle) acknowledges his debt to Russian culture, and in particular to Chekhov's *Seagull*, in Ronald Bryden's (183) characterization, the "bankrupt house, undisciplined servants, impending disaster." Just as Shaw had earlier done, Sokurov moves laterally from one fragile imperial household to another (now from Russia back to England), reproducing Shaw's Ark-Mansion but with a porthole and swathed in fishing nets, a mansion intercut with associative shots of a large ocean liner. As in Shaw's play, the military zeppelin's threat, hovering overhead, suggests a certain ideological affinity between itself and the mansion. The three vectors—impending death, imperial England, privileged culture—structure both Shaw's and Sokurov's complex systems.

Sokurov's title, *Mournful Unconcern*—and its Latin rendition as *Anaesthesia psychica dolorosa*—has been explicitly linked in interviews with the fading of loyalties. It allegedly refers to a pathological condition of emotional disconnection from kin, home, and homeland, an unconcern toward familiar, collective identifications. Sokurov ("Avtory") writes:

> The name of the film is taken from the realm of medicine. . . . If you were a psychiatrist and someone came to you by appointment and said: "Doctor, it seems to me that I have lost all sense of affection for those close to me; the creaking sound of the door to my native home does not affect me; the color of the clouds over my homeland leaves me indifferent; and the death of a fellow soldier from my own land does not concern me; the smoke from its conflagrations does not make my eyes tear up . . . ," you would know that before you stands a patient who is seriously ill, and that this illness is called "mournful unconcern."

This condition, medicalized by Sokurov in a fashion similar to Muratova's asthenic syndrome, functions as both personal and political symptom. As his characters engage in erotic frivolities amid shelling, sniper bullets, zeppelin overflights, and the eventual explosion of the mansion itself, they exhibit the condition of Sokurov's psychopolitical disease, failing to conjure up the loyalties and affiliations that would bind them together as loved ones, citizens, and national subjects. Cultural and economic beneficiaries, they suffer nevertheless from imperial languor.[37] The mansion-ark-empire, with its indifferent visitors-passengers-patriciate, is an easy target for the zeppelins overhead. "Balthazar . . . flood," mutters Shotover as he stumbles around the mansion, his words invoking the fall of the Babylonian Empire and the impending noadic apocalypse.[38]

The ship-house as a metaphor for the beleaguered British Empire had been suggested by Shaw himself, as well as by Shaw scholars.[39] As Bryden (194) remarks, "There has scarcely been a year since in which Shaw's extraordinary theatre poem, as authentic a myth for imperial Britain as Blake's prophetic books, has not seemed cannily relevant to the civilization whose end it foresaw."

In Sokurov's appropriation, the vessel, shot from repeated low-angle vectors in "the style of a tragic epoch, marking a farewell to the grandiosity of the 19th century" (D'iachenko 107), is wholly suitable for the imperial elite of a different era and ideology, as Iampol'skii ("Kovcheg" 114) evocatively suggests, "tragic in the face of historical catastrophe, to which it cannot counter-pose authentic values." The final explosion of the mansion and its submersion into the ocean—its surviving passengers adrift at sea—anticipate the final sequence of *Russian Ark*, with its metaphors of flood and endless sea voyage.

Without belaboring one might similarly see Hitler's grandiose and isolated alpine fortress as a similar spacious vessel, a metonym for the political ship of state, or Lenin's state-requisitioned Morozov estate,[40] or Hirohito's imperial palace, adrift in a sea of social and moral calamity, carrying a haphazard manifest of privileged voyagers. In Hitler, Lenin, and Hirohito themselves we see the fragile carapace of political power that produces, sustains, and is in turn produced by the empire over which it momentarily rules. In each case the mansion-ark's residents are transient, passengers rather than inhabitants: Hitler comes for a one-night visit; Lenin is there only to convalesce (that is, to die); the Hermitage visitors are invited for the evening; Hirohito is temporarily stranded between his evacuated family and his increasingly burdensome palace duties.

Stacked inside one another, the empire, the mansion-ark, the political figurehead, and finally the beleaguered physical body, with all its real, imagined, and psychic ailments,[41] are embedded renderings of the imperial coil, an unwieldy, sin-ridden husk of earthly indulgence, the fleeting physical embodiment of political power, all too cognizant of its inevitable death.

Death-Empire-Culture: Other Arks

By the time of *Moloch*, filmed at the 1939 Kehlsteinhaus fortress near Berchtesgaden in the Bavarian Alps,[42] Sokurov's death motifs had already become a
signature, as familiar as Abrashitov-Mindadze's locomotives or Muratova's
identical twins. Death hovers over Hitler's dinner conversation, drawn in
part from Picker's *Hitler's Table Talk in the Central Headquarters* (*Hitlers Tischgespräche im Führerhauptquartier*): the vegetarian ruler describes broth as
"corpse tea" (*Leichnam-Tee*); he drolly explains that crabs are best caught using
dead grandmothers as bait. *Moloch*'s narrative frame is a litter of newborn puppies, presented to Hitler on his arrival and to which he reacts with disgust. At
his departure he is told they have died "from the plague," though the scene is
deeply ambiguous. The puppies' death prompts the film's last scene: in Hitler's
words, "We will beat death."[43]

Still, *Moloch*'s richest death scene is a dialogue between Hitler and a priest
who comes in vain to advocate for a deserter's life. Their dialogue is visually
accented by a double-sided human sculpture at the base of the staircase. Each
man's argument, like each face of the stone figure, is sufficient unto itself: the
crucifix versus the swastika; the tragic sacrifice of youth versus the necessary
sacrifice of maggots; the advent of Christ's reign versus the victory of the Third
Reich. Where Christianity would transcend death in the name of eternal life,
Nazism would conquer death with a thousand-year empire, substituting for
Christ's empire.[44] When the priest appeals to Hitler "as if you were Christ himself," their dialogue resembles a distorted exchange between Pilate and Christ,
one in which Hitler is *both* Christ *and* the adjudicator of Judea.[45] Hitler's culminating retort, "Who can explain this paradox? Those who worship a crucifixion

FIGURE 6.2. Sokurov. *Moloch*. Guarding the thousand-year Reich.

do not want to die!," might have been uttered by Sokurov himself, albeit in a different register. Sokurov's response to this paradox is his entire oeuvre: those who worship the crucifixion must come to terms with death, and in particular with their own mortality.[46]

In Sokurov's next film, *Taurus*, Lenin's impending death is foreshadowed by his dream encounter with his dead mother, her breath foul from the grave's putrefaction, his "rehearsal," to use Sokurov's term, for both Lenin and the viewer.[47] Death saturates the screen: as Krupskaia reads aloud to Lenin a description of the death throes of Marx, the cognitive limits of the nonbeliever are revealed in his sharp interrogation of her, the conundrum of secular consciousness, struggling to think beyond itself: "So, you intend to live after me? How do you imagine that life?" ("Vy chto, sobiraetes' zhit' posle menia? Kak vy predstavliaete sebe etu zhizn'?"). Sokurov's visual and aural reduction of Lenin, with cattle mooing in a fashion eerily similar to Lenin's sclerotic bellows, displays a pitiless quality worthy of Lenin himself. "The difference between animals and humans," as Sokurov ("The Solitary Voice" 75) has insisted on more than one occasion, "is that dogs don't realize they are mortal. After death, a human starts his second life in the remembrance of those who have lost him."

There is no more complex topic for contemporary Russian cinema than Lenin.[48] Unlike the image of Stalin, who was repeatedly the critical subject of film during the *perestroika* period,[49] Lenin's image was comparatively untouched in cinema. "Lenin in the form of a character," suggests Aronson ("Giperdokument" 173–74), "is more than just a theme. It is a difficult complex of social neuroses that cannot so easily be neutralized by political equanimity or a disinterested viewpoint." The classic Lenin films still remembered today share the big-concept Lenin of a typical Mosfil'm production from the mid-Soviet period.[50] Lenfil'm's *Taurus* responded to this cultural myth as, in Matizen's formulation, "an artistic answer of the former [dynastic] capital to the current capital [Moscow], which had had the exclusive right to do Lenin films" (*Novye Izvestiia*, February 28, 2001). *Taurus* therefore signaled a shift to a new stage of Leniniana: if the first stage (arguably 1924–87) was marked with varying styles of ritualistic adoration, and the second stage (from roughly 1987 onward) with the irreverence of the anecdote,[51] then this third stage, marked by a mixture of grotesque irony and detached contemplation, was the first serious treatment of this figure in the post-Soviet period. It broke new ground in a fashion different from Sokurov's subsequent representation of Hirohito, yet both cinematic renderings were produced in a context of visual prohibition that bordered on the cultic.

A similar sequence in *Taurus* and *Sun* underscores their parallel structures: Lenin's necro-dream of his mother and Hirohito's necro-dream of U.S. bombers as sinister, flying specimens from his own ichthyological research. But this manifest homology—death dream (*Taurus*) and death dream (*Sun*)—is offset by their respective endings. In *Taurus* the great leader, having long disavowed God, faces mortality toward the end of life. In *Sun* the great leader, disavowing his own Godhood, faces mortality as a new life. Hirohito's final words are spoken to his wife with characteristic minimalism: "We are free. . . . Now I am not god. I have relinquished that fate" ("My svobodny. . . . Teper' ia ne bog. Ia otkazalsia ot etoi uchasti").[52] This deliberate asymmetry is the deeper point of comparison between the cultic dimensions of these two films.

In a sequence that anticipates Hirohito's mortal transfiguration he recites a poem written by his grandfather, the 122nd Emperor Meiji, on the eve of the Russo-Japanese War: "The ocean to the north and south, / to the west and east / heaves with waves. / Our people await a time / when the storm will subside."[53] The recitation signals Hirohito's search for a political solution, but not at any price. By the film's end he has finished his own poem, now about death, which he sends to his son: "In winter, the snow resembles / the *sakura* in March; / indifferent time wipes away / both one and the other." This poetic dyad—the grandfather's poem of imperial war and the grandson's poem of inevitable death—is reproduced on a larger scale as Sokurov's own film, in which the imperiled empire, the inevitability of death, and the artistic text are inescapably intertwined.[54]

The film's muted composition—the colors, the cloistered, shuttered, sunless lighting of the mise-en-scène—allows for the climax to occur in a similarly muted fashion: the Sun tilts his head impossibly close to MacArthur so as to light his first cigar. No longer Sun and earthly mortal, they are transformed by Sokurov into two men smoking. In this film where the sun had been absent throughout, the moon finally appears, integrating Hirohito into the natural order, in the upper-right corner of the frame as Hirohito reaches the decision to repudiate his divinity.

At stake in these films is one of Sokurov's core questions: How does culture properly mediate our place in the world, including our own mortality, life's sovereign boundary? Sokurov's answer involves a delicate negotiation between secular overreach and cultural value, an autoreferential solution, as Jameson ("History and Elegy" 7) would put it. Emblematically, Sokurov's cultural text mediates our place in the world, including our mortality, by its musings on the secular hubris of three political figures: Hitler's desired victory over death, Lenin's final dictatorship of the proletariat, and Hirohito's rule as immortal Sun God.

The *Ark* Itself

An odd fact is that Sokurov's birthplace in Podorvikha was eliminated through controlled flooding ("Aleksandr Nikolaevich Sokurov" 41). In the world of vulgar sociological criticism, Sokurov's *Russian Ark* might be seen as a response to that social fact. On a larger scale, however, Sokurov's film is concerned with the stubborn survival of cultural value, not its submersion in the waters of political tumult. Both technologically and ideationally this survival takes the form in *Russian Ark* of the filmmaker's re-seizure of the Winter Palace. I have in mind a comparison neither with the historical 1917 nor with Sergei Eisenstein's *October*, about which much has already been written (e.g., Drubek-Meyer; Kujundzic), but instead with a related cultural phenomenon: the reenactments of the Winter Palace seizure.

Most ambitiously, the Soviet playwright and director Nikolai Evreinov (1879–1953) staged a grandiose storming for the three-year anniversary of the October Revolution in November 1920, a variant of political reenactments that can be traced from the seizure of the Bastille.[55] Evreinov's event, with eight thousand participants, a live orchestra of five hundred musicians, and an estimated audience, sadly reduced in numbers due to inclement weather, of 100,000 spectators, one-fourth the population of Petrograd at that time, was an extraordinary cultural and technical feat employing so many spotlights that Petrograd electricity had to be shut off in several sections of the city during the event (Taylor 9; von Geldern 199–207).

Sokurov's effort, staged eighty years later and a decade after the collapse of Marxism-Leninism, engaged a cast and crew of 4,500 participants, including 867 professional actors, three live orchestras, and a thousand extras, requiring ten buses for transportation. Fifteen trucks were needed to transport the props. The 250-member lighting crew worked for twenty-four hours to set the lights in thirty-six halls; fifty makeup artists and sixty-five costume designers meticulously prepared the cast so that the high-definition video would not pick up any flaws in their uniforms and ball gowns. Like Evreinov, Sokurov included historical figures as well as actual persons historically associated with the Winter Palace.[56]

Evreinov's 1920 enactment was crowned by "the new sound of the *Internationale* as sung by the forty-thousand-member chorus" (Rudnitsky 44). Sokurov's musical apex was the Mariinskii Theatre Orchestra, conducted by Valerii Gergiev, who had flown in from New York on the eve of the shooting. In place of Evreinov's Military Revolutionary Committee, with its rifles, machine guns, and bayonets, Sokurov choreographed an imperial cotillion, strongly suggestive of the Romanov tercentennial ball of 1913, the last grand event of the dynasty before world war, revolution, civil war, and the onset of socialism.[57] Not since 1913 had the Russian elite danced on the parquet of the St. Nikolai Hall; not since then had the fireplaces burned logs or Christmas trees decorated the hallways. The return of the aristocracy to the Winter Palace was of course symbolic: the extras were no more aristocrats than Evreinov's extras were Bolsheviks, but the celebration had an important symbolic function in reclaiming that space for a post-Soviet consciousness that stressed historical continuity over rupture, empire over federation, elite culture over mass culture, even if oxymoronically recorded in the mass medium of Sokurov's auteur cinema.

One cannot argue that Sokurov had Evreinov in mind, but the seizure was a shared ritual in which the accumulated cultural mythology passed at critical moments through the all-consuming machine of the imperial palace. It is an otherwise superficial comment that the real protagonist of the film is the Hermitage itself. This remark takes on greater nuance when we ask: Why do the Stranger and Time Traveler hurry from room to room? What compulsion motivates the motion forward? The answer is unclear; something is missing. In fact, it is the structure of the Hermitage itself that draws us ahead from room to room. Its enfilade sucks the camera, the actors, and the viewers forward, but not forward historically: we reencounter Catherine II, for example, *after* the 1943 Siege of Leningrad; we move from the anachronistic encounter of three twentieth-century Hermitage directors (Iosif Orbeli, Boris and Mikhail Piotrovskii) *back* to a nineteenth-century military exercise, then onward to the early twentieth-century Romanov family. We are architecturally drawn forward according to the museum's physical structure, toward its own event in the St. Nikolai Hall, the crowning moment in the Winter Palace's autobiography. The act of filming is the building's movement forward to the past, from the dismal year 1943 onward to the bright 1913, to a time when Russia might recapture the attention of Sokurov's ("In One Breath") chosen audience—in his carefully chosen word order, the "cultured public in *Europe and Russia*" (emphasis mine).[58]

FIGURE 6.3. Sokurov. *Russian Ark.* "We battled Napoleon, not the Empire style."

Accordingly, the soundtrack—original music by the contemporary St. Petersburg composer Sergei Evtushenko and nonoriginal music by Glinka, Purcell, Tchaikovsky, and Telemann—attempts an integration of imperial European with Europhile Russian culture similar to its project in the visual arts: work by Russian composers is interedited with works by Purcell and Telemann and performed by the Mariinskii Theatre Orchestra, a cinematic antidote to Europe's indifference and arrogance toward its maligned and neglected kin.[59] Still, in Sokurov's rendering this Russo-European reentanglement has its darker side: as the French Stranger dances with Pushkin's wife, Natal'ia Goncharova, one might recall another Frenchman's flirtation and duel, which led to Pushkin's murder by Georges-Charles de Heekeren d'Anthès.

Russian Ark is not, therefore, an introductory tour of the Hermitage, but the highly selective passage of the Hermitage through its European self.[60] This architectural flow explains the otherwise weakly plotted narrative, its vulnerability to dismissal as a museum travelogue, its underdeveloped characters. Its effete cast retains a lifeless, wax museum quality; they are avatars in a retro video game navigating corridors and hallways, encountering historical figures but, more important, viewing priceless art. Indeed, architecture is only one element in Sokurov's tribute to a range of arts that preceded cinema and to which his cinema pays homage. Apart from the many paintings, the film inventories Catherine II's theater, the poet Pushkin, the playful ballet of the former Kirov dancer Alla Osipenko, the appreciative caresses of the blind sculptress Tamara Kurenkova, and finally Valerii Gergiev's symphonic conducting, a pantheon of the imperial arts, in which Sokurov's cinema now aspires to take its place.[61]

The film's chilly emotional tenor, its displacement of the human in favor of the material, supports the flow of architectural space. The enfilade of rooms permits the viewer to identify neither with the fey Stranger—the bearer of Europe's indifference and arrogance, of which Sokurov has spoken in interviews—nor with the Time Traveler, invisible and remote, restricting himself largely to ironic reiterations of the Stranger's judgments.[62] Both are otherworldly beings. The Stranger has been compellingly described as vampiric, and the Time Traveler has an equally spectral stature, as if the two were matched dark and light beyond-the-grave visitations.[63] The blind sculptress, moreover, is "an angel." Her intimate, tactile knowledge of the Hermitage holdings, her ability to read its allegories (Harte 54)—the partridge means X, the apples mean Y—holds out to us an object lesson: though we ourselves be spiritually blind, we are yet capable, caressing Sokurov's digital recording as she does the statue, of analogous devotion to cultural value that would heighten our inner powers of vision, narrowing the gap between our mortal existence and the immortality that the imperial museum may reveal but only religion fulfills.[64]

The film's architectural tunnel, within which past and future are visually available, sets up a kind of retrospective futurism, a linkage of imperial nostalgia with the high-tech expertise of a Sony HDW-F900, symptomatic of a larger neotraditionalism in Sokurov's work.[65] As the director had suggested several years earlier in his interview with Edwin Carels:

> I consider myself first and foremost someone who is very much bound by tradition. This is what I deliberately want in every film, to connect with tradition. So please do not call me an avant-gardist. The avant-garde wants to ignore tradition as much as possible. . . . The evocation of a certain continuity is perhaps the only intellectually constructed element in my work. . . . But tradition, that is the most important thing. (Sokurov, "The Solitary Voice" 73)[66]

This "evocation of a certain continuity" finds its central articulation in the Time Traveler, the role Sokurov (a self-described "traditional person"; "Tvorcheskii alfavit" 74) notably reserved for himself.

A major task of this neotraditional video maze is to make visible the connections not simply between, for example, Catherine II and her acquired oil paintings, but more globally between, say, Peter I and Rembrandt in a seamless visual narrative—in Sokurov's terms, a single breath (*v odnom dykhanii*).[67] This "one breath" manages to reduce the Bolsheviks to nil: they pass by the camera as an unrecognizable, shaded blur. Sokurov could have eliminated altogether their seizure of the Winter Palace, yet he comments instead on their historical significance by his allocation of screen time. This directorial decision performs a curious inversion: history is subject to montage, but the film is not.[68]

It is surely true, as Harte (44) has suggested, that "this Russian vessel of world art will help ensure the survival of the country's own cultural values," yet it is worth asking: *Which* cultural values? This is not a wooden Russia, nor need it be, but rather a gilt and marble Russia that survives the Soviet deluge in Sokurov's cinema. What is noteworthy for our purposes here is not the fact of survival, but the structure and conditions of survival in the specifically imperial refuge.

In the final sequence, "Farewell, Europe," we encounter Sokurov's most sensitively rendered paradox: bidding adieu, the film reestablishes its claim to Europe.[69] Sokurov's film sets the conditions for the waters to subside in the very act of its own production: an integrated European production crew, multilingual technicians, international soundtrack and technology, and global marketing, distribution, and exhibition. Sokurov's final scene and the leave-taking—from the tercentennial ball, but more important from early twentieth-century Europe—is the clarifying moment toward which the film has been moving for the previous eighty minutes. The ark with its precious cargo, adrift under conditions of early twentieth-century catastrophe, is reunited with Europe through the fact of the film's production.

Church-Military-Museum

In Sokurov's later work the triangular cluster of death, empire, and culture finds more explicit expression in three specific institutions: the church, the military, and the museum. These three are the stopping points, for example, in Sokurov's *Elegy of a Voyage*, an oneiric memory trip whose narrative has little function other than—in a fashion similar to *Russian Ark*—to convey its own narrative voice westward. The itinerary includes the St. Mariia Monastery at Valdai, the customs crossing at the Russo-Finnish border, and eventually Rotterdam's Boijmans van Beuningen Museum, a final visit that occasions a lengthy disquisition on art akin to that in both *Hubert Robert* and *Russian Ark*.

These three institutions—the church as keeper of immortality, the border guard as keeper of the polity, the museum as keeper of high culture—are held in a studied alignment that is affirmed by the ritual practices of the film's production. If this line of argumentation is turned backward to earlier films, new connections link the religious tenor to military and political life: Why would *Spiritual Voices* name a film about the military border patrol at the Tadzhik-Afghan frontier? Why would *Confession* be a film about a naval patrol ship?[70] Why would *Evening Sacrifice*—the Orthodox vespers' canticle of repentance ("Let my prayer arise in Thy sight as incense. / And let my hands uplifted be an evening sacrifice"; Psalm 141:2)—turn out to be a film on the Soviet May Day demonstrations?

In *Hubert Robert: A Fortunate Life*, Sokurov's interest in the artist's work— "Robert des ruines," as the painter was called because of his preference for ruins—reveals an affinity with Robert's declaratively commemorative intent as artist and Keeper of the King's Pictures, Keeper of the Museum, who fell precipitously with the end of the Ancien Régime.[71] Sokurov's Robert, a painter of the fallen empire, produced works of immortal architectural decrepitude that count among the Hermitage Museum's prized holdings.[72] Sokurov reminds us at the end of *Elegy of a Voyage* that historical time moves irrevocably forward, that these holdings are our only constant link with life itself: "The sun has changed position. There is no going back. But the canvas is still warm."

Atheism-Colonialism-Cinema: The Modernist Crisis

Japan is in no way an Asiatic country. It is an eastern Great Britain.
                              —Aleksandr Sokurov, "Nastoiashchee" (2005)

I can well understand the feelings of a man, to a large extent an atheist,
destroyed by the Modern style at the beginning of the century: it was that
[Modern style] by which Chekhov was destroyed.

—Aleksandr Sokurov, "Glavnym" (1994)

The early twentieth century saw the rise of cinema, a medium that emerged
within the practices of modernism, the military possibility of total war, and
the colonial expansionism of Europe. "Filmmaking was unlucky," Sokurov
("Tvorcheskii alfavit" 84) remarks, "that it was born in the epoch of modernism,"
a time that "pushed Europe toward world war, toward a particular existence of
community," a time whose impact on such writers as Chekhov, Sokurov suggests, was only deleterious.

Elsewhere Sokurov ("The Solitary Voice" 73) gestures at the connection he
sees between modernism and early twentieth-century imperial grandeur:

> Modernism gave birth to the avant-garde and to the new historical
> concept of the "world war"; modernism emerged as a form of pride
> within one culture in relation to others. Europe as distinct from Asia,
> for example. Because Europe considered itself the better civilization,
> it was unable to understand the essentials of the other. . . . The de-
> sign and costumes of orientalism are all expressions of a grandiose
> lack of understanding. . . . The first signs of this new, distorted rela-
> tionship were to be found in the culturally-historically determined
> style of modernism.[73]

The "grandiose lack of understanding" by an Orientalizing Europe is most
radically staged in *Mournful Unconcern*, with its quaint kimonos and African
documentary footage, the function of which is not to provide some universal
humanity but to present practices that are parallel, yet fatally unrecognizable as
such through European eyes: the dances and song, the self-ornamentation and
music making. A similar Orientalizing distance is maintained by the camera
in *Days of the Eclipse*, where local Turkmen initially appear, in Jameson's (*Geopolitical* 93) stark description, "as sick and feeble as the survivors of Auschwitz,
grinning toothless at the apparatus, sitting against the mud walls in emaciated
inanition, a population of in-bred freaks and mutants."

It is in an entirely different register that Sokurov figures Japan in the
three Japanese stories and in *Sun*, where his residual Orientalism is infused
instead with adoration. Japan is, as the epigraph suggests, "in no way an Asiatic
country," but rather "an eastern Great Britain" (Sokurov, "Nastoiashchee" 97).
Indeed, in Sokurov's circumlocutory system, Japan is an alternative Russia, a
culture that is by extrapolation also "in no way an Asiatic country," but, incon-
stantly and imaginatively, "an eastern Great Britain." Sokurov's turn to Japan
as a compatible stand-in for Russia brings into clearer focus certain affinities

of the two cultures in Sokurov's work, where they are perpetually infused with condescension, yet enthralled by their own colonial ambitions.

Cinema Is Not Necessary

There are no leaders. In those situations when it is hard from their standpoint for people . . . then a leader is thought up, a psychological feeling . . . that is transferred from the people to a concrete and utterly mortal person.

—Aleksandr Sokurov, "*Moloch*: Interview with
Alexander Sokurov" (1999)

Cinema is not necessary. Painting is necessary; music is necessary; literature is necessary; but cinema is not necessary.

—Aleksandr Sokurov, "*Moloch*: Interview with
Alexander Sokurov" (1999)

Sokurov's negations—the nonexistence of leaders and the nonnecessity of cinema—are related phenomena. They point first of all to Sokurov's penchant for a rhetoric of negation. There is, however, potentially more than this, since these demotions are made not just by anyone, but by someone who is a leader in cinema. We can of course prove nothing, but, taken together, his demotions suggest a potential demiurgic connection between the political leader and the cinema director.

With an oddly insistent tone, Sokurov ("Tvorcheskii alfavit" 82) has often contended that cinema has little to offer elite culture: "Cinema is derivative" ("Kino vtorichno"). For Sokurov, painting, music, and literature are a source of great cinematic inspiration and guidance.[74] His television program *Island of Sokurov* (1998–99) attempted, among other things, to locate the proper place for the "tenth muse" in Russia's elite cultural traditions and to make sense of the way it too could produce social and, above all, ethical meaning. His focus on the relationship between cultural value and political power—between the inspired, immortal text and the profane system within which the text is produced—finds that relationship to be a deeply asymmetrical one. The cultural text, perpetually embedded in a system of power that both sustains and contaminates it, provides a glimpse into a larger, transcendent land-after-life, to which the political world is blind, even hostile. In *Mournful Unconcern* the piano may at first obediently comply with public commands to play Chopin's Waltz in C sharp minor and Rachmaninov's Prelude for piano and orchestra in C sharp, but it soon breaks down and cannot get through Mendelssohn's *Spinning Song*. So culture more broadly, if attuned to social command, falters in its primary task.

It is this inequity between a supererogatory political power and an equally magnificent but spiritually transcendent culture that prompts two of

Sokurov's core questions: How does the artistic text answer for the conditions of its production? Is there some way to undo culture's perpetual complicity, to distinguish Purcell, Telemann, Glinka, Tchaikovsky—or, more important, contemporary artists (and by extension, Aleksandr Sokurov)—from the systems that produced and sustained them? These questions take on a particularly urgent tone for Sokurov with regard to cinema. "Filmmaking is a purely Russian business," he writes, "the same as automobile-making for Americans. Russian cinema has a fundamental and highly artistic legacy that no other people have. . . . Cinema will always thrive in Russia" (quoted in Avdeyeva).[75]

Cinema, then, is for Sokurov a way for Russian culture to renegotiate a place in the world (that is to say, vis-à-vis Europe) that is reducible to neither imitation nor exceptionalism, reintegrating itself into a European culture where its imperial heritage had long been inadequately recognized. As a young art, however, cinema in Sokurov's understanding has no choice but to counterpose itself to the historical weight of the European cultural tradition.

If for Sokurov there are no political leaders, but merely a demotic transfer, rendering collective power to an utterly mortal person, then his unfinished tetralogy sets out to reverse this operation: to revert Hitler, Lenin, and Hirohito to their ordinary status. In so doing Sokurov raises a related and more awkward question: What can be said, by contrast or similarity, of the film director as demiurge? Is his artistic power also the result of a similar transfer (as Sokurov says of the politician, "from the people to a concrete and utterly mortal person"), or is it made of some other substance, some adamant different from political power?

Sokurov's films themselves, it must be argued, enact that difference. The difference between the political leader and the artist is signaled in a number of ways, but the most evident symptom is the political leader who inexplicably "does not know": Hitler "does not know" about Auschwitz; Lenin "does not know" who Stalin is; Hirohito "did not know" about Pearl Harbor. One may always, of course, be distracted by the historical evidence, but historical evidence is not the matter at hand.[76] Instead, the recurrence of the political leader who "does not know" points by contrast to the film director who *does* know. What the director knows is, first, the leader's utter ordinariness and, second, the blindness of the demotic transfer that produces such overweening political power. This is where "honorable cinema," to use Sokurov's term, would overcome its otherwise unnecessary status, tracing the supererogatory acquisitiveness of its political counterpart and distinguishing the artistic leader from the political one.

In this regard several critics have suggested a harsher interpretation of Sokurov's portraits of political leaders. "In [his] heightened interest in Führers of various kinds," suggests the poet Lev Rubinshtein, "I perceive [Sokurov's] own Führer tendencies" (quoted in Gladil'shchikov et al. 65). The journalist Iurii Gladil'shchikov has made a similar comment with regard to Sokurov

as Sun-God.[77] And yet to ascribe Sokurov's history of ambitious and senten-
tious contrarianism to an affinity for Hitler or Hirohito is to misassign it. It is
deeply a matter of interpretation, of course, but let me choose two moments
in Sokurov's comments to argue for a different model, less in his defense than
in pursuit of this line of thought. "When an artistic image appears," Sokurov ("*Moloch*: Interview with Alexander Sokurov") insists in his commentary
to *Moloch*, "it is impossible to explain its appearance by analytic means. It may
only be explained by a *collective process*" (emphasis mine). He continues: "It an-
noys the audience, as they believe cinema is created *for the viewer*" (emphasis
in the original).

Paradoxically committed to collectivism yet resistant to a cinema "created
for the viewer," Sokurov uncannily reproduces the conditions in which his
cinema was forged, a culture that exuded abstract enthusiasm for *narodnost'*
without answerability to the *narod*. His insistence on a complete—even, some
would argue, capricious—autonomy over the immured cultural artifact as a
collectively inspired yet insular totality has less to do with the symptoms of
Hitler or the Sun God than with the symptoms of the late Soviet period—with
its adoration for high culture, its imperial ambitions, its museum-like posthis-
tory, its elegiac love of the strong state—in which Sokurov's own conflicts were
fought out. Sokurov's insistence on the radically independent utterance, an-
swerable only to itself, reveals traces of his own ensnared dependency of the
late Soviet years. As his own work suggests, he is more closely aligned with
such wounded figures as Solzhenitsyn, with whom he has conducted extensive
dialogues (*Conversations with Solzhenitsyn*), than to Hitler, Hirohito, or Lenin.

"Sokurov was the first in our cinema to formulate the idea of imperial collapse and the idea of the Other," writes Mikhail Trofimenkov ("Nigde i vsegda"
130), "but also the apocalyptical mood that took hold of the large part of the
intelligentsia in those years." Such associative linkages, particularly with the extravagant image of Babylonian collapse, have been echoed by a number of other
scholars (e.g., Iampol'skii, "Kovcheg" 111; Shilova, "Posle posmotra"). The idea of
the empire, with its overweening assimilations of value; the unreflective popular
transfer of power to an ordinary mortal as a symptom of collective crisis; the
moral failure of culture to extricate itself from the structures of political expedi-
ency; and the yearning for a museum-stasis outside of history and indistinguishable from "death, the banal leveler" (Sokurov, "Death" 64)—these elements form
the basis for Sokurov's creative economy: death, empire, culture, contained in a
film-artifact that would aspire at the same time to point a way out.

Most emblematically in *Moloch, Taurus,* and *Sun* a single day, homologous
to a human life, traces how a mortal has wielded this enormous power, insen-
sate to that transcendent invisible empire beyond his perceptual capacities, the
empire of his own immortality. In Sokurov's vision our refusal to contend with
death prevents us, in Jameson's (*Geopolitcal* 112) memorable phrasing, from successfully "getting the corpse out of the apartment." Sokurov's ("Interview" 18)

cinema offers itself as an opportunity to practice just that: "Life in film is another life." Much of his cinema seeks to replicate the sanctuary of death beyond the passage of historical time. His job—through that most visually dynamic medium available to us—is to make that invisible and immortal seen, holding up the lens that would refract some small amount of light in such a way, as in a séance, that we may dimly see the figures from the other side.

FILMOGRAPHY

Note: Documentaries are marked with an asterisk.

*Call Sign R1NN (Pozyvnye R1NN). Television documentary. 1975.

*The Most Earthly Cares (Samye zemnye zaboty). Television documentary. 1975.

*The Summer of Mariia Voinova (Leto Marii Voinovoi). Television documentary. 1975.

*The Automobile Gains Reliability (Avtomobil' nabiraet nadezhnost'). 1977.

The Lonely Human Voice (Odinokii golos cheloveka). 1978, released 1987.

*Mariia: Peasant Elegy (Mariia: Krestianskaia elegiia). 1978, released 1988.

*Sonata for Hitler (Sonata dlia Gitlera). Short. 1979, released 1989.

Demoted (Razzhalovannyi). Short. 1980.

*Dmitrii Shostakovich: Viola Sonata (Dmitrii Shostakovich: Al'tovaia sonata). Codirected with Semen Aranovich. 1981, released 1986.

*And Nothing More (originally titled Allies; I nichego bol'she). 1982, released 1987.

Mournful Unconcern (Anaesthesia Psychica Dolorosa) (Skorbnoe beschuvstvie [Anaesthesia Psychica Dolorosa]). 1983, released 1987.

*Evening Sacrifice (Zhertva vecherniaia). Short. 1984, released 1987.

*Patience Labor (also known as Patterns on the Ice; Terpenie trud). Short. 1985, released 1987.

*Elegy (Elegiia). Short. 1985, released 1986.

*Moscow Elegy (Moskovskaia elegiia). 1986, released 1988.

Empire Style (Ampir). Short. 1987.

Days of the Eclipse (Dni zatmeniia). 1988.

*Petersburg Elegy (Peterburgskaia elegiia). Short. 1989.

Save and Protect. (Spasi i sokhrani). 1989.

*Soviet Elegy (Sovetskaia elegiia). 1989.

*To the Events in Transcaucasia (K sobytiiam v Zakavkaz'e). Short. 1990.

Second Circle (Krug vtoroi). 1990.

*Leningrad Retrospective (1957–1990) (Leningradskaia retrospektiva [1957–1990]). 1990.

*A Simple Elegy (Prostaia elegiia). Short. 1990.

*An Example of Intonation (Primer intonatsii). Short. 1991.

Stone (Kamen'). 1992.

*Elegy from Russia (Elegiia iz Rossii). 1992.

Whispering Pages: From Themes of 19th Century Russian Prose (Tikhie stranitsy: Po motivam russkoi prozy XIX veka). 1993.

*Spiritual Voices (Dukhovnye golosa). Television documentary. 1995.

*Soldier's Dream (Soldatskii son). Short. Excerpt of Spiritual Voices. Television documentary. 1995.

*Eastern Elegy (Vostochnaia elegiia). Short. 1996.

*Hubert Robert: A Fortunate Life (Rober: Schastlivaia zhizn'). Two versions (26 min. and 12 min.). Short. 1996.

Mother and Son (Mat' i syn). 1997.

*Petersburg Diary: Inaugurating the Dostoevskii Monument (Peterburgskii dnevnik: Otkrytie pamiatnika Dostoevskomu). Short. Television documentary. 1997.

*A Humble Life (Smirennaia zhizn'). 1997.

*Petersburg Diary: The Kozintsev Apartment (Peterburgskii dnevnik: Kvartira Kozintseva). Television documentary. Short. 1998.

*The Knot: Conversations with Solzhenitsyn (Uzel: Besedy s Solzhenitsynym). 1999.

*Confession (Povinnost'). Television documentary. 1997.

Moloch (Molokh). 1999.

*dolce . . . (dol'che . . .). 2000.

Taurus (Telets). 2000.

*Elegy of a Voyage (Elegiia dorogi). Short. 2001.

Russian Ark (Russkii kovcheg). 2002.

Father and Son (Otets i syn). 2003.

*Petersburg Diary: Mozart. Requiem (Peterburgskii dnevnik: Motsart. Rekviem). 2004.

Sun (Solntse). 2005.

*Elegy of Life: Rostropovich. Vishnevskaia (Elegiia zhizni: Rostropovich. Vishnevskaia). 2007.

Aleksandra. 2007.

7 ✳

Aleksei German: Forensics
in the Dynastic Capital

Introduction: Seeing Bad Things

My father [Iurii German] was more naïve than I am. He had a harder time
seeing bad things.

—Aleksei German, "Kino" (1986)

A decent account of Aleksei German's work is intertwined with the biography
of his father, Iurii German. I therefore ask for the reader's patience with this
short detour. One of the major works devoted to the director's films is, after all,
Lipkov's *German, Son of German* (*German, syn Germana*). It is less that Aleksei
German's father was an important man, though he was a well-known writer of
his generation, than that the son's cinema concerns a way of thinking about the
Soviet past, for which the father is a touchstone.

Born in 1910, Iurii German was a grown man in his late twenties during
the Purge years of 1937–38.[1] In 1953, the year Stalin died, Iurii was forty-
three; his son was not yet fifteen. Among the many visitors to the Germans'
home were former gulag prisoners, newly released after 1953 and 1956. The
father, author of quasi-journalistic police and military stories of the Stalin
era, on which some of the son's scripts are based, had an intimate knowledge of "bad things," as the filmmaker son calls them, and must therefore

185

have had a good deal of practice *not seeing* them in the Soviet 1930s and 1940s.

The son seems to suggest that he himself, by contrast, had the luxury of greater scrutiny and the skepticism of a later, more placid age. Bad things could be seen by the filmmaker son without that element, whatever it was that had protected or hindered his father's sight. What was that something? Idealism? Ideology? I would like to bracket this question for the moment, if only to avoid an imprecise and premature answer.

In Aleksei German's *Lapshin* and *Khrustalev* the maturing child protagonist is witness to conversations and events the meaning of which becomes evident over decades (original titles and production information provided at the end of the chapter). Neither the child nor the adults seem to understand the magnitude of their contemporary historical moment: in *Lapshin* it is the eve of the Purges; in *Khrustalev* it is the death of Stalin. A similar ignorance, the filmmaker suggests, can be traced in his earlier *Trial*: "One could say that the *protagonist's ignorance* is primary for us" (German, "Kino" 153, emphasis mine). At issue is not precisely a lack of information, though it is also this, but rather a manner of processing information that the passage of time might provide. German's cinema is concerned with the nature of that process: how the present moment is perpetually in excess of our capacity to understand its content.

In its critical reception German's cinema has gone through an oddly analogous accumulation of meaning. Though critical hindsight is operative for any cultural text, it holds true with particular intensity for German's cinema. Most obviously at the level of plot we have a much firmer sense of the films' intentions than we could have had at the moment of their premiere. As the massive screening exodus at the 1998 Cannes International Film Festival (and the ensuing press reviews) painfully suggests, the audience saw *Khrustalev* in a very different fashion at that time than we see the film today. *Khrustalev* remains, as Viktor Matizen ("*Khrustalev*" 21) put it, a film "threatened neither by oblivion nor by understanding," and yet the Cannes critics were as lucky as they were undiscerning: they saw German's work naïvely, ignorantly, in a fashion no longer available to us.[2]

German's contribution is a very specific one: he narrates stories collected by those who *became* the Soviet intelligentsia to an audience who, however unintentionally, *ceased to be* the Soviet intelligentsia. Set at mid-twentieth century—the 1940s (*Trial* and *Twenty Days*), the 1930s (*Lapshin*), the early 1950s and 1960s (*Khrustalev*)—German's films draw on the memories of one generation back, the generation of such family friends as the poet Nikolai Zabolotskii (1903–58), the film director Iosif Kheifits (1905–95), the playwright Evgenii Shvarts (1896–1958),[3] the writer Il'ia Il'f (1897–1937), and the film and theater director Grigorii Kozintsev (1905–73; German, "Kino" 133–35; Lipkov, "Proverka" 224). This was the generation that expended its talents on building a wholly Soviet intelligentsia and whose children lived to see its demise.

For the highly educated, metropolitan children of this first Soviet generation, the future, as conceived by their fathers, gradually became a thing of the past, a weakened operative concept. This shift was not therefore a matter of depression, indifference, or loss of hope. Rather, the future ceased to be a point of primary orientation, a discursive resource for authority or for conjuring up a lifestyle in the present tense. "We'll clear the land of scum and plant an orchard, and still have time to wander in that orchard," announces our beleaguered Lapshin as he drives his motorcycle through the relentlessly bleak and treeless winter landscape, a season typical of German's films. Lapshin himself would never be mistaken for the intelligentsia, but his representation—the ritual of his inscription and reinscription in the short stories, film, and contemporary criticism and scholarship—serves as a measure by which these two generations made sense of their relationship both to the future Lapshin had seen (as archaic as it was unshakeable) and also to the Soviet future more broadly as a wildly enthusiastic simulacrum. That Soviet future is recaptured by German as an homage *en arrière* to the verdancy, ignorance, and naïveté of the fathers.

If I therefore devote somewhat more space to the biographical section of this chapter than I have in other chapters, this is in part driven by an effort to contextualize the naïveté and ignorance no longer available to German's contemporary audience, for whom a grasp of the past is the only compensation. German's challenge to the medium of feature film—the very medium, after all, of Grigorii Aleksandrov's jolly and deceitful 1938 *Volga-Volga*—was to use it against itself, to convey a completely different set of memories, the forgotten life of the 1930s, to a cinema public who still associated the 1930s with the successes of *Volga-Volga*. As Tony Wood (103) puts it, "How are we to retell our history without disgracing our forefathers?"

As in previous chapters, my analysis here for the most part proceeds from an effort to see German's work as a single, common text with internal variations. There are a number of arguments for this approach; as Arkus ("German Aleksei" 252) points out, the films share a similar voice, "the voice of the narrator, who in all the films seems to be the same person," running through three of German's four single-authored films. At the same time a distinct divide exists between the two earlier films (*Trial* and *Twenty Days*) and the two later ones (*Lapshin* and *Khrustalev*) and will inform this analysis. In the two early films German's more typical devices are muted; in the later two his signature becomes more stylized, less concerned with convention, further individuated from what he has described as "plotted, actor's cinema" (quoted in Vail' 7). And although *Lapshin* and *Khrustalev* are different from each other in a number of obvious respects that will be clear in passing, their devices are closely linked in ways that might allow a description of one film's techniques to stand in for the other.[4]

Biographical Remarks: The Writer's Little Son

Aleksei German was born in Leningrad on July 20, 1938. During the war, his early childhood, he lived in Arkhangel'sk, where the family spent five years, then at Poliarnoe, the Northern Fleet's base near Murmansk, where wartime sailors would return from submarine operations on the White Sea (Lipkov, "Proverka" 203; Razguliaeva).[5] The family returned to Leningrad in 1945.

As a young man German ("Razrushenie" 154) intended to become a doctor, his mother's profession, but at his father's urging he turned to the theater and then to cinema. "I never wanted to be a cinema director," he reflected later. "I wanted to be a doctor. I experience terror in the face of this profession [of filmmaking]. I am always unhappy when I have to shoot. It's as if—every day—you had to drill teeth" (quoted in Gladil'shchikov, "Uzh polnoch' blizitsia . . ."). With some unwillingness (and the intervention in the admissions procedure by the poet Ol'ga Berggol'ts, his mother's friend), German went through the examination process and was admitted to the Leningrad State Institute of Theatre, Music and Cinema (LGITMiK) in 1955.

German has maintained that a critical factor in the formation of his unusual cinematic practice is the fact that he did *not* receive the standard professional education in cinema, which would normally have taken place at Moscow's All-Union State Institute for Cinematography (VGIK). Instead, at LGITMiK he joined the Directing Section, where he studied with Grigorii Kozintsev and Aleksandr Muzil'. His practical work included a student assistantship for Iosif Kheifits while the latter was filming *My Dear One (Dorogoi moi chelovek*; Lenfil'm, 1958). As German describes it, his principal job on the set was mouse handler: he was assigned to guard the mice that would crawl over the body of the actor Aleksei Batalov (Razguliaeva).

German's first independent theater production was Evgenii Shvarts's play *An Ordinary Miracle (Obyknovennoe chudo)*. It caught the eye of Georgii Tovstonogov, head of Leningrad's prestigious Bolshoi Drama Theatre (known by its initials BDT), and, after German's graduation from LGITMiK in 1960 (and a short stint at the Smolensk Drama Theatre), the encounter led to several years as Tovstonogov's assistant at the Leningrad BDT. Even as a "writer's little son" ("pisatel'skii synok"), as German ("Aleksei German" and elsewhere) puts it with characteristic self-deprecation, he found success at BDT by no means assured. "I bore a stigma of talentlessness," he recalls of that time, "that neither my high grades [at LGITMiK], nor *An Ordinary Miracle*, nor anything else could overcome" (quoted in Razguliaeva).

Leaving BDT in 1964 for the position of assistant director at Lenfil'm Studio (professionally, a step backward), German worked for a number of film productions, including Vladimir Vengerov's enormously successful *Workers' Settlement*

(*Rabochii poselok*; Lenfil'm, 1965). After Vengerov's film premiered German was much in demand: "At the studio I earned myself the reputation of 'outstanding assistant director,'" he quipped (quoted in Fomin, *"Polka"* 110). But he wanted to shoot his own work. Together with his father, then already ill with cancer, he wrote a script from his father's novella *Operation "Happy New Year,"* the original title of what was much later to become his first film, *Trial on the Road.*[6]

A brief addendum on German's father is necessary here. An author since 1931, closely associated with the journal *Young Guard* (*Molodaia gvardiia*), Iurii German first began writing for cinema in 1936. His fate was extremely unstable during much of his creative life. On the one hand, he was awarded a Stalin Prize recognizing his script for Grigorii Kozintsev's *Pirogov* (Lenfil'm, 1947), about the life of the surgeon anatomist. On the other hand, he was threatened with exclusion from the USSR Writers' Union and apparently came so close to being arrested for his story "Lieutenant Colonel from the Medical Service" ("Podpolkovnik meditsinskoi sluzhby") that he went to live for a time with the writer Konstantin Simonov (German, "Kino" 140, 143). An intimate part of the Leningrad intelligentsia, Iurii German's name figured periodically in government documents and newspaper articles from that era.[7] He was, in Gladil'shchikov's ("Uzh polnoch' blizitsia . . .") description, "a representative of . . . the high middle-class of the Stalin-Khrushchev empire," with access during his son's childhood to a chauffeur, a nanny, and a maid. Two of Aleksei German's scripts (*Trial* and *Lapshin*) were adaptations of his father's work, based on personal encounters. A third script (*Khrustalev*), although based initially on

FIGURE 7.1.   German. *Khrustalev, the Car!* "When Nero dies, my dear . . ."

Iosif Brodskii's autobiographical essay "In a Room and a Half" (1985), became also in some respects a portrait of German's father.[8]

Iurii German's illness precluded the completion of their screenplay, and Aleksei, unwilling to seek a substitute cowriter, turned instead to a different project altogether, codirecting *Seventh Satellite* with Grigorii Aronov.[9] German would consider Aronov to be the first director of *Seventh Satellite*.[10] "Some things I learned while working on that film," German recounts, "and some things I rejected. But already then it began to be clear to me that everything that is called the profession—montage, the storyboard, everything of which I had been so fearful—is not the profession, whereas that which *is* the profession definitely cannot be taught" (quoted in Lipkov, "Proverka" 204). With the completion of *Seventh Satellite* Aronov and German intended to co-shoot a second film based on Nina Kosterina's diary, which had appeared several years earlier in the literary journal *New World* (*Novyi mir*); failing to secure permission from Goskino, they went their separate ways.[11]

Iurii German died from cancer in 1967. The director Nikolai Rozantsev had asked to take over the task of producing a script from *Operation "Happy New Year"* as his own project. Blessedly for German's work, Rozantsev's screenplay fell through and German returned to the project, asking the scriptwriter Eduard Volodarskii to work with him on it (Fomin, *"Polka"* 110–11). Their resulting script was amplified by the stories of Aleksandr Nikiforov, a former partisan-participant in operations similar to those described by German's father; the core episode of the trial by road, for example, was taken from Nikiforov's account of partisan warfare.[12]

During these early years German's future wife, Svetlana Karmalita, whom he had met in 1968, was a graduate student, writing her thesis on German documentary theater of the 1960s, but she decided to leave academia and join her husband in Kalinin to work on *Trial*. She has been German's coresearcher and shooting partner ever since, as well as the scriptwriter for such war films as Rudol'f Fruntov's *There Lived a Brave Captain* (*Zhil otvazhnyi kapitan*; Mosfil'm, 1985) and Mikhail Nikitin's *My Battle Crew* (*Moi boevoi raschet*; Lenfil'm, 1987).[13]

After several adjustments to the 1969 script of *Operation "Happy New Year,"* Lenfil'm moved the film to the next administrative stage in January 1970. The worst was yet to come. Despite unflagging support from the Lenfil'm Studio director I. N. Kiselev, as well as from Konstantin Simonov,[14] Tovstonogov, Kheifits, the film director Sergei Gerasimov, and the partisan war hero Major-General Aleksandr Saburov, German encountered enormous difficulties in getting *Operation "Happy New Year"* approved by Goskino. The extensive documentation, protocol, and other details of this protracted struggle are available elsewhere.[15] The most vocal opposition, led by Boris Pavlenok, head of Goskino's Central Bureau for Feature Cinema, was successful, at least in the short term, in shelving the film.[16] "I pledge my honest word," Pavlenok is said to have remarked, "that while I am alive, that scum will not appear on the screen" (quoted in Lipkov, "Proverka" 208).

The film's topic was indeed a controversial one: the voluntary return in December 1941 from Nazi captivity of a Soviet POW seeking to redeem himself by serving in a partisan unit in the occupied northwest territories of the USSR during the winter of 1941–42. Such returnees were considered traitors. On August 16, 1941, Stalin had signed Order 270: Soviet soldiers who were taken prisoner rather than fighting to the death were considered guilty of treason and subject to imprisonment, if not execution (and the accompanying repression of their families). The enduring Soviet perception of returning POWs as traitors to the homeland ensured a chilly reception at Goskino for German's story line.

But the fact that its subject is controversial is not a satisfactory explanation for the film's difficulties. After all, the protagonists of Sergei Bondarchuk's war film *Fate of Man* (*Sud'ba cheloveka*; Mosfil'm, 1959) and Grigorii Chukhrai's war romance *Clear Skies* (*Chistoe nebo*; Mosfil'm, 1961) had also been Nazi war captives. As early as 1962 Fedor Poletaev, a Soviet POW who had escaped his Nazi captors to join the Oreste guerrilla brigade, was given a Hero of the Soviet Union award; streets were named after him in both Moscow and Riazan'. Sergei Smirnov's collection *Stories of Unknown Heroes* (*Rasskazy o neizvestnykh geroiakh*), published in 1964 and republished in 1973, addressed this theme.[17]

A more serious problem was the fact that German does not permit the viewer to believe that Lazarev was a wholly passive figure during the time of his captivity. As Youngblood (177) points out, German's protagonist, Lazarev, unlike the protagonists of the two films mentioned above, had "been fighting with the Germans and surrenders to the partisans wearing a German uniform." Moreover, German's film portrays the partisan brigade as well established in December 1941, whereas the official Soviet position insisted that such brigades came into being only gradually in response to Stalin's appeal of July 7, 1941.[18]

But principal among German's mistakes, and certainly more lethal than the returning POW, was the film's core conflict between the partisan commander Lokotkov (a Chapaev-like figure) and his political commissar, Petushkov, senior ranking yet subordinate within the partisan unit. As émigré partisan memoirs of the era confirm (Liddell-Hart 164–65), considerable friction often divided central military authorities from partisan brigades, especially in the early war days that German chooses:

> This spontaneous partisan movement was at first semi-autonomous with regard to the central Soviet authorities. At first Moscow's attempts to take over the leadership of the movement met with considerable resistance. The history of some partisan units tells us that many political commissars and officers sent out from Moscow were killed by the partisans when they tried to enforce the will of the centre. (Captain N. Galay quoted in Liddell-Hart 164)

The film's contradiction in military hierarchy—whereby the major from the center vies to subordinate the partisan commander in circumstances conditioned by the regular army's temporary retreat—comes to unmanageable crisis around the return of the POW, appropriately named Lazarev.

The contentious relationship between partisan commander and major was recast by German several times in an effort to appease Goskino, but its underlying problem could not be resolved. As Goskino saw it, the film's plot was fatally predicated on the Red Army retreat (Lipkov, "Proverka" 207). In Pavlenok's caustic words, "We have to congratulate Lenfil'm on a film about the people who lost the Great Fatherland War" (quoted in German, "Aleksei German" 205).

In the larger context of the film's production German's problems concerned the still narrow range of alternative views on the Great Fatherland War. German's challenge to the ideological status quo was very different from those of earlier, humanizing Thaw films, such as Grigorii Chukhrai's war drama *Ballad of a Soldier* (*Ballada o soldate*; Mosfil'm, 1959) or Mikhail Kalatozov's war romance *Cranes Are Flying* (*Letiat zhuravli*; Mosfil'm, 1957). With the exception of Andrei Tarkovskii's war drama *Ivan's Childhood* (*Ivanovo detstvo*; Mosfil'm, 1962), German's *Trial* was without allies. In the early 1970s the cinematic environment was such that the reigning measure of ideological probity, as German ("Aleksei German" 199) and others, including such cultural conservatives as Central Committee secretary Peter Demichev, have pointed out, was Iurii Ozerov's numbing epic, the eight-hour World War II film *Liberation* (*Osvobozhdenie*; DEFA and Mosfil'm, 1969). Such later iconoclastic war dramas as Larisa Shepit'ko's *Ascent* (*Voskhozhdenie*; Mosfil'm, 1976) and Elem Klimov's *Come and See* (*Idi i smotri*; Mosfil'm, 1985) were not yet in circulation. Pavlenok summed it up with characteristic bile: "Many war films make various mistakes. This one [German's film] is unique in having gathered together all the mistakes that are possible to make" (quoted in Lipkov, *German* 98).

Trial went through four major stages of revision, resubmission, and negotiation; late in the negotiations, German was struck from the film, which was then reassigned to the director Gennadii Kazanskii, until Lenfil'm Studio director Kiselev agitated successfully—contributing to his own peril—to have this assignment reversed.[19] In the end, however, Goskino director Aleksei Romanov signed the final order to shelve the film. Lenfil'm was forced to absorb the financial losses; the film's crew was required to forgo their bonuses (Lipkov, "Proverka" 209); and the film's negatives, positives, soundtrack, and all outtakes were to be returned to Gosfil'mofond (Fomin, "Polka" 132). Only in 1986, some fifteen years later, was *Operation "Happy New Year,"* now under the title *Trial on the Road,* finally released. Although the film is sometimes erroneously counted as one of the unshelved films of the Conflict Commission convened in the wake of the Fifth Congress of the Filmmakers' Union, it in fact appeared just prior to the events recounted in chapter 2. *Trial on the Road* was eventually awarded a USSR State Prize in 1988, by then the second of two major state prizes awarded German.[20]

In the early 1970s, however, German was adrift. *Trial* had been shelved and he had few prospects in cinema. Konstantin Simonov extended a hand, proposing that German shoot one of the older writer's stories. German had admired such novellas as *Panteleev* and *Levashov* but was drawn to Simonov's newly written *Twenty Days without War*, part of the author's quasi-autobiographical cycle *From Lopatin's Notes* (*Iz zapisok Lopatina*), set in part in 1942 wartime Tashkent, where strategic sectors of the defense industry had been located. German's attraction to the cycle was partly because of the long monologue of the aviator, Iura Stroganov (brilliantly performed by Aleksei Petrenko in German's film), which Simonov eventually cut from the novella (German, "Postizhenie dobra" 140).

Simonov's offer to collaborate was an attempt to protect German, to keep him in the profession, but the task was not an easy one.[21] Despite Simonov's prestigious name and ranking within the government hierarchy, the film once again encountered considerable resistance at Goskino, which held up release for a year. Eventually Goskino capitulated to pressure from German's formidable admirers, and the film premiered in 1976.[22]

In light of German's distribution problems it should be noted for clarity's sake that the order in which the cinema public—those outside immediate professional circles—came to know his work was therefore substantially different from the order of its production. The production order was *Trial*, *Twenty Days*, and *Lapshin*, but metropolitan audiences first knew German's work in 1976 from his putative "debut" with the literary senior statesman Konstantin Simonov. Then nothing by German appeared for nearly a decade, while *Trial* languished on the shelf. Long after German's "first" (in fact, second) work with Simonov, the director shot his father's well-known novella *Lapshin*, finally released after a two-and-a-half-year delay in 1984, and only then the "later" (though in fact his first) and more controversial *Trial* was released as a "third" film. Bull-headed and stubborn by his own description,[23] German had begun his cinematic career with his most provocative topic in *Trial on the Road* and only then was privileged enough to have been mentored through *Twenty Days* by Simonov, without whose subsequent appeal to Filipp Ermash at Goskino German would not have gained permission to begin work on *Lapshin* (German, "Postizhenie dobra" 143; Lipkov, "Proverka" 218).

The screenplay for *My Friend, Ivan Lapshin*, originally called *Head of Operations* (*Nachal'nik opergruppy*), was begun as far back as 1969, just after *Seventh Satellite* (Fomin, *Kino i vlast'* 219).[24] Shot in Astrakhan', the film is set in 1935 in the fictional provincial port town of Unchansk, where Lapshin heads up the Seventh Brigade of the militia, a transposition of Iurii German's original setting in Leningrad of 1936–37. Iurii German's original novella was based in part on stories told by the retired Leningrad police commissar Ivan Bodunov, another of the many family friends who had populated the German household. Although

Bodunov had managed to survive the Purges, his entire police team—including the figures named Okoshkin, Bychkov, and Pobuzhinskii in the film—had subsequently been arrested and shot in 1937–38 (German, "Kino" 148, 154), as had the film's writer Khanin, based on the translator Valentin Stenich.[25] Several episodes, such as the scene in which Khanin fishes newspaper out of Adashova's homemade soup, are based on the German family history (German, "Kino" 149).

German's shift of the film's time frame backward from 1937 to 1935 was one of several causative factors in the delayed release of *Lapshin*. Leningrad Party Chief Sergei Kirov had been assassinated in December 1934. Whether or not the assassination was carried out by the NKVD at Stalin's behest, as has often been alleged, the year 1935—after the assassination but before the Purges were under way—was retrospectively seen as a time of relative peace and innocence on the eve of the Great Purges of 1936–38. In an extended interview with El'ga Lyndina German ("Razrushenie" 153) recounts a comment by an unnamed Goskino official:

> "I want to explain, Aleksei, where your misfortune lies. There exist certain myths about time periods. There exists a myth about the war; it satisfies one person; it doesn't satisfy someone else. In *Twenty Days without War*, you struggle with that myth. But that's half your misfortune. A myth exists about the 1930s. [In *Lapshin*] you have chosen the happiest time period—1935! And you try to dissect it. We won't give up this period to you."

Completed in 1981, the film met considerable obstacles at Goskino before its eventual release in 1984. *Lapshin*, the director's favorite film (German, "Kino" 148), was finally awarded a Russian Federation State Prize in 1986, as well as three prizes at the Locarno International Film Festival that same year, the Festival's Bronze Leopard, the FIPRESCI prize, and the Ernest Artaria award.

German's fourth film, *Khrustalev, the Car!*, begun in 1991, was completed only in 1998. Its thematic focus is the so-called Doctors' Plot and the events in the wake of the anticosmopolitan campaign from roughly 1948 onward.[26] The film takes its name from the figure of Vasilii Khrustalev, who had replaced General Nikolai Vlasik, arrested on December 16, 1952, after more than two decades as one of Stalin's trusted bodyguards (Hoberman 53; Wood 103). The film, as long and obscure as it is magnificent, is in every respect, to quote Evgenii Margolit ("'Ia okom stal'" 20), "a grandiose close to Soviet cinema."

Since 1999 German has been working on *History of the Arkanar Massacre*, based on the Strugatskii brothers' novella *Hard to Be a God* (*Trudno byt' bogom*), a text in which he has been interested since childhood (German, "Boius'" 10). Even under relatively good working conditions, German is a film director who moves slowly, some would say—including the director himself—making problems for himself at every turn. *Twenty Days*, his quickest film, took two years to shoot (Razguliaeva), requiring 316 shooting days at a time when the average shooting schedule for a normal Soviet film was between sixty and eighty shooting days (Lipkov, "Proverka" 215).[27] *Lapshin* required four years to shoot (Anemone 203); *Khrustalev* took seven years.

In the meantime German finally began to enjoy some degree of professional stability, first as artistic director of the Studio of First and Experimental Films at Lenfil'm (1988–92), where his students included Aleksei Balabanov (whose work is examined in this volume), Maksim Pezhemskii, and Lidiia Bobrova, and then (together with Svetlana Karmalita) conducting a directors workshop at the Graduate Courses for Scriptwriters and Directors (Arkus, "German Aleksei" 250; Gladil'shchikov, "Uzh polnoch' blizitsia . . .").

In addition to the Russian (1986) and USSR (1988) State Prizes for *Lapshin* and *Trial*, respectively, German has received several other significant awards. In 1987 the Rotterdam International Film Festival awarded him its KNF (Critics') Award for his three existing films (*Trial, Twenty Days*, and *Lapshin*). *Khrustalev* was nominated for the Golden Palm award at Cannes in 1998 but did not win. Among his domestic awards are the Golden Aries for Best Director from the Russian Guild of Cinema Scholars and Critics in 1999 and a Nika for Best Director and Best Feature Film for *Khrustalev* in 2000.

It is a testimony to German's work as a force to be reckoned with that in 2000, when *Khrustalev* was entered in the Nika competition, Sokurov withdrew *Moloch*, nominated for Best Director, and Mikhalkov withdrew *Barber of Siberia*, nominated for Best Feature Film (Sul'kin, "Khrustalev" D-8). In Gladil'shchikov's ("Uzh polnoch' blizitsia . . .") assessment, "By the 1990s, after the death of Tarkovskii and the intelligentsia's massive disenchantment with Mikhalkov, Russia's Number One film director was tacitly acknowledged to be precisely German."

The Leningrad Text

I put the left glove
On my right hand.

—Anna Akhmatova, "Song of the Last
Meeting" (1911)

A central dynamic in German's work is his settling of accounts with the Leningrad heritage out of which he emerges. I have in mind two specific registers of meaning. Most narrowly, it is the Leningrad school of cinema, for which Iosif Kheifits and (in German's own generation) Il'ia Averbakh (1934–86) are the chief references.[28] Younger figures strongly identified with Leningrad cinema would include, most obviously, Aleksandr Sokurov, but also Konstantin Lopushanskii, Sergei Sel'ianov (as a director rather than as a producer), and Viktor Aristov.[29]

The profile of Leningrad's major studio, Lenfil'm, is of course varied in the extreme, and some might question whether a Leningrad "school of cinema" exists at all. For all its diversity, however, Leningrad cinema—principally Lenfil'm and the Leningrad Documentary Film Studio, where Sokurov often worked—is commonly viewed as a potential refuge from opportunism, careerism, and (later) commercialism, a film community where the art of absolutely unprofitable auteur films might still be taught, supported, made, and screened, a locale farther away from the festival circuit and from the corrosive influence of Hollywood than its Moscow competitors.[30] Central to its sensibility is the cult of perpetually delayed or unfulfilled artistic talent, a myth with even greater currency in Leningrad culture than in Russian culture more broadly, and of which German and Sokurov are perhaps the most extravagant examples in cinema. It is a myth that combines introversion, reclusiveness, and apparent disavowal of ambition. In his work on Averbakh, D. Bykov ("Toska" 135) describes Leningrad as the ideal site for such cinema, "the alternative, abject capital of the intelligentsia, a city of the background," a "polemical retort to [the Mosfil'm director] Sergei Gerasimov." Sergei Dobrotvorskii ("Proverka" 9) has described Leningrad cinema as "a precise reconstruction—almost like a protocol—of the epoch, the flow of life, dusted over with imperceptible poetry, fidelity to the most minute detail."[31] Dobrotvorskii's description captures two key, if apparently incongruent features of Leningrad cinema: fidelity to detail and a lyricism "dusted over" life yet capable of great affective richness.

As for the second (and larger) register of meaning for the Leningrad heritage, I refer to Akhmatova's 1911 poem, undoubtedly familiar as a similar encounter between minute detail and intense lyric affect: leaving her lover's apartment for the last time, the distraught narrator struggles to pull her glove on what turns out to be the wrong hand. This second register of meaning, then, is located in the broader Leningrad intertextual environment, legatee of the Petersburg text as the "mythologized counter-model" (Toporov, "Peterburg" 7) to Moscow.[32] The broader Leningrad cultural tradition is most pronounced in the poetic lineage that extends from Anna Akhmatova to Iosif Brodskii, Aleksandr Kushner, and Evgenii Rein, one that sustains a similar tension between minute observation and lyrically infused representation, often steeped in spiritual asceticism and elegiac fatigue.[33] Writing about Averbakh's "lyrical rationalism," for example, Finn (148) describes it as "somehow akin to Leningrad poetry—justified above all by the strength of its intellect, deeply and incisively understanding both emotion and sensibility." As Aleksandr Shpagin puts it with characteristic pathos, "Leningrad preserved a spirit of moral stoicism; it strove to sustain itself, its honor and worth, its culture, its stance, well-honed for many years, of the honest pauper-philosopher. And of course the Leningrad ivory tower sometimes was reminiscent of a hermetically sealed flask, engendering its own phantoms."

This is, of course, a much larger field of analysis than can be attempted here, but it is nevertheless the cultural (and dominantly poetic) environment within which German stages his work.[34] His complex biography, both the obstacles he encountered and those to which he contributed, is utterly compatible with this myth of delay, disavowal, and reclusion. German is, to borrow his own description, a "record-holder" among directors whose films met difficulties.[35] Much of his work before *Khrustalev* shares the muted restraint often identified with Leningrad culture, the intense emotional and formal discipline often accompanied by rigorous attention to empirical detail.

This resonance of German's "everyday asceticism" (Buttafava 279) with the Leningrad poets is a critical element that contextualizes the common characterization of his "scrupulous realism" (Pozdniakov 4) or "hyper-documentalism" (Gladil'shchikov, "Tak" 75), his extreme but highly selective attention to ephemeral detail as an evocative resource for the lyric. Visual specificity and lyricism—the left glove on the right hand as a sign of intense emotional distress—work as dual, related features, suggesting barely restrained, neoromantic vapors just above the austere surface, evident in the subjective camera work of Valerii Fedosov, until finally in *Khrustalev* German's style engages in a long overdue bacchanalian excess and profanation of restraint.

The Lyric Conjuration

We hurry back on the suburban train
from Vyritsa to the imperial capital,
where the Russian crown frightened the world
for two hundred years, where now there is just a regional,
provincial city.

> —Evgenii Rein, "Aunt Tania"
> ("Niania Tania") (1990)

German's investment in the lyric is more that a belief in a source of inspiration for his individual cinema. Poetry, he has maintained, shares a deep kinship with cinema in general through their mutual engagement in montage, the juxtaposition of manifestly dissimilar images and their latent intelligibility to each other. Poetry in particular is a critical resource for cinematic sensibility. "Cinema does not grow out of cinema; it grows out of literature, out of poetry. . . . Whatever the level of understanding a director has of literature, of poetry, that level will determine his cinema," he insists (German, "Kino" 125). While German's poetic tastes are catholic, with no preference for Leningrad poets over others, his primary orientation toward poetry as a kind of cultural and ethical bedrock, a place of cinema's origins, is very much in the broader spirit of both Petersburg and Leningrad culture from at least the early twentieth century forward.[36]

German has often described the cinematic atmosphere during the shooting stage as resembling the poet's efforts to conjure poetry. When he was on location for *Twenty Days* his recitation to cameraman Valerii Fedosov of Nikolai Zabolotskii's early poetry would establish the mood for a panorama shot (German, "Razrushenie" 163).[37] The lyrical prose of Ivan Bunin's story "In Paris" ("V Parizhe") also served as stylistic inspiration for this film (German, "Kino" 126). At times, lines of poetry, for example, from Zabolotskii's "Portrait," were set up as enactments of specific episodes in *Twenty Days*. Boris Pasternak's poetry ("For me at that time, these verses were like the Bible" [German, "Kino" 127]) and Anton Chekhov's lyricism defined the ambiance of *Lapshin*. The poetry of Osip Mandel'shtam and Aleksandr Tvardovskii, the lyric prose of Iurii Trifonov's novellas *House on the Embankment* (*Dom na naberezhnoi*) and *The Long Farewell* (*Dolgoe proshchanie*) repeatedly served as models for German's understated stylistics. German and Svetlana Karmalita have sometimes written short, draft poems as aural enactments of a scene's mood, improvising free verse that German would recite aloud to a patient Valerii Fedosov (German, "Kino" 127). In one interview German ("Kino" 129) quotes a line of verse from the Leningrad poet Mariia Petrovykh, whose untranslatable laconism expresses the lyric saturation that the director sets for himself as a goal: in Petrovykh's words, she struggles to "remain silent so long that verse occurs" ("domolchat'sia do stikha").[38]

One might see in *Lapshin*, then, the free-associative, repetitive rhymes— "Capablanca . . . blanka, maranka, manka, ranka, perebranka"; "au revoir, reservoir, samovar"—chanted by the boy's father and his coworker Vasilii Okoshkin as related to German's creative play, a kind of extemporaneous, automatic muttering, as if the linkage of rhymed utterances would lead them to something that they otherwise would not say or could not recall. Their improvisational muttering is a habit in *Lapshin* that elsewhere in the film surfaces in Khanin's random recitation of Pushkin's *Ruslan and Liudmila* (*Ruslan i Liudmila*).

It is for this reason—to turn for a moment to German's later and most ambitious work—that Aleksandr Blok's (*Sobranie* 2: 193) verses, recited in the opening shot of *Khrustalev, the Car!*, must be seen neither simply as an extradiegetic voice-over nor as a mere frame, but as something more, namely, the conjuration of poetry as a necessary remnant left over from the shooting stage itself, now crossed over into the film:

Всё; всё по старому; бывалому;	Everything, everything is
И будет как всегда:	and will always be the same:
Лошадке и мальчишке малому	To the little horse and the little boy
Не сладки холода.	The cold is not sweet.

Blok's 1906 verses from "In October" ("V oktiabre"), recited by the sixty-year-old narrator in the opening frames of *Khrustalev*, function as several related classes of repetition. The poem, *itself about repetition*, is the elderly narrator's repetition of verses heard in childhood. It is simultaneously the young boy's memory of his grandmother's recitation, itself a memorization over a lifetime that shared a generation, if not a life span, with Blok's own short life (1880–1921). The recitation of Blok's verse at the film's outset analogizes Blok's October as German's March.[39] Because October and March are not without ideological valence in Soviet mythology they inevitably evoke the historical stretch from Lenin's October to Stalin's March.

Cited at the outset of the film, Blok's 1906 poem is in fact the film's organizing text, just as lines from Zabolotskii's "Portrait" had played a key organization role in *Twenty Days*. As German playfully turns verse into film, the lyric line balloons into gargantuan cinema. Blok's line "to the little boy, the cold is not sweet" appears as the NKVD officer's suggestion that young Alesha suck sugar while sticking his bare behind out the window ("There's ice cream for you"). Blok's lament "And without any grounds, they drove me into the attic" becomes the innocent family's unexplained eviction from their home to a communal apartment. Blok's human flight, "And real life begins / And I will have wings! . . . I cried out . . . and I fly!," becomes Klenskii's sudden flight to freedom. Blok's final lines, "Everything, everything is always be the same, but only without me!," anticipate Klenskii's final emancipating disappearance.[40] In another director this would perhaps be coincidence or a scholar's procrustean stretch; from what we know of German's shooting practices (including his enactments of poems in previous work) it surely is neither.

At the outset of *Khrustalev* the *intelligent* narrator of *Khrustalev* recalls two things. First, as a child he had misattributed Blok's 1906 verses to his grandmother, who had often recited them. The aging narrator knows his attribution to be false; still, his inscription of authorship into his own genealogy in some higher sense rings true. The narrator's second memory is the smell of the neighborhood lilacs, now forgotten by everyone but him. The two memories are inversions of each other: in the first, individual memory (his grandmother as poet) is faulty where collective memory holds true; in the second, individual memory retains the lilacs where a faulty, common memory fails.

While the verbal text recites Blok's 1906 poem the camera provides a visual citation to Blok's most famous poetic line, "Night, street, lamppost" ("Noch', ulitsa, fonar' "). This line, from Blok's 1912 poem—also, incidentally, attributed to October (*Sobranie* 3:37)—was known by heart from early school years by every Soviet *intelligent*, pickled into earliest memory and thereby strongly signaling the cultural community within which the Russo-Soviet spectator, a distant kin of both the narrator and the director, is situated.

"Why the [Blok] citation in *Khrustalev*: 'Everything is and will always be the same'?" German ("Trudno" 6) asks rhetorically. "Journalists have written '1953, 1953.' . . . I didn't write about 1953." Of course, steeped in Blok's concern for cyclical time and eternal return,[41] German both did and did not write about 1953. In the film's final shot everything in 1963 indeed is "always the same": even Klenskii's final transformation—from a high-ranking military surgeon to a train conductor, a *vobla* speculator and hobo king—reproduces in mock form all the key elements of his previous life, from his cognac "tea" and network of unofficial privileges to his status as presiding leader of an insular, carnivalesque band.

These poetic allusions—now verbal, now visual—collapse any useful distinction between poetry in the production process and in the film's diegetic space, as if production leaves its lyrical mark on the finished product. The casting of the conceptualist poet Dmitrii Aleksandrovich Prigov as the Jewish doctor Vainshtein serves as the director's ludic notice that the lyric mode may be humorously redeployed at any moment. The children's lyrics that Klenskii recites as he furtively hovers outside his own hospital to evade arrest fulfill a similar commentary, underscoring the gulf between naïve children's poem and the film's sinister context. Pushkin's lyrics likewise render parodic the attempt by Varvara Semenovna, herself a Russian literature teacher, at impregnation by Klenskii.

It is significant that, as German ("Aleksei German" 208) looks at the post-Soviet cinematic landscape, with its heightened opportunities and freedoms for postcommunist film, he turns, as ever, to a literary frame of reference:

> Please, say anything you want today, and say it any way you want. But such a plateau of literature has emerged—Platonov, Akhmatova, who wrote *Requiem* during the Stalinist epoch, Mandel'shtam, Grossman, Pasternak, Dombrovskii, and especially Shalamov, who, for me, leads them all in his moral strength. . . . Just try nowadays to feel yourself to be a leader against the background of such giants.

German's comparative rubric—Akhmatova, Mandel'shtam, Shalamov—form a loosely knit community, also impeded in their time, of Soviet schismatics who conserve the liberal intelligentsia's alternative cultural heritage, steeped in citations of inherited lines, known by heart and reinscribed as family genealogy. The films' periodic verses, often without obvious motivation, suggest themselves as a counterrecitation back to the state's slogans, a place for the mind to reside other than in the staff offices. Here Shpagin's earlier description of the "Leningrad ivory tower sometimes . . . reminiscent of a hermetically sealed flask, engendering its own phantoms" might well have been a description of German's filming practices and the world he seeks to protect from dispersal. German's cinema is an elegy to a *way* of remembering, a memory structure in generational wane for whom poetry had an adaptive, everyday function.

Cinema of the Background

The lyrical, intertwined with quotidian detail, has often elicited two critical assertions about German's work, assertions that are opposed but credible despite their incompatibility. The first holds that German cares a great deal about historical fidelity. Even in *Khrustalev*, for example (despite its visual excess and tone of hysteria), German was transfixed with material accuracy: the twelve black ZIS-110 automobiles, each carrying one member of the twelve-person Politburo; the precise replication of Stalin's dacha at Davydkovo; the historical authenticity of the doubles, prepared by the security police as part of an impending case against the accused; and Stalin's consultations with an imprisoned cardiologist.[42]

Indeed, the fascination with physical accuracy has a long prehistory in German's work. During his theater years, long before he joined Lenfil'm in 1964, his concern for authentic props resulted in considerable uproar when he brought real machine guns into a Sholokhov production at the Leningrad BDT, over the loud objections of the audience (German, "Razrushenie" 158). In *Trial on the Road* he insisted on the replacement of metal rail ties by wooden ties. For *Twenty Days* he acquired a train car from the war years, set on the same rail lines near Dzhambul, pulled by a steam engine from the early 1940s. His crew, traveling in the same cold compartments as in the war years, caught cold, did without hot water, endured cramped conditions, but filmed an atmosphere—the sound of the rails, the steam coming from the actors' mouths—that would not have been present in a studio setting. As for costumes and props, German and Karmalita put out a call on Leningrad radio and in Tashkent newspapers asking the citizens of Tashkent to sell clothes and household objects from the war period (Lipkov, "Proverka" 211; Zorkaia 11).

For *Lapshin* an authentic 1930s tram was acquired and shipped from Leningrad to the filming location in distant Astrakhan' (Lipkov, "Proverka" 220). The filming crew attended appointments at the forensics morgue where local family members identified corpses (Lipkov, "Proverka" 220). His father's Moika apartment, equipped with Iurii German's typewriter, globe, and photographs, was replicated for the communal apartment in *Lapshin*. German's scrupulous efforts to conjure up the air of 1941–42 (*Trial*), of 1942–43 (*Twenty Days*), of 1935 (*Lapshin*), and of 1953 and 1963 (*Khrustalev*) were concerned with the physical air—rather than its metaphor—hovering in clothing, books, and furniture of the historical period, in photographs from the medical archives. The objects, meticulously collected by German and Karmalita for *Trial*, *Twenty Days*, and *Lapshin* from second-hand stores, transformed the director into amateur archivist, from archivist to laboratory chemist, isolating and extracting the elements of the historical period.

And yet a second credible assertion insists that German does not care at all about fidelity to historical events. Again, to choose *Khrustalev*, according to reliable accounts Beria was not present at the historical moment of Stalin's death (Anninskii, "Khrustal'naia noch'" 4). Lindenberg, a Swedish journalist for *Scandinavian Workers' Paper*—the historical figure was a messenger from the German family's Jewish relatives abroad (German,

"Khrena-nakhrena!")—was not murdered, as in the film, but lived on to old age (German, "Izgoniaiushchii d'iavola" 125). Even the weather was not right, one critic grumbled (Listov 8). Indeed, such major critics as Viktor Matizen ("*Khrustalev*" 21) took German to task, asking why "a film, so demonstrably claiming authenticity, would just as demonstrably deviate from existing descriptions of the leader's death."

The incompatibility of these two assertions cannot be reduced to the filmmaker's preference for props over history. It is rather that the fidelities of props and history—the "correct" object versus the "correct" account of events—bear different valences. The historical object begs historical contingency. The accumulation of correct objects—objects *from* the time; failing that, objects precisely *replicating* those of the time—matters because at stake is memory, for which the object, and not history, is everything.

German's "physiognomy of space," his "maniacal striving for accuracy" (Aronson, "Po tu storonu kino" 219) was precisely the quality that incurred such objections from Goskino for his "superfluity of background" ("izlishestvo vtorogo plana"; Shmarina 125). Unsurprisingly, German ("Boius'" 10) saw it differently: "I always liked making the background. [Goskino] even wrote about me . . . that I present the background as if it were the real cinema. But that background is indeed the most important; it is life itself. I do indeed film a 'cinema of the background.'"

In this light we may look again at the child protagonists of *Lapshin* and *Khrustalev*, mentioned at the outset of this chapter. Critically important to the tenor of the film but without a key role in the narrative, they observe and note, a human embodiment of German's "most important" background, the human passage of time that is life itself, the place where naïveté and ignorance might be outgrown.

In another register too cinema of the background signals German's recusal from the symbolic main event of Moscow, metropolitan cinema. A committed Leningrader even in his Moscow setting for *Khrustalev*, German insists on the "the alternative, abject capital of the intelligentsia, a city of the background," as D. Bykov ("Toska" 135) earlier described the tradition. In his focus on the literal cinematic background German stages in physical terms Leningrad's polemical retort to Mosfil'm and to Moscow as the new imperial capital, contrasting it with a space for those imperial abnegators who would choose to inhabit the background, "where the Russian crown had frightened the world for two hundred years, where now there is just a regional, provincial city" (Rein 113).[43]

Given German's attention to historical detail, it is useful to note the difference between his work and the phenomenon of retro cinema. The latter, most familiar from the stylistically driven retro films of, say, Mikhalkov, with its extravagant costumes, late imperial preferences, effete nostalgia, and high gentility, bears no relation to German's fanatical, even shamanistic obsession with the objects themselves.[44] In contrast to retro cinema German's lyrical forensics tend to examine the moment when the fathers were still alive and their young sons were listening keenly. His impulse is to locate precisely the moment when the poetic impulse, familiar since early memory, expresses itself most palpably on the material world.

Here the props have a deeply talismanic function rather than the decorative or ornamental role they play in retro cinema. German's rough, phantasmagoric nervousness and its excessive, disorienting, and periodically inaudible subject matter are incompatible with the glossy Stalinism of, say, Ivan Dykhovichnyi's *Moscow Parade* (*Prorva*; Mosfil'm, 1992), Pavel Chukhrai's *The Thief* (*Vor*; NTV-Profit, 1997), and Mikhalkov's *Burnt by the Sun*. In large measure German's differences from retro cinema are rooted in the very different demands of art cinema from those of genre cinema, which more easily lends itself to retro style. But more than this, Mikhalkov's 1930s in *Burnt by the Sun*, typically for retro cinema, mourns the loss of a past—and by extension the 1870s to 1890s figured in *Mechanical Piano, Barber of Siberia*, and so forth—whereas German's 1930s in *Lapshin* mourns the loss of an imagined, socialist future that, by German's 1980s, had become outmoded, a very different anachronistic poignancy than could be mastered by the slick delights of retro cinema. What stood in place of this 1930s future—not as a replacement, but simply as something that had grown out of the sons' experience—was a regard, simultaneously respectful and bemused, for the fathers' naïveté, as one would respect a child for once having tried to change the world.

Critical to German's effort to align the lyric with material history is his dogged collection of photographs detailing life outside the official realm. However much he has insisted in certain interviews (e.g., German, "Razrushenie" 165) that he relies solely on personal and family photograph collections, he elsewhere discusses a more intriguing process of selection. In *Trial* he moved from watching Nazi archival footage, news chronicles, and propaganda films—a normal research stage—to large boards of archival photographs, pinned up so as to track the acquisition or reproduction of specific objects.

It was here that German first saw images that would inspire the barge scene in *Trial*, his most famous shot: "columns of our prisoners, filling the roads as far as the horizon" (German in Lipkov, "Proverka" 204). According to cameraman Iakov Sklianskii, hundreds of regular Soviet prisoners close to their release dates played the POWs on the German barge. "We wanted to give a real feeling of those sad eyes, so people would understand the size of the tragedy, so they would wonder why we did so much harm to so many people," the cameraman explained (quoted in Stone, "A First Glimpse" 21).[45] As the camera draws back to pull in the full scope, the barge of captured men suggests a microcosm, an utter inversion of its official meaning.[46] Compared to this single shot—the centerpiece of the film—Lazarev is an utterly peripheral figure, an

FIGURE 7.2. German. *Trial on the Road*. Soviet convicts playing Soviet POWs.

instance of the circumstances of the barge scene, which occurs without him and (as a flashback) *before* his appearance. A virtual McGuffin, Lazarev is incidental to the problem, which existed before and without him.[47]

Rich sources of evidence in German's forensics, therefore, were technical and instructional photographs and footage:

> We searched for the background's truth in technical photographs, for example, the construction of city pipelines around Ligovka in 1935. Only the pipelines interested the photographer, but passers-by happened into the shot. They were not posing; they did not know that they were being filmed. . . . This was everyday life, not on the screen of [the film] *Volga-Volga*. (German, quoted in Lipkov, "Proverka" 224)

Here we can see German's reverse-processing, appropriating incidental passersby from the official context, into which they had blundered unawares, so as to exploit their unintended presence as raw material for the cast, costume designer, and hair stylist. Repositioning the incidental figure from the visual periphery to the cognitive center, from the distracting to the scrupulously studied, German shifts the figure's function from the accidental to the contemplative. The official photograph, having already undergone a double processing of technical darkroom and ideological darkroom, is appropriated by German to redefine a human presence no longer extraneous to the camera's technical eye.

It makes sense, therefore, that, searching after *Trial* for the right cameraman, German would eventually find Valerii Fedosov, then known for his scientific and technical camera work (Lipkov, "Proverka" 210). At stake in German's work, therefore, was not the political opposition of the family snapshot to the agit-prop glossy, but the more basic relation of background to foreground, rooted first in perception itself and only secondarily as a political relation.

In this respect German's product is in no way documentary. In fact, highly structured and fetishistically orchestrated, his films are documentary in reverse. In the preparation stage he may select a photographic document. But by the shooting stage he is engaged in restaging a historical moment that had long ago lived out its own life cycle:

> For me, one of the postulates is the apparently unorganized illustra-
> tion of reality, which in fact [in my film] is organized down to the
> millimeter. It is a precise handling of the camera. It is the precision
> of the view through the camera, the precise choice of the person
> who will look at the camera. Whereas in a newsreel, the filming is
> somehow incidental: someone waves his hand and the filming starts.
> (German, "Razrushenie" 164)

German's work is a renegotiation of center and periphery, a counterstaging of the fixed historical narrative from the periphery. To state subjectivity he poses something else: an anonymous, potential extrapolation, plural but uncodified. The director's abuse of the official image—its layout, its focus, its cropping— heightens this misalignment between sponsored consciousness and an amorphous, lyric memory.

The soundtrack functions according to a similar principle, allowing ambient sound to move out from the background to occupy our attention. "The background noise is more important than the basic dialogue, precisely for its submersion in time," German ("Kino" 152) remarks.[48] In dialogue with his producer Guy Séligmann, German confirms a curious inversion: the background noise is often selectively enhanced, whereas the foreground noise is at times deliberately muted (German, "Izgoniaiushchii d'iavola" 128).

Enfranchised from both the camera's eye and the narrative, the soundtrack is punctuated by aural events, often off-camera, that the camera was seemingly not quick enough to catch. Just as things get in the way of the camera, set up to film at the "wrong angle" for the shot, voices are mumbled. The visual impairment thus finds a corresponding device in aural impairment, sounds inadequately recorded or irrelevant to the discursive and narrative regimes. In *Lapshin,* for example, we overhear one conversational scrap after another: "They lost a wheel"; "Where's my petrol can"; "He's completely blind; there'll be an accident"; "It's not over; it hasn't even begun"; "Don't be rude to your grandmother"; "She used to be a wonderful dancer"; "If you break it, I'll kill you." As one of German's early critics laments:

> The film's essential and sole direct utterances of a given character
> can be broken off, interrupted by another's speech. . . . Everyone is
> constantly talking on the screen simultaneously and unintelligibly.
> Some unknown person's broken phrase flies in to the shot, some-
> times incomprehensible, unlinked, sometimes pertaining to fate, but
> someone else's fate that has no link to the given subject. (Quoted in
> German, "Kino" 151–52)[49]

By *Khrustalev* Russian critics were complaining that they required a subtitled print, that they felt locked in an "information prison" like the characters themselves (Matizen, "*Khrustalev*" 21). As this was exactly the film's purpose, these objections phased neither the director nor Svetlana Karmalita, who enigmatically replied that cinema is not literature; not everything need be audible (D. Bykov, "German" 49, 52). After *Trial* extradiegetic music was replaced by the clang and crash of life, as everyday objects impede, constrict, and intrude upon human agency.[50] The mirror falls in *Lapshin,* and by *Khrustalev* there is a whole cascade of accidents: the falling washtub; the electric short that throws Fedia Artemov to the ground; Lesha's brief, accidental fire in the bathroom; the shattering of light bulbs and dishes; the mother's broken beads; Polina's scarf caught in the descending lift; the clothes racks collapsing under the winter coats. Like tiny gags in a larger comedy, these accidents are micro versions of a larger disaster to which the characters have only limited conceptual access.

German's final product requires of the viewer an analogous renegotiation of center and periphery in viewing practices. His apparently "unfinished" presentation forces the audience to replicate his own earlier struggle with the archival photographs, creating an isomorphism between his preparatory research and the viewing practices that he requires of the spectator. The writer Tat'iana Tolstaia (16) characterizes her own reaction thus: "Where should we look; what should we hear; what is important; what is not important; what is it necessary to remember and what can we skip for the time being? Or can we skip nothing, but how is that possible?"[51] Staging central events at the visual periphery, or the obverse, admitting peripheral characters momentarily to grandstand for the camera,[52] German forces the spectator to sort out what is important, without benefit of a more traditional camera's discursive nudge. So too, by implication, his characters struggle with the world in which they operate, wherein the raw material of life only contingently and momentarily adheres to the regime of their individual desires and anticipations.

Although more pronounced in *Lapshin* and *Khrustalev,* the background appears as a kind of provincializing force from the very beginning of German's cinema. As Arkus ("German Aleksei" 251) points out, *Trial* is set in "a nameless, strategically insignificant region of occupied territory." Lopatin's diaries (in German's selected rendition) focus on events at the rear, in distant Tashkent, not the front. *Lapshin* is moved from Leningrad, the setting of Iurii German's stories, to the periphery, a fictional small port city called Unchansk. "We decided to transpose the place of action from Leningrad to a small town," German explains. "The smaller the town, the more insignificant the supervisor, the more the history itself—as we felt it—would be sadder and more truthful" (quoted in Lipkov, "Proverka" 221). Lapshin, based on Leningrad police commissar Ivan Bodunov, is likewise demoted to small-town policeman. Lapshin's execution of the serial murderer and cannibal Solov'ev—an otherwise sensationalist topic, as is Khanin's gruesome and extended suicide attempt—likewise shifts to the periphery of the narrative, dismissed by the characters and not mentioned again. In place of these acts of violence, the background's flow of life seizes the spectator's attention, allowing us only haphazardly to integrate what the camera offers us. The limited knowledge evinced by such characters as Natasha Adashova, brightly anticipating the production quotas for Abrau-Diurso champagne,[53] is reproduced by our own expectation of clear sightlines, blocked again and again by the camera's "unintentional" blundering. We are keenly aware of our own ignorance, like the protagonists whose "ignorance is primary for us" (German, "Kino" 153).

Even the very title of *Khrustalev* is a study in periphery. The name is called out by Beria to his trusted subordinate (perhaps the same historical figure who administered poison to Stalin)[54] as Beria leaves Stalin's deathbed. Khrustalev and Stalin exist as an odd pair of contradictions. Khrustalev is peripheral, a person without a body; he never appears on camera, but names the film. The dying Stalin is central, but a body without a person; present throughout the historical period, he is a mere cameo in the film.

In its extreme grotesqueries and peripheral distractions, as Gladil'shchikov ("Tak" 75) has suggested, *Khrustalev* resembles German parodied by Kira Muratova. We might indeed see a superficial similarity of German's "voodoo practices" with those of his colleague, in the tendency in both filmmakers to lay out the physical properties of the mise-en-scène with the obsessive attention of a spell.[55] Yet where Muratova's odd objects, such as her dolls, tend to be eccentric and diegetically unmotivated, German's odd objects, such as the self-opening umbrella, are eccentric and diegetically credible.[56] There are reasons, however tenuous, for German's girls in the cupboard and for the Klenskii double, where in Muratova these would be merely the pleasures of domination or a love of twins. German's objects are attentive to the Weltanschauung of the era; his goal is the conjuration of lyrical associations that linger in physical objects; his historical props serve as lures. In Muratova, by contrast, there is no equivalent to the interplay of received history and memory; there is, rather, the Anti-position: fluid, strategic, protean, contingent, but adequate to itself.

Hence their instances of grotesque play have quite different agendas: for Muratova, the joy of destruction; for German, the mulish insistence that memory is a shared, lyric realm, something more than individual witness or state memory alone. Whereas Muratova chooses contemporary life, to which she has no commitment of verisimilitude whatsoever, substituting instead a kind of ecstatic desecration, German's work is relentlessly historical, concerned with cognition and memory, in the ways things were recalled through the noise of time.[57] His is a project of contemplation, an interview (was it this way or that?) with his father's generation, with the received codes of a state film institution where he did not study, and with the very nature of the way perception is conventionally inscribed in film.

If German and Muratova share common ground it is their Gogolian heritage with its unabashed superfluity of background detail. In German's ("Iz rechi" 25) remarks at the August 27, 1999, screening of *Khrustalev* at the Aurora Cinema in St. Petersburg, he prepares his audience accordingly:

> Do not consider this cinema gloomy, frightening, anti-Russian. . . .
> It is simply a humorous film. Sometime in the future it will indeed
> *be* humorous, although very frightening. But it is cinema made with
> love. Once such a thing was called the Russia-Troika [a reference to
> Nikolai Gogol''s novel *Dead Souls*]. We attempted to approach the
> genius of Gogol'.[58]

By "the genius of Gogol'," as the intelligentsia in the cinema hall would understand, German implied inclusion of (what has come to be known, from Leont'ev forward, as) the second line of Russian literature: from Gogol' to the early Dostoevskii, Belyi's *Petersburg*, Kharms, Zoshchenko, Bulgakov. After all, the Doctors' Plot included accusations no less grotesque and imaginative than Gogol' or Kharms might have invented.[59] The second line of literature, in its grotesque and imaginative play, has historically been the intelligentsia's refuge, an alternative, carnival retort to official Soviet culture.[60]

The Plural Self

And even now, when the dreams begin dreaming, my little brother, my little sister, my girlfriend . . . It is terribly difficult to recollect it.

—Peasant woman's voice-over in
Trial on the Road (1985)

Looking back over the history of German's "framing voices," we realize in retrospect that they were present in all four films. The one we are likely to forget is the narrative frame voice in *Trial*, whose opening shots are narrated by the voice of an old peasant woman recalling her losses. German does not retain this elderly speaker in the narrative, and we soon forget her. By *Twenty Days*, however, that framing voice is more strongly developed: it brackets each end of the film and, in its enunciation and vocabulary, more closely resembles our own, that is to say, the profile of German's educated, art house audience. It is, as Arkus ("German Aleksei" 252) describes it, "a bit deaf, a voice slightly cracked [*nadtresnutyi*], with the *ancient-régime* articulation of the intelligentsia." It is in fact the voice of Konstantin Simonov himself, who frames the opening and closing with his own memories:

> God only knows why you remember one thing and not another.
> Even though after the landing at Feodosiia there was the house, and

Stalingrad, and two wounds, yet why, for example, in my memory
suddenly again there is that winter, foggy dampness over the
sea, . . . that soldier with his words about Hitler and Pasha Rubtsov,
in that hat of his, looking like a captured officer. (German, "Postizhenie dobra" 141)

In German's next two films, *Lapshin* and *Khrustalev*, the elderly protagonist
recalls his childhood, attempting to make sense of the fathers' world. In *Lapshin*
the narrator's frame comments, set in 1983, are "my declaration of love to those
people beside whom my childhood had passed, five minutes' walk from here
and a half-century ago."[61] In *Khrustalev* a similar nostalgic tenor is struck:
"There never was and will never be anything better than this in my life."

German's child protagonists are nearly the same age: Aleksandr (*Lapshin*)
is nine; Lesha (*Khrustalev*) is eleven, almost twelve. Bearing the same name as
the director, the child narrator of *Khrustalev* is slightly younger than the filmmaker would have been in February 1953, when the film first opens. In both
films the director intermittently suggests that it is the boy's memories that are
narrated in the films and that the boy is himself. In each case the director has
striven for a kind of intense autobiographical accuracy in his staging of the
boy's home, using objects from the German family household or replicating
the apartment layout. In *Khrustalev* the maid Nadia was indeed the Germans'
family maid. As in the film, Nadia bore a son, Boria, from a German lover in
1942. The family chauffeur was Kolia, who would chide Nadia for that foreign
liaison, which had indeed landed her a stint in prison (German, "Izgoniaiushchii" 125). Even certain deviations from this autobiographical dimension tended
to be strategic: the protagonist's name is changed from Glinskii, the surname
of German's aunt, to Klenskii, for fear of offending the family.

To argue that either of these two films, *Lapshin* or *Khrustalev*, narrates the
boy's memories, however, is to leave unexplained the overwhelming number
of episodes in which the boy is not present, the events of which he could have
no memory, and things of which he could not have heard.[62] More important, as
even German's most astute supporters have opined,[63] it is to leave unexplained
the filmmaker's transparent lack of interest in staging the camera work so as to
represent the boys' memories or points of view.

Given German's unqualified insistence—in "Izgoniaiushchii" (122), for instance, "The boy is me"—that the narrative lines follow the boy's point of view,
the question inevitably shifts: What is meant by the boy? What is meant by the
boy are the cumulated stories overheard, nightmares, gossip, family lore, newspaper articles, wishful thinking, neighbors' secrets, fantasy, fears, the totality of
social discourse passing through the intermittent presence of a child who is the
sign of shared memory, a lateral slice of history for which there is no correct account, only correct objects and the ritual of recounting—uncodified, unofficial,
contingent, and unprofessional.

That recounting of the plural self in all its multiple versions, its unmanageable and unaccountable elusiveness, is German's primary charge. The shifting, handheld camera work, the use of nonprofessional actors, the black-and-white footage, the gathering in of the visual and aural peripheries are, in this respect, instrumental to the capture of common knowledge, things both overheard and (more often) underheard, the reconstruction of the *sensation* of memory, in particular its construction where it could not have existed.

Between the child's individual spectatorship, inadequate by itself, and official state history is the child *as a plural self* (hence its continuation in his absence), his belonging to a larger cultural community, where the objects endure to mediate their intergenerational existence—the existence, in all its variety and incoherence, of the midcentury, urban intelligentsia—perpetually caught between individual and state memory systems. As German biographically is in a position to know, that intelligentsia is a collectivity self-consciously very different from, if intimately interdetermined by, state-constituted collectivity.

That Stalin died, for example, on an earlier date and not, as the announcer Iurii Levitan officially declared, at 9:50 p.m. on March 5, 1953, matters in this film not for historical rectification, but because both versions, inhabiting the common knowledge of the intelligentsia, must necessarily be present simultaneously.[64] Accurately chosen, German's objects can draw out common knowledge, knowledge not intended to be correlated with notions of historical accuracy: what the intelligentsia knew, in all its mutually contradictory codices, simultaneously present to the child, a sign of shared memory with all its encodings, self-deceptions, and aggrandizements. In *Khrustalev* the script begins at 5:00 a.m. on the day "not known" in official history, having been occluded by the known date. And because it was officially "not known" by the metropolitan intelligentsia, intermarried as they were, the occluded date was eventually also known by them exactly as such.

That individual knowledge can never be adequate to this task accounts in part for the enormously intense (and of course wholly unproductive) public furor around German's contested accuracy in capturing popular memory.[65] Such a charge is commonplace for a culture whose imposed aesthetic canon for sixty years had been a kind of monist realism, a culture that then in the *perestroika* years condignly privileged a range of emergent realisms as "moral antidotes." As we know, those members of the intelligentsia whose texts—historical, literary, televisual, painterly, cinematic—addressed the Stalin period were especially vulnerable to accusations of inaccuracy. In the space between the autobiographical and state memory systems, actual fiction became, conversely, documentation because it was overly invested in the veracity of individual categories of truth, truth unconsecrated by the state.

German's intended target, then, is less state truth than the countervailing fashion that individual witness is a uniquely adequate instrument to capture the shared memory of the intelligentsia. In contrast, German's cinema strives to produce the plural knowledge of the metropolitan intelligentsia.

Errant Discourse

Mikhail Iampol'skii ("Diskurs" 175) has written at length about the distinction in *Lapshin* between the camera's discursive regime and the film's narrative, a term that he understands as plot, but also the characters' behavior and relations, their dialogues:

> The very fact [in traditional cinematic discourse] that the camera moves after a particular person indicates that the given character is central for that given narrative. An incidental passer-by falls out of the shot without acting on the camera's work regime; that is why precisely the camera's movement relegates to him the status of "incidental."

Characteristically in German's work, camera discourse does not serve narration; each is accorded an independent existence: "One recounts, another shows," Iampol'skii (178) provisionally suggests. The radical resistance of German's camera to the requirements of the narrative creates the impression variously described by critics as a kind of perceptual and conceptual fragmentation: "mosaic . . ., carousel-like, motley, kaleidoscopic" (Pozdniakov 4). This quality, a strategic misalignment of two knowledge systems, is muted in the early work (*Trial* and *Twenty Days*) for reasons that have as much to do with Soviet cultural politics as with individual filmmaking style, but gives way in *Lapshin* and, to an even greater extent, in *Khrustalev* to a camera that blunders around the diegetic space.

Avoiding the conventional reverse-angle shots, the camera, which seems perpetually "not to know" in its glances and misglances, is sometimes willfully incompatible with the narration of the characters' blundering impulses. The cognitive dissonance between camera and narrative voice (in Iampol'skii's sense of plot, dialogue, and characters' actions)—a dissonance expressed in the camera's apparent verdancy toward the requirements of the visual field and its corresponding hypersensitivity to peripheral knowledge—accounts in part for the repeated remark that German has somehow reconstituted the physiological experience of recall, of things being simultaneously new and residual in deep memory structures, the simultaneous experience of discovering and remembering. In this dyad of discovering and remembering the camera discourse is often assigned the function of demonstrating what it had once been like (as at Cannes in 1998) *not* to know.

In its *not* knowing, the camera is neither our eyes, informed of history yet ignorant of the diegetic narrative regime, nor the characters' eyes, confident in their intentions, and of an imagined future, yet oblivious to what we know now. The camera is a third element, belonging neither to our world nor theirs. Characters go about their narrative business with few clues to their intentions. We know little of what they know; they know little of what we know. The camera, which traditionally mediates these relations, here records a third thing: the paucity of shared knowledge.

This is precisely why German's signature shot—a character's direct gaze at the camera—is so effective. It may be traced from the opening scene of *Trial*, in which the German officer and soldier look directly at the camera (and implicitly at the partisan rifle sights). "The device of the glance at the camera, which I used so much in *Twenty Days without War* and in *Lapshin* in general, became the most important thing: the entire film was built around it," German explains. "The glance at the camera is the glance of those people from over there, from out of that time period towards me and into my soul" (quoted in Lipkov, "Proverka" 222). The gaze, described by Galichenko (43) as bearing "all the innocence of the naïve candid, captured in early documentaries and newsreels," bridges in the imaginary realm that which remains in history the unfathomable gulf between us and the past.

Replicating Ignorance

Finally, I would like to return to the first epigraph of this chapter. German tells us that his father's generation could not see bad things, that their *ignorance* is primary to our understanding of the son's cinema. His films suggest that what had blinded his father's generation was their own radiant future, a bright virtuality into which they stared. In retrospect the boy witness could see their future without its radiance, as an expired condition that had impeded vision, something that the fathers had observed to the point of blindness. The narrator's recollecting voice, years beyond that imaginary future, takes upon itself an account of its beauty and impairments.

In this regard the self-imposed restrictions of German's cinema—its frequently inaudible soundtrack, its blocked camera angles, its chaotic, handheld camera, its incoherent narrative line, its visual and narrative distractions, its unidentified characters—play out in the technical realm the cognitive limits of characters who operate ignorant of the real, historical future into which they are blundering. The films' technical absences—an avoidance of color, of extradiegetic music, of establishing shots and bright lighting plans (in favor of dark or high-contrast shots)—replicate in a different register the ways the characters have to fend for themselves.

By *Lapshin*'s end the hero's impending political refresher course (*perepodgotovka*) is a cruel comment on how 1936–37 would lethally "refresh" the likes of Lapshin.[66] The writer Khanin, who cannot believe Maiakovskii's death was a suicide, is someone—though not just someone, but a writer himself—who will soon attempt suicide. In *Khrustalev* a gerontologist, specializing in extended life, dies at a young age. And as for us, we film viewers are in a similar condition,

FIGURE 7.3. German. *My Friend, Ivan Lapshin*. "We'll clear the land of scum . . ."

at a loss to anticipate how the films will move forward, since they will adhere neither technically nor narratively to the norms we may expect from the camera's familiar regime. Until German's films, we have watched cinema much as Adashova predicted champagne production quotas, or as Lapshin anticipated strolling in the socialist orchard: confidently, but without any understanding of the range of real possibilities.

The intentional irony is in German's foreclosing to the viewer the one thing the intelligentsia does well: know. German gives us a portrait of shared cognitive limitation, when even the brain surgeon in *Khrustalev*, a skilled trepanator who can balance a cognac glass on his head, is as powerless as he was at Stalin's bedside. The mental disorientation of the educated elite (and us as viewers) meshes historical knowledge with hallucination, society gossip, common knowledge, dreams, scraps of newspaper, and overheard underworld songs, where the background's lush detail, "life itself," in German's terms, pushes forward to disrupt what we had thought of as the conventional plot.

In German's cinema the citational world of the late Soviet intelligentsia, as arcane as it is unprofitable, stages a rebellion that assumes no real likelihood of escape. Shifting from the early, isolated landscapes of *Trial* to increasingly claustrophobic interiors and insular, cloistered space of *Twenty Days* and *Lapshin*, *Khrustalev*'s crowded quarters—the endless, narrow hospital corridors, cupboards that serve as temporary home, the communal apartments, the paddy wagon, the shrunken replication of Stalin's bedroom—all extend to a historical interiority: "I wanted to be *in* history, not above it," German ["Izgoniaiushchii" 126] remarks about his task in *Khrustalev*. "So Jonah must have felt," comments the critic Zhanna Vasil'eva ("Chrevo kita"), "in the belly of the whale." The film's visual and aural hindrances are linked to this compositional feature: everything present is simultaneously also "in the way," although what "the way" is remains unresolved.

Pressing in on this relentless interiority, this slim likelihood of escape, public space intrudes into private space. Characters live in partisan encampments (*Trial*), temporary military assignments (*Twenty*), state-issued staff apartments (*Lapshin*), or residences staffed by government informants (*Khrustalev*). The major characters are men in uniform and holding rank: Adamov (*Seventh Satellite*) is a military lawyer; Lokotkov (*Trial*) is a partisan commander; Lopatin (*Twenty Days*) is a military war correspondent; Lapshin (*Lapshin*) is a police investigator and the boy's father was a police doctor; Klenskii (*Khrustalev*) is a military surgeon. State slogans, "Let Us Rejoice!" ("Raduemsia!"), float in the soup they eat at assigned quarters (*Lapshin*). Slogans resound in the "Hymn of the Comintern" they repeatedly sing ("Factories, arise! . . . To the battle, proletarian!") and are performed by the brass orchestras that play the patriotic and military songs throughout German's films ("an orchestra for each inhabitant," as Adashova puts it in *Lapshin*). Awake, Lapshin dreams that Solov'ev is executed by International Workers' Day; asleep, he dreams his own near death in an airplane crash and a civil war shelling. Okoshkin mutters administrative orders in his sleep ("Hurry to the transfer platform").

Here German's detractors and supporters agree in one respect. In response to German's Nika award for *Khrustalev* from the Russian Academy of Cinema Arts and Sciences, one unsympathetic journalist asks:

> To the respected academy members I have accumulated a sum-total of one single question: How could you choose as Best Feature Film something that almost no one has seen; almost no one has understood; from which the audience walked out; and which was not even widely printed due to its utter lack of commercial viability? (Gvozdev)

And yet a staunch supporter of German's work, Liubov' Arkus ("Vopros ekspertam" 29), had a remarkably similar comment: "The film will have no distribution. This was intentional. It will have no broad success. This was intentional. A certain number of people, who will be called the elite, will recognize it. Of those, some seventy per cent will not say what they think of it, because it is already accepted to say that it is a good film."[67]

Arkus's careful phrasing—"a certain number of people, *who will be called the elite*" (emphasis mine)—is worthy of attention. She insists upon a distinction between the intelligentsia, whom she would see misidentified as the elite, and the new economic elite at a time when the intelligentsia has undergone considerable devaluation. In a different cultural context her assessment might be taken as dispirited; in the inverse logic of Leningrad culture it is the highest recognition, an acknowledgment of German's exquisite portraiture of the stratum to which she herself belongs, in German's words, "the most unprotected—and the most despised—part of the country's population" (quoted in Moskvina, "Chelovek" 55).

"I wanted something to remain on the earth after my death," German ("Izgoniaiushchii d'iavola" 125) says. "The world that is around me and in me will cease to exist. The only means to preserve that world is to leave it on a piece of film. Even if it is a world that is thought up and refracted." Arkus, therefore, is both right and wrong: what German has left behind is a cinema of the Soviet *cultural* elite. This cinema of and for the late Soviet intelligentsia is not therefore *about* itself. In *Trial*, for example, we are asked to believe that the philosophical and nuanced Lazarev is a taxi driver, though nothing in his bearing makes this belief an easy task. Instead, German's films are a cinema of and for the late Soviet intelligentsia as a way of knowing the world: its lyric orientation toward experience, its insistent attention to empirical truth, its mix of delicate hermeticism and brutality, its rarified air of erudition.

Claustrophobia and incipient disappearance, inscribed both in German's films and in the conditions of their production, are rearticulated in the films' relative unavailability—in copies and in substance—to a broad spectatorship. The intense condensation of cultural resources within a narrow, metropolitan circle—culturally privileged, if not therefore materially privileged—are inseparable in the films' inaccessibility to distribution and consumption. *Khrustalev*'s painstaking and protracted seven-year process, roughly 1991 to 1998,[68] produced an object simultaneously of intense citational insularity and unprecedented visual grotesque. The small theater venues where the film has been exhibited are symptomatic of the films' terms, articulating an intelligentsia that knows itself to be collectively unable to effect a substantial change of status. "As far as the intelligentsia is concerned," German ("Pochemu ia ne snimaiu") remarks, ". . . I do not believe in its capacity for cohesion and resistance. The only things of which it is capable are to go to the camps or to leave the country. Individual instances are capable of self-immolation." This is the most intriguing paradox to German's work: his evident regard for individuals of a congregate in whose capacity for plural action he fundamentally cannot bring himself to believe, though its key plural act is precisely the production of extraordinary individuals from the Leningrad intelligentsia who formed the lyric fabric of his texts.

FILMOGRAPHY

Seventh Satellite (*Sed'moi sputnik*). Codirected with Grigorii Aronov (lead
     director). 1967.
Trial on the Road (also known as *Checkpoint* or *Roadcheck*) (*Proverka na
     dorogakh*). Original title *Operation "Happy New Year"* (*Operatsiia "S
     novym godom"*). Completed 1971, released 1985.[69]

Twenty Days without War (*Dvadtsat' dnei bez voiny*). 1976.

My Friend, Ivan Lapshin (*Moi drug Ivan Lapshin*). Completed 1981, released 1984.

Khrustalev, the Car! (*Khrustalev, mashinu!*). 1998.

History of the Arkanar Massacre (*Istoriia arkanarskoi resni*). In production.

Aleksei Balabanov: The Metropole's Death Drive

I only want to make negative things, because that is how I was born.
—Aleksei Balabanov, quoted in Clarke (1999)

Introduction: No "In the Name Of"

The critic Tat'iana Moskvina ("Pro Ivana i Dzhona" 25) has proposed that Balabanov's characters share one trait—the fact of having nothing to lose:

> There, on the enemy side, ideology is necessary, energy, a constant pumping of faith, ecstasy, devotion, a feat. Here [in Russia] nothing is needed. Here there is no "in the name of" or "for the sake of," nothing narcotic, but there is emptiness, cold, power, a lonely person who by his own free will can destroy the "enemy" by the rules of the game, without hate.

Moskvina's assertion ("no 'in the name of'") is the first half of the quandary that interests me. The second half concerns Balabanov's putative nationalism, a characterization that appears in most assessments of his work.

Certainly, in isolation, examples abound of Balabanov's nationalism and xenophobia: "I am against things foreign," he explains in an interview with

Clarke. Yet what kind of nationalism is founded on the recurrent desire to "make only negative things"? And if the practices normally associated with the stirrings of nationalism—the romantic galvanizing of a common language and orthography; the throwing off of an older, oppressive force; the sacred memories of battles lost or won; the newly optimistic rediscovery of holy sites and customs—are either absent, or mocked, or lauded as evidence of imperial superiority, then from what alien, repressive force is the imaginary nation to be wrested? This chapter is, in part, an exploration of that question. As we move toward a fuller answer let the temporary assertion be that, amidst Balabanov's insistent repudiations, we do not yet understand how the aspirations of his so-called nationalism exist side by side with malaise and the insistent, reclusive negativity of his work.

The generation coming of age after 1991, including those who would discover Balabanov's cinema, entered a time when the encounter with the state would be profoundly different from the experience of their elders. The youth league and Party meetings, state parades, volunteer brigades, official rallies, and demonstrations of the Soviet years had been relegated to historical footage. Unlike their parents', this generation's pragmatic and relatively de-ideologized encounters with the state were principally located at the bureaus of marriage, divorce, birth, and death.

Balabanov's cinema seized on this reduced and routinized contact to elaborate its gothic potential. Between birth and death, his characters tend to encounter the state through the army, the prison, and the police, institutions of compulsion requiring no exquisite ideology to galvanize their ranks; conscription and conviction served admirably in its stead. In its largest dimensions, Balabanov's cinema came to inhabit what is sometimes described as a postideological space, a place where violence and the accrual of power, itself the galvanizing idea, was newly sufficient.[1]

Not surprisingly, then, Balabanov's heroes often share a kind of anonymity or erasure: the hero of Happy Days (serially named Sergei Sergeevich, then Petr, then Boria) doesn't know his own name. His head injury has erased his past; he seems to come from nowhere. The hero of Castle is known by little else than his moniker of Surveyor; the eponymous hero of Trofim is a passerby whose image is discarded by the film editor. Danila in Brother is a cipher of a different sort, "a loner, . . . acting without reason" (Beumers, "To Moscow!" 83). His false identity as a clerk during the war—a claim made to his brother, whom he loves dearly; and to Sveta, for whom he has affection—is exposed to us in private as he fashions a handmade silencer with alacrity and skill. War's anonymous craftsman, he recommends to us a certain caution with respect to other conclusions we might draw.

In a similar fashion the innocuously named Ivan in War is someone who, as Moskvina ("Pro Ivana i Dzhona" 25) notes, does not long to wed his fiancée, has no job to which he would return, no intact family to welcome him, no cohort of hometown veterans to share his experiences, and no prospects that would engage his skills. And then, in *Cargo 200*, there is the mysterious Captain Zhurov, less a human being than a malignant force in the universe.

For *Brother, Brother 2, Dead Man's Bluff, Cargo 200*—in the absence of a literal battlefield or military encampment—the city serves as the default battlefield, the contested area left from the collapsed state. In *Brother 2* and *War* the battlefield expands to take on a global character: in *Brother 2* Chicago's tenements and corporate offices; in *War*, as Horton ("*War*") points out, the Chechen War moves "far beyond Grozny and Moscow and into the proper drawing rooms of upper middle-class Brits."

In these conditions Balabanov's heroes—in particular Danila, Ivan, and Mitia in *It Doesn't Hurt*—exhibit what Alena Solntseva has called the David complex, "when the putatively weaker one turns out to be stronger than the one considered strong" (Arkus et al., *Seans Guide* 155). If the David complex holds true for these figures, it equally holds true for Balabanov himself, whose David complex drives his assault on the privileges and resources of Hollywood cinema.

Following this logic for the moment we might insist that Balabanov's work operates in two parallel registers: his politics of Russian domestic conflicts and his politics of global cinema. In the former he functions as a member of the imperial rabble, keen on keeping old superiorities in place. In the latter, global regime Balabanov is the provincial provocateur, the David who would fight for a world in which the elite cinematic indulgences of a Quentin Tarantino, David Lynch, or Sam Peckinpah—with each of whom he is occasionally compared— are not the exclusive prerogatives of American Hollywood directors alone.[2]

Of course, Balabanov's films, extraordinarily varied and complex, include both art house films (*Happy Days, Castle*, and the unfinished *River*) and genre cinema (*Brother* and *Brother 2, War, Dead Man's Bluff, It Doesn't Hurt*, and *Cargo 200*). Whereas other filmmakers have a history of shooting films difficult to ascribe to one cinema or another (Abdrashitov is a prominent example in this volume), Balabanov shoots films that are strongly marked as one or the other. In exploring the issues introduced briefly above, I focus primarily on his genre cinema and the later films. Among the early art house films *Happy Days* in particular will serve as a touchstone for key features of the director's work.

Biographical Remarks: From *Happy Days* to *Cargo 200*

Born in Sverdlovsk (now Ekaterinburg) on February 25, 1959, Aleksei Balabanov studied at the Translation Department of Gor'kii (now Nizhnii Novgorod) Pedagogical Institute, considered in the late Soviet period among the best departments for translation training in the USSR. Graduating as a military translator in 1981 he served in Africa and the Middle East. Returning to his hometown he worked from 1983 to 1987 as a director's assistant at Sverdlovsk Film Studio, then in 1987 entered the Graduate Courses for Scriptwriters and Directors (VKSR) in Moscow, where he studied in the Auteur Cinema experimental workshop of Lev Nikolaev and Boris Galanter (Director's Sector). Graduating in 1990 he returned to Leningrad to shoot his first feature film, *Happy Days*,[3] the product of Lenfil'm's Studio of First and Experimental Films, with which he was associated during Aleksei German's tenure (1988–92). *Happy Days* was followed by *Castle*, an even more sharply auteurist work based on Kafka's unfinished novel and set, in Jonathan Romney's ("Brat-Pack") wry characterization, "in an anachronistic non-place somewhere between the early 1900s and Brueghel's Middle Ages." Although reviewers were generally kind (see Belopol'skaia, "V tverdom pereplete"; Dobrotvorskii, "Uznik"; Drozdova; Kharitonov), the film is considered Balabanov's weakest, including by the director himself ("Portret" 220). In 1994, together with fellow director-producers Sergei Sel'ianov and Viktor Sergeev, Balabanov founded the St. Petersburg production company CTV, with which his work has been closely associated since that time.[4]

Balabanov's next work, *Trofim*, was one of four short works that together compose the compilation film *Arrival of a Train* (*Pribytie poezda*; CTV, 1995), shot to celebrate cinema's centenary.[5] Balabanov's contribution was hailed by many critics as the best of the four shorts, but it was his next work, the action film *Brother*, that marked the start of his international visibility. *Brother* was a sharp turn away from a darkly auteurist mode toward genre cinema.

Brother was a hit both at the box office and in video copies, of which some 400,000 *legal* copies—nota bene—were sold in the first five months of its release (Romney, "Brat-Pack"). It was followed by one of Balabanov's most controversial films, the stylized historical drama *Of Freaks and Men*, which, despite winning the Nika award for Best Director and the Best Picture in 1998, encountered severe distribution problems both in Russia and internationally because of its disturbing content, such as the shots of two naked children, the putative conjoined twins.[6] As one critic put it, echoing the conservative reaction to German's *Khrustalev*, "I am very glad that I live in an emancipated country where the highest cinema prize is given to a film for which broad distribution (and correspondingly popular success) is impossible by its very definition" (Ustiian 49). Turning to a more commercially viable mode, Balabanov shot the sequel *Brother 2*.

The year 2002 held both promise and tragedy for Balabanov. He finished *War*, a fictional episode from the First Chechen War (1994–96), and began his next work, *River*, "a nanook film," as he describes it in Clarke, adapted from the Polish author Wacław Sieroszewski's novel.[7] *River* was set in the 1880s in Iakutia (Siberia), an area Balabanov had come to know during his travels for Sverdlovsk Film Studio. The film was interrupted because of a car crash that killed his lead actress, Tuinara Svinobaeva, and severely injured the director's wife. His next film, *The American*, was also left unfinished because of schedule disruption, but the ensuing three years saw a major film each: the crime spoof *Dead Man's Bluff*, the melodrama *It Doesn't Hurt*, and the crime thriller *Cargo 200*. *Brother* and its sequel, *Brother 2*, together with such disturbing films as *Of Freaks and Men*, on the (largely fictive) early pornography business, and *Cargo 200*, about a maniacal killer, provoked sharp, new disagreements among critics about cinema's ethics, its heroes, and its influence in the new society.[8]

Balabanov's major prizes have included the Best Film Award in 1992 for *Happy Days* at Moscow's Debut Festival. *Brother* won the Grand Prix at the Open Russian Film Festival (Kinotavr) at Sochi in 1997 and a Special Prize in the Feature Film Competition of the Cottbus Festival of Young East European Cinema. His *Of Freaks and Men* was awarded both Best Picture and Best Director in the 1998 Nika competition, and in 2002 *War* was awarded the Golden Rose at Sochi. The Russian Guild of Cinema Scholars and Critics awarded him their prize for *Cargo 200* in 2007 (shared with Aleksei Popogrebskii's *Simple Things* (Prostye *veshchi*). Three of his films have been selected for inclusion in the programs at Cannes (*Happy Days, Brother, Of Freaks and Men*).

Magnetic Topography: Balabanov's Metal City

Petersburg is a provincial city. All the power is in Moscow.
                                        —Viktor Bagrov to Danila, in *Brother* (1997)

The city takes away power.
                                        —Hoffman to Danila, in *Brother* (1997)

As these two epigraphs suggest, Viktor Bagrov and Hoffman in the film *Brother* are oddly paired. Killer and cemetery inhabitant, "Tartar" and German, they function as two contrasting mentors with two different views on the city: for Viktor the big city is a lure; for Hoffman any city is a danger. For both these men, however, the city has magnetic power: for Viktor the city draws everything toward it ("All the power is in Moscow"); for Hoffman the city sucks power away from even the strong ("The city takes away power"). An unstoppable machine, a magnetized instrument, Balabanov's city in *Brother* and elsewhere operates as a collection of moving parts in a larger, relentless modernity.

Indifferent, indefatigable, these moving parts are figured as early as *Happy Days* in the recurrent battered trams and *Trofim* in the steam engine. They reappear as the freight tram of *Brother,* the arriving and departing of the steam engines and the belching coal-fueled steamboat of *Freaks,* the endlessly repetitive automobile sequences of *Dead Man's Bluff,* the magnificent industrial shots of the motorcycle and side car in *Cargo 200* that stream exultantly past the monstrous, intricate wasteland of Leninsk, and the identical shot of freight trains outside both Captain Zhurov's and Artem's apartment windows.

FIGURE 8.1. Balabanov. *Brother*. Cargo tram car.

It is inside this urban machinery that Balabanov's peasant Trofim, a wronged husband and rustic avenger, is led away to be hanged; that Danila (*Brother*), a provincial soldier well prepped for violence, is sharpened into a hired killer. In *Freaks* the first intertitle—"Iogan passes through Immigration Control and *goes out into the city*" (emphasis mine)—is not mere narration; it is a diagnostic warning. In this film Balabanov's city, repeatedly shot from the windows of a well-to-do household (oddly) overlooking the train station, is the theater of destruction for two genteel, St. Petersburg families, the site of Liza Radlova's transformation from a virgin to—not a prostitute, as one might expect, but—a client of sexual servility. By the time of *Dead Man's Bluff* Balabanov's urban setting has become a killing field—eighteen murders and fifty liters of fake blood—from its second scene to its penultimate one. And in *Cargo 200* his extravagant, industrial diorama is the larger death force that hosts the carnage in this late Soviet celebration of sexual sadism. "Is it not plausible," the later Freud (54) asks in "Beyond the Pleasure Principle," a line of questioning compatible here, "to suppose that this sadism is in fact a death instinct which, under the influence of the narcissistic libido, has been forced away from the ego and has consequently only emerged in relation to the object? It now enters the service of the sexual function." In many of these films Balabanov's city, staging an iron inevitability on the behavior of individuals, draws out of them those drives of which they had been unaware, processing them to their logical extreme, and imposing the appropriate punishment in a delirium of lethal aggression and sexuality.

In his essay "Walking in the City" de Certeau writes about:

the creation of a *universal* and *anonymous* subject which is the city itself; it gradually becomes possible to attribute to it, as to its political model, Hobbes's State, all the functions and predicates that were previously scattered and assigned to many different real subjects— groups, associations, or individuals. "The city," like a proper name, thus provides a way of conceiving and constructing space. (94; emphasis in the original)

Balabanov's characters, tending toward anonymity and effacement, are ide- ally suited to this modern environment. His city, typically a dynamic, modern ironworks of unrelenting repetition, of aggressive and mechanized return, pro- cesses its human material by recurrent modes of mindless compulsion. "There is no development of humankind at all," insists Balabanov, "and never has been" (quoted in Clarke). Balabanov's city is the metal id, amoral, primal, compelled toward acquisition and gratification. In no way the crowning achievement of human progress, Balabanov's city is instead the articulation of the human's primal drives, dominant among them, the death drive, that "urge inherent in all organic life to restore an earlier state of things," the preorganic, as Freud ("Beyond the Pleasure Principle" 36) describes it.

In this common project, *Happy Days, Brother,* and *Brother 2* cumulatively document that Balabanov's city is configured according to a topography differ- ent from the one we might know empirically: In *Brother 2* Chicago is not the city of the Sears Tower, but of abandoned buildings, fire escapes, and back hallways. Balabanov's St. Petersburg, too, is most typically a city of rundown tenements and dark courtyards. The two cities, so unlike in real life, rhyme with each other in Balabanov's work; the hero slips with comparable ease from one to the other, at home as long as the urban conditions are sufficiently degraded.

"My Homeland!"

FIGURE 8.2. Balabanov. *Brother 2.* Urban fire escape.

This city is not always the central feature in Balabanov's work. It recedes to mere backdrop in his melodrama *It Doesn't Hurt*, a modern rendition of Dumas *fils*'s 1848 novel *La Dame aux camélias*.[9] Melodrama is an unlikely genre for Balabanov and not an altogether successful one.[10] Even his most dedicated critics saw it as a deviation from his signature brutality. "The terrible and magnificent Balabanov, the most provocational of Russian directors," writes Elena Plakhova, "has made a soft, lyrical, and sorrowful film. The beast within turned out to be affectionate and tender, though there is no reason to deceive ourselves: he will still show his fangs" (quoted in *"Mne ne bol'no"* 33).

Balabanov's next film, *Cargo 200*, proved Plakhova right. In this work, and more typically throughout his cinema, the city's ominous presence is registered in the camera's frequent independent references, unmotivated by plot. The camera's glances suggest that the city leads its own existence, capable of driving the action, disgorging plot and characters as by-products of its constant operation.

The city in decay, de Certeau (96) argues further in the same essay, affords unique opportunities for what he describes as

> microbe-like, singular and plural practices, which an urbanistic system was supposed to administer or suppress, but which have outlived [the city's] decay. . . . Far from being regulated or eliminated by panoptic administration, [these microbe-like practices] have reinforced themselves in a proliferating illegitimacy, developed and insinuated themselves into the networks of surveillance.

De Certeau's description, in evident dialogue with Foucault[11] is oddly compatible with Balabanov's cinematic rendering of the city. A "proliferating illegitimacy" of soldiers-turned-criminals (in *Brother* and *Brother 2*), punks-turned–hit men (*Dead Man's Bluff*), and militia-turned-killers (in *Cargo 200*) confirm, in Bogomolov's ("Killer" 31) words, that "the human has been lost, but the City has been found—a kind of anonymous strength, the accumulation of the will and soul of lost people."

Bogomolov's capitalization of "City" confirms a certain compatibility with de Certeau's proposal: that the City ("like a proper name," as de Certeau says), a microcosm that in Hobbes's Leviathan or Hegel's State is the embodiment of reason, but here is seen in reverse, an instrument gone mad, that which is, without contradiction, both sacred and evil. And so while some might see in *Brother,* with its church cemetery and marketplace, an evocation of Dostoevskii's church and Hay Market,[12] the "belly of St. Petersburg," as it was popularly known, where, at the crossroads, Raskol'nikov first repented his killing, we find a problem. Here—in Balabanov's world where there is no "development of humankind at all"—Danila undoes Raskol'nikov's act, returning there not to repent but to kill.

The Brothel, the Crypt, and the Battlefield

A portion of the [death] instinct is placed directly in the service of the sexual function, where it has an important part to play. This is sadism proper.
—Sigmund Freud, "The Economic Problem
of Masochism" (1924)

In *Happy Days,* a film about the impossibility of shelter, the camera's strong vertical axis is our only respite from Balabanov's oppressive city: a high crane shot captures the cityscape, periodically surveying the state of things. Balabanov's recurrent shot of the St. Petersburg skyline allows us a magisterial position from which to take in the metropolitan vista, to absorb the panorama in a fashion not available to the characters at the street level. These crane shots are accompanied by the film's gravest melodic line, a recording of Wagner, distorted by skips and scratches that aurally mimic the *veduta*'s double exposure. This vertical axis belongs to us alone.

In contrast is the film's long horizontal axis of the tram lines, their cars shuttling characters back and forth across the city, severing relations and carrying the characters away from one another. The jazz song "Too Many Tears" underscores the complex pain of these adult relations,[13] while a third melodic line, the hero's music box tune, provides private comfort. These three musical registers—Wagner, the jazz song, and the music box melody—structure the film's three visual registers: the city vista, the personal couplings, and the private retreat. It is the first of these, the city as an object of contemplation, orchestrated by its own soundtrack, that becomes Balabanov's prominent cinematic signature, evident still in *Cargo 200,* where the industrial city of Leninsk, tracked by the extensive dolly shots, exults in its own melodic interludes.

FIGURE 8.3. Balabanov. *Cargo 200.* Captain Zhurov returns to Leninsk.

Meanwhile, at street level in Balabanov's city life usually operates amid primitive homelessness and death. The nameless, transient hero of *Happy Days* shuttles between the prostitute's house-cum-brothel and the cemetery. This linkage of brothel and crypt continues elsewhere. In *Trofim* the rustic hero is led from the urban brothel to the gallows. In Balabanov's most satisfyingly perverse film, *Freaks*, two delicate, educated families are destroyed by the invasive solicitations of pornographers, who turn one elegant home into a pornography studio until, by the film's end, Liza follows the line of this logic to the brothel and Iogan commits suicide. In *Cargo 200* Captain Zhurov's sexual exploitation of the heroine continues until he himself is murdered.

Veterans of prison and army alike seek transient shelter in Balabanov's St. Petersburg, Moscow, Chicago, Tobol'sk, and Leninsk. Danila, a convict's son from 22 Station Street—a name that itself suggests transience—is demobbed from the army, sidesteps the militia, and drifts instead into crime. Such lateral shifts allow for the perpetual substitutability of the prison, the army, and the police. In *Brother, Brother 2, War, Dead Man's Bluff*, and *Cargo 200* the distinctions become smudged between soldier and bandit, battle and crime, motherland and turf, division and mob, thug and government deputy, business deals and contract killings, banking and money scams, police uniforms and gang clothing. By *Dead Man's Bluff* the commonalities among prison culture, military culture, and the militia are virtually erased: the militia man has a picture of Stalin hanging on his wall; the shady businessman has a picture of Stalin tattooed on his chest. Their shared skills and training are figured in Balabanov's script as uniquely suited to urban life, which becomes thereby another field of battle in a state of endless war. In *Brother* oddball characters—Viktor Bagrov and Hoffman's crackpot elderly lodger—operate in a periodic hallucination (now playful, now serious) in which World War II is still very much in progress. By *Brother 2* even Danila himself understands his world in terms of war commitments. "In wartime we don't listen to music like that," he admonishes Irina Saltykova for her taste, though it is peacetime. "Russians in war do not abandon their own," he tells Dasha.

War, accordingly, is merely a pastoral variant of the urban battlefield from *Brother, Brother 2*, and *Dead Man's Bluff*, with the narrative units in a different order. In *War*, as in *Brother*, the Chechen antagonist is killed, a rescue effort is launched for someone else's beloved, an older mentor offers initial wisdom, an inept sidekick provides inconstant help. In *War*, as in *Brother 2*, the geopolitical conflict is played out across global expanses—Moscow, Chicago, London, Groznyi, Vladikavkaz, Tobol'sk—in a permanent war to fend off vulnerabilities left from imperial collapse. Balabanov's permanent state of war does not *require* a city for its staging, but the city provides infinitely varying visual and narrative opportunities to figure the ways the collapsing empire, turning itself inside out, moves Chechens from the periphery to the St. Petersburg marketplaces (*Brother*), to Moscow and Samara restaurants (*War*), just as it had sent Danila

(*Brother*), Ivan (*War*), Oleg (*It Doesn't Hurt*), and Angelika's fiancé (*Cargo 200*) to Chechnia.

By *Cargo 200* Leninsk is exquisitely suited for this urban site of permanent war. At the end of the Soviet Union, the twilight Leninsk, the City of Lenin is contrasted with ex-con Aleksei's imaginary City of the Sun,[14] the religious utopia that he defends to the professor of scientific atheism Artem Kazakov (another of Balabanov's utterly despised *intelligenty*). Here communism's janissary is the crazed Captain Zhurov, neither a thug nor a lone maniac, but, as several preparatory episodes suggest, a local militiaman routinely acting at the edge of accepted codes of misbehavior, the violent, material extension of Artem's ideology, which, if expressed toponymically, is the degraded industrial modernity of Leninsk.

I am reminded here of Sinyavsky's remarks on a similar urban, toponymical perversion. After Kirov's assassination, the writer recounts in *Soviet Civilization*, Stalin began to rename cities in Kirov's honor (Kirovsk, Kirovograd, Kirovokan). It "wasn't just a function of Stalin's wanting to cover his tracks," Sinyavsky (101–2) writes, "but above all, in my view, an exercise in black humor. As if Stalin were compensating the dead Kirov by making him a national hero . . . his way of thanking Kirov for having been murdered." Balabanov's love of sordid transgression draws on sources from a range of historical periods (including the prerevolutionary writer Aleksandr Kuprin [1870–1938]).[15] But most of all its sadomasochism draws on this Stalinist legacy, with which it is intimately, even erotically intertwined.

How Balabanov Is Different

If you are given lined paper, write across the lines.
—Aleksei Balabanov, *Cargo 200: CTV release* (2007)

Situated at the end of this volume, Balabanov belongs to a different era of cinema than those directors whose work we examined earlier and those differences are worth brief notation here. Most obviously, of course, Balabanov is significantly younger than the others, but generation alone and in the abstract is not a wholly satisfactory explanation. After all, the other directors themselves belong to various generations: the 1930s (Muratova and German), the mid-1940s (Mikhalkov and Abdrashitov), and the early 1950s (Sokurov).[16]

Lev Anninskii ("The Sixties" 13) has suggested that a generational cohort is marked, if only associatively, by three key moments: its date of birth, its "confirmation" (a common event that organizes early adulthood), and its finale, the last moment around which a subject's full professional potential coheres. Implicit in Anninskii's model is a delicate negotiation between the historical event and how an individual is positioned to respond to the moments that Anninskii calls the confirmation and finale.[17]

Anninskii's model is useful in its capacity to cluster cultural generational figures, aligning them approximately to historical events, but it is inadvertently useful too for the prominent exceptions for which it fails to account. Muratova (b. 1934) and German (b. 1938) belong to Anninskii's generation, for whom the early 1960s would have been youthful confirmation. In Muratova's and German's case, however, delays in their work muddle Anninskii's categories in all but a strictly numerical sense. History would assign them to the Thaw; cinema politics would do something else. We would not describe Muratova and German as having been "young Thaw directors," in the way that Evtushenko was the "swallow" of Thaw lyrics, or that Anninskii himself, in a different fashion, has been characterized as a quintessential Sixties critic.[18] Though completing their film training at the height of the Thaw (in 1959 and 1960, respectively), Muratova and German became casualties of the Stagnation period, undergoing a delayed public confirmation, to use Anninskii's term, only as middle-aged directors during *perestroika*.

Mikhalkov (b. 1945) and Abdrashitov (b. 1945), both younger and less controversial filmmakers, were in late adolescence as the Thaw was coming to an end. Graduating from VGIK in 1971 and 1974, respectively (roughly ten to fifteen years later than Muratova and German), their confirmation took place on time, as it were, in the Stagnation period. The late 1970s and early 1980s were very productive years: Mikhalkov shot seven poststudent films during this period; Abdrashitov shot five.

For Sokurov (b. 1951) the generational ascription becomes oddest of all. Born at the very end of the Stalin period, Sokurov, the paradoxicalist would argue, enjoyed greater productivity in the late 1970s and early 1980s than either Mikhalkov or Abdrashitov, completing ten feature and documentary films by 1985. But of Sokurov's ten films, nine were shelved, some for as long as a decade, until the deliberations of the Conflicts Commission released them. And so, despite a *production* history quantitatively comparable to Mikhalkov's and Abdrashitov's, Sokurov shares a *distribution* history that is chronologically timed with and more similar to German's and Muratova's (some seventeen years his senior), for whom a late confirmation begins only in the second half of the 1980s.[19]

In any event, it is on this already highly differentiated terrain that we find the sharpest point of contrast between these five filmmakers and Aleksei Balabanov. Some eight years younger than Sokurov, Balabanov completed his first feature film in 1991, the year the Soviet Union ceased to exist. Other than his student films, Balabanov's work has only ever been post-Soviet cinema.

In terms of the economics of cinema, Balabanov's confirmation period—the period of *Happy Days*, *Castle*, and *Trofim* (1991–95)—took place after the industry had utterly collapsed, when even the day-to-day food supply had become uncertain. Balabanov shot his early films by patching together funds, friends, and improvisational shooting locations. Any argument that his films were "unafraid" would have to proceed from a notion of fear—more economic than ideological—different from those filmmakers who preceded him. The experience of banned films (for Muratova and German), of circumspect or subdued social commentary (for Mikhalkov and Abdrashitov), of obscurity and stubborn recalcitrance toward Goskino (for Sokurov) were ancient history by the mid-1990s.

As Balabanov is set apart by the economic state of the industry into which he enters, and by the collapse of state ideology, so too is he set apart by his audience's reception of his films. Whereas his first three nonstudent films were narrowly art house in their orientation, set in a historical or indefinite past, and circulated principally on the festival circuit, his 1997 *Brother* was a genre film with a contemporary setting and box-office appeal. It quickly became the lead example of new cinema, eclipsing such competitors for "new post-Soviet film" as Aleksandr Rogozhkin's *Peculiarities of the National Hunt* (*Osobennosti natsional'noi okhoty*; Lenfil'm, 1995) and Sergei Bodrov Sr.'s *Prisoner of the Mountains* (*Kavkazskii plennik*; Boris Giller, 1996).

Whereas Balabanov's film education took place under conditions that were utterly lacking a future, his work and his jointly owned film studio, CTV, that produced his cinema were instrumental in constructing a future, bringing young Russian viewers back to domestic films watched in film venues. As eighteen-year-old Evgenii Gusiatinskii (30–31), a second-year student at VGIK, wrote of *Brother* and *Brother 2*:

> How we lived earlier without the brother is completely incomprehensible. It seems as if he had always existed. It is just *we* who had gone astray, set off down the wrong path. But with our brother it is possible no longer to be afraid; he will always point out exactly the right road. . . . *Brother 2* is quite possibly the most important picture in the entire history of post-*perestroika* cinema. . . . The lead character is not Danila Bagrov, but each person sitting in the hall.

Such responses abound in young cinema-goers' television interviews, message boards, and blogs.[20] Lines from the film entered the street vocabulary of those more or less the age of Balabanov's hero, Danila Bagrov, two decades younger than Balabanov, viewers for whom Balabanov's cinema was a reference point in their own youthful confirmation, at a time when cinema was resurrecting itself, and constitutive of that very resurrection.

Balabanov's lead actor for *Brother* and *Brother 2*, Sergei Bodrov Jr., likewise emerged as a figure "emblematic for his generation" (Bogomolov, "Killer" 28), an "anti-hero icon with young Russian audiences" (Romney, "Brat-Pack"). Bodrov's career trajectory—first in his own father's film, *Prisoner of the Mountains*, and then in *Brother* and *Brother 2*, followed several years later by his tragic death in 2002—confirmed his status as Russia's leading cult figure since Viktor Tsoi and strengthened the claim of *Brother* and *Brother 2* as the lead visual manifestoes of the younger generation.[21]

As Gusiatinskii (32) suggests of *Brother 2*, the appeal to the younger generation stemmed in particular from the film's orientation toward "two parallel realities, without which it is difficult to imagine life today—television and computer life." The film's electronic hyperreality—life intermingled with television, the computer game, the music video, and the video game—is enhanced by the fact that both the director and the lead actor bring to *Brother* and *Brother 2* a mash-up of their own real-life backstories and previous film texts. Balabanov, originally an effete art house director with the stereotypical preoccupations of the Soviet intelligentsia—Beckett and Kafka—had learned a different way to connect with a provincial and deracinated, demobbed youth. In making *Brother* Balabanov became a new kind of director for those same Danilas who had up to now forgotten about Russian cinema.

As for Bodrov Jr., his previous acting role in *Prisoner of the Mountains* transferred that diegetic combat experience from the edges of the empire in Chechnia home to Tula and St. Petersburg (in *Brother*), Moscow and the United States (in *Brother 2*), and eventually back to Chechnia (as Medvedev in *War*). In different ways for both Balabanov and Bodrov, biography and script fused into a functional continuum. Balabanov, the former *intelligent,* pampered whiner of the collapsed Soviet center, was finally able to understand the veteran who had defended the borders of the creaky imperial structure.

The mass appeal of this duo of Balabanov and Bodrov was one to which none of the art house directors—Muratova, German, Abdrashitov, and Sokurov— aspired and one that Mikhalkov's increasingly mass-culture ambitions chose not to master. If an earlier face-off, therefore, between German and Mikhalkov could be understood as the opposition of art house to mass culture, then the face-off between Balabanov and Mikhalkov could be understood as the opposition of two box offices. "*Brother 2* is noteworthy," writes the young Gusiatinskii (33), comparing it to Mikhalkov's hit of two years earlier, "in its utter eclipse of the recent mega-project by the name of *Barber of Siberia*, which also painstakingly resurrected our glorious history. . . . It turns out that, in our genetic makeup, the Tsars have long ago and forever been replaced by the Brothers."

A final key difference in Balabanov's work that sets him off from the other five directors is his relationship to the intelligentsia. The other five directors have little in common, yet, in a mercilessly reduced fashion, one could summarize it thus: Mikhalkov tends to pillory the intelligentsia as weak and ineffectual, disconnected from real political power. Abdrashitov sees their rationalist inclinations as nobly misguided. Muratova tends to berate the intelligentsia as philistine, while German cherishes a particular subset of it. Sokurov, in many ways the quintessential, absorbed *intelligent,* has seemed not to notice them, focusing instead on more incandescent matters.

In contrast to this internally diverse set, Balabanov came to share mass culture's contempt for the intelligentsia. Not for nothing are the cultured conjoined twins (*Of Freaks and Men*) shown pornographic postcards to the strains of Prokof'ev's elite *First Ball of Natasha Rostova*. The opening lecture scene of *Dead Man's Bluff*, for example, piteously mocks its incapacity to account for its own economic conditions. Indeed, for good measure, the negative portrayal specifically of filmmakers is a recurrent feature of Balabanov's cinema.[22]

It is tempting to compare Balabanov's disrespect for the intelligentsia with Muratova's, given her delight in negative things and her abiding suspicion of redemptive motives. Balabanov's oft-quoted maxim—"If you are given lined paper, write across the lines"—might well be Muratova's motto. Like Muratova, Balabanov is interested in the moment when the humanist, sufficiently provoked, becomes a carnivore. In Balabanov's press conferences this exchange is played out as the moment when the film critic and *intelligent* discards any pretense of being a viewer and, rising to his feet, instead becomes a Soviet-style moral orator. Meanwhile, Balabanov is on the side of the new barbarians, whoever they might be.

But if Balabanov, like Muratova, lives to provoke the intelligentsia, his provocations occupy an entirely different forum, taunting them in the medium of mass culture, lacking Muratova's arcane inscrutability. Provoke as she might, Muratova shoots art house cinema; Balabanov is different, and unlike other "new Russian directors" with whom he is often compared, including Rogozhkin and Bodrov Sr., Balabanov has been ostentatiously uninterested in a dialogue of mutual understanding with critics, middle-brow viewers, or the intelligentsia more broadly.[23]

A consequence of Balabanov's confrontational style is that he has often been taken at face value when, in press conferences, interviews, and elsewhere, he has baited his educated listeners with nationalistic, racist, sexist, or anti-American retorts, inviting shocked (and largely unreflective) reactions.[24] They have responded, not unreasonably, by labeling him a bigot without regard for his performative enthusiasm.

Here the cinema scholar Evgenii Margolit ("Golyi nerv") registers a useful objection:

> Balabanov is not that simple. . . . Balabanov doesn't insist upon
> anything—he vividly demonstrates the absence of a stable world. . . .
> In *Brother* he says, "Look, here is your hero with a capital H, and you
> are in agreement with him." And indeed, everyone identifies with
> this character. Yet for all that, the real values remain somewhere on
> the sidelines, and the author, in general, talks about this openly.[25]

If this is so, then what are these "real values"? How would we know, in the "absence of a stable world," that we were correct?

Foremost in Balabanov's cinema, we can perhaps agree, is his mock-serious tone, undercutting poignant moments with a burlesque register that hampers our heartfelt identification and instead encourages ridicule, invoking the literary tradition that includes such figures as Gogol', early Dostoevskii, and

Kharms. In *Happy Days*, as in Gogol''s *Overcoat* (*Shinel'*), the undercurrent of mockery warns us that only the middle-brow would shed sentimentalist tears on behalf of the text's disenfranchised.

Hence in *Happy Days* any smug pity for the nameless hero is offset by our laughter at his efforts to pay the rent by allowing glimpses of his injured head. In *Trofim*, the hero's presumed execution is undercut by his comic, second "execution" at the hands of (a bitter choice!) the filmmaker and editor Aleksei German, who plays a cameo role. In *Freaks* any compassion for the Siamese boys is compromised by the perverse sight of one dead drunk and the other in love. Our despair for Liza is constrained by the comic perversity of her hired flagellator in leather pants and long hair.[26] This tradition—by now, highly exaggerated—descends from Akakii Akakievich's mock-spooky ghost, which once prevented us from mourning the poor clerk's passing from St. Petersburg life, or Kharms's plummeting old women, who were a source of mirth rather than humanistic compassion.[27]

Thus, as we watch the closing shot of *Freaks*—Iogan afloat on the ice, heading toward his voluntary death—the question arises: Where is the director in this shot? Is this the same familiar mockery, or (at last!) the director's righteous punishment of Iogan for the trouble he has caused?

We cannot answer unambiguously—or rather, it is incorrect to do so—but two facts are these: first, the pornographic footage staged a puritanical whipping as a necessary pretext for arousal; second, Balabanov's film, calibrated to the pornographic footage it contains, thrashes us in a similar fashion. Voluntarily entering the cinema hall we have allowed him to smuggle his pornographic postcards into our intellectual lives, prompting the lament by one critic that it would have been better had the film never existed (Basina 48).

To see the film's ending as merely puritanism, therefore, errs in two respects. First, the interpretation does no justice to the erotic satisfaction of watching Iogan's death *for its own sake*. After all, the subject's destruction of himself, Freud ("The Economic Problem," 170) reassures us, "cannot take place without libidinal satisfaction," primarily our own satisfaction at his impending death. But second, the insistence on a monologic puritanical interpretation does not do justice to the stubborn mockery of Balabanov's cinema. The "real values," then, to return to Margolit's assertion, must accommodate this double voicedness; it must preserve its refusal of resolution.

The Putative Nationalist

Nothing is funnier than unhappiness, I grant you that. . . . Yes, yes, it's the most comical thing in the world. And we laugh, we laugh with a will, in the beginning.

—Nell, in *Endgame* (1957)

FIGURE 8.4. Balabanov. *War.* "You've given back the Ukraine, Kazakhstan . . ."

In light of this commitment to mockery, I would like finally to return now to the question of Balabanov's nationalism. If it is billiards, as Sergei says in *Dead Man's Bluff*, then let it be Russian billiards. The Chechen warrior Aslan tells Ivan (*War*) that Russians fight poorly because they do not fight for their homeland. Our concern here is not the veracity of the truth claim, but rather the villain's functional distinction between his own tribal nationalism and the status of Russia's imperial legatee.

Brother and *Brother 2*, key films in the debates about Balabanov's putative nationalism, bear titles that, as Beumers ("To Moscow!" 83) astutely points out, are parodic to the core. Falsehood and betrayal mark the brothers' relations throughout the two films. Just as Danila lies to Viktor about his combat experience, so Viktor lies to him, cheaply subcontracting a killing to Danila with a false story about Viktor's own endangerment. And Danila? "Russians in war do not abandon their own," Danila explains sententiously (*Brother 2*), before abandoning his newly arrested brother to the U.S. court system and returning—presumably forever—to the homeland. We are poor readers if we do not savor these contradictions.

"I am against things foreign," Balabanov explains (quoted in Clarke). We are certainly justified in taking his press statements at face value; such astute insiders as Balabanov's own mentor does. As Aleksei German puts it, "I read in the newspaper Balabanov's interview with absolutely racist opinions against Jews and people from the Caucasus. As someone with a shortcoming characteristic of a scoundrel, Balabanov is not so talented that he can count on my attention. He is not a Wagner" (quoted in "Portret" 226).

But beyond Balabanov's performative mode, does it make sense therefore to insist on such a similar literalist reading of imaginative texts? Danila is playfully hostile to a foreigner yet a friend to Hoffman. He is anti-American but enacts a Hollywood action script. In this Hollywood script he cannot discern a Frenchman from an American, a trope later repeated three times in *War*, when John is mistaken for an American. In *Brother 2* Danila is anti-Black but sleeps with the African American television reporter Lisa Jeffrey. Having killed innocent musicians, Danila has the opportunity to kill the U.S. businessman Richard Mennis, whom he believes responsible for the death of his veteran-friend, yet he walks away without narrative explanation.

Eventually our improvisational logic, struggling to keep up with Balabanov's, becomes so self-evidently defective, so unable to account for its own extemporaneity, that a different set of questions must be asked, questions that approach Balabanov's work with no expectation of ideological consistency. The absence of expectation, I would argue, not only serves us better as readers of his work, but it also productively comments on the argument that Balabanov is a nationalist.

Shedding those expectations, we can see that Balabanov's hero in *Brother* and *Brother 2* is someone who, innocent of the law, nevertheless takes this un-known thing into his own hands. Danila is what is left when the army and prison survive but the civil state is absent. Clannish, untouched by such no-tions as legal consistency, he is an endearing regression to local loyalties. Here "American" is all negative values such as universality, liberalism, and fairness. Consistency for Balabanov is not only an unnecessary constraint; it is lethal, the heart of moral masochism, liberalism itself.[28] The scholar who would make order out of the films' ad hoc inclinations misses the function of the utterance, which has to do with other things: provocation, impulse, individuation, and a stubborn political incorrectness.

For liberal critics, therefore, to chastise Balabanov for his hero's reckless murder of innocent lives—the young musicians at the end of *Brother 2*, for example, in the Metro Club—is to ask for moral consistency when a different principle is presiding. Danila's victims are neither innocent nor guilty, but ob-stacles that retard the pacing. This is no longer the Danila of *Brother*, advised by his mother to visit his older brother in "Leningrad."[29] Nor is it the same Danila who asked Hoffman, "What do we live for?" Instead, it is the Danila—executing tasks, navigating the maze, and eliminating the obstacles—who makes it back to Home Base, mission accomplished.

And what, incidentally, was that mission? Perhaps one of Balabanov's younger admirers, another VGIK student, is correct about Danila's true goal:

> The action takes place on enemy territory. The war is conducted over zones of influence: there are Blacks, there [are] Ukes, and now there is us, Russians, thanks to the representation of the Bagrov Brothers. And our mission is to seize that land of grace. I will never believe that Danila went to the States only to return money to a duped hockey player. He went to scope out the battle. America will be ours. Chicago we will rename New Biriulevo.[30] (Shchigolev 35)

Danila's victory is twofold. First, he beats the American Mennis (the homophone is surely intentional). Second, he enacts Balabanov's cinematic victory over Hollywood, its genre norms, its pacing, production values, and action figure, which he appropriates to suit local needs. In this realm Danila is Balabanov's avatar, a freedom fighter battling for his cinema's emancipation from Hollywood, where the imperial center holds the outposts in sway, distributing to its own domestic elite those privileges that Balabanov's periphery would seize for itself: the right, for example, to shoot Michael Cimino's *Deer Hunter* (Universal, 1978) or Ridley Scott's *Black Hawk Down* (Revolution Studios 2001).[31]

This anticolonialist battle is a different matter from Balabanov's pronouncements of superiority *within* the space of the Russian polity vis-à-vis other ethnicities, where, hardly a freedom fighter, he is in fact its opposite. Eggplant, the African ("Ethiopian") figure in *Dead Man's Bluff*, straddles these two worlds. On the one hand, his ritual humiliation is a deliciously egregious violation of Hollywood norms. On the other hand, his ritual humiliation relegates him to inferior status with a retrograde ex-Soviet imperium.

Such a split—to put it crudely, anticolonial abroad (against Hollywood), colonial at home (against the "peripheral ethnicities")—helps to account for the semantic richness of the children's poem in *Brother 2*, first heard at Fedia Belkin's school recital: "I learned that I had / An enormous family."[32] The poem, typical of Soviet pedagogy, is described by one critic as "a new socialist realist mantra for the 21st century" (Seckler). It becomes Danila's war chant. He recites it first as the Chicago pimps climb the stairs to retrieve their prostitute; second, as he himself climbs the fire escape to confront Mennis. The poem exquisitely functions in several registers of contradiction: a child's poem, mockingly recited by an adult; official Soviet verse, mockingly pronounced by a young post-Soviet criminal; a provincial Russian poem, mockingly chanted by an international avenger against U.S. villainy. In the last of these we can see Danila's role as stand-in for Balabanov himself, colonized but also mocking and lawless, challenging Hollywood's global empire.

These internal contradictions in Balabanov's performative style—in global cinema, Russia's radical emancipation from Hollywood's rule; in the domestic arena, Russia's retrograde superiority over other subjects—must not be resolved. Above all, it must not be resolved in the name of anything resembling humanism, an orientation that would falsely lighten the filmmaker's darker side and frustrate his metatextual assaults on Hollywood. Undoubtedly with the best of intentions, several critics (Dolin "À la guerre"; Moskvina, "Pro Ivana i Dzhona") have positioned *War*, for example, somewhere between the conciliatory register of Bodrov Sr.'s *Prisoner of the Mountains* and the statist-patriotic manifesto of Aleksandr Nevzorov's ideological *Purgatory* (*Chistilishche*; ORT, 1998). While I would not debate this location in purely descriptive terms, Balabanov's text must not be mistaken for an ethical message, for a film that is, in Dolin's ("À la guerre" 29) words, "absolutely anti-war." In an effort at consensus, Dolin writes:

> War is an elemental force, transforming a human being into a cunning and cruel animal. That is the single, unambiguous conclusion that one could draw from the film. It would be interesting to know, who would dare to disagree with this conclusion? (29)

As far as this filmmaker is concerned, I would be one who would cautiously disagree. First, Balabanov does not necessarily see the cunning and cruel animal as a bad thing. Second, the Balabanov I have watched sees no transformation at all: his human already *is* a cunning and cruel animal; his films set out to remind us that we are as well.

FILMOGRAPHY

Egor and Nastia (Egor i Nastia). Documentary. 1989.
On Aeronautics in Russia (O vozdukhoplavanii v Rossii). Documentary. 1990.
Happy Days (Schastlivye dni) 1991.
Castle (Zamok) 1994.
Trofim. Short. From *The Arrival of a Train (Pribytie poezda)*. 1995.
Brother (Brat). 1997.
Of Freaks and Men (Pro urodov i liudei). 1998.
Brother 2 (Brat 2). 2000.
War (Voina). 2002.
The River (Reka). Unfinished but released. 2002.
The American (Amerikanets). Unfinished, not released. 2003.
Dead Man's Bluff (Zhmurki). 2005.
It Doesn't Hurt (Mne ne bol'no). 2006.
Cargo 200 (Gruz 200). 2007.
Morphium (Morfii). 2008.

9 ✳

Postscript

My task in writing this volume has been to ask whether Russian culture as imaginatively shaped by the experience of empire is traceable through the work of six leading contemporary filmmakers. Despite the grandeur of the topic I proceed from the more self-contained speculation that the cultural experiences of empire, variously articulated in content, structure, and the practices of production, have been naturalized to the point of near invisibility for a variety of reasons, ranging from the globally ideological to disciplinary convention.

It is one matter for a political scientist or a historian to remark on a deeply subjective stratum that runs through the debates on empire. This subjective stratum and resistance to strict definition, long considered a scholarly vulnerability, is more recently recognized by some social scientists and historians to be a source of methodological richness, linking their research more densely with work in contemporary cinema, literature, and the visual arts.[1]

In contrast, culture analysts practice in a different environment. To put the matter provocatively, most historians assume some relationship, however attenuated, between the historical document and the social reality that generated it. In cultural analysis, by contrast, the claim always remains potentially available that the text, as Viktor Shklovskii (39) once overstated the case, "has always been free of life."[2] That is to say, less consensus exists regarding a necessary and self-evident correlation between the artistic text and the circumstances of its production; no method confirms that a text operates by a certain mimesis rather than displacement, inversion, disavowal, appropriation, occlusion, or any other tricks of the imaginative trade. The relationship of evidence to argument (as well as their relative weights) is perpetually volatile.

Edward Said has suggested that, as metropolitan cultures of the British and French Empires came to a gradual understanding of the limits and external pressures on the imperium, it was the contestations of native peoples and a growing awareness of *other* empires different from their own that accelerated this process, marking that waning metropolitan culture with signs of their presence:

> I venture the suggestion that when European cultures finally began
> to take due account of imperial "delusions and discoveries" . . .
> [they] did so not oppositionally but ironically, and with a desperate
> attempt at a new inclusiveness.[3] It was as if, having for centuries
> comprehended empire . . . to be either taken for granted or cele-
> brated, consolidated, and enhanced, members of the dominant
> European cultures now began to look abroad with the skepticism
> and confusion of a people surprised, perhaps even shocked by
> what they saw. (*Culture and Imperialism* 189)

Here one might object that, unlike the case with England and France, Russia's modern periods of imperial collapse—1917 and 1991—are marked by somewhat different features. After all, Russia's intellectual historians and philosophers, its cultural producers and administrators, situated at the edge of Europe, could at no time be described as *unaware* of other empires, whether historical or contemporary to it. The cultural appropriations of Englishness, for example, and in particular the seafaring glory of the thalassocratic empire, were part of a

FIGURE 9.1. Aivazovskii. The Mary Caught in a Storm.

common Russian identity practice of the elites from the late sixteenth century onward, strengthening what Said (*Culture and Imperialism* 52 and elsewhere) himself would call "structures of attitude and reference" in a complex "web of affiliations" (125).

All the same, what strikes me as relevant in Said's comments has to do with the idea that the era of imperial collapse—arguably the last two decades of Soviet Stagnation—is accompanied by distinct forms of cultural play. Speaking of the British and French imperial demise (and with it, the flourishing of modernism), Said broadly identifies three forms of cultural play: a "circularity of structure"; a "novelty based . . . on the reformulation of old, even outdated fragments . . . from different locations"; and a renewed emphasis on irony that "draws attention to itself as substituting art and its creations for the once-possible synthesis of world empires" (*Culture and Imperialsim* 189). Said continues:

> When you can no longer assume that Britannia will rule the waves
> forever, you have to re-conceive reality as something that can be
> held together by you, the artist, in history rather than in geography.
> Spatiality becomes, ironically, the characteristic of an aesthetic
> rather than of political domination. (189–90)

These comments are, of course, conjectural, however much Said may extensively shore them up in textual practice.[4] Literalist that I am, I might wish for a closer textual reading than he is inclined here to provide. At the same time I also cannot help but recognize that the filmmakers under examination here, witnessing their own country's imperial cascade, respond with impulses, manifestly diverse but sharing a common engagement with that process, whether that engagement is expressed as a move toward nostalgic conservation, apocalyptic acceleration, undoing what has been done, transcoding it into a different symbolic register with different valences, or other forms of serotine play.

In the context of Said's comments, for example, Mikhalkov's enjoinments to us to engage together with him in a pastoral, leisurely story of imperial repetition and continuity proffer a compensatory counternarrative to collapse. Rather than catastrophe or apocalypse, the Russian empire, his films often seem to insist, is only episodically fragile within a larger and "more meaningful" cultural continuum staged on the estates and summer homes of an insufficiently marshaled elite. As consumers of Mikhalkov's narratives of dynastic and socialist Russias, we would be foolish to see this proposition as a neutral and descriptive category, an accounting of fact. Instead, from what we know of his work, it is an offer to participate in a restitutive belief system with real social consequences, politically distinct from those proposed by other filmmakers. Mikhalkov's narrative of imperial continuity is testimony in its own way to more foundational evidence of extreme discontinuity, to which his imaginative project reacts by revealing its anxieties and ambitions.

Sokurov, though also a neotraditionalist, responds in an utterly different fashion to the circumstances of collapse than does Mikhalkov. These two directors might be seen as sharing a number of features: nostalgic elitism, a love of state and military, and an elevated regard for high European art. Yet where Mikhalkov stages an elaborate genealogical spectacle, Sokurov stages a different kind of spectacle on an abstract plane, conditionally figured as the secular markings of a pure and free immortal soul. Where in the end Mikhalkov would reside in the profane world, Sokurov would not. Where Mikhalkov's cinema is grounded in social fact, melodramatic afflatus, and unbroken historical time, Sokurov's cinema is a timeless visual sanctuary, the locus for static allegory.

Sokurov, "the first in our cinema to formulate the idea of imperial collapse," as Trofimenkov ("Nigde i vsegda" 130) claimed, renders that collapse through the elegies, the drama of British imperial catastrophe, and the recurrent tales of death. Yet his rendition of "the apocalyptical mood that took hold of the large part of the intelligentsia" (130) nevertheless seeks to work on that sensate apocalypse to transcode it as the transcendent empire *beyond* death, the realm of the immortal that confounds Hitler's ambitions to overcome the kingdom of death, Lenin's denigration of "life eternal," and Hirohito's theocratic status. Sokurov's creation of a timeless, cloistered space, analogous to the timeless, cloistered spaces of the church monastery and the museum, simultaneously arrests the historical moment of collapse and sublates it to a higher, spiritual realm of artistic genius and potential immortality, to life without end.

And here is the paradox: Muratova's cinema too is in its own way a cloistered, private space of artistic creation. Any comparison of Muratova with Sokurov—a comparison of atheist to Orthodox, of reprobate humorist to humorless prohibitor—might seem odd. After all, Muratova will not deliver the redemptive episode because she knows there is no one in whose name it could be delivered. All the same, the two filmmakers share an intense absorption in the emancipatory potential of art. For Muratova, art emancipates us in real-time, eccentric improvisation; for Sokurov, art emancipates us in a ritual of reverence, liberated from profane time. Here the skeptic and the believer, the ludic miscreant and the gnomic augur share a sense of cinema—through the many ideological and critical obstacles they have similarly faced—that is a sovereign realm, marked by its utter insularity, a world they seek to shutter off for the sake of its own practices. Muratova, the self-declared narcissist ("Egoism is the essence of my métier" [quoted in Frodon 72]), and Sokurov, the stubborn visionary of "non-procedural passions" (Arkus in Arkus and Savel'ev, *Sokurov* 21), produce comparably intractable cinemas, marked as much by the official ideology that shut them out as by their own responsive practices. In both cases there is no question as to who holds mastery; each takes as fitting a certain autocracy, commensurate with the conditions they have endured. If these two filmmakers share a kind of monologic imperviousness, that feature emerges from the conditions of political volatility in which their skills were honed.

Abdrashitov and Mindadze, by contrast, who had a less confrontational history with the Soviet authorities, bear an entirely different relation to their viewer, one predicated on dialogue, a lament for an imagined *communitas*. Staging in their cinema a repeating allegorical accident that suggests a larger collective mishap, Abdrashitov-Mindadze pose the anguished question "Are we worth it?" (to which Muratova has already answered unequivocally "No" repudiating available ways of belonging: loyalties, patriotism, collective sentiment, family ties). What for Abdrashitov-Mindadze is a failure of communal formation is for Muratova a fraudulent category from the outset. Where Abdrashitov-Mindadze would elevate the community, hoping to overcome its social amnesia, Muratova would dismiss that collectivity as a set of electrical charges.

The state, so admired by Mikhalkov and Sokurov, bears a different meaning for Abdrashitov-Mindadze. Its collapse, often figured as a legal accident, is lamented only in the sense that the pliable subject is ill prepared to stand on its own. Shell-shocked and contused, Abdrashitov-Mindadze's citizens can neither function individually nor sustain a set of relations absent the ministrations of the state. "Our children will still meet each other again just as we met," a Caucasian partisan casually remarks to a Russian veteran in *Time of the Dancer*. Devoid of malice, his words acknowledge their status as a stalled imperial relation, a generic, drifting dyad, demobbed from state wars and temporarily vitiated of antagonism. The characters of Abdrashitov-Mindadze return again and again to some missing element: kinship, camaraderie, loyalty. Their characters remain in a suspended state, for which nineteenth-century literature represents the only remaining memory system.

In German's work it is not memory but knowledge that is missing. His characters are not the somnambulants or the posttrauma casualties, incompetent to reconstitute the past, as in Abdrashitov-Mindadze's cinema. They are hampered instead by a naïveté toward their present and its implied future. If Lapshin walked the long way to work—through the provincial town's victory arch, though it meant a detour—he did so to confirm his unshakeable optimism in the future, unshakeable (in German's cinematic logic) *because* it exists just before the onset of the Terror. In detailing the naïveté and ignorance on the catastrophic threshold of the 1930s and 1940s German creates the conditions for us to consider our own naïveté and ignorance in the course and aftermath of the Soviet collapse, when these films, against considerable odds, were painstakingly made. In sharp contrast, therefore, to Mikhalkov's continuities, German's cinema is a eulogy to a way of remembering, a portrait of a mid-Soviet identity—ignorant and cultured, foolish and noble—by those who saw it out.

Of course, one cannot compare these creative renditions as if they were inert, empirical objects in the social domain, established points of reference or agreed-upon things. If German cherishes the fragile network of the intelligentsia, whereas Muratova expresses toward it a brutal contempt, these two directors in no sense disagree; they do not undertake a common reference to the same social stratum (nor indeed to the intelligentsia at all, some would argue), but are addressing a larger economy of existing myths, argued positions, and prior texts in circulation. One need not, therefore, find the two filmmakers in conflict because their systems of representation differ; to do so is to mistake imaginative engagement for a social platform.

Yet here is where Balabanov's work marks a new turn in contemporary cinema. If one were to continue Said's line of thought—that imperial collapse generates distinct patterns of artistic play that cannot therefore be foretold as a set of inevitabilities, but may be read retrospectively as individually legible about the historical moment—Balabanov's work suggests a particularly dark variation. In the chapter on Balabanov's work I argued against a view of his cinema as a kind of emancipatory nationalism, a project of collective, celebratory self-realization. An alternative view derives from recent research on ultranationalisms of a different order. Roger Griffin and other theorists of twentieth-century German and Italian politics have debated the merits of palingenesis as a newly productive model of modernist ultranationalism that derives ideological power from the imaginative resurrection of an earlier empire whose legitimacy is placed beyond investigation, in a space of eternity, origins, or other naturalized inertness.[5] The most familiar example of modernist palingenesis is the Third Reich, whose imaginative power lay in part in its promise of having superseded the Holy Roman Empire and Bismarck Germany. Italian fascism likewise found in the Roman Empire a source for palingenetic inspiration. Such figures in the historical avant-garde as the modernist writers Thierry Maulnier and Georges Valois participated in a right-inflected version of modernist production, compatible both with ultranationalism and, under the influence of Charles Maurras, with fascist ideology.[6] Russia too we will remember, is not without its engagement with Rome, a legacy that traces itself through Byzantium and Russia's dynastic period potentially to the present day.

Do we find in Balabanov's cinema a newly assertive confidence about old imperial superiorities? However steeped in protective irony, Balabanov's cinema offers a kind of provocational crypto-imperialism, an ostentatious disdain for ethnic minorities and a pugnacious appetite for cultural dominance that imaginatively resurrects from the early twentieth century a demiurgic modernism, now as a right-wing avant-gardism. It is an interpretation that would provide a conceptual bridge between Balabanov's earlier neomodernist recyclings—Samuel Beckett (*Happy Days*) and Franz Kafka (*Castle*)—and his later work, with its fascination for such modernist categories as the city, for machinery, industry, transport, metal landscapes, as well as its concerns with power, mastery, hierarchy, and (particularly in *Cargo 200*) paranoia. Balabanov's iron modernity revisits and completes early communism's dark legacy: Lenin, once described by H. G. Wells as "this little man at the Kremlin [who] sees the decaying railways replaced by a new electric transport, [and] a new and happier Communist industrialism arising again," is refashioned by Balabanov as Leninsk, the crepuscular, second life of communist industrialism, the anonymous urban machine. His regressive vision is that of the cultural *refusé*, an alienated path-breaker in search of spiritual regeneration, rejecting the conventions of the recent past so as to forge a new, brutalist art, one that might satisfy the resentments of a right-wing neomodernism.

A quarter-century ago Harold Isaacs (6–7), commenting on the legacy of the European empires, suggested:

> [Empires] laid much more than a political imprint on the peoples
> they ruled. The mystiques by which they governed for so long in-
> cluded whole cultural systems that survived in many shapes and
> measures of their real or assumed superiorities, or by the sheer trans-
> forming power of what they brought with them. They left as legacies
> styles of life as well as of government, often of language, art, religion,
> and philosophy of the spirit.

The refractions of the empire explored here do not imply that the examples by these six directors exhaust the range of imaginative play. Chosen for their prominence rather than for any anticipated results of the research (such as a premeditated taxonomy), they suggest an unpredictable variety of such imaginative play and serve as a caution against any claim that a limit, a unity, or a template is achieved here. We may debate the textual evidence or the interpretation brought to contemporary culture, but it would be difficult to respond to Isaacs that the "mystiques by which they governed for so long" did not bear traces of the imperial imagination that has been so much a part of Russia's history and culture.

Notes

1. Hall's (64) work, based most directly on Mayall, posits the three great ages of nationalism as the early nineteenth-century establishment of new Latin American states, Woodrow Wilson's Versailles enlargement, and midcentury decolonization.

2. For a debate on this topic, see Gayatri Spivak's exchange with Chernetsky, Condee, and Ram in Chernetsky et al. The term "second world" refers to the (former) socialist states, including the Soviet bloc, but often also including China, Cuba, Albania, North Korea, Mongolia, and North Vietnam. The term is an extrapolation from "third world," the origins of which are debated but most often ascribed to an article by the French demographer Alfred Sauvy (*L' Observateur*, August 14, 1952), comparing third world countries to the Third Estate: "ce Tiers Monde ignoré, exploité, méprisé comme le Tiers État" (this ignored Third World, exploited, scorned like the Third Estate). The most common competing attribution is to Charles de Gaulle.

3. Where a younger generation of scholars might see a similarity between them, Anderson would see a sharp difference here between Gellner's "invention" ("he assimilates 'invention' to 'fabrication' and 'falsity'" [Anderson 6]) and his own imagining. For a useful elaboration of this point, see Hall 4.

4. For a concise but productive overview of the semantics of "nation," see Zernatto's classic essay.

5. In a similar modernist spirit, Hobsbawm (10) writes, "Nationalism comes before nations. Nations do not make states and nationalisms, but the other way round."

6. For a useful assessment of the contending strains of nationalism in the 1990s, see Tolz, *Russia* 235–69; Tuminez 199–201.

7. Most attempts to define "nation," as Tishkov and Olcott (81) astutely remark, founder on their own eagerness to convert an emotional state into an objective category, together with the related assumption that a preexisting nation gives voice to its own emotive nationalism rather than, as post-Marxist sociologists have suggested in

polemics with Miroslav Hroch, Anthony Smith (*Ethnic Origins; Theories of Nationalism*), and others, that the nation is imagined in part through the discursive practices of nationalism. This emotional state, which is in fact nationalism, remains strategically unstable and protean, immune to logic, subject to wild claims of uniqueness, prone to sudden shifts and generational recalculations, with a passionate conviction about the presence of a stable reality that in fact is not necessarily present and is never stable, but rather, as Said has productively argued, is a combination of the "empirical and the imaginative," "constantly being made and unmade" (*Orientalism* 331, 333). This claim to fixity, like claims of historical continuity and uniqueness, is symptomatic of its larger hallucinatory quality that is paradoxically its most enduring trait.

8. One must mention first of all the seascapes of the late nineteenth-century painter Ivan Aivazovskii (1817–1900; see Blakesley). One might speculate that Aivazovskii's many seascapes functioned in part as a practice of imaginative cross-identification with British maritime power. See also descriptions by the historian Vasilii Kliuchevskii (1841–1911), who depicts the Russian imperial subject dreaming of "the level, empty fields, which appear to curve around the horizon like the sea" (70). For an extensive description of landscape as a marker of Russian identity, see Ely; Rosenholm and Autio-Sarasmo. On landscape and other collective identities, see Shama; Kaufmann (United States and Canada); Zimmer and Kaufmann (Canada and Switzerland); Lekan (Rhineland); and Edensor 37–68.

9. On the second modernity, see, among other writings, *Theory, Culture and Society* 20.2 (April 2003), especially the essays by Ulrich Beck, Wolfgang Bonss, and Christoph Lau; Bruno Latour; and Scott Lash. See also Lash; Carleheden. For a brief, useful overview of the word "modern," see Williams 208–9; for an exhaustive discussion, see Compagnon.

10. For an interesting debate on this modernist approach, itself by no means unified, see Gellner, "Adam's Navel" and Anthony Smith's response ("The Nation" 36–42). Smith, a student of Ernest Gellner, is further along what might be described as the primordialist-modernist continuum than his constructivist mentor.

11. Geographic determinism is perhaps a topic more suited for poets and extremists than for scholars. Nevertheless, the scholarly literature on the political and economic implications of Russia's size and climate is rich and interesting. Excellent recent scholarly work includes Lynch (in particular chapter 6, "What Future for Russia? Liberal Economics and Illiberal Geography"). For an example of political extremism based on the fatalism of geography, see Dugin.

12. For an elaboration of this argument, see Lieven, *Empire* 4–5. I will note here, but make no attempt to resolve, the issue of whether the United Kingdom is itself a nation-state or a multinational state within which distinct national institutions—such as the Scottish Parliament, the Church of Scotland, the Scottish educational system—preserve a complex range of cooperation and participation in the unitary state. For an intelligent discussion of this ambiguity, see Nairn, *After Britain* and *Break-up*; MacCormick 133–35; Colley.

13. Doyle (45) writes, "Empire . . . is a relationship, formal or informal, in which one state controls the effective political sovereignty of another political society. It can be achieved by force, by political collaboration, by economic, social, or cultural dependence." Most research on empire returns to four features: a composite polity;

a core-periphery system (unlike federation or confederation), with a dominating center and a dominated periphery; a tendency to expansion and periodic collapse; and a *mission civilisatrice*. See, for example, Ionescu 7 (a strong political center, religious or ideological coercion, a sense of final purpose); Lieven, "The Russian Empire" 608 and *Empire* 3–26 (a great power with expansionist temptations) Szporluk, "The Russian Question" 66–67 (a great power with different people under different legal and administrative systems, endowed with a sense of ideological or religious mission).

14. As Lieven (*Empire* 231) maps out, the Russian 1550s annexation of the khanates was not the first suppression of non-Slav, non-Orthodox peoples, but was nevertheless the conquest of more highly organized and powerful states that, as Tatar and then Muslim empires, had dominated Russia for nearly three hundred years and had led to imperial drives into Siberia and south to the Caucasus. With his characteristic love of precision, Hosking (*Empire* 5) marks the foundation of the empire with Ivan's 1552 construction of the Cathedral of the Annunciation in Kazan. The relevance of his choice for this study lies in Ivan's inscription of culture onto military and administrative conquest. The 1550s—1559, to be precise—likewise mark the establishment of the first Russian fortress in what is now Chechnia (Eremenko and Novikov 209–32). For an account of this period mindful of its larger significance in the emergence of the empire, see Kappeler's *Russland* 24–56. For Hosking (at least at the time of his writing), the empire's end-point comes 439 years later with Yeltsin's speech of September 4, 1991: "The Russian state . . . will never be an empire. . . . It will be an equal among equals" (*Summary of World Broadcasts*, SU/1168, September 4, 1991, I, quoted in Hosking, *Empire and Nation* 5). As Yeltsin's later pronouncements demonstrated, however, equality proved a less interesting project when the alternative was regional hegemony. Already by December 1991 the Yeltsin press office issued the claim that all borders with Russia, with the exception of the Baltics, were subject to Russian revision (Tolz, "Conflicting" 286). By his September 14, 1995, decree ("Strategic Policy of the Russian Federation towards CIS Member States"), Russian supremacy over the territory of the former USSR was again cautiously invoked (Tolz, "Conflicting" 285), a practice that has sporadically continued under Putin.

15. In fact Peter had been using the title as early as 1710. See *Polnoe sobranie*, items 2287, 2298, 2301 (pp. 543–45, 560–67, 575–77).

16. The varying pace of state cohesion, to be sure, had its own geographic priorities. To return to the example of Chechnia, its script, based on Arabic, was Romanized only in 1925, then shifted to Cyrillic in 1938 (Tishkov 74–76).

17. This shift from a 1920s policy of *korenizatsiia* (indigenization or "going to the roots") to *sliianie* (fusion or "drawing together") has been the subject of Western debate at least since the work of Lowell Tillett in the late 1960s. For more recent, polemic debates, see Suny and Martin. Perhaps the most often cited essay is Yuri Slezkine's "The USSR as a Communal Apartment."

18. For the more narrowly educated among us, Jean-Bédel Bokassa (1921–96) was the military ruler of the Central African Republic (1966–79), which he renamed the Central African Empire in 1976, hoping to make the country stand out from the rest of Africa, and crowned himself Emperor Bokassa I the following year.

19. An accompanying historiographic shift can be traced after the work of the leading Marxist historian of the 1920s, M. N. Pokrovskii, whose school fell from favor

after 1934, and the reemergence of such historians as Sergei Bakhrushin, Vladimir Picheta, E. V. Tarle, and B. D. Grekov (Markwick 40–41; Shteppa 90, 97–98).

20. The most nuanced treatment of Soviet Russian class ascription can be found in Fitzpatrick, "Ascribing Class."

21. The term "symbolic ethnicity," from Gans's work, describes a way of being ethnic largely through symbols, coexistent with substantial adaptation to a dominant culture.

22. One might argue that the "Internationale," composed as the very counter-vention of a (sovereign) national anthem, performed a delicate operation in the early Soviet years, when (until 1944) it served as the USSR anthem. As an anthem, the "Internationale" confirmed Soviet relations *within* the polity for "nations" subsumed under the imperial umbrella, while at the same time aspiring, in the name of interna-tionalism, to transcend Western sovereign boundaries as conceived of by bourgeois nationalism.

23. Similarly, the translation of *narod* tends to avoid "nation" in favor of the con-ceptually less confusing "people" or "folk," an issue to which I return below.

24. See Doyle 32–39, 42, 45, 135 for an extended discussion of these distinctions.

25. David A. Lake (57) presciently argued the likelihood of Russia as a newly con-stituted informal empire: "As they mature, relations between the successor states are unlikely to resemble those between the autonomous, sovereign states often thought to characterize international politics. To understand the future, we must return to the study of imperialism."

26. For a more detailed discussion of this phenomenon in the late Soviet period, see Rywkin.

27. The RSFSR branch of the Writers' Union was founded in 1958, three years *after* the Moscow branch, in part to offset the liberal politics of its metropolitan resi-dents (Garrard and Garrard 3, 79). The RSFSR Writers' Union—significantly—then became the principal source from which members of the all-union Litburo (Bureau of the Writers' Union Board), the key governing structure of the Union's administra-tion, were chosen during the stagnation period (86). Only in mid-*perestroika* were the Moscow and Leningrad branches "emancipated" to enjoy administrative status on a par with the republican unions. More than this, during the stagnation period at least, the chairs of the governing councils in the *non-Russian* republican unions were consistently Russian, whereas the vice chairs tended to be from the relevant ethnic community (148).

28. See Dunlop, *The Rise of Russia* 16–20, for an extensive treatment of this issue.

29. The distinction between russocentrism and russification comes out of de-bates surrounding David Brandenberger's work, specifically whether the later Stalinist period (1945–53 in particular) was one of pragmatic russocentrism rather than either russification or Russian nationalism. See also Mitrokhin for the early post-Stalin years in particular and Brudny for the later Soviet period. I am grateful to Ellen Mercer for a series of discussions on this topic.

30. An early instance of conservativism as unintentional modernization, I would argue, was the Great Schism of 1666–67, triggered by efforts at backward reform, as both parties argued a return to their respective constructed pasts. One might argue that the dissolution of the USSR, in which the conservative coup played a precipitating

role in inadvertent modernization, was another example, the culmination of the process begun in the mid-1960s.

31. See, for example, *Izvestiia*, June 2, 1989, 9; *Sovetskaia Rossiia*, June 7, 1989, 2, respectively. The term "russophobia" (*rusofobiia*) entered into more active circulation as a result of Igor' Shafarevich's *samizdat* work of the same title, written in 1978–82 and published in the conservative journal *Nash sovremennik* 6 (1989): 167–92 and 11 (1989): 162–71.

32. Dominic Lieven, *Empire* (124), likewise characterizes the distinction between *rossiiskii* (Russian state and ruler) and *russkii* (Russian people and culture) in ways that resonate with Hosking's (*Empire* 8–9) argument about Russia's imperial and demotic identities.

33. See Richters for an analysis of related strains in the Estonian Orthodox Church. See also Werth for an excellent account of Georgian Orthodox autocephaly and ethnic fragmentation.

34. Quoted in *Novoe vremia* 22 (1991): 13. It is perhaps significant that Russian Orthodox liturgical music becomes codified precisely *after* Petrine Westernization; in other words, what might be misperceived as Russia's most "national" music emerges in a context of Westernized imperial culture (see Frolova-Walker in S. Franklin and Widdis 124).

35. The central issue, captured in Paul Goble's (79, 81) succinct formulation "What is Russian and who are Russians?," must take into account, among other things, the diasporic community of 25 million Russians throughout the former empire. Regional conflict therefore can be adequately addressed neither with reference to the Russian polity nor to Russian ethnicity, but rather to the very geographic noncorrespondence between those two categories that is the weightiest legacy of the empire.

36. Key features of totalitarianism—"a system of autocratic rule for realizing totalistic intentions under modern conditions" (Friedrich et al. 126)—in much of the relevant scholarship include a totalist ideology, a single mass party, a system of terroristic police control, state monopoly over mass communications, and centralized control of the economy. The most comprehensive discussion of the historical trajectory of this scholarship is contained in Gleason. See also Cohen.

37. For an elaboration of this argument, see Condee, "From Emigration." In addition to the discrepancies between market-driven and state-driven modernization such as those listed above, one might add other discrepancies, such as Western valorization of individual subjectivity (including the individual work ethic and the striving toward individual autonomy), socialist valorization of collective subjectivity and the vanguard class. On the related debates around socialist modernization and/or neotraditionalism, see Martin, "Modernization."

38. For a lively and useful discussion of this topic, see Arnason's "Communism and Modernity" in the special issue of *Daedalus* focusing on multiple modernities. See also Clermont.

39. Suffice it to mention capital flight, electronic communication, terrorist networks, mass migration, and the drug and weapons trade.

40. This new writing on Russia, by such scholars as Rogers Brubaker, David Laitin, Terry Martin, Yuri Slezkine, and Ronald Grigor Suny, productively engages

several sources, the most formative of which are Ernest Gellner and Benedict Anderson and, more distantly, Karl Deutsch.

41. The appeal of the phrase "evil empire" lies as much in the cheesy stylistics of assonance as in its semantics, which, as Dominic Lieven (*Empire* 7) aptly comments, "surely owed something to science fiction."

42. There is considerable debate among our colleagues in the social sciences concerning the inevitability of the Soviet collapse. Mau and Starodubrovskaya, for example, see the process as highly deterministic and indicative of a foreseeable logic of the revolutionary process (the English Civil War, the French Revolution, and 1917). George Breslauer, by contrast, has characterized the last decade of the USSR as a volatile one in which the emergence of Gorbachev and Yeltsin played a pivotal role in precipitating change.

43. For a thorough set of citations contrasting descriptive versus normative usages of "empire," see Suny, "Empire" fn. 3 and 4.

44. One exception to this tendency is the extensive comparative treatment contained in Lieven, *Empire*.

45. It should be noted at the same time, however, that the impulse to be indisputably imperial in Russian texts often took the form of English affectation. The appeal of Englishness was surely, among other things, its unambiguous, material separation of metropole from colony by the enormous expanse of ocean. As S. Franklin and Widdis (52) remark, "Statements about Englishness can often be read as coded statements about the self."

46. As Dominic Lieven (*Empire* 318) remarks, "In the Soviet case [as distinct from the British Empire] a clearly defined Russian nation did not exist, did not possess genuine self-governing national institutions, and certainly did not control the imperial state. The latter was run by an imperial Party elite, largely Russian in ethnicity but Soviet in loyalty." In a later footnote, Lieven adds that the presence of Russian ethnicity in the ruling elite varied widely at different historical periods: in 1917–21, the only Russians among the leadership were Lenin and Nikolai Bukharin; in 1988, by contrast, the only non-Slav full member of the Politburo was Edvard Shevardnadze (440 fn. 51).

47. These polls were conducted in February 1995 in Moscow and eighteen regions of the Russian federation. See Tolz "Conflicting" for further information and extensive details on these and other opinion polls.

48. Hirschman's classic study, *Exit, Voice and Loyalty*, encounters interesting challenges in the Soviet context: "It makes no sense," he writes, "to speak of being loyal to a firm, a party, or an organization with an unbreakable monopoly" (82). For much of Soviet history, the opposite was true: being loyal to a Party with an unbreakable monopoly was, for many of its citizens, sensible in the extreme.

49. See, for example, E. P. Chelyshev, quoted in Slobin (524): "Literature abroad can, to a degree, be called Orthodox literature."

50. The first question ("Tam ili zdes'?") refers to Vladislav Khodasevich's 1925 essay. The second, ("Odna literatura ili dve?") refers to the 1978 University of Geneva symposium and its subsequent volume, edited by Georges Nivat. A third key text is the extraordinarily valuable volume by Matich and Heim, *The Third Wave*.

51. Hubertus Jahn notes, for example, that the poet Aleksandr Pushkin, traveling in the Caucasus, "explicitly referred to the Caucasus and to the newly conquered

territories as 'Russia.' In other words, he understood 'Russia' as a multiethnic empire. On the other hand, he constantly described the Caucasus as foreign and exotic and clearly as a part of the so-called Orient" (quoted in S. Franklin and Widdis 55).

52. Among the best work on identity formation during the bleakest years of the Stalinist period is Kotkin, Hellbeck, and Eric Naiman. See also two edited volumes, the first by Sheila Fitzpatrick and Yuri Slezkine, the second by Véronique Garros, Natalia Korenevskaya, and Thomas Lahusen.

53. Let us conditionally identify key features of civil society as autonomy and an institutionalized capacity for critique. See Lewin's (262) definition of an "aggregate of networks or institutions that either exist or act independently of the state."

54. Staraia Ploshchad' (Old Square) was the location of the Central Committee Headquarters of the CPSU.

55. Tsipko, *Nezavisimaia gazeta,* February 9, 1995.

56. Hosking nevertheless has cogently defended the wisdom that projects an eventual transformation of contemporary Russia to a nation-state:

> In Russia the sense of solidarity associated with nationhood would do much to diminish . . . the bitter political conflicts which still disfigure its internal order. I do not pretend, of course, that the process of strengthening national identity in Russia can be wholly reassuring either for her neighbors or for the international community at large. But I believe it is preferable to any attempt at rebuilding empire, which I take to be the only serious alternative. (*Russia* xxvii)

57. "Одна его часть как бы прикинулись иностранцами, в их самом страшном и угрожающем облике, и принялось следовательно и радикально преследовать все русское и и насаждать все самое для того времени модернизированное и западное, чего реальные иностранцы, если бы они действительно завоевали Россию, вероятно делать бы не стали. Однако в результате этой жестокой прививки, Россия действительно спаслась от реальной колонизации превосходящим ее в техническом и военном отношении Западом."

58. "Народ был Другим. Он выключился из публичной сферы и отношений обмена. Он подлежал надзору и заботе; классификации и дисциплинированию. Он говорил на русском языке . . . но те же слова произносил иначе и вкладывал иные значения."

59. For a lively and thoughtful polemic with Etkind's work, see Engelstein, a self-described "old historicist." Reviewing Etkind's *Knout* (*Khlyst*), Engelstein (482) aims her critique at Etkind's participation in the "catchall genre of interdisciplinary cultural studies," a discomfort that implicitly extends to such work as "The Shaved Man's Burden" ("Bremia britogo cheloveka"), under discussion here.

This incompatibility with an emancaption narrative need not be the case universally. Mario Barrera's account of internal colonization, for example, in *Race and Class in the Southwest* ("a form of colonialism in which the dominant and subordinate populations are intermingled, so that there is no geographically distinct 'metropolis' separate from the 'colony' " [194]) retains thereby an emancipatory potential.

60. In the realm of political—rather than cultural—theory, one might find the roots of this argument in Lenin's *The Development of Capitalism in Russia* (172–77,

269, 363ff), and Gramsci's "The Southern Question" in *The Modern Prince*. For a more recent handling of this model, though with radically different conclusions, see Hechter's (8–9, 166, 342–51) analysis of England's internal colonization of Wales, Scotland, and Ireland.

61. "Русский дворянин в петровскую и послепетровскую эпоху оказался у себя на родине в положении иностранца — человек, которому во взрослом состоянии искусственными методами следует обучаться тому, что обычно люди получают в раннем детстве непосредственным опытом. Чужое, иностранное приобретает характер нормы. Правильно вести себя — это вести себя по-иностранному, то есть некоторым искусственным образом, в соответствии с нормами чужой жизни. Помнить об этих нормах так же необходимо, как знать правила неродного языка для корректного им пользования. . . . Надо было *не быть* иностранцем . . . , а вести себя *как* иностранец."

62. I am thinking, to cite one well-known example, of Fedor Abramov's *Wooden Horses* (*Dereviannye koni*), in which the metropolitan narrator visits an unfamiliar hinterland in his capacity as a collector of peasant artifacts. The story underscores the gap between the educated protagonist's metropolitan expertise and the peasants' un-examined, organic, local knowledge. This parallelism is established through the device of the ethnographic journey to a location simultaneously old and new, originative yet awaiting first discovery, and thus "forgotten," an ethnically homogeneous, primordial memory system renewed by the journey itself.

63. I will spare you the examples. The best and most comprehensive research on this topic is by Kathleen Parthé, especially 202–8 ("Childhood") and 61–63 ("Child-hood Time"). See also Peterson, especially 92–94 ("Utopia II: Perfection in the Past") and 94–95 ("Utopia III: The Legendary World of Childhood").

64. For an insightful discussion of this thread in Russian culture, see Janet Kennedy 93.

65. Inverting Said's famous characterization of the Orient ("a theatrical stage affixed to Europe" [*Orientalism* 63]), we might say that St. Petersburg was built as the Newly Shaven Man's theatrical stage affixed to Russia.

66. As Lotman ("Poetika") mentions in passing, the copresence and interdependency of these unbridgeable collective identities are performed in the many tales of Peter's behavior, reputed to shift erratically between a stylistically Europeanized and a supposedly natural, peasant register.

67. See, for example, note 45 on the textual appeal of "Englishness" under social conditions that hardly resemble England.

68. On the complexities inherent in the shift from "nation" to "nationalism," see Greenfeld, *Nationalism* 4–12.

69. The most interesting recent work in English on this topic has been done by Stites, *Serfdom*.

70. *Ostaf'evskii arkhiv kniazei Viazemskikh* (St. Petersburg, 1899), quoted in Knight (50). For an extensive discussion of this issue, see Leighton 48–51.

71. Institute of Russian Literature, or Pushkinskii Dom, f. 93, op. 3, no. 881, l. 10, quoted in Knight (55).

72. For a fuller discussion of Uvarov's *narodnost'* see Riasanovsky. See also Whittaker; Lincoln. For a larger, comparative discussion of the phenomenon of official

narodnost', see Seton-Watson *Nations*, especially 148, as well as his *Russian Empire*. As Jahn points out (in S. Franklin and Widdis 62–63), the principal shift from Uvarov's *narodnost'* of the 1830s and the Panslavist *narodnost'* of the late 1860s on was from an "ethnically neutral populism" to a Russian primacy with imperial aspirations.

73. I bracket here, though it in no way contradicts my argument, the figure sometimes identified as the writer Nikolai Gogol', clothed in a red robe and situated at the back of the crowd. The most valuable discussion of the painting and its cultural context may be found in Gray 107–24.

74. Berdiaev's work, written late in his emigration years (1946), appeared in his homeland only in 1990, in *Voprosy filosofii* 1 (1990): 77–144 and 2 (1990): 87–154. For the second resurgence of interest in the Russian Idea in the late communist period, see Aizlewood. For a discussion of its relevance to late Soviet and post-Soviet culture, see Condee "No Glory" 31–33 and 190, fn 27. The best historical treatment of the concept of Holy Rus' is Cherniavsky, "'Holy Russia.'"

75. See references. For Chernetsky, see also the following unpublished monograph and edited volume (in progress): "Second World Postmodernity: Literary Paradigms of a Cultural Transformation" and *Postcoloniality and the Second World: Postcolonial Theory Encounters Contemporary East European and Post-Soviet Culture*, edited and with a contribution by Chernetsky. See also Barrett; Ulbandus 7. Of interest but somewhat less relevance is Pavlyshyn.

76. Прощай, немытая Россия,
    Страна рабов, страна господ,
    И вы, мундиры голубые,
    И ты, им преданный народ.

    Быть может, за стеной Кавказа
    Сокроюсь от твоих пашей,
    От их всевидящего глаза,
    От их все слышащих ушей.

77. Among oft-cited examples of such colonial texts are Pushkin's three southern poems—*Prisoner of the Caucasus* (*Kavkazskii plennik*), *The Fountain at Bakhchisarai* (*Bakhchisaraiskii fontan*), and *The Gypsies* (*Tsygany*)—as well as his later parodistic travelogue *Journey to Arzrum* (*Puteshestvie v Arzrum*); Bestuzhev-Marlinskii's *Stories of the Caucasus* (*Kavkazskie povesti*), such as *Ammalat-bek*, *Letters from Dagestan* (*Pis'ma iz Dagestana*), and *Mulla-Nur*; Lermontov's *Hero of Our Time* (*Geroi nashego vremeni*), as well as his many short lyrics; Lev Tolstoi's *Prisoner of the Caucasus* (*Kavkaskii plennik*), *Cossacks* (*Kazaki*), and *Khadzhi-Murat*. This "*Prisoner* tradition" is continued in Leonid Gaidai's film *Prisoner of the Caucasus, or Shurik's New Adventures* (*Kavkazskaia plennitsa, ili novye prikliucheniia Shurika*; Mosfil'm, 1966), Vladimir Makanin's novella *Prisoner of the Caucasus* (*Kavkazskii plennyi*), and Sergei Bodrov's film *Prisoner of the Mountains* (original Russian title, *Prisoner of the Caucasus* [*Kavkazskii plennik*], Karavan, 1996).

78. Implicit in the structure of this argument is Jameson's critique of Claude Lévi-Strauss in "On Interpretation" (*Political Unconscious* 77–80). I am grateful to Petre Petrov for several extended discussions on this topic.

79. See Daniel 5:5–31. King Balthazar, son of Nebuchadnezzar, sought the meaning of the words "Mene mene tekel upharsin" (translated by the Jewish prophet Daniel

as "Thou art weighed in the balance and found wanting"), written on the wall of his palace by God's disembodied hand.

80. "Так двадцать стройных танцоров превращались в цветущих делегатов его национальной политики, точно так же, как дети, бегущие к Мавзолею, где он стоял по праздникам, превращались в гонцов будущего, в его розовые поцелуи. И он умел это ценить, как никто другой, поражая окружающих своей неслыханной широтой."

81. A similar conceptualism is at play as the children are ideologically recast as "heralds of the future" (*gontsy budushchego*) of historical determinism. Note the conceptualist compatibility with Dmitrii Aleksandrovich Prigov.

82. Ланцелот. В каждом из них придется убить дракона.

Мальчик. А нам будет больно?

Ланцелот. Тебе нет.

1-й горожанин. А нам?

Ланцелот. С вами придется повозиться.

Садовник. Но будьте терпеливы, господин Ланцелот. Умоляю
вас — будьте терпеливы.

83. In a very different register from Chiaureli's, the poet-conceptualist Dmitrii Aleksandrovich Prigov, as he chose to call himself, engages in a mock-serious imperial display that similarly "demotes" the sovereign nation to the status of an imperial substate. In his "Kulikovo Field," the narrator, who functions on an ideological continuum with God, the Autocrat, and Stalin, positions his national tokens—the Poles, the French, and the Germans, much as in Chiaureli's film—on the playing field of war.

Вот всех я по местам расставил
Вот этих слева я поставил
Вот этих справа я поставил
Всех прочих на потом оставил —
Поляков на потом оставил
Французов на потом оставил
И немцев на потом оставил. (92)

("See how I have put them all in their places / These here I have put on the left / These here I have put on the right / All the rest I have left for later / The Poles I have left for later / The French I have left for later / And the Germans I have left for later.")

As those schooled in Russo-Soviet culture and Prigoviana in particular will appreciate, the humor of this poem is structured by the neat overlay of two voices: that of the infantile and distracted boy-narcissist with his toy soldiers and the detached, military confidence of the autocrat with his imperial ambitions, exercising his "unheard-of expanse" (as Iskander would have it) over the Poles, the French, and the Germans as if they were such mere subordinate ethnoterritories, the citizens of Armenia, Tadzhikistan, or the Moldavia on the Soviet imperial playing field. Prigov ironizes, on the one hand, the leader's deluded global megalomania while elevating the boy to a position of mock mastery over these states.

84. Mosfil'm, Russia's best-known film studio, dates from the cinema production units of A. A. Khanzhonkov and I. N. Ermol'ev. The studio was named Mosfil'm

Cinema Factory in 1935 and renamed Mosfil'm Cinema Studio on January 4, 1936. See www.mosfilm.ru.

Goskino, the acronym for the Government Committee for Cinema Affairs of the USSR Council of Ministers (Gosudarstvennyi komitet po delam kinematografii pri sovete ministrov SSSR), was responsible for virtually all preproduction, production, and postproduction: script commission, selection, and approval; ideological and financial supervision; copies, distribution, and release coordination. Under its umbrella Goskino also administered film institutions such as VNIIK (the All-Union Research Institute for Cinema Art), VNITIK (the All-Union Institute for the Theory and History of Cinema), NIKFI (Research Institute for Film Equipment and Technology), VGIK (the All-Union State Institute of Cinema), and LIKI (the Leningrad Institute of Film Engineers), as well as the industry's major periodicals, *Cinema Art* (*Iskusstvo kino*) and *Soviet Screen* (*Sovetskii ekran*).

The All-Union State Institute of Cinema (Vsesoiuznyi gosudarstvennyi institut kinematografii; http://www.vgik-edu.ru/), better known as VGIK, is the first and oldest state cinema institute, founded as the State Cinema School (Goskinoshkola) in 1919 under the prerevolutionary director Vladimir Gardin (1877–1965), director (with Vsevolod Pudovkin) of VGIK's first full-length feature film *Hammer and Sickle* (*Serp i molot*; Goskinoshkola VFKO, 1921). Among the names associated with VGIK are the Soviet Union's leading film and theater figures, including Lev Kuleshov, Sergei Eisenstein, Vsevolod Pudovkin, Aleksandr Dovzhenko, Mikhail Romm, Sergei Gerasimov, Konstantin Stanislavskii, Evgenii Vakhtangov, and Vsevolod Meierkhol'd. VGIK's list of students includes virtually all established Soviet and Russian filmmakers, including those examined in this volume, with the exception of Aleksei German and Aleksei Balabanov. For an interesting portrait of pre-*perestroika* VGIK, see the interview with Sokurov in Bokshitskaia.

85. For a list of the dates of founding for the republican studios, see Passek 301–25.

86. I use the term Filmmakers' Union rather than the more frequent translation, Union of Cinematographers, both for brevity and clarity, to avoid confusion between the English meaning of cinematographer (cameraman, DoP) and the Russian meaning (cinema professionals). The USSR Filmmakers' Union, which numbered about 6,500 members in the mid-1980s, included directors, scriptwriters, cinematographers, and film composers, as well as film critics and historians. Founded in 1965, the Filmmakers' Union was one of the last Soviet unions of the creative intelligentsia. See http://www.unikino.ru/. The first, the Writers' Union, was founded by the famous April 23, 1932, Decree of the Central Committee of the CPSU and held its inaugural conference in 1934. The Architects' Union, also founded in 1932, was followed by other such unions only after the death of Stalin: the Artists' Union (1957), the Journalists' Union (1959), and the Filmmakers' Union. See Garrard and Garrard; Hingley 189–259; Christie, "The Cinema"; Nepomnyashchy.

87. Pushkin's (287) letter reads: "There is no doubt that the division of churches separated us from the rest of Europe and that we did not participate in a single one of the great events that shook it, and yet we had our own, special predestination. [Нет сомнения, что схизма (разделение церквей) отъединила нас от остальной Европы и что мы не принимали участия ни в одном из великих событий, которые ее потрясали, но у нас было свое особое предназначение]."

88. Pushkin (288) writes: "I swear on my honor that for nothing in the world would I wish to change my fatherland or have a different history from that of our ancestors, such history as God has given to us." ["Но клянусь честью, что ни за что на свете я не хотел бы переменить отечество или иметь другую историю, кроме истории наших предков, такой, какой нам бог ее дал."] In 1974, at the height of Soviet third-wave emigration (though still a decade before Tarkovskii's own nonreturn), this sentence resonated loudly with Soviet contemporary issues of mandatory citizenship.

CHAPTER 2

1. As the attentive specialist will already know, production figures vary somewhat from source to source, depending on how the parameters are defined (coproduction contribution, release date, etc.). This figure is based on Segida and Zemlianukhin's 2004 *Fil'my Rossii: Igrovoe kino/TV/video (1992–2003)*, updated from their earlier 2001 *Filmy Rossii, 1995–2000*.

2. Dondurei ("Kinodelo" 127) points out that this figure is influenced to a minor extent by the fact that cinema attendance at two-part films (over 1,000 meters) required the purchase of two tickets, and thus two statistical "visits," even when the two-part film was watched from beginning to end in a single sitting.

3. In 1921 twelve films were produced; in the following year, the number rose to sixteen. In 1948 seventeen Soviet films were released; in the following year the number rose to eighteen, only to fall in 1950 to thirteen. In 1951 nine films were released, the smallest number since 1918. Segida and Zemlianukhin, *Domashniaia sinemateka* 6.

4. The best attempt is made here to present the state of the industry based on the most reliable cross-checked sources available. Nevertheless, most leading scholars would agree with the film sociologist Daniil Dondurei ("Artistic Culture" 269–70) that inconsistency and debates plague this effort, especially on cinema of the early 1990s, a time without "any credible system of accounting that would allow a *bona fide* investor or economist to make an informed judgment about industry conditions. There is no national statistic agency to track the data and report on federal and local trends."

5. Boris Durov's *Pirates of the 20th Century* drew an audience of 87.6 million; Vladimir Men'shov's *Moscow Doesn't Believe in Tears* drew 84.4 million. For figures pertaining to other Soviet blockbusters, see Kudriavtsev, *Svoe kino*; see also http://www.kinokultura.com/plus/prokat1.html; http://www.kinokultura.com/plus/prokat2.html, as well as *Soviet and Russian Blockbuster Films*, a special issue of *Slavic Review* 62.3 (Fall 2003).

6. By way of comparison, an average Hollywood production year might yield 150 films, of which a select seven might have been chosen for exhibition in the USSR in the late Soviet period (Dondurei, "Mestobliustiteli" 5).

7. This quotation, from a 1922 private conversation between Vladimir Lenin and Commissar of Enlightenment Anatolii Lunacharskii, and attributed by the latter to the former in a later interview, is one of the most contested utterances in the history of cinema. Its source is G. M. Boltianskii, ed., *Lenin i kino* (Moscow, 1925), 16–17. See also Taylor and Christie 56.

8. In 1986 eight full-length feature films were able to draw more than 20 million viewers; see http://www.kinokultura.com/plus/prokatı.html.

9. See accounts in Lawton, *Kinoglasnost* 66; Christie, "The Cinema" 45; Laurent 81–84.

10. Klimov's best-known films are *Agony* (*Agoniia*; Mosfil'm, completed 1974, released 1981; distributed in the United States as *Rasputin*), *Farewell* (*Proshchanie*; Mosfil'm 1982), and *Come and See* (*Idi i smotri*; Mosfil'm, 1985).

11. *Farewell* had originally been the project of Larisa Shepit'ko, Klimov's film-maker wife, who died in an automobile accident in 1979; the film was taken over by Klimov after her death.

12. One of the few reliable reasons for a film's shelving was the emigration or expulsion of a prominent participant. This was the cause even in the case of Ivan Pyr'ev's ultra-Stalinist collective-farm musical comedy *Kuban Cossacks* (*Kubanskie kazaki*; Mosfil'm, 1949), after the exile of the theater director Iurii Liubimov, who played Andrei in the film and founded Moscow's experimental Taganka Theatre in 1962. See R. Bykov 15.

13. Kulidzhanov's best-known films include *The House in Which I Live* (*Dom v kotorom ia zhivu*; Gor'kii Studio, 1957), *When Trees Were Tall* (*Kogda derev'ia byli bol'shimi*; Gor'kii Studio, 1961), and *Crime and Punishment* (*Prestuplenie i nakazanie*; Gor'kii Studio, 1969). Among his students was Vadim Abdrashitov, who had earlier studied with Mikhail Romm. For valuable historical commentary, see Arkus, "Mai"; Arkus and Savel'ev, "13 mai." Newly elected members of the Union secretariat were Abdrashitov, Rolan Bykov, Grigorii Chukhrai, Igor' Gelein, Gleb Panfilov, Andrei Plakhov, El'dar Riazanov, Andrei Smirnov, and Sergei Solov'ev ("Who's Who").

14. Although Iakovlev does not enlarge on this theme, one might reasonably assume, given the cultural processes traceable as early as summer 1985, that "intellectualization" involved greater administrative tolerance toward ambiguity and indeterminacy, as well as certain formal qualities—structural open-endedness, experimental montage, abstractionism, auteurism, polystylistics, atonality, and so on—historically associated with the tastes of the elite, educated metropolitan consumer.

15. The stenographic record is published in *Piatyi s'ezd kinematografistov SSSR, 13–15 maia 1986 goda.* An edited (and censored) version of the proceedings can be found in *Iskusstvo kino* 10 (1986): 4–133. See also *Sovetskaia kul'tura* 15 and 17 (1986) and *Osnovnye napravleniia.* For an English-language summary and commentary on the May 1986 Fifth Congress of the Filmmakers' Union, see *Current Digest of the Soviet Press* 38.20 (1986): 1–8, 20; Lawton, *Kinoglasnost* 53–69.

16. As Faraday (59, 216 fn. 36) and Graffy ("Literary Press") point out, similar vested interests operated in the other culture industries. Literary royalties were paid out according to print runs, not sales, a system designed to maintain the practice of enormous payments to politically loyal literary administrators, authors of so-called secretarial literature. The purchase by state museums of artwork by senior artist-administrators held in place a similar system of consecration. See also Korobov; Lovell.

17. See Plakhov, "Dva goda zhizni" for his account of this period. See also Arkus and Plakhov; Batchan, "Andrei Plakhov"; Christie, "The Cinema"; Graffy, "Recent Soviet Cinema"; Robinson; Young, "Soviet Filmers"; and "Soviet Union to Review Censored Films," *New York Times,* June 21, 1986. For invaluable documentary materials and analysis, see Fomin, *Kino i vlast'* and "*Polka.*"

18. The three best-known examples of mutilated films are Mikhail Shveitser's *The Tightly Tied Knot* (*Tugoi uzel*; Mosfil'm, completed 1957, released in a restored version 1988; also known as *Sasha Steps Out into Life* [*Sasha vstupaet v zhizn'*]), based on Vladimir Tendriakov's novella of the same title; Marlen Khutsiev's *Il'ich's Gate* (*Zastava Il'icha*; Gor'kii Studio, completed 1962, released in 1965 under the censor's title of the mutilated version *I Am Twenty* [*Mne dvadtsat' let*], then restored and re-released 1988); and Andrei Tarkovskii's historical drama *Andrei Rublev* (Mosfil'm, completed 1966, limited release 1971; re-release 1988).

Among the underdistributed films four deserve mention here: Otar Ioseliani's *Pastorale* (*Pastoral'*; Gruziia Film Studio, 1975), which had been released only in Moscow in a single print; Aleksandr Rekviashvili's *Road Home* (*Put' domoi*; Georgian title, *Gza shinisaken*; Gruziia Film Studio, 1982); Elem Klimov's 1965 comedy *Adventures of a Dentist* (*Pokhozhdeniia zubnogo vracha*; Mosfil'm, 1965), and Tengiz Abuladze's romantic drama *The Plea* (*Mol'ba*; Georgian title *Vedreba*; Gruziia Film Studio, 1967), the first part of his trilogy, of which the successive two were *The Wishing Tree* (*Drevo zhelaniia*; Georgian title *Natvris khe*; Gruziia Film Studio, 1977) and *Repentance* (*Pokaianie*; Georgian title *Monanieba*; Gruziia Film Studio, completed 1984, released 1986). In some cases, as with Konchalovskii's *The Story of Asia Kliachina*, a mutilated version of which had been released as *Asia's Happiness* on three screens of three small cinema clubs for three days (H. Kennedy 35), the distinctions between mutilation, underdistribution, and shelving are more complex.

19. Other films, contemporary with the Conflicts Commission's deliberations and problematic principally for their sexual content, were Savva Kulish's *Tragedy in Rock Style* (*Tragediia v stile rok*; Mosfil'm, 1988) and Isaak Fridberg's psychological drama *Little Doll* (*Kukolka*; Mosfil'm, 1988).

20. For an account of the particular difficulties encountered by Askol'dov *even after* the Conflicts Commission had unshelved his film, see Lawton, *Kinoglasnost* 117-18. It should be noted that three Stagnation-era films are routinely misidentified in scholarly literature and the trade press as having been unshelved by the Conflicts Commission, but they were in fact released earlier. These are Aleksei German's *Trial on the Road* (original title *Operation "Happy New Year"*; *Proverka na dorogakh* [*Operatsiia "S novym godom"*]; Lenfil'm, completed 1971; released 1986); Elem Klimov's *Agony*; and Gleb Panfilov's *Theme* (*Tema*; Mosfil'm, completed 1979, released 1986). Because they contained what came to be viewed as *"perestroika* themes"—Soviet POWs in World War II (German); political and sexual intrigue in the court of Nikolai II (Klimov); Jewish Third-Wave emigration (Panfilov)—and were released in proximity to the Commission's work, these three works are often erroneously folded into the Commission's list of unshelved films.

21. Most noteworthy among these (now twice) underprinted and underdistributed films are Iurii Il'enko's *Spring for the Thirsty* (*Rodnik dlia zhazhdushchikh*; Dovzhenko Film Studio, 1965); Kaljo Kiisk's *Madness* (*Bezumie*; Estonian title *Hullumeelsus*; Tallinnfillm, 1968); Bulat Mansurov's war film *There Is No Death, Boys!* (*Smerti net, rebiata!*; Turkmenfil'm Studio, 1970); Vladimir Motyl''s *Forest* (*Les*; Lenfil'm Studio, completed 1980, released 1987), based on Aleksandr Ostrovskii's play; Tolomush Okeev's *Sky of Our Childhood* (*Nebo nashego detstva*; Kirgizfil'm, 1966), based on the story by Chingiz Aitmatov; Larisa Shepit'ko's (1938-79) *Homeland of Electricity* (*Rodina elektrichestva*;

Dovzhenko Film Studio, completed 1967, released 1987), based on a story by Andrei Platonov and constituting the first cine-novella of the trilogy *Beginning of an Unknown Age* (*Nachalo nevedomogo veka*; ECS/Dovzhenko Studio/Mosfil'm, 1967, released 1987), a portmanteau production of Grigorii Chukhrai's Experimental Creative Studio at Mosfil'm (discussed below); and Andrei Smirnov's *Angel*, based on a story by Iurii Olesha and constituting the second cine-novella of the same trilogy. See *Variety,* July 1, 1987. See also Plakhov, "Vtoroe rozhdenie." Originally intended as a multipart commemoration of the fiftieth anniversary of the October Revolution, the resulting trilogy also included Genrikh Gabai's panel *Motria*, after the novella of the same name by Konstantin Paustovskii. *Motria* only appeared two years later as a television production (Woll 202).

22. Analogous administrative reforms can be traced in the other creative unions and related branches of the culture industry. In late October and early November 1986 the newly restructured Union of Theatre Workers of the Russian Republic elected the liberal Kirill Lavrov as head. In March 1987 the Architects' Union of the Russian Federation followed suit, with changes in the political orientation of its newly elected administration. See *Sovetskaia kul'tura,* May 15 and 17, 1986; *Pravda,* December 5, 6, and 7, 1986; Buzychkin 12; Nepomnyashchy 134, 148 ffn. 13–15.

It would be a mistake, however, to perceive changes (or their absence) in the creative unions as a sole measure of cultural reform. Two contrasting evidentiary cases are the Artists' Union and the Composers' Union, the latter of which in early 1990 reelected the conservative Tikhon Khrennikov, who had led the Union for over a half-century (since 1948). In these two cases the radical changes in the culture industry cannot be adequately assessed by examining the internal union politics, but rather by tracing the transnational flow of work and producers circumventing the union structure. In contemporary art, the July 7, 1988, Sotheby auction is the most evident instance. See three short articles by Gambrell in *Art in America*; Nepomnyashchy 136–37. The rate of reform's acceleration in these culture industries was such that the respective unions were already relics of the socialist bureaucracy, for which (unlike cinema distribution) emerging substitutes were already functioning.

23. Although Aleksandr Kamshalov's appointment was largely seen by the liberal intelligentsia as a step forward, Kamshalov was by no means their political ally. From 1962 to 1970 secretary of ideology on the Young Communist League (Komsomol) Central Committee, Kamshalov had been known for his conservative tastes. Later, as head of the Cinema Sector of the Cultural Department of the Communist Party Central Committee (1970–86), he largely ensured that foreign films were screened no more broadly than to an audience of his Central Committee cohorts. Indeed, the list of Soviet directors whose work was delayed due in part to Kamshalov's participation is long and impressive, including Mikhail Romm (*Ordinary Fascism* [*Obyknovennyi fashizm*]; Mosfil'm, 1965) and Andrei Tarkovskii (*Andrei Rublev*, as well as work by Iurii Il'enko, Mikhail Kalik, Otar Ioseliani, Gleb Panfilov, and Sergei Paradzhanov). Kamshalov's bland assurances in July 1987—already six months in office and more than a year after the May 1986 revolt—that the priorities of a reformed Goskino were to "examine [the new economy] from the ideological viewpoint" and to "encourage production of musicals and sci-fi films" (*Variety,* July 1, 1987) suggests he had not read of recent changes in the industry press. The principal merit of Kamshalov's selection was that

he inherited a system stripped of its power. The most detailed and intelligent account of the change of power from Ermash to Kamshalov is Arkus and Matizen.

24. See *Sovetskaia kul'tura*, September 10, 1987. The artistic directors—Iurii Arabov, Sergei Bondarchuk, Rolan Bykov, Valentin Chernykh, Georgii Daneliia, Sergei Kolosov, Vladimir Men'shov, Vladimir Naumov, Iulii Raizman, Karen Shakhnazarov, and Sergei Solovi'ev—provide brief sketches of their associations in *Soviet Film* 5 (1988): 8–9, 12–17. For similar sketches by the artistic directors of Lenfil'm, see *Soviet Film* 8 (1988): 16–17.

25. Among the more familiar films of Chukhrai's experimental studio were Vladimir Motyl''s *White Sun of the Desert* (*Beloe solntse pustyni*; ECS/Mosfil'm/Lenfil'm, 1970), Leonid Gaidai's *Ivan Vasil'evich Changes Profession* (*Ivan Vasil'evich meniaet professiiu*; ECS/Mosfil'm, 1973), and the two aforementioned contributions to *Beginning of an Unknown Era*, Larisa Shepit'ko's and Andrei Smirnov's panels, *Homeland of Electricity* and *Angel*, respectively.

26. See Fisher 240; see also Kapralov 3. Although work continued until 1976, the years 1972 to 1976 were significantly less productive. The fateful moment came with the 1972 renaming and reorganization of the Experimental Creative Studio as the Mosfil'm (*nota bene*) Experimental Creative Association. See Lawton, *Kinoglasnost* 77–78, 245 fn. 16.

27. For an unusually interesting roundtable on *Repentance*, including contributions by Lev Annenskii and Irina Shilova, see the VGIK volume edited by Dymshits and Troshin, 138–64. See also Bozhovich, *Pokaianie*.

28. Fisher suggests that Mikhalkov's *Dark Eyes* (*Ochi chernye*; Excelsior Films, Adriano International Corporation, 1987) had been a strong contender for the 1987 Cannes Golden Palm. Mikhalkov, an outspoken critic of the reformers at the May 1986 Fifth Congress, was on poor terms with new Union First Secretary Elem Klimov, who sat on the 1987 Cannes jury. Fisher (241) speculates that Mikhalkov's loss of the Golden Palm to Maurice Pialat's *Under Satan's Sun* (*Sous le soleil de Satan*; Action/CNC, 1987) was due in part to Klimov's lobbying efforts. Mikhalkov's only award was the Prize for Best Actor, awarded to lead actor Marcello Mastroianni. The other Soviet Cannes prizewinner for 1987, Tengiz Abuladze's *Repentance*, was awarded Cannes's Grand Jury Prize and the FIPRESCI Prize. See also Bollag.

29. Six Thaw films in particular won "international" (i.e., Western) acclaim. Grigorii Chukhrai's debut film *Forty-First* (*Sorok pervyi*; Mosfil'm, 1956), a remake of Iakov Protazanov's 1927 film, based on a novella by Boris Lavrenev, won a Special Prize at the Cannes Film Festival in 1957. Chukhrai's next film, *Ballad of a Soldier* (*Ballada o soldate*; Mosfil'm, 1959), won two 1960 prizes at Cannes (Participation and Youth Prizes), as well as the 1960 Grand Prize at London and awards at festivals in Milan, Mexico, Tehran, and Athens (Woll 238). Iosif Kheifits's screen adaptation of Anton Chekhov's novella *Lady with the Lapdog* (*Dama s sobachkoi*; Lenfil'm, 1960) shared with Chukhrai's *Ballad* the 1960 Cannes prize for Participation. Mikhail Kalatozov's *Cranes Are Flying* (*Letiat zhuravli*; Mosfil'm, 1957) won the Golden Palm at Cannes in 1958. Tengiz Abuladze's *Someone Else's Children* (*Chuzhie deti*; Gruziia Film Studio, 1958) won First Prize for Debut Film at the London Film Festival in 1960. Aleksandr Alov and Vladimir Naumov's *Peace to Him Who Enters* (*Mir vkhodiashchemu*; Mosfil'm, 1961) won a Special Jury Prize (Gold) at the Venice Film Festival in 1961.

30. Under the slogan "Cinema: The Renewal of Artistic Consciousness," the Plenum brought several prominent figures of renewal to the event, including the émigré writer Andrei Siniavskii, the Polish director Krzysztof Zanussi, and the British producer David Puttnam. Viktor Demin spearheaded the movement to excise from the Union charter the statute that stipulated "only those filmmakers [who] stand for Socialist Realism may be members of the Union" (Lawton, *Kinoglasnost* 92).

31. Managers of urban public baths were in a similar situation, in practical (if not always juridical) possession of vast downtown space, the legal supervision of which was virtually nonexistent.

32. Though inferior in quality, Elektronica VCRs, at roughly $1,800, were nearly half the price of most Western models, which sold for an average of $3,000 (*Variety*, July 1, 1987).

33. See "Spisok fil'mov, kotorye obsuzhdalis' Konfliktnoi komissiei i sekretariatom Soiuza kinematografistov do nachala avgusta 1988 goda," *Kinostsenarii* 4 (1988). The 1990 figure is cited in Graffy, "Unshelving" 261 fn. 2.

34. For the sake of comparison, Soviet films sold abroad in these years numbered at a fairly stable figure of 585 in 1985 and 500 in 1986 (*Variety*, July 1, 1987).

35. See *Variety*, July 9–11, 1989, 59. See also Faraday 225 fn. 59 for a useful discussion. Dondurei ("Mestobliustiteli" 5) cites a noticeably lower production figure of $50,000 during the years 1989–91.

36. Dondurei ("Artistic Culture" 275–76) cites $1 million as the average production cost for the end of 1994.

37. As Dondurei remarks, "We seem to have got accustomed to a festival-centered model of Russian filmmaking, where a single screening at Locarno, Nantes, or Rotterdam substitutes for runs in Cheliabinsk or Syzran'" (*Nezavisimaia gazeta*, April 10, 1993). By the mid- to late 1990s this statement would have to be amended: although the films would still not run in Cheliabinsk cinemas, an annual festival might.

For a list of regular festivals as of 2003 see *Spravochnik "Kinofestivali Rossii,"* which lists from two to eight major festivals each month in the Russian Federation and near abroad. The top festivals to emerge (or reemerge in substantially different form) from this decade include the archival festival *White Posts* (*Belye Stolby*; White Posts, near Moscow, January); the audience-elected festival *Long Live Russian Cinema!* (*Vivat, Kino Rossii!*; St. Petersburg, May); the politically conservative festival *Golden Knight* (*Zolotoi Vitiaz'*; location varies, May); the highly competitive post-Soviet competition *Cinesaurus* (*Kinotavr*; Sochi, June); its nearest competitor, *Kinoshock* (*Kinoshok*; Anapa, September); the animation festival *Krok* (Kiev and elsewhere in Ukraine, September); the (now) annual, "grandmother," *Moscow International Film Festival* (Moscow, June); the panoramic (feature, documentary, animation) *Window to Europe* (*Okno v Evropu*; Vyborg, near St. Petersburg, August); the long-standing documentary festival *Russia* (*Rossiia*; Ekaterinburg, October); the retrospective of recent prizewinners, *Festival of Festivals* (*Festival' festivalei*; St. Petersburg, June).

38. Beumers works with a 1996 production figure of twenty-eight films for 1996. This number has been updated here to thirty-four, reflecting more recent research in Segida and Zemlianukhin, *Fil'my Rossii* 245.

39. For a list of Russian CNC applicants and results (1990–94), see *Iskusstvo kino* 8 (1994): 42–47.

40. See Graham 23 ffn. 1–2 for a broadly ranging account of this word's various semantic fields. The essay is the best English-language scholarship on *chernukha*, exploring its early literary association with the writings of Liudmila Petrushevskaia and others (9). See also Zorin on *chernukha* as a broader cultural trend.

41. Graham (13) comments, "In place of [socialist realism's] pure idealism, logocentric optimism and 'conflictlessness' (бесконфликтность), [*chernukha*] offers pure naturalism, mute pessimism and omnipresent conflict (всеконфликтность)." See also Faraday 176–77.

42. Tumanishvili's *Solo Voyage* was widely distrubted and pulled an audience of 40.7 million (Kudriavtsev, *Svoe kino* 416).

43. By the mid- to late 1990s, by contrast, the noncorrespondence between audience's genre preferences and directors' choices became a more manageable, if nevertheless neglected, task. As Beumers comments:

> Audience surveys show that comedies and adventures rank above any
> other genre in the popularity of both cinema and video preferences. . . .
> Yet Russian producers and film-makers responded to audience taste with
> reluctance and some delay, producing instead mainly thrillers, action movies
> and melodramas: the search of new releases by genre classification shows
> that only 10 comedies were produced in 1996, six in 1997 and none in 1998.
> ("Cinemarket" 895)

Late in 1998, as Beumers adds in a footnote (895 fn. 36), Aleksandr Rogozhkin's *Peculiarities of National Fishing* (*Osobennosti natsional'noi rybalki*; CTV, 1998) would raise this last figure to a single comedy for 1998.

44. *Lumière Express*, for example, reported that 47 percent of respondents to its questionnaire cite the quality of films (of which *chernukha* was the most frequently mentioned culprit) as their overwhelming reason for nonattendance, while only 22 percent cite the discomfort of the debilitated theater space ("Poidut li moskvichi v kinoteatr?," *Kino atel'e* 3 (1996): 66–67, quoted in Beumers, "Cine-market" 884.

45. *Little Vera* was listed as numbers 33–34 (as a two-series film) for audience attendance, drawing 56 million viewers for each half (Kudriavtsev, *Svoe kino* 413), one of only two *perestroika*-era films to exceed 50 million. The second blockbuster, Alla Surikova's "comedic Western" *A Man from Boulevard des Capucins* (*Chelovek s bul'vara Kaputsinov*; Mosfil'm 1987), pulled an audience of 50.6 million (Kudriavtsev, *Svoe kino* 414).

46. The more serious scholar should consult, respectively, http://us.imdb.com/title/tt0083628/ and http://us.imdb.com/title/tt0089689/.

47. Filippov (*Ogonek*, March 10, 1991, 30) cites ASKIN as an (inaccurate) acronym for a slightly different variant, the All-Union State Cinema and Video Association (Vsesoiuznaia gosudarstvennaia kinovideoassotsiatsiia).

48. See Filippov 31. Other Tiskino productions include the young Azeri director Murad Ibragimbekov's *Waltz of the Golden Tauruses* (*Val's zolotykh tel'tsov*; Tiskino, 1992), based on a novella by his father, the writer Maksud Ibragimbekov; and Valerii Akhadov's melodrama *I Promised I Would Leave . . .* (*Ia obeshchala, ia uidu . . .*; Tiskino, 1992), based on the short stories of Evgenii Kozlovskii.

49. With characteristic bureaucratic caution, Goskino chief Kamshalov issued an order that ASKIN's establishment be postponed (*Izvestiia*, April 17, 1990). See also *Current Digest* 42.31 (1990): 14–15.

50. Gubenko's two best-known films are *The Orphans*, also known in English as *The Winged Birds* (*Podranki*; Mosfil'm, 1976), and *And Life, and Tears, and Love . . .* (*I zhizn', i slezy, i liubov' . . .*; Mosfil'm, 1984).

51. The director Aleksei German ("Pochemu ia ne snimaiu"), whose work is discussed in detail in chapter 7, describes ASKIN as "a peculiar restoration of the former Party apparatus of Goskino. A victory of the former minister and his deputies, bloodless and without furor, has already taken place."

52. See Rudnev. Rezanov and Khoroshilova report that 637 guests attended at ASKIN's expense.

53. Khudonazarov is credited with only one poststudent film, *Beneath the Melting Snow Is the Sound of the Brook* (*V talom snege zvon ruch'ia*; Tadzhikfil'm, 1983). He is primarily known for his camera work in such films as Boris Kimiagarov's epic three-part series *Tale of Rustam* (*Skazanie o Rustame*; Tadzhikfil'm, 1971) and Valerii Akhadov's *Who Is Going to Truskavets* (*Kto poedet v Truskavets*; Tadzhikfil'm, 1977), based on a story by the Azeri writer Maksud Ibragimbekov. One cannot help but be curious about the intersection in the early 1990s among three figures: Valerii Akhadov, whose 1992 film, *I Promised I Would Leave . . .* (mentioned above) was one of the last financed by Tiskino; Maksud Ibragimbekov, whose son's 1992 *Waltz of the Golden Taurusus* (mentioned above) was also financed by Tagi-zade; and Khudonazarov, newly elected (1990) head of the Filmmakers' Union, who had earlier worked as cameraman to both directors.

54. The Motion Picture Association of America, representing the interests of the seven major U.S. studios, is responsible for issuing film ratings, lobbying the federal government, and protecting the copyright interests of its member studios. The Motion Picture Association (changed in 1994 from its original 1945 name, the Motion Picture Export Association of America) is the international arm, handling issues of foreign exhibition of U.S. films as well as protectionism and piracy issues.

55. Blockbuster prereleases or screeners were often obtained by so-called *kazachki* who were employed in the U.S. studios during the production process to obtain advance or marketing copies, some still with the time code in the corner. More typical were "rags" (*triapki*), the product of camcording inside the U.S. theater, thoughtfully accompanied by audience comments and coughs. By far the most widespread form of video piracy was a third method, involving the purchase abroad of a legal copy, which was then mass-produced in a domestic studio. See Fix 14; S[ul'kin], "'Gorbushku'". For a useful technical summary of these and other forms of piracy (signal theft, broadcast piracy, etc.), see www.mpaa.org/anti-piracy. See also Klein.

56. Only with the collapse of the Soviet Union were many well-known U.S. films, such as *Gone With the Wind*, publicly screened for the first time. Marilyn Monroe was at best a dimly acknowledged figure from her one screen appearance in the USSR in 1966 in Billy Wilder's *Some Like It Hot* (Ashton Production/Mirisch Corporation, 1959). See Turovskaia in Dondurei, *Otechestvennyi* 71. Such classic films as Howard Hawks's *Gentlemen Prefer Blondes* (20th Century Fox, 1953) and Joshua Logan's *Bus Stop* (20th Century Fox, 1956) were widely available only in the early 1990s; thus Marilyn Monroe was known only as an ancient forerunner of Madonna (*Moscow Times*, May 29, 1993, 7).

57. The sociologist Daniil Dondurei ("Kinodelo" 128; "Posle imperii" 33–39), re-counts how his research firm, Double-D (Dubl'-D) conducted a 1992 survey of 140 pro-ducers. Among the survey topics was a question concerning their advance work with distribution networks and independent distributors prior to the start of production. As one might by now expect, not a single producer had made even the most rudimentary agreements before the start of filming. Nor, one might argue, would it necessarily make sense for any producer to do so. As Aleksandr Golutva, former head of Lenfil'm Studio, then (as of 1997) deputy minister of Goskino, remarked:

> With film directors forced to make long intermissions in shoots due to financial difficulties and therefore not knowing when they will end the shooting, the distributors can hardly plan their work. We need representa-tive distributors operating with large movie packages in order to be able to agree with cinemas and replace a film whose release is postponed with an-other one. (Johnson's List 7300, August 26, 2003, 1993)

58. In fact, some trade organizations, such as the American Film Marketing As-sociation, never joined the 1991 MPA/MPAA boycott in the first place. Its president, Jonas Rosenfield, did not endorse the boycott on the grounds that his hundred mem-bers would not support its imposition and there was no way for its domestic enforce-ment (Hift 12).

59. Solov'ev's *Anna Karenina* eventually appeared in 2007 as a Channel One tele-vision miniseries production.

60. Even an abbreviated list for the years 1994–96 is striking. For 1994 it would include Dmitrii Dolinin's adaptation of Anton Chekhov's short story "In the Ravine" ("V ovrage") in his *Little Ring of Gold, Bouquet of Scarlet Roses* (*Kolechko zolotoe, buket iz alykh roz*; Lenfil'm, 1994) and Sergei Solov'ev's adaptation of Anton Chekhov's play *Three Sisters* (*Tri sestry*; Patmos [Russia]/Aurora [Germany], 1994). For 1995 adaptations included Roman Balaian's of Ivan Turgenev's short story . . . *First Love* (. . . *Pervaia liubov'*; Ostrov/Innova-Film [Germany], 1995); Nikolai Dostal''s of Fedor Sologub's novel *Petty Demon* (*Melkii bes*; Vremia [Mosfil'm], 1995); Aleksandr Proshkin's of Alek-sandr Amfiteatrov's play *Black Veil* (*Chernaia vual'*; Ritm [Mosfil'm], 1995); and Sergei Ursuliak's of Maksim Gor'kii's play *Summer-house People* (*Dachniki*), retitled *Summer People* (*Letnie liudi*; Kovsag, 1995). As for 1996, the major film of the year was Sergei Bodrov's liberal adaptation of three similarly titled works by Aleksandr Pushkin, Lev Tolstoi (both works entitled *Caucasian Prisoner* [*Kavkazskii plennik*]), and Vladimir Makanin (*Caucasian Prisoner* [*Kavkazskii plennyi*]), for which the film version was titled *Prisoner of the Mountains* (*Kavkazskii plennik*; Karavan, 1996). The year's production also included Sergei Gazarov's adaptation of Nikolai Gogol's play *Inspector General* (*Revizor*; Nikita i Petr, 1996); Sergei Lomkin's adaptation of Mikhail Bulgakov's story *Fatal Eggs* (*Rokovye iaitsa*; Ada-Fil'm, 1996); Vladimir Motyl''s adaptation of Anton Chekhov's short stories *Gone with the Horses* (*Nesut menia koni*; Arion, 1996); Samson Samsonov's adaptation of Aleksei Tolstoi's short story "Love," entitled *Sweet Friend of Years Forgotten Long Ago* (*Milyi drug davno zabytykh let*; Ritm [Mosfil'm], 1996). On this sudden explosion in literary adaptation, see Condee, "Dream"; Faraday; Johnson 282–83; L. Karakhan, "Cinema without Controls" 11; Karriker 291.

61. Dondurei ("Kinodelo" 133) cites a range in 1995 of 150 to 200 million rubles for the purchase of new Russian feature releases, as opposed to a range of 10 to 15 million rubles for a recent Hollywood feature film.

62. See Knox-Voina 286 on "kind cinema" and the "trend of optimism," particularly the films Dmitrii Astrakhan's *Everything Will Be All Right* (*Vse budet khorosho*; Fora-Fil'm/Lenfil'm, 1995); Georgii Daneliia's *Heads and Tails* (*Orel i reshka*; Ritm [Mosfil'm]/Dialogue International [U.S.], 1995); and Gennadii Baisak's *Agape* (Akter Kino, 1996).

63. See "On Government Support of the Cinema Industry" ("O gosudarstvennoi podderzhke kinematografii"), *Rossiiskaia gazeta*, August 29, 1996.

64. One of the key articles in the Law on Authors' Rights concerns film property, whereby films made between 1964 and 1992 were the property of the studio and post-1992 films belonged to the director. Beumers, "Cinemarket" 877.

65. The Penal Code was finally passed in 1997. The relevant articles are 146 (breach of authors' rights) and 171 (illegal business). Beumers, "Cinemarket" 895 fn. 15.

66. Iurii Moroz directed the political detective film *Black Square* (*Chernyi kvadrat*; Shans [Gor'kii Film Studio], 1992), based on Fridrikh Neznanskii's novel *Fair at Sokol'niki* (*Iarmarka v Sokol'nikakh*) and not to be confused with Iosif Pasternak's *perestroika*-era documentary *Black Square* (*Chernyi kvadrat*; Moscow Central Documentary Studio, 1988) on the historical (1910s–1920s) and late (1960s) Soviet avant-garde.

67. Sel'ianov directed *Angel Day* (*Den' angela*; Lenfil'm, 1980–88), *Whit Monday* (*Dukhov den'*; Golos [Lenfil'm], 1990), *The Time of Sorrow Has Not Yet Come* (*Vremia pechali eshche ne prishlo*; Lenfil'm, 1995), and *The Russian Idea* (*Russkaia ideia*; CTV [Russia]/BFI [UK], 1995). Sel'ianov's Petersburg-based production company, CTV, was founded in 1994. Its earliest project, in cooperation with the filmmaker Aleksei Balabanov and the French producer Guy Seligman, was Georges Bardawil's *Secrets Shared with a Stranger* (*Ispoved' neznakomtsu*; Flash Film [France]/CTV, 1994; French title *Confidences à un inconnu*), based on the Symbolist writer Valerii Briusov's novella *Last Pages from a Woman's Diary* (*Poslednie stranitsy iz dnevnika zhenshchiny*). On CTV's impressive list of successes are four major hits by Aleksandr Rogozhkin: *Operation "Happy New Year"* (*Operatsiia "S novym godom"*; with MNVK [TV-6 Moscow], 1996); *Checkpoint* (*Blokpost*; CTV, 1998); *Peculiarities of National Fishing* (*Osobennosti natsional'noi rybalki*; CTV, 1998); and *Cuckoo* (*Kukushka*; CTV, 2002). Its other major films include films by Aleksei Balabanov—*Of Freaks and Men* (*Pro urodov i liudei*; CTV, 1998); *Brother* (*Brat*; CTV, 1997); *Brother 2* (*Brat 2*; CTV, 2000); and *War* (*Voina*; CTV, 2002)—and Pavel Lungin's *Tycoon* (*Oligarkh*; CPD [France]/CTV, 2002).

68. Among Markovich's clients was the U.S. businessman Paul Tatum, whose murder in 1996 was linked to disputes around the Moscow Radisson Hotel Business Center.

69. The Americom is now the America Cinema.

70. National Amusements is the parent company of Viacom, with 1,350 screens in the United States, United Kingdom, and throughout Latin America.

71. The major stations were the state-owned ORT and RTR, 2 x 2, and TV6, but not NTV. The discussion here on Latin America concerns only the television broadcasting of feature films, not soap operas.

72. Menashe (10) reports that in October 1997 all ten of the top best-selling videos on the Russian market were copies of foreign films.

73. On ticket and video prices, see Larsen, "In Search" 194. Beumers ("Cinemarket" 887) cites an estimate for the late 1990s of 30 to 33 percent VCR ownership for Russia as a whole and 43 percent for Moscow households.

74. Federal Law on Cinema (126-FZ, Article 7), quoted in Beumers, "Cinemarket" 873.

75. Golutva refers here to Vladimir Men'shov's 1979 popular Mosfil'm melodrama, which won the 1981 Oscar for Best Foreign-Language Film.

76. NTV-Profit was a subsidiary of NTV, the television network and, in the late 1990s, the flagship of media magnate Vladimir Gusinskii's investment company Media-Most.

77. Birgit Beumers ("Cinemarket" 889), the most serious Western scholar writing on the film industry, cites an average 1998 television return of no more than $25,000 for contemporary Russian feature films.

78. The Kremlin Palace of Congresses—now the State Kremlin Palace—was constructed in 1959–61 and designed by Mikhail Posokhin and Ashot Mndoiants inside the territory of the Moscow Kremlin. The building's sleek design provides a subdued contrast of Soviet international style to the surrounding tsarist architecture. It is precisely this tension of how to hold the Soviet and tsarist culture simultaneously within view that seemed to absorb Mikhalkov's attention around this event, and not only there, as the next chapter will explore. From the early 1960s on during the Soviet period, it was the site of CPSU congresses and sessions of the USSR Supreme Soviet. Its main conference hall, the venue for the Union Congress, was at the time of its construction the largest in Europe and among the most technologically advanced for simultaneous translation.

79. See *Iskusstvo kino* 8 (1998); Beumers, *Russia on Reels* 50–53 and "Cinemarket" 875–76, 893. For additional information, see Menashe 13, 17.

80. For comparison's sake, the average Russian domestic production in the late 1990s ran from $700,000 to $1.5 million, rising to a higher range of $1.5 million to $5 million by 2002, compared with an average of $10 million for European productions and $100 million for major Hollywood productions. Johnson's List 7300 (August 26, 2003); www.gazeta.ru, July 5, 2002.

81. Although founded under the tsars in 1864, the New Dawn Perfume Factory is more closely associated with the Stalin era, when more pungent perfumes were the mode. Two years before Mikhalkov's special-order Junker eau-de-cologne, New Dawn had produced an earlier (1997) special-order olfactory triumph: Mayor Cologne, named after Moscow mayor Iurii Luzhkov, "the burly, baldheaded man who looks about as likely to represent sweet smells . . . as does the average pipe fitter" (Spector).

82. Rosbusiness Consulting reports the 2003 federal budget allocation for domestic film production as just under $50.53 million (July 15, 2003).

83. See "Russia Warned," CBS News, broadcast October 9, 2003; "Putin Urges." These analyses deal almost exclusively with video *sales* rather than the rental industry; the increasingly legal video rental business has emerged less out of respect for the law than because of the speed at which pirated copies wear out.

84. Special 301 refers to the section of the 1988 Trade Act empowering the U.S. government to enact a variety of retaliatory actions in cases of piracy and access problems involving intellectual property. See www.mpaa.org/anti-piracy for April 30, 2001: "MPA Hails USTR 'Special 301' Report: Taiwan, Malaysia, Russia on 'Priority Watch List.'"

For film industry losses, see http://www.mpaa.org/PiracyFactSheets/PiracyFactSheetRussia.pdf. See also "Russia Warned," CBS News, October 9, 2003. The International Federation of the Phonographic Industry (IFPI) cites a 2002 figure of $311 million for the Russian pirate music industry (Nicholson), compared to a legal Russian industry of $274 million (Holdsworth). In addition to these U.S. losses must be counted the estimated $100 million in taxes uncollected by the Russian government (December 2003 estimate). See www.mpaa.org/anti-piracy for December 10, 2003: "Valenti Meets with Russian Prime Minister."

85. In mid-2003 Soiuz-Video had sixty-five Moscow outlets, many at British Petroleum gas stations, and four in St. Petersburg (Holdsworth).

86. This estimate applies to the city as a whole. Markets such as Gorbushka and Mitino offer a much higher rate of pirated goods, estimated at 70 percent (Sul'kin).

87. Dondureyi and Venger (32) cite 101 and 79 full-length feature films for 2004 and 2005, respectively.

88. The industry generally defines a multiplex as a cinema with five or more screens.

89. See http://www.kinostardelux.ru/about/about.shtml.

90. The CIS figures for 2002 were $111.7 million (Maternovsky, "U.S. Giant").

91. By comparison, the average Russian production cost has risen from $700,000 to $1 million in 2002 to a broader range of $1.5 to 5 million in 2003.

92. From top to bottom, the leading five European countries are the United Kingdom, Germany, France, Italy, and Spain. Maternovsky ("U.S. Giant") cited a higher projected figure for 2007 of $580 million but does not provide information on his analytic source. Projected profits for 2011 are $900 million (*New York Times*, 2 June 2008).

93. By contrast, the low range for ticket prices at unrenovated or underrenovated Moscow cinemas was $1.50 (www.gazeta.ru, July 5, 2002).

94. According to *The Guardian* (Walsh), *Tycoon* alone garnered $407,514 in its first week, exceeding returns on any other Russian-language film. See Johnson's List 7300 (August 26, 2003).

CHAPTER 3

1. The title *"Slave of Love"* includes quotation marks because the narrative recounts the early twentieth-century production of a silent film by that title.

2. For those interested in a shorter route, two excellent pieces touching on the explicitly imperial preoccupations of *Barber of Siberia* are Gerasimov and Razlogov.

3. Surikov is author of such well-known paintings as *Morning of the Strel'tsy's Execution* (1881, Tret'iakov Gallery), *Boiarina Morozova* (1887, Tret'iakov Gallery), *Men'shikov in Berezov* (1883, Tret'iakov Gallery), and *Sten'ka Razin Sailing in the Caspian* (begun in 1910, Russian Museum). Konchalovskii is best known for his historical drama *Siberiade* (*Siberiada*; Mosfil'm, 1979), the romance *Maria's Lovers* (Cannon,

1984), the action adventure *Runaway Train* (Golan-Globus, 1985), and most recently *House for Fools* (*Dom durakov*; Bac, 2002).

4. See Beumers, *Nikita Mikhalkov* 3 for an account of Mikhalkov's more elaborate claims. This is in general an indispensable volume on Mikhalkov's work.

5. "A strange and unpleasant figure" is a typical characterization (Nikolaevich 59).

6. It is telling that Razzakov's biography of Mikhalkov has recently taken this phrase for its title.

7. *Urga*, released in the West as *Close to Eden*, will nevertheless be referred to here as *Urga, Territory of Love*, the English translation of its Russian title (*Urga, territoriia liubvi*). *Urga* is the Mongol word for a hunting and herding pole. Planted upright in the ground, it can also mark off an area for love-making.

8. These include both major and minor parts in *At Home*, "*Slave of Love*," *Mechanical Piano*, *Kinfolk*, *Urga*, *Anna*, *Burnt by the Sun*, *Barber of Siberia*, and 12.

9. See http://www.trite.ru/trite.mhtml?PubID=2. "TriTe" ("three T's" in Russian) stands for "Work, Comradeship, Creativity" (Trud, Tovarishchestvo, Tvorchestvo). TriTe's international partners have included MGM, Pathé Entertainment, Warner Bros., HBO, Universal Studios, Paramount, and Camera One (France).

10. See in particular its *History of the Fatherland in Testimony and Documents 18–20cc.* (*Istoriia otechestva v svidetel'stvakh i dokumentakh, XVIII–XX vv.*), 12 vols. (1991–2003).

11. See http://www.trite.ru/mikhalkov.mhtml?PubID=59. Domestic awards and prizes include a People's Artist of the RSFSR (1984), a Grand Prix at Kinotavr Film Festival (1992) for *Urga*, which also won the Nika Director's award (1993), and a Russian Federation State Prize (1994) for *Burnt by the Sun*. A second State Prize was awarded in 1999 for *Barber of Siberia*. In 2005 the Sixteenth Kinotavr Film Festival awarded Mikhalkov a Lifetime Achievement Award, and in the same year he received the Aleksandr Nevskii Medal.

12. It was Jean-Nicolas Pache (1746–1823), briefly mayor of the Paris commune (1794), who first painted the slogan on the commune walls.

13. Gerasim Petrin (*Mechanical Piano*), the cook's son, is the slogan's more formidable interlocutor, an opponent on the one hand of Shcherbuk's entrenched privilege and on the other hand of the liberals' Westernizing idiocies. Petrin, a peripheral truthsayer—like Konstantin (*Dark Eyes*), the Russian veterinarian who delivers one of the film's final monologues—performs the filmmaker's distinction between equality and equal rights. Simultaneously proud to be seated at the table of his social superiors and resentful that his father's labor paid for luxury to which he has only fleeting access, Petrin recognizes that his acceptance at the estate is attributed to his intellect, work, and talent rather than because men deserve equality. Unlike Shcherbuk, Petrin's intervention constitutes Mikhalkov's real settling of scores with both the indolent wealthy and the radical egalitarians.

14. Rustam Ibragimbekov, initially best known as the scriptwriter for *White Sun*, went on to work with Mikhalkov in a long a productive collaboration that included *Hitchhike*, *Urga*, *Burnt by the Sun*, and *Barber of Siberia*.

In her excellent article on *At Home among Strangers*, Prokhorova (171–72) pointed to borrowings from such classic Westerns and spaghetti Westerns as Sergio Leone's *The Good, the Bad, and the Ugly* (*Il buono, il brutto, il cattivo*; Arturo González Producciones Cinematográficas, 1966) and *Once Upon a Time in the West* (*C'era una volt al West*; Finanzio San Marco, 1968), as well as George Roy Hill's *Butch Cassidy and the Sundance Kid* (Campanile and Twentieth-Century Fox, 1969) and domestic Soviet varieties, most obviously Vladimir Motyl''s *White Sun of the Desert*.

15. The structural similarity of these groups invites the viewer's comparison: the five Red Cavalry officers (Kungurov, Lipiagin, Sarychev, Shilov, Zabelin) are matched by five White counterrevolutionaries (Belenkii, Lebedev, Lemke, Solodovnikov, Turchin). The anarchist band is less coherent, but their leader, Brylov, is routinely shot side-by-side with four helpers, including Kaium and Brylov's boy servant.

16. For background information, see Egorova 219; Suminova 141.

17. Surikov's best-known canvases precisely address key moments of Russian historical rupture or schism, including events relating to the actual seventeenth-century Schism, such as the 1671 seizure of Boiarina Morozova, the late seventeenth-century Cossack rebel Sten'ka Razin, the 1698 revolt of Peter I's sharpshooter regiments, and Aleksandr Men'shikov's 1727 disgrace and exile. These canvases cannot stand in for the entirety of Surikov's work; nevertheless, his best-known paintings were often a critical articulation of state crisis (the Schism, peasant revolt, regimental rebellion, a palace coup).

18. The name of the mysterious philosopher (B. Tos'ia) whose perorations bracket the film's beginning and end is widely interpreted to mean "God—that is, I" (Bog—to est' ia).

19. See Beumers, *Nikita Mikhalkov* 29–30 concerning Khamdamov's original project and its relations to Mikhalkov's finished product.

20. Brooks grounds his argument in French melodrama of the postrevolutionary period of the early nineteenth century, tracing it in particular from writings of playwright René-Charles Guilbert de Pixérécourt, whose first and best-known melodramatic play was *Coelina, or The Child of Mystery* (1800). To this early moment I would add Victor Dacange, author of *Thirty Years, or, The Life of a Gambler* (1827) and *Theresa, or, The Orphan of Geneva* (1821). For all intents and purposes, the "Russian Pixérécourt" is considered to be the German playwright August von Kotzebue (1761–1819), author of *Misanthropy and Repentance* (1788) and *Child of Love* (1796), Kotzebue's first St. Petersburg production (Stites, "The Misanthrope" 31). On other dramatists who wrote melodramas in Russia, including Rafael Zotov and Nikolai Polevoi, see Buckler 75–76.

Consistent with Brooks, Lang, and others I take melodrama neither as a transcendent category nor as a transhistorical mode to mean any performance of great expressivity or affective excess, such as theater as such, or (the argument has been made) the entire belief system of Christianity (see Lang's discussion 14–15 fn. 2). Instead, I prefer to see melodrama more narrowly as a historically grounded mode marked by the frequency of certain formal and thematic features that articulate a modern sensibility in conditions of (and response to) a post-Enlightenment emphasis on rationality, secularity, and progress.

Singer (7) identifies a cluster of five key elements: pathos, moral polarization, overwrought emotion, sensationalism, and a nonclassical narrative form. The recurrent preoccupations of melodrama are more numerous than those examined in this chapter, which is not intended as an exhaustive account of the melodramatic mode's rich practices but rather an argument about Mikhalkov's selective preferences and their potential investments. Finally, my framework situates itself in dialogue with the shift, from the mid-1970s (that is, from Elsaesser) onward, to an understanding of the wider range of ironic and camp melodramatic modes and a more ideologically ambivalent understanding of melodrama's allegedly Manichaean polarities. I would like to express thanks to Dawn Seckler, at whose initiation a seminar on Russian melodrama for the 2007 Russian Film Symposium: Melodrama and Kino-Ideology was organized, encouraging me to return to this topic.

21. Lunacharskii, "O frantsuzskoi drame," cited in Bagrov, "Soviet Melodrama." There was no question that Lunacharskii, himself a playwright of some note, had an educated and well-developed notion of melodrama, which he identifies in terms strikingly similar to such leading contemporary theorists as Peter Brooks. Lunacharskii describes melodrama as "characterized by artificially burning affects, frequently accompanied by charged music, a sharp contrast between good and evil, with lots of action, and with a poster-like crudity in the entire thing" (quoted in Bagrov, "Soviet Melodrama"). Cf. Peter Brooks (xiii): "the extravagance of certain representations, and the intensity of moral claim, . . . a heightened hyperbolic drama, making reference to pure and polar concepts of darkness and light, salvation and damnation." On Lunacharskii's plays, see Fitzpatrick, *The Commissariat*, 152–61; Von Szeliski.

22. Melodrama was not alone is its poor fit with the new ideology. As Savel'ev ("Out of Ideology") points out, "Several Western 'players' in the game of genre cinema—for example, the horror film . . .—did not have the opportunity to enter into the 'playing field' for ideological reasons: they were totally incompatible with the existing canons of socialist reality; they lay outside of Soviet life."

23. See Trofimenkov ("Origin") in a similar vein: "Officially considered during the Soviet period to be an ideologically foreign, bourgeois genre, [melodrama] always existed, mimicking, pretending to be something else, but existing all the same."

24. It is a fraught and complex question whether melodrama *necessarily*—that is to say, intrinsically, by its very nature—maintains social stability through reconciliation. For a lively treatment of this issue, see Mulvey 75–79. To the extent that this debate touches upon Mikhalkov's work, the implications of the argument here are that this reconciliation in the name of social stability is indeed at stake.

25. See Prokhorov for an excellent analysis of melodrama and its development in Thaw cinema.

26. On Vera Kholodnaia, see Prokof'eva, especially chapter 5 ("Taina smerti," 149–95) and the essays in Ziukov, especially N. Brygin, "Krasnaia koroleva" (97–101). See also the film scholar and montage director Oleg Kovalov's *Island of the Dead* (*Ostrov mertvykh*; Soiuzitalofil'm, 1992), which includes footage of Kholodnaia.

27. Cf. Trofimenkov's ("Origin") wry comment on the success of melodrama in the 1920s and the 1960s: "These periods, albeit short, in which elements of market relations (as in the 1920s) or the development of bourgeois humanism (as in the 1960s) were permitted in our country . . . confirm . . . the dogmatic position of Soviet ideologues who considered melodrama to be a bourgeois genre."

28. See Beumers, *Burnt* 64–65 and more generally for the best in-depth account of this film. In addition to Mitia's hidden identity as an NKVD officer, he also conceals a romantic identity, most suitable for melodrama, as Marusia's former (and first) lover. Masked identities, one of melodrama's hallmarks, can be found already in *At Home* (the secret traitor of the CheKa), *"Slave of Love"* (the underground cameraman and

Bolshevik), *Mechanical Piano* (Platonov's concealed love affair with Sonia), and *Five Evenings* (Aleksandr Petrovich's true occupation).

29. Films set in a later period, such as *Five Evenings*, replace these period props with the genteel bric-a-brac of their time, to which both camera and script insistently direct our attention. *Five Evenings*, set in 1958 (as we know from broadcasts of Van Cliburn winning the First International Tchaikovsky Piano Competition), provides a virtuosic example. A television fashion host, proffering advice on home decorating, disapproves of a now "old-fashioned" set of small ornamental elephants. In the film's final moments, as the heroine delivers her most poignant monologue, the camera lingers ironically on her bric-a-brac, including the same small ornamental elephants that had been dismissed by the television fashion world.

30. These resonances are heightened by Mikhalkov's deliberate insertion of anachronisms: the use of electric guitar to accompany a repetition of the signature song in *"Slave of Love"* and Eduard Artem'ev's contemporary melody on ship building, sung by a well-known, fashionable Soviet musician, Aleksandr Gradskii (*At Home*). This film's anachronistic dimension is intensified by narcotics as a key element of the story line, lending it a contemporary overlay. Neuberger (262) does not mention, but her well-crafted argument would support a stunning example of this resonance, when the film crew of *"Slave of Love"* laments a time of "plentiful film stock, high revenues, and the happy old days," a prescient description of how Stagnation came increasingly to be viewed in retrospect.

31. "Already in '*Slave of Love*,'" Mikhalkov writes, "in a number of scenes depicting the everyday life of the cinema group, we tried to find a Chekhovian intonation, an ironic quality, sensitivity, the ephemeral quality of human relations characteristic of that writer" (quoted in Sandler 211).

32. The Chekhovian sources were most evidently "Lady with the Lapdog" but also included elements from "Anna on the Neck" ("Anna na shee"), "Gooseberries" ("Kryzhovnik"), and "Names Day" ("Imeniny"; Bogemskii 16).

33. Since 1911 more than ninety adaptations, including for animation, children's films, and television films, have been made of Chekhov's work. Among the best known are Ivan Dykhovichnyi's *Black Monk* (*Chernyi monakh*; Mosfil'm, 1988), Kai Hansen's *Romance with a Double Bass* (*Roman s kontrabassom*; Pathé, 1911), Sergei Iutkevich's *Subject for a Short Story* (*Siuzhet dlia nebol'shogo rasskaza*; Mosfil'm, 1969), Iulii Karasik's *Gull* (*Chaika*; Mosfil'm, 1970), Iosif Kheifits's *Lady with the Lapdog* (*Dama s sobachkoi*; Lenfil'm, 1960), Andrei Konchalovskii's *Uncle Vania* (*Diadia vania*; Mosfil'm, 1970), Vladimir Motyl''s *Gone with the Horses* (*Nesut menia koni*; Arpon, 1996), Iakov Protazanov's *Ranks and People* (*Chiny i liudy*; Mezhrabpomfil'm, 1929), Abram Room's *Belated Flowers* (*Tsvety zapozdalye*; Mosfil'm, 1969), Samson Samsonov's *Grasshopper* (*Poprygun'ia*; Mosfil'm, 1955) and *Three Sisters* (*Tri sestry*; Mosfil'm, 1964), and Sergei Solov'ev's *Family Happiness* (*Semeinoe schast'e*; Mosfil'm, 1970) and *Three Sisters* (*Tri sestry*; Aleksandr Bukhman, 1994). See Shatina and Antropov 269–75.

34. On the cinematic Austen, see MacDonald; Troost and Greenfield.

35. The theme of property dominated such stories as Chekhov's "Belated Flowers" ("Tsvety zapozdalye"; 1888), "Other People's Misfortune" ("Chuzhaia beda"; 1886), and "A Visit with Friends" ("U znakomykh"; 1898) and was informed by Chekhov's family history of financial disaster and ensuing loss of home.

36. Mikhalkov comments:

They [Goskino] would hardly have entrusted us, young artists, with the production of *Cherry Orchard*, all the more so given that we were not the first filmmakers who wanted to produce that film. In "Fatherlessness" ["Bezotsovshchina"] on the other hand, what attracted us was the fact that, in comparison with the other plays, this work was weak, immature; it was written when the writer was only seventeen. And this gave us the right to be maximally free in our reading of it. Never mind the fact that the form in which the play existed made it impossible to film—it was huge, more than 277 pages. (Quoted in Lipkov, *Nikita Mikhalkov*)

The script was developed from an unpublished draft, discovered in 1920 when Chekhov's heirs moved his papers from family ownership to state archives. First published by Tsentrarkhiv in 1923, the play was attributed to the years 1877–78, when Chekhov was a gymnasium student in Taganrog, editing the student journal *The Stutterer* (*Zaika*; Chekhov 393–402). This manuscript is an earlier version of an 1881 manuscript, usually staged as "Platonov," after its principal character, or "A Play without a Title," the words written on the folder containing the draft itself and so named in the twelfth volume of the 1949 edition of Chekhov's collected works. "Whenever one hears of a play by Chekhov one cannot quite place," Karlinsky (68) comments, "it is a sure sign that somebody else has tried to trim down [Chekhov's] untitled 1881 play [*sic*] to manageable size. The manuscript young Chekhov once discarded is thus gradually becoming an inexhaustible source of new Chekhov plays." Despite the enormity of the "raw material" contained in the voluminous *Platonov*, Mikhalkov also drew liberally from such Chekhov sources as "At a Country House" ("V usad'be"), "Teacher of Literature" ("Uchitel' slovestnosti"), "Three Years" ("Tri goda"), and "My Life" ("Moia zhizn'").

37. The pattern will continue in *Burnt by the Sun*, with its musical citations from Leoncavallo's *Pagliacci*, and in *Barber of Siberia*, with its citations from Rossini's *Barber of Seville*.

38. "Human ephemerality and physical permanence," as Neuberger (264) puts it.

39. The quotation in the title of this section is from Mikhalkov, "Ia sdelal kartinu" 18. The epigraph, from Mikhalkov's documentary film *Anna*, invites a comparison between the daughter's childhood and that of Iliusha Oblomov. Returning to this topic at the film's conclusion, the narrator suggests that "what divided them was faith and godlessness." Neither abstraction figures prominently in the textual lives of either child.

40. Although I agree with Valentino (161) in his essay on *Oblomov* that the film, and Mikhalkov's work more broadly, engages in a "lament on the disappearance of the pre-modern, old Russian, communal, familial, estate values that characterized life at Oblomovka," I disagree that *Casta Diva* in Mikhalkov's work is therefore "morally pernicious, for it is part of the secular, imported Western culture." Instead, Mikhalkov's delicate negotiation proposes that it retain features of its status as a recognized *European* empire without therefore being a Western culture. In this configuration *Casta Diva* is merely an engaging composition of a transimperial, elite culture.

41. *Urga* instantiates all three: the pristine Mongol steppes, the characters' growing dependency on the city, and the Russians' irretrievable loss of homeland; as the yet unborn child recounts, "Last year my wife and I went to Baikal *where the Russians used to live*" (emphasis mine). On this elegiac Russia, see Moskvina, "Russkaia mysl'."

42. Mikhalkov's *Oblomov* deviates from more common interpretations of Goncharov's novel in his sympathetic treatment of both protagonists. Oblomov's childhood and character exude warmth, kinship, and love of the countryside; Stoltz's childhood and character exude discipline, initiative, and a thirst for foreign travel. Mikhalkov's scripting of their defining childhood moments as (respectively) summer and winter suggests that he would see them as interdependent figures. That the film's end dwells on little Andriusha, sired by Oblomov but raised by Stoltz, might be seen as a fanciful way of staging the mating of these two male types, for whom the inclusion of Ol'ga, a reproductive female but not the mother, is a necessary element for the sake of cinematic decency. For a valuable discussion of this issue, see Beumers, "Mikhalkov Brothers' View" 143.

CHAPTER 4

1. The most thorough and reliable English-language biography and analysis is Taubman, *Kira Muratova*. See also Bozhovich, *Kira Muratova*. See Abdullaeva, *Kira Muratova*, for the most interesting Russian-language engagement with Muratova's work.

2. In reference to the authorship of *Our Honest Bread*, however, Muratova has been unequivocal: "I didn't consider myself the real author of that film" (quoted in Taubman, *Kira Muratova* 3).

3. To Zhukhovitskii's romance of a geologist and a local farm girl Muratova added the complicating parallel romance of the geologist with an urban professional woman (Bozhovich, "Rentgenoskopiia" 54; Sirkes 93),

4. Taubman, *Kira Muratova* 4. For documents pertaining to the fate of *Long Farewells*, see Fomin, "*Polka*" 92–109.

5. For an excellent discussion of the flashback sequences and the film more broadly, see Larsen, "*Korotkie vstrechi*."

6. During this time in the mid-1970s Muratova was to have filmed *Princess Mary* (*Kniazhna Meri*), based on Mikhail Lermontov's short story. Rustam Khamdamov, who shares with Paradzhanov a love of elaborate visual ornamentation, was to have done the costume design. Beyond the bright ornamentalizations of Paradzhanov and Khamdamov, critical influences in Muratova's work have been diverse in the extreme. The filmmaker repeatedly identifies Charlie Chaplin's comic sadness and Fellini's aesthetic eye as key elements in her work. It is no surprise that Eisenstein's cinema of attractions and his late, highly mannered *Ivan the Terrible* have been cited as formative in her creative work, particularly her films from 1978 onward, beginning with *Getting to Know the Wide World*. See Bollag and Ciment 12; Taubman, *Kira Muratova* 9–10, 27.

7. "Ivan Sidorov" functions in some respects as the Russian equivalent to the film pseudonym Alan Smithee, that is, a name substituted when the real director or actor disavows his or her work. For historical background, see Lesli Klainberg's television documentary *Who Is Alan Smithee?* (Orchard, WinStar, 2002).

8. See Iutkevich 284, which lists only her two early codirected films (the short *Steep Ravine* and *Honest Bread*), as well as *Brief Encounters* and *Getting to Know the Wide World*. At the time of Iutkevich's writing, *Long Farewells* was still shelved and *Among the Grey Stones* had appeared under "Ivan Sidorov."

9. Only *Enthusiasms*, to which I will return, provides an extended congenial environment, with its long outdoor shots, seaside institution, and extended walkways, vaguely similar to *Long Farewells*. Unlike *Long Farewells*, however, each mammal in *Enthusiasms* is institutionalized in his or her own most suitable fashion.

10. Others include the little Lilia Murlykina (*Three Stories*), as film scholar Maia Turovskaia has repeatedly suggested in public film discussions, and the young, retarded Misha (*Minor People*), who avidly collects detritus.

11. Erofeev ("Proshchanie" 94), who served on the Kinotavr jury for the Sochi International Film Festival when Muratova's *Three Stories* was an entry, fought hard if unsuccessfully to award it the Grand Prix.

12. I of course realize that "minimalism" is hardly a descriptor one would normally assign to this director, with her love of ornament and complexity. Here I have in mind not her visual staging of a shot, but rather her civilizational standards.

13. In this vertical montage, using music to underscore the associative link between two apparently contrastive shots, we can see a specific example of her affinity with Eisenstein's later work.

14. Similar interspecies face-offs occur in Muratova's *Chekhovian Motifs* between the father and his pig (with intercuts between human lips and pig lips); in *Minor People* when a male character engages in a prolonged kissing scene with an ape; and in *Two in One* when the father and the family dog take turns urinating on the daughter's threshold. For an excellent analysis of this and other moments, see Graffy at http://www.kinokultura.com/2007/17r-dvavodnom2.shtml.

15. In *Chekhovian Motifs* the ritual bickering—are the workmen building a store or a barn ("Magazin!" "Sarai!")?—enacts a similar contestation over human and animal. Though based in part on Chekhov's one-act play *Tat'iana Repina* and his short story *Difficult People* (*Tiazhelye liudi*), the original texts are barely discernable in Muratova's rendition. Muratova's end product is such that it no more matters that *Chekhovian Motifs* originated in Chekhov than that *Tuner* originated in Arkadii Koshko's memoirs. Koshko, a sort of Russian Sherlock Holmes, was chief of the Moscow Investigation Department in the first decade of the twentieth century.

16. As Muratova's work matures, these episodic disciplinarians become more mannered in their mindless banality. In *Long Farewells* the groundskeeper, Vasia, berates guests for using sporting equipment, and the social worker (*obshchestvennik*) upbraids the civic behavior of young Kartseva. *Sentimental Policeman* includes a lengthy, repetitive lament by an episodic figure whose disciplinarian mother will not admit him after 11:00 p.m.; in *Three Stories*, the episodic disciplinarians include the disapproving older woman of "Ophelia" who, standing in the courtyard, intones, "This is not a toilet."

17. As the critic Nina Tsyrkun astutely points out, *Three Stories*, read backward, tells of a little girl who commits murder, who matures into an adult with her own philosophy of murder, and who, as a mature woman, is finally herself murdered: crime and punishment, but narrated in reverse.

18. In *Getting to Know the Wide World* "the building site is chaos, a place where culture has not yet been created" (Bozhovich, "Iz zhizni" 15).

19. Not for nothing is the lethargic Nikolai (*Asthenic Syndrome*), Muratova's emblematic victim of *asthenia*, a state high school English teacher.

20. The well-to-do farmer's home, the setting for the first half of *Chekhovian Motifs*, offers a rural variant to this genteel environment: its lace curtains, china, family icons, and linens embroidered with didactic proverbs invite an analogous desecration to the urban *intelligent*'s cozy, carefully furnished flat.

21. Murlykina, whose surname in Russian evokes a kitten's purr, appears in the film under her real name and recites her real address, as if she had no more need of a diegetic name and address than would any other pet in Muratova's menagerie. The more traditional intermixing of professional and nonprofessional actors is thus extended in Muratova's work to a more ambitious intermixing of reality systems. A related instance, in *Asthenic Syndrome*, is the character of the "film actress" Ol'ga Antonova, played by the film actress Ol'ga Antonova.

22. "In Bergman I find a lack of barbarity" ("V Bergmane mne ne khvataet varvarstva"; quoted in Plakhov, "Kira Muratova" 206).

23. In a 1991 interview with Jane Taubman, Muratova describes *Sentimental Policeman* as "the polar opposite of *Asthenic Syndrome* in all respects. I'm always drawn from the sweet to the sour. This is a small, closed, chamber tale and very sentimental" (*Kira Muratova* 63–64).

24. "I don't understand; I don't understand," repeats Evgeniia Vasil'evna early in *Long Farewells*. Later, in an angry scene over a rejected translation job, she attempts to interrupt and silence her interlocutor with repetitive irony: "I understand, I understand." Nikolai (*Asthenic Syndrome*), rueful of his student's reaction, compulsively repeats, "He didn't understand me" and, several scenes later, "No one understands me, no one understands me."

25. A similar instance of irresolvable, discursive surfeit is the nameless dwarf (Oksana Shlapak) in *A Change of Fate*, who is described by Larsen ("Encoding Difference" 120) as a "'double' . . . [who] aids and abets all of Maria's actions."

26. Critics disagree whether this figure is the school administrator *chez soi* or a different character altogether. I am not convinced that, for Muratova's work, the question itself is correctly formulated.

27. "You are so tired . . . I love your smell . . . you are like an angel."

28. For an interesting pursuit of this line of thought, see Aronson, "Ekstsentrika" and "Mezhdu priemom."

29. The film is shot in Tadzhikistan near Isfara.

30. See Shilova, "Renata Litvinova" for one of the best analyses of the actress's work and persona.

31. See also Litvinova, "Monologi medsestry."

32. In *Two in One*, for example, this inventory includes a mannequin, nude dolls, nude paintings, nude sculptures, and pornographic photography.

33. Cf. Berry (449), who refers to the dolls as "simulated humans."

34. And, conversely, corpses, as in *Minor People*, may at any moment revert to life.

35. See Anninskii, "Ar'ergardnyi boi" and *Shestidesiatniki i my*.

36. The key essay from which the term "other prose" (*drugaia proza*) stems is by Sergei Chuprinin. See also Condee and Padunov, "Pair-A-Dice Lost" 86 and "Perestroika Suicide" 77.

37. "There are things I like," says Muratova, who apparently counts her colleague Petrushevskaia among her favorite things. "For example, Liudmila Petrushevskaia" (quoted in Plakhov, "Mne nuzhna" 10). There is more than a superficial resemblance between the work of Muratova and Petrushevskaia, particularly between Muratova's later cinema and Petrushevskaia's plays (*Three Girls in Blue, The Stairwell, Cinzano*). A cluster of features—for example, the memorable, unredeemable female characters, presented in an unromantic yet often highly sexualized fashion by these two women artists of the same generation—is only the start of a comparison. Both gather their material anecdotally (in Petrushevskaia's terms, as "incidents" [*sluchai*]) from their circle of friends and acquaintances. Like Muratova, Petrushevskaia is fascinated by aspects of the psyche left out of more traditional Russian narration, for example, recreational prostitution, infanticide, and alcoholic debilitation. But where Muratova engages in ludic pleasure, Petrushevskaia aims at a more gothic orientation. For an interesting discussion of their similarities and differences, see Taubman, *Kira Muratova* 62, 117; D. Bykov, "Kira Muratova: Chto-to." As problematic as any comparison across media may be, this kinship is a more sensible project than any comparison of Muratova with other women filmmakers, such as Dinara Asanova or Larisa Shepit'ko.

38. Litvinova, who worked with the Aleinikov brothers on their filming of Gleb Aleinikov's *Tractor Drivers* (*Traktoristy*, 1992), maintains a persona in real life at least as intriguing and impenetrable as Prigov's own. Although Sul'kin ("Renata" 17) does not use the colloquial term *steb*, his interview with Litvinova stresses elements of her retro style that precisely capture the multiple, layered consciousness of *steb*: its generational disjuncture, love of "totalitarian kitsch" (Kundera 251–57), and faux obliviousness to changing fashion.

39. See Taubman, *Kira Muratova* 46–47 for a brief account of the details. For insightful comments by Andrei Plakhov, chair of the Conflicts Commission, on the furor surrounding the profanities in *Asthenic Syndrome*, see Batchan, "Andrei Plakhov"; Condee and Padunov, "*Makulakul'tura*" 84, 89–90; Plakhov, "Soviet Cinema" 81.

40. In a similarly reflexive fashion, a respectable, middle-aged couple, leaving the cinema, implicitly from Muratova's own film, comment to one another, preempting the viewers' reaction: "I don't understand why we have such sorrowful films. I don't feel so great myself as it is. I am tired from work, I want to relax, listen to music . . . but there they go once again, wandering around, complaining, burying people, talking about all kinds of things."

41. It is a triple abyme in this sense: we ourselves watch Sasha, who is watching his mother, who is watching slides of Sasha and his father. The most interesting work on the textual phenomenon of abyme is found in Dällenbach.

42. Muratova's ("Iskusstvo rodilos'" 96) first visit to the pound, about which she has written and spoken considerably, occurred during her filming of *Brief Encounters*.

43. Muratova's assistant director, Nadezhda Popova, performs the obscene monologue.

44. The project of transforming Muratova from a director into an essentialized woman director involves remarkably contradictory moves. An early claim that she

represented a "genuinely female perspective" marshaled precisely the qualities absent in her postcommunist work: "compassion and mercy . . ., warmth," a director's view that is "reassuring . . ., respectful" (Attwood 192). Another analysis makes the opposite claim, attributing to Muratova a "'masculine' approach . . . common amongst women directors . . . who felt they had a 'male type' lodged inside them" (Attwood 234). Yet another takes refuge in more generalized expectations: the catalogue for the Berlin 47th International Film Festival characterizes *Three Stories* as a "feminist thriller" (cited in Beumers, *Russia on Reels* 199).

Although Muratova's example may inadvertently encourage other women in the field, even the best arguments (such as Sabrodin and Messlinger's) for a continuity of women's cinema—let's say Iuliia Solntseva, Lili Brik, Ol'ga Preobrazhenskaia; then a problematic leap forward to Larisa Shepit'ko, Dinara Asanova, Muratova, Lana Gogoberidze, and on to Natal'ia P'iankova, Lidiia Bobrova and Larisa Sadilova—tells us little more about that continuity than what their first names already convey.

45. N. Vlashchenko, "Kira Muratova: Garmoniia—eto narushenie vsekh zakonov," *Den'* (1997), quoted in Taubman, *Kira Muratova* 106.

46. "I am not a social critic," Muratova insists to Judy Stone ("Soviet Director" 33). "I believe in . . . art as a game and by no means art for a social cause."

47. In *Minor People*, for example, the mafia figure is a former Russian teacher.

48. One of Muratova's earliest "episodic eccentrics" (*Brief Encounters*), a portrait of gentle, impaired helplessness, is the old man who compulsively recounts how his children were killed by the fascists. This character bears a kinship resemblance to the episodic blind man in *Long Farewells* who requests Evgeniia Vasil'evna's help in writing out a lengthy message to his children, as well as the two blind men in the last shot of "Ophelia" (*Three Stories*) to whom Ofa hands her drowned mother's cane.

49. "A luxury, opium, a narcotic—so what?" (Sirkes 90).

50. According to Taubman (*Muratova* 42), the dancers were cut from Muratova's *Among Grey Stones* and therefore reinserted in *A Change of Fate* and *Enthusiasms*. The paintings in "Ophelia" are the work of Evgenii Golubenko, who contributed to the scripts of *Sentimental Policeman*, "Boiler Room No. 6" (the first panel of *Three Stories*), *Chekhovian Motifs*, *Tuner*, and the first panel of *Two Stories*. He also played a minor acting role in "Ophelia." Golubenko's paintings first appeared in *A Change of Fate*.

Retrospectively, the amateur song and guitar performance of Lermontov's "The Sail" at the end of *Long Farewells*, however diegetically motivated, marks another such amateur interpellation.

CHAPTER 5

1. A complete filmography for Abdrashitov and Mindadze—including entries for Mindadze's early, independent scenarios for film shorts—as well as an extensive bibliography of interviews, reviews, and articles on their work, separately and together, up through *Time of the Dancer* (1998) can be found in *Kinograf* 5 (1998): 34–73.

2. Abdrashitov was in the last generation of VGIK students to study under Romm, whose other VGIK students included directors Tengiz Abuladze, Vasilii Shukshin, and Andrei Tarkovskii.

3. Abdrashitov's footage was cut when Romm's project was taken over by Elem Klimov, German Lavrov, and Marlen Khutsiev. Completed in 1974, the film was released under the title *And All the Same, I Believe* (*I vse-taki ia veriu*). On the finished product, see Abdrashitov, "A chto" 80. For Romm's comments on the young Abdrashitov's work, see Romm 62.

4. See Kudriavtsev, *Svoe kino* 412. *Parade of the Planets*, their most controversial film for which they are best remembered, reached an initial audience of only 2–3 million viewers (Hardy).

5. The opening subtitle of *Parade of the Planets* describes the film as "An Almost Fantastic Story" ("Pochti fantasticheskaia povest'"). Its cosmological fantasy derives less directly from the vast telescopic machinery of the opening sequence than from a single sheet of paper—the army reserve notice of a seven-day training session—that flutters out of the astronomer's postbox as he returns home from observing the distant stars.

Other critics have dubbed this style variously as "a tendency to elliptical speech [*inoskazanie*], mystico-metaphorical generalization" (Mark Kushnirovich in "Kritiki," *Seans* 11 [1995]: 5), "programmatic metaphorism" (Sirivlia 45), "existential" (Maslova 25), "mysticism" (Stishova, "Konets" 84), and "fantastic realism" (Donets 52), to cite some of the more common descriptors. Dobrotvorskaia ("Povorot" 7) captures the ambiguity in her characterization of their style as "social symbolism."

6. Pavlik Morozov (1918–32) was a thirteen-year-old peasant boy murdered by villagers for allegedly betraying his father to the state. The best research on Morozov is Kelly.

Abdrashitov ("Pliumbum" n.p.) comments:

The picture, to be sure, divided viewers into two categories. One group of viewers thought: anything can happen in life, and it's not out of the question that in an extreme situation it would be necessary to interrogate one's own father. The other category [of viewers] decided that this cannot be done under any circumstances, in no social order, under any government. These second viewers understand the picture as we ourselves do, and consider Pliumbum to be an anti-hero. As do we.

7. The defendant Valia Kostina (*Speech*) first spies the infidelity of her partner, Vitalii Fediaev, set against the proscenium frame of a theater performance. Her attorney, Irina Mezhnikova, first notices the rudderless drift of her life as she watches her younger self, framed in the home movies; her abandonment of her fiancé is framed by the train's window, within which she observes him as her train pulls away. A similar frame shot in *Train* positions its characters within the train's window frame in order to posit the key question of the film: "Are we worth it?"

8. Indeed, Mikhail Trofimenkov ("Ostanovilsia" 6) has remarked that their creative biography neatly divides into two decades of five films each. The first—from Abdrashitov's 1973 diploma film *Stop Potapov* to Abdrashitov-Mindadze's 1982 *The Train Stopped*—was a period of "concise, cold, insightful social dramas . . . simple, albeit borderline situations, simple people, simple words, a restrained moral position." The second decade—through *Play for a Passenger* (1995), the time of Trofimenkov's essay—was

one in which "human movement lost its former physiological-social definition. The precise dramatic structures began to slide."

9. For an extended analysis of the relevance of this notion to contemporary Russian cinema, see Beumers, *Russia on Reels*, especially Kovalov (in Beumers 12–21) and Condee ("No Glory" 25–33); see also Sergei Sel'ianov's 1996 film *The Russian Idea*, commissioned by Colin MacCabe (British Film Institute) in 1995 for the centenary of cinema; see also McDaniel.

10. Abdrashitov's immediate reference here is to the scene in *Time of the Dancer*. The preoccupation with "revenge gone wrong"—wrong because it is not properly a human prerogative in Abdrashitov-Mindadze's world—first surfaces in *Play for a Passenger*: Nikolai's attempts at revenge against the former judge consistently ameliorate his intended victim's life.

11. An exception is *Magnetic Storms* (2002), which, however undefined in its temporal coordinates, suggests the late 1980s, some fifteen years before its shooting. Abdrashitov has kept the film unyoked from an event at specific place and time, yet insistently cites such factory battles during the period of late *perestroika* and the early 1990s. On factury unrest (principally of an earlier, post-Stalinist period), see Kozlov, in particular chapters 12 and 13 on the June 1962 Novocherkassk riots, the best-known example of Soviet factory unrest.

12. An early example of this juxtaposition of leisure and violence is the scene in *Train* in which the investigator Ermakov and the journalist Malinin spend a Sunday at the beach together. Cameraman Iurii Nevskii's lens focuses on the two men in casual conversation set against a backdrop of the railroad bridges, a constant reminder of the violent train accident that had brought them together.

13. The rational explanation—that German Ermakov must have acquired (and already memorized!) the information from his fellow investigators—is nowhere supported by the film. Ermakov has no interest in Malinin's background, nor is Malinin a suspect in the investigation.

14. In the screenplay the line takes an ironic tone. "'I am Petrov,' [Nikolai] said. 'A rare name. It would have been easier to guess it than to remember it'" (Mindadze 505). This casual opposition of "guessing" and "remembering" captures a key preference in their work for the reliability of an intuitive gamble over memory's trace.

15. Other examples abound: in *Parade of the Planets* the reservists are mistaken for a repair crew at the pensioners' home. Leaving, they encounter a figure whom they mistake for a rural fisherman, but who turns out to be a chemist. In *The Armavir* Timur is called a "horseman," claims to be a graduate student, but turns out to be a thief. The cruise entertainer Rusalka is actually a shipboard thief. Aksiusha, officially a ship's mate, is a pimp. In *Play for a Passenger* Oleg Petrovich was a Soviet judge who became a train conductor and then a night watchman. Nikolai, the student-accordionist, became a petty criminal, then a convict, then a wealthy entrepreneur. "Inna," the part-time prostitute, presents herself as a singing teacher. Kuz'min ("Batia"), Nikolai's criminal "father," has identity papers under the name "Gurfinkel." In *Time of the Dancer* Valera goes from soldier and welder—or so he tells his wife—to nightclub owner. Andrei goes from a television repairman to military ensemble dancer to nightclub entertainer. Fedor was a miner before he was a soldier; then he became a bus driver. Katia moves from nurse to part-time prostitute. Temur,

once a pediatrician, became a rebel separatist. His wife, Tamara, a Russian literature teacher, is passed off as Andrei's fiancé. And so on.

16. This subjective moment is more explicit in the screenplay, narrated by the protagonist attorney, Irina Mezhnikova, who observes herself in the film as an alien woman:

> There, on the white screen, still at the very beginning of her journey, an unknown, provincial girl already seems to be measuring herself for the incipient decade. Already there, sitting together with everyone else at the festive table, she seems to be overcoming the barriers facing her. . . . It seems to me at some moment our eyes even meet and she looks at me without a smile, severely, and indeed with disapproval. (Mindadze 93)

Here too one can discern the dual registers, wherein the spectral younger self is coded as the elusive, higher judge of the real, contemporary self.

17. The term "parade of planets" refers to the rare phenomenon of planetary conjunction, when the planets, circling the sun at different speeds, are positioned in the sky such that a large number of them—usually four or five, but here, implicitly, six—can be seen at one time from the Earth. The film's six reservists pass through distinct settlements on their journey home. These settlements have been extensively debated by critics as signaling the Ages of Man, key sites of Greek mythology, or levels of the biblical world. See El'iashev and Lapshin; Grashchenkova.

18. The train as a space for self-revelation resonates with a number of nineteenth-century Russian literary works, most notably Dostoevskii (*The Idiot*) and Tolstoi ("Kreutzer Sonata," *Anna Karenina*). In the transient demimonde of Abdrashitov-Mindadze's films, however, the confession is inevitably further reinvention.

19. "Fox hunting" and "pelengation" refer to the sport of tracking radio signals through a country terrain by means of radio receivers mounted as headphones.

20. To this list I suppose one could add the self-described "dead," victim reservists of *Parade of Planets*, who, ambushed by enemy rocket fire during their military exercises, are sent home early.

21. On the trope of the mutilated Soviet hero, see Kaganovsky, *How* and "Bodily Remains"; I. Smirnov. The rich topic of masculinity, impairment, and state violence is explored, with varying degrees of indebtedness to Sontag's *Illness as Metaphor*, in Bourke; Gillespie; Mitchell and Snyder; and Quayson.

22. The title of this section is from Abdrashitov, quoted in Stishova, "Konets" 84.

23. The censor's discomfort with such films as *The Train Stopped* and *Parade of the Planets* led to their limited distribution rather than outright removal. Abdrashitov ("Kazhdyi raz" 9) comments, "When a viewer would write to the newspaper, 'Why do we read about *The Train Stopped*, but we can't see the film anywhere?,' as a rule, they would answer, "Comrade, you don't know your own city. Out at the city limits the picture was given one screening.'"

24. Their theatricality, so starkly different from the bravura and theatricality of Mikhalkov, is heightened in *Play for a Passenger* by the fact that the actors Sergei Makovetskii (who plays Oleg) and Igor' Livanov (Nikolai) are a full decade younger than their forty-year-olds' roles. The actors are thus the same age as their characters when

they first met as judge and defendant. This studied effect further distances the viewer from the events on the screen, framing them as if time had stood still, recycling the old plot with the roles reversed. A similar flattening out of time is at work in *The Armavir*, in which the father and the son-in-law are contemporaries. Their arguments about the past—Marina's youth, the moral compromises of their common military experiences—cast them in a horizontal relationship as generational and professional equals.

25. Similar camera work in the war games and the dance scene in *Parade* suggests a latent similarity of these projects: the wordless, crepuscular movement of bodies, ill coordinated and inexperienced, cautious and mutually instructive. Each scene is followed by the river swim: close-up shots of heads swarming in the river, then a pulling back of the camera to survey their collective flailing. Such camera work is evident in Shevtsik's visual treatment of the pensioners, alternating close-up head shots with high-angle crane shots at the entire group, their goodwill infused with a kind of zombie-like somnambulance.

CHAPTER 6

1. As Aleksandra Tuchinskaia has provocatively suggested about *Days of the Eclipse* and *Second Circle*, "It is a different climactic zone of the country, once united by a common trouble." See http://www.sokurov.spb.ru/island_en/feature_films/krug_vtoroi/mnp_kvt.html. For the most detailed bibliography of director's materials (scripts, diaries, articles, working notes, reviews, letters), as well as interviews, memoirs, and critical articles through 1996 (*Mother and Son*), see Rakitina.

2. Sokurov ("The Solitary Voice," 73–74) has mentioned, for example, his early inspiration from Robert Flaherty's 1934 *Man of Aran* and Jean Vigo's 1934 *L'Atalante*, each of which, in different ways, stages its drama around the figure of the boat and a life on the water. Here one might see the very beginnings of the interpretive cluster (the ocean or river, the ship, the flood) that will become articulated variously in *Confession*, as well as the endings of both *Mournful Unconcern* and *Russian Ark*.

3. The second epigraph of this section is taken from Sokurov's website located at http://www.sokurov.spb.ru/isle_ru/isle_ftr.html. Sokurov ("Nastoiashchee" 97) traces his interest in Hirohito to his history studies during the early 1970s while at Gor'kii University.

4. Multiple reasons are usually given for the film's unacceptable status apart from its unconventionality. First, Sokurov was an enrolled documentalist submitting an artistic film for his graduation work; second, Platonov's political status in the 1970s was still a precarious business. See "Aleksandr Nikolaevich Sokurov" 41.

5. See Arabov's mordant comment: "The film was secretly carried out of the editing studio, and its negative was substituted, it seems, by the negative for *Battleship Potemkin*. It was a conceptual substitution that was carried out. Did they erase *Battleship Potemkin*? Entirely possible. And from then on—despair" (quoted in Arkus and Savel'ev, *Sokurov* 30). For a bibliography of works by and about Iurii Arabov, see Andreeva. For Arabov's collected screenplays, including the unfinished tetralogy, see Arabov, *Solntse*. *Lonely Human Voice* was subsequently hidden in the director Aleksei German's editing room at Lenfil'm when it was not covertly "on tour," as Oleg Kovalov describes. I am indebted to Mikhail Trofimenkov for additional information on this series of incidents.

6. Cameraman Sergei Iurizditskii, who had worked with Sokurov on the ill-fated *Lonely Human Voice*, maintains that Sokurov's substituted diploma film was not *Summer of Mariia Voinova* but a modest documentary film, *The Automobile Gains Reliability*, about a car factory. See Iurizditskii's conversation with Anastasiia Leshchenko in *Kinovedcheskie zapiski* ("Mne zhizn' interesna sama po sebe," at http://www.kinozapiski. ru/article/52/). I am grateful to Aleksandr Shpagin, who first alerted me to this early film, which figures nowhere in the standard Russian filmographies.

7. This later *Mariia* consists of two chapters: the color footage (dating from Gor'kii City Television) and the second black-and-white chapter. It is sometimes bundled together with the 1978 documentary *Last Day of a Rainy Summer* and the twosome is referred to as *Elegy of the Land* (*Elegiia zemli*).

8. On Sokurov's diploma defense, see Liviia Zvonnikova's account in Arkus and Savel'ev, *Sokurov* 31–32. It was Zvonnikova who introduced Sokurov and Arabov; see Arabov's account in *Solntse* 506. Zvonnikova was one of three VGIK colleagues, together with Paola Volkova and Polina Lobachevskaia, who hotly defended *Lonely Human Voice* and successfully sought support from Andrei Tarkovskii and Konstantin Simonov (Arabov, *Solntse* 507).

9. For additional details, see http://www.sokurov.spb.ru/island_en/bio.html on Sokurov's website *Island of Sokurov* (*Ostrov Sokurova*), http://www.sokurov.spb.ru/ index.html. *Island of Sokurov* was the name of the director's 1998–99 television show, which dealt inter alia with the topic of cinema's role in contemporary society and its place vis-à-vis the other arts.

10. See, e.g., Sokurov, "Nastoiashchee" 101–2 and "Glavnym" 72. "Authentic film does not need a viewer," Sokurov ("Tvorcheskii alfavit" 80) has insisted. "The book cannot exist without the reader. Cinema, fortunately or unfortunately, can exist without a viewer." Commenting on *Stone*, his film on Chekhov (on Chekhov's ghost, to be more precise), Sokurov characteristically remarks, "*Stone* is a film that would never search for the audience: its voice is too quiet. This film will meet with its audience only if the audience searches for it." See http://www.sokurov.spb.ru/island_en/feature_ films/kamen'/mnp_kam.html.

11. See the series of articles on *Russian Ark* in *Artmargins*, in particular essays by Drubek-Meyer and Kujundzic. See also Ian Christie's cautionary remarks (*Russkii kovcheg* 244–45).

12. See Belopol'skaia, "*Mariia*" 143–46, for an extended discussion of this conundrum.

13. See http://www.sokurov.spb.ru/island_en/feature_films/tikhie_stranitsy/ mnp_tst.html. Confirmation of Tuchinskaia's insight might be gleaned from Sokurov's comment in "Cinema and Painting" that something must always be held back from the viewer and that "art is only where this reticence exists, a limitation of what we can actually see and feel. There has to be a mystery" ("Cinema and Painting," commentary to the DVD of *Elegy of a Voyage*).

14. The same could be said of Sokurov's 1991 documentary on Yeltsin, *An Example of Intonation*. On this topic, see Iampol'skii's remarks in "Istina tela" 165–66. An English version of this essay appears as Iampolski, "Truth in the Flesh."

15. As with his earlier compilation film, *Sonata for Hitler*, which draws extensively on Mikhail Romm's *Ordinary Fascism* (*Obyknovennyi fashizm*; Mosfil'm, 1965), Sokurov

is concerned with editing existing footage rather than presenting previously unseen images. On this, see Turovskaia (*Sonata* 147). Sokurov's compilation film *Leningrad Retrospective*, thirteen and a half hours covering thirty-four years of Leningrad film chronicles, contains three short segments not integral to the official series *Leningrad Cine-Chronicle* (*Leningradskaia kinokhronika*), from which he edits his own film. Two sections are filmed by Sokurov's own students in 1988; a third section is filmed in 1990 by Sokurov himself. See Savel'ev, "Leningradskaia." in Arkus and Savel'ev, eds. 158.

16. Or, similarly, the opening sequence to *Mother and Son*, as Kujundzic notes, runs for eight minutes in silence and virtual immobility. The theater director Kirill Serebrennikov (151) describes such passages as Sokurov's making "visible through cinema the presence of the invisible."

17. The title *Island of Sokurov* now refers to his website, http://www.sokurov.spb.ru/isle_ru/isle_ftr.html.

18. On the essay-film, see Lopate. Sokurov comments on *Soviet Elegy*, "[It] can hardly be called a documentary film in the proper sense. Of course, the author guarantees the accuracy of chronology, but he insists on an artistic mode of thinking, not on a political or historical investigation." See http://www.sokurov.spb.ru/island_en/documetaries/sovetskaya_elegiya/mnp_sel.html. Elsewhere Sokurov ("Tvorcheskii alfavit" 77) writes, "Cinema itself is similar to a paired organ, like eyes. One eye is the documentary form. The other is artistic. I am interested neither in purely documentary nor in purely artistic cinema."

19. See Aleksandra Tuchinskaia's intriguing comment that their common plot is the "permanent co-existence of everyday life . . . with messages or messengers from nowhere." See http://www.sokurov.spb.ru/island_en/feature_films/dni_zatmeniya/mnp_dnz.html. Elsewhere Sokurov ("Teni zvuka" 13) has proposed a different trilogy, consisting of *Second Circle*, *Stone*, and *Whispering Pages*.

20. Sokurov's *Aleksandra*, though not explicitly part of this family trilogy, is in some ways its thematic continuation. The film's intimate, at times erotic portrait of grandmother and grandson strongly affiliate it with *Mother and Son* and *Father and Son* through multiple registers (camera work, the visual texture of the images, acting, narrative structure, pacing).

21. Sokurov's eleven elegies to date are *Mariia: Peasant Elegy*, *Elegy*, *Moscow Elegy*, *Soviet Elegy*, *Petersburg Elegy*, *Simple Elegy*, *Elegy Out of Russia*, *Oriental Elegy*, *Elegy of a Voyage* (the English-languge title of *Elegiia dorogi* or "Elegy of the Road"), and *Elegy of Life*. One might also count *Elegy of the Land* since it is a combination of two shorter documentaries, *Mariia* and *Last Day of a Rainy Summer*. After several elegies were completed, Sokurov ("The Solitary Voice" 75) considered uniting them under a single title, intending to produce a total of twenty-five, the age at which one begins to live consciously. "The elegy," Sokurov ("Tvorcheskii alfavit" 93) asserts, in one of his perpetual searches for a marker of homeland, "is a very Russian, emotional form."

22. I will resist the temptation to argue that his *Aleksandra*, starring Galina Vishnevskaia, belongs to the cluster of artists' portraits. Given the strong diegesis, the film falls more comfortably into his clusters of family films and military life.

23. One might equally include *Aleksandra*, set at a Russian military outpost in Chechnia, in this cluster. Military figures and military operations play a role at the

periphery of many other works. *Mournful Unconcern* is replete with military footage, one of three subsidiary visual planes to the film. *To the Events in Transcaucasia* concerns the mothers of young recruits to the Caucasian wars. The two lead characters of *Father and Son* are a veteran and a recruit; the family friend Sasha is from a military family. *Russian Ark* is awash in sailors and soldiers, as is *Elegy of a Voyage*.

24. "Well, I would never have put it like that, but yes. . . . I feel as if there were two personalities inside me. One is very active, versatile, and exuberant; the other is sober, strong, and almost ascetic" (Sokurov, "The Solitary Voice" 73).

25. Elsewhere Sokurov remarks of the title characters in *Father and Son*, "Their love is almost of mythological virtue and scale. It cannot happen in real life. This is a fairy-tale collision." See the author's preface at http://www.sokurov.spb.ru/island_en/feature_films/otets_i_syn/mnp_ots.html.

26. See Savel'ev, "Krugi" 60 for a discussion of this aspect of the film. For Sokurov's comments on Mamardashvili, see Sokurov, "Teni zvuka" 16.

27. Significantly, Boss Mangan's fainting episode is rescripted as death by Sokurov in *Mournful Unconcern*.

Dobrotvorskii ("Gorod i dom" 194) sees *Second Circle* as a kind of radical intensification of this practice: "The former Sokurov," he writes, "filmed houses like graves and cemeteries like cities. The Sokurov of *Second Circle* no longer sees a difference between [our] current residence and that on the other side." Some of the best work specifically on this topic is Iampol'skii, "Smert' v kino"; Rubanova.

28. "It's mandatory in the film that there should be an episode of observing Tiutchev's funeral; in fact everything should be reproduced in detail that accompanies this ritual in Russia of the nineteenth century. And the funeral should be luxurious: horses with black funerary horse-cloths, liveries, black morning coats" (Sokurov, "Tiutchev" 452).

29. The original order was intended to have been *Taurus, Moloch, Sun* (Sokurov, "Nastoiashchee" 95), but the actual order for logistical reasons was *Moloch, Taurus, Sun*. The producers for *Taurus*, anticipating a controversial domestic reaction to the Lenin film, set out to raise its entire budget from Russian sources without foreign investments (Ogurtsov). Because of delays associated with this strategy, this (would-have-been) "first" film was completed only after *Moloch*.

30. I should mention for the sake of clarity, since it has been the source of some critical confusion, that *Taurus* is not the story of Lenin's death day, but rather the story of the summer of 1922, after his May 26, 1922, stroke. Lenin died on January 21, 1924.

31. If one cared to argue an *original* metanarrative running through the *intended* order, it would (characteristically, for Sokurov) move chronologically *backward*, beginning with decrepitude (*Taurus*), moving to the acme of mature political power (*Moloch*), and ending with the childlike Hirohito—the "shrimp" (*smorchok*, literally "small morel"), as General MacArthur calls him—who, coming to an understanding of his mortality, is permitted to start life anew.

32. On the importance for Sokurov of color selection, range, and contrast, including a color's history in the work of Rembrandt, Goya, the German Romantics, and the French Impressionists, see the lengthy interview accompanying the DVD of *Moloch*, "*Moloch*: Interview with Alexander Sokurov."

33. Sokurov has repeatedly underscored his resistance to narrative structure as a principle for organizing film art. "If the film is based on the principle of the story, the narrative," he insists, "it is not art" ("An Interview" 18). His frequent scriptwriter Iurii Arabov confirms this preference. "A large part of the films of world cinema," he responds in an interview with Irina Liubarskaia, "are anchored in the plot. Aleksandr Nikolaevich goes against this flood" (Arabov, "Stsenarist" 110).

34. The film's annotation, like Shaw's play before it, is unequivocal on this score: "The house itself is a ship" (*Sam dom—korabl'*; Annotation, *Skorbnoe beschuvstvie*, Krupnyi Plan, restored DVD version, 2005).

35. See also Iampol'skii, "Kovcheg" 109–15.

36. Osipenko is the central figure in Sokurov's short *Empire Style* and appears later as herself in *Russian Ark*. See http://www.ballerinagallery.com/osipenko.htm.

37. Cf. Sokurov's ("The Solitary Voice" 76) comment on *Second Circle*: "The main character represents the modern Russian people, wilting under the stress of the current climate, who turn apathetic and just sit and stare." A sharper articulation is offered in *Aleksandra*. The eponymous heroine, an elderly grandmother visiting her officer grandson in Chechnia, finds herself in dialogue with young Russian soldiers on whether or not Chechnia is the homeland. This dialogue inter alia suggests that the borders of the empire may have stretched beyond that which could be considered homeland, and that the absence of affect—elsewhere, *Anaesthesia psychica dolorosa*—is a psychological symptom of that sovereign overreach. For an extended argument of this point, see the review of *Aleksandra* in Condee, "Sokurov's Chechnia." For an argument that situates this film in the context of a larger international film history, see Christie, "Grandmother's Russia."

38. In *Mournful Unconcern* Balthazar is the wild boar that roams the mansion, one of the many exotic creatures loose in the house. Balthazar the boar (and parodically the king of Babylonia) is visually associated with the capitalist entrepreneur Boss Mangan (Iampol'skii, "Kovcheg" 111), suggesting the impending collapse of Mangan's capitalist empire as part of the larger, looming catastrophe. The unmotivated presence of such creatures undergirds the interpretation that the mansion is indeed not simply a ship, but an ark.

39. In the opening scene Shaw (*Bernard Shaw* 75) describes Heartbreak House as resembling "an old-fashioned high-pooped ship with a stern gallery." The mansion walls are identified as "the starboard wall" and "the port side of the room"; the sofa is "oddly upholstered in sailcloth." The mansion's owner is a former captain and the play encourages a larger interpretive frame: as Hector cries in Act Three: "And this ship that we are all in? This soul's prison we call England?" (146). Shaw (*The Bodley Head* 5: 185) himself, on the eve of the play's 1921 London opening, remarked to the *Sunday Herald*, "The heartbreak begins, and gets worse until the house breaks out through the windows and becomes all England with all England's heart broken."

40. The estate in *Taurus* was the former property belonging to the widow of the industrialist and philanthropist Savva Morozov (see Vasil'eva, "Leonid Mozgovoi"). Relocated to Moscow, Morozov's widow left the only local property in the region equipped with a telephone and its own electric station, an unintentional commentary on Lenin's core requirements of modernity: appropriated property plus the electrification of the entire estate.

41. I would mention Hitler's constipation and psychosomatic vapors, Lenin's disabling dementia, Hirohito's psychological symptoms, his twitches and the involuntarily moving lips. As the lead actor, Issei Ogata, describes the symptoms:

> During the shooting Aleksandr Nikolaevich [Sokurov] many times directed my attention to Hirohito's mouth. The Japanese somehow do not notice it, but his mouth was in fact completely beyond his will [bezvol'nyi]. His lips were limp, twitching. . . . He did not have the right to show anyone his suffering: God, after all, could not suffer. And this hidden torment distorted his body. It led to an unnatural shuddering of his lips. And Sokurov felt that very keenly. ("Solntse: Portret fil'ma" 187)

42. Some confusion exists in cinema criticism concerning the name of the shooting location. Kehlsteinhaus, located at the top of Kehlstein Mountain, is the fortress shot in Moloch. Hitler seldom stayed in Kehlsteinhaus, in part because of his fear of heights. The nearby town (often confused with Kehlsteinhaus) is Berchtesgaden. A small chalet on Obersalzberg is Berghof, which had been Otto Winter's holiday home, then was purchased by Hitler in 1933 with proceeds from Mein Kampf. Hitler often stayed at Berghof.

43. One might see a similar death frame in Sun: the day begins with a Radio Tokyo broadcast on the heroic deaths of Japanese students; it ends with the ritual suicide of the radio dispatcher.

44. As Joseph Goebbels explains to Martin Bormann during the group's brief Ausflug (the "Witches Sabbath," as Hitler describes the outing), "The thousand-year Reich is nothing more than the thousand-year reign of the Just in the Gospels." A few moments later, invoking a garbled version of the Gospel of John (presumably 3:14), Goebbels explains that the end of the world will arrive when Jesus strikes down the serpent. Goebbels's Apocalypse anticipates Hitler's eschatological diatribe: "The whip for all beasts! I won't allow calm! I will lash out again! Thirty years! Forty years! Until the beast finally becomes human! . . . Because the sky is so close!" The antipathy of the historical Hitler to Christianity has been a matter of long and irresolvable debate. Though baptized a Roman Catholic, he is often quoted as having an aversion to Christianity. See Mitcham 137; Koch 39, as well as Henry Picker's (largely) 1941–42 Hitlers Tischgespräche im Führerhauptquartier (Hitler's Table Talk in the Central Headquarters). Hitler's Table Talk draws on the notes, supervised by Martin Bormann, by such stenographers as Heinrich Heim and Henry Picker (depicted in the film), the latter a German officer who took notes on Hitler's table conversations from March 21 to August 2, 1942 (consonant with the film's setting). In "Moloch: Interview with Alexander Sokurov" the filmmaker says that much of the historical materials came from the memoirs of Albert Speer.

45. In Nazi folklore it was not uncommon for the historical Hitler to be rhetorically linked with Jesus.

The synoptic gospels—Matthew, Mark, Luke—are similar (hence the term), but it is John that is most akin to this scene and perhaps more broadly in Russian culture, in part because of Mikhail Bulgakov's novel Master and Margarita, as well as Nikolai Gei's well-known 1890 painting What Is Truth? (Chto est' istina?), depicting the confrontation between Jesus and Pilate. The association of Hitler with Pilate is earlier prepared for in Sokurov's *Sonata for Hitler*, which includes a sequence of Hitler washing his hands over and over again, a reference, it might also be argued, to Pilate in Matthew 27:24.

46. Note the similarity of Hitler's cry to Sokurov's own monologue in *Elegy of a Voyage*: "I ask him [a monk] why did Christ pray that his Father not send him to his sacrificial cross? Why did Christ want to avoid crucifixion? If he so loathed being crucified, then how can I accept his crucifixion?"

47. The theater premiere excluded this dream sequence, which was later added to the video and DVD versions.

48. Sokurov's lead actor, Leonid Mozgovoi, who plays Lenin, recalls in interviews his pride at having gained admittance into the Communist Youth League at thirteen and a half instead of the usual fourteen and his early activism as the school's Komsomol organization secretary (Bezrukova; Vasil'eva, "Leonid Mozgovoi"). For Russians of this generation, the film's subject matter required a rewriting of their own collective autobiography: their relation to the (multiple) Soviet Lenins, the satiric late *perestroika* Lenin, and the relative oblivion into which this pivotal historic figure had lately fallen.

49. The best known *perestroika*-era films on Stalin include Tengiz Abuladze's *Repentance* (*Pokaianie*, 1987; Georgian title *Monanieba*); Semen Aranovich's documentary *I Served in Stalin's Bodyguard or Songs of the Oligarchs* (*Ia sluzhil v apparate Stalina, ili pesni oligarkhov*, 1990); Iurii Kara's *Balthazar's Feasts, or A Night with Stalin* (*Piry Valtasara, ili Noch' so Stalinym*, 1989); Tofik Shakhverdiev's documentary *Is Stalin with Us?* (*Stalin s nami*, 1989); and Sergei Solov'ev's *Black Rose Is an Emblem of Sadness, Red Rose Is an Emblem of Love* (*Chernaia roza emblema pechali, Krasnaia roza emblema liubvi*, 1989). For a chronological list of earlier Stalin representations in Soviet feature films from 1937 to 1953, see Bagrov, "Ermler"; Taylor and Spring.

50. By contrast, few Lenin films came out of his namesake studio, Lenfil'm. The two best known are Sergei Iutkevich's *Man with a Gun* (*Chelovek s ruzh'em*, 1938) and Grigorii Kozintsev's *Vyborg Side* (*Vyborgskaia storona* 1939). Both feature Maksim Shtraukh as Lenin. Shtraukh also appeared as Lenin in two Mosfil'm productions, Sergei Iutkevich's *Tales of Lenin* (*Rasskazy o Lenine* 1957) and Iutkevich's *Lenin in Poland* (*Lenin v Pol'she*, 1966). Other major Mosfil'm Lenins include Boris Shchukin, who played Lenin in Mikhail Romm and Dmitrii Vasil'ev's *Lenin in October* (*Lenin v Oktiabre*, 1937) and in Romm's *Lenin in 1918* (*Lenin v 1918-om godu*, 1939); and Iurii Kaiurov, who played Lenin in Sergei Iutkevich's *Lenin in Paris* (*Lenin v Parizhe*, 1980) and in Viktor Georg'ev's *Kremlin Bells* (*Kremlevskie kuranty*, 1970).

51. An early violation of the Lenin cult came in 1987 with the publication of the scandalous "mousetrap montage" in *The Spring* (*Rodnik*), showing Lenin's head smashed in a mousetrap.

52. For the film script of *Sun*, see *Kinostsenarii* 1 (2005): 4–35; Arabov, *Solntse* 383–430.

53. This episode was based on historical fact, although the incident took place at one of the imperial conferences, held on September 6, 1941.

54. Sokurov's humor often goes unnoticed in the context of overriding moral sententiousness, but his use of passages from Wagner's *Götterdämmerung* here is surely caprice.

55. For a historical account, see Evreinov 4–5; Evreinoff 426–30. On the Bastille, see Ozouf.

56. For Evreinov, the historical figures included Lenin and Kerenskii; Sokurov's historical figures included Peter I, Catherine I, Catherine II, Nikolai I and his wife, Nikolai II and his wife, Anastasiia and Aleksei Romanov, as well as the other children, and the poet Aleksandr Pushkin and his wife Natal'ia Goncharova, neither of whom, curiously, appear as characters in the credits. It is perhaps significant that Sokurov, whose voice is the Time Traveler, is, like Pushkin, also uncredited.

Evreinov included a number of the actual 1917 participants; Sokurov included the current director of the State Hermitage Museum, Mikhail Piotrovskii, as well as a number of other prominent St. Petersburg cultural figures of this circle, such as the doctor Oleg Khmel'nitskii (St. Petersburg Postgraduate Medical Academy), the sculptress Tamara Kurenkova, and former Kirov ballerina Alla Osipenko.

57. It would be a mistake to assume that the ball was in any sense a historical replication, since Pushkin and Natal'ia Goncharova figure among the dance partners. Rather, as Evreinov suggested with respect to his own reenactment, "The directors did not consider reproducing exactly a picture of the events. . . . Theatre was never meant to serve as history's stenographer" (Zufit 272, quoted in von Geldern 201).

58. It should be mentioned in this regard that *Russian Ark* is Sokurov's *second* Hermitage film. His first was *Hubert Robert: A Fortunate Life*, the documentary on the French Rococo painter (1733–1808) whose work is well represented in the Hermitage.

59. Not content to leave this project of reintegration without comment, Sokurov registers the Stranger's allergic reaction to Russian music: it gives him hives. A similar interediting of Russian (Glinka, Tchaikovsky, and, this time, the contemporary St. Petersburg composer Sergei Slonimskii) with Western European music (Mahler, Chopin) also structures the soundtrack of Sokurov's *Elegy of a Voyage*.

60. See Birgit Beumers's trenchant commentary in *Kinokultura* on the ideological determinates of Sokurov's film: http://www.kinokultura.com/reviews/Rark.html.

61. Sokurov's reverential acknowledgment of elite culture reaches its apex in *Elegy of a Voyage*. At the end of the film, its otherwise routine production credits include Pieter Bruegel the Elder's 1563 *Tower of Babel* and van Gogh's 1885 *Lane with Poplars* (presumably in recognition of their contribution to sequences filmed in Rotterdam's Museum Boijmans Van Beuningen) alongside the lighting director and others.

62. The Stranger is based on Marquis Astolphe de Custine, author of the 1843 four-volume *La Russie en 1839*. Europe, Sokurov ("Tvorcheskii alfavit" 78) has suggested elsewhere, "is interested in [Russia] geographically, encyclopedically, exotically, [whereas] we have a human interest in it," a human interest that, as *Russian Ark* suggests, is not reciprocated.

63. Of the Stranger/de Custine, the *Artmargins* roundtable participant Ulrich Schmid writes, "Sokurov designs him as a vampire. . . . Custine wears a black suit and spreads his long fingers like Murnau's Nosferatu. Custine is dead and so is his artistic taste: he prefers *natures mortes*."

The Time Traveler, invisible to us but a beneficent figure nonetheless, speaks of awakening from misfortune, an account that, beyond the collective misfortunes of 1917 and 1991, suggests a personal passage from life to death: "I open my eyes and

I see nothing. I only remember there was some accident. Everyone ran for safety as best they could. I just can't remember what happened to me."

64. "Only culture and only spirituality," writes Sokurov ("Tvorcheskii alfavit" 88), "are able to reconcile the human being to the inevitability of departure into the higher realm. And they [culture and spirituality] prepare him in as elevated a state of mind and soul as possible. All my films are about this."

65. One might see a similar instance of retrospective futurism in *Sun* where computer graphics animate the paleo-ichthyological dream sequence.

66. Elsewhere he writes, "I am also sometimes called an avant-gardist, but I do not consider myself to be one" (Sokurov, "Tvorcheskii alfavit" 74).

67. This phrase is the title to the accompanying documentary film to *Russian Ark* and Sokurov's characterization of his efforts in that feature film. The most familiar effort of similar ambition is Alfred Hitchcock's 1948 *Rope*, with its eight-minute continuous shots, mandated by the length of a single reel. The closest Russo-Soviet analogue is Andrei Tarkovskii's *Sacrifice* (a Swedish-produced film), for which the final eight minutes are a single shot.

68. For a more developed argument, as well as a lively polemic, see the exchange between Kujundzic and Eshelman.

69. The Time Traveler, read by Sokurov, utters the line "Farewell, Europe!," thus completing a verbal frame around the film: in the early moments of the film the same word (*proshchai*) was uttered by the Stranger as he attempted to part immediately from his Russian companion.

70. See Totaro's argument on Sokurov's interest in St. Augustine.

71. Arrested in October 1793, Robert escaped the guillotine only by error and was released from prison in 1794, after the removal of Robespierre. On the representation of ruins, see Ginsberg; Jackson. See also Iampolski, "Representation."

72. Among the Hermitage holdings are Robert's *Ruins* (1758), *Laundresses in the Ruins* (early 1760s), *Ruins of a Doric Temple* (1783), *Ruins on the Terrace in Marly Park* (1780s), *Inhabited Ruins* (1790s), *Artist amongst the Ruins* (1796), *Ancient Ruins Used as Public Baths* (1798), and *Landscape with Ruins* (early nineteenth century). See additional commentaries by Kujundzic.

73. In light of these and other comments, I am intrigued by Fredric Jameson's cautious proposal in *Critical Inquiry* that Sokurov be considered "the last great modernist auteur" ("History and Elegy" 10), one of the last "to renew the claims of high modernism" (1). Jameson's usual deft characterization does not account for Sokurov's resistance to avant-gardism. "Please do not call me an avant-gardist," he said ("Solitary Voice" 73). See also his comments from *Andere Cinema* (Rotterdam 1991) at http://www.sokurov.spb.ru/island_en/crt.html). This rejection of the avant-garde, even more than Sokurov's ("Tvorcheskii alfavit" 84) explicit resistance to modernism and the modern, leaves us to claim a modernism that would embrace tradition as its primary feature.

74. For a more extended set of comments on representation in relation to montage, see Sokurov, "Izobrazhenie i montazh." See also "Interview" 14 ("For me, the strongest sensations in the arts are always produced by painting and symphonic music") and "Tvorcheskii alfavit" 84 ("I can live without cinema, but I cannot live without music").

75. Elsewhere Sokurov ("Interview" 15) argues, "Cinema as art is not an American idea, it's not American cinema's destiny. It's the old world that carries this idea of art, and the new world has a harder time with this ancient conception, constantly producing an art that is less compelling because its genesis and its history aren't as fundamental."

76. By now we can see the futility of arguments around Sokurov's historical accuracy. See, for example, Mcnab's objections that Sokurov ignores Hirohito's atrocities, such as the 1937 Rape of Nanjing. Sokurov is primarily concerned neither with historical accuracy nor historical inclusivity, but with a set of conditions—an analogue in some sense to laboratory conditions—for consideration of a specific set of ethical problems. For similar objections to *Russian Ark*, see Petrovskaja. For a thoughtful response, see Alaniz.

77. "I suspect that Sokurov often feels lonely in that role of Sun-God, which his admirers have cultivated" (Gladil'shchikov, quoted in "*Solntse*: Portret fil'ma" 151).

CHAPTER 7

1. Iurii German's legal name was Georgii German, hence the occasional inconsistency in Aleksei German's own patronymic (that is to say, in official documents, the filmmaker is Aleksei Georgievich; in public situations, Aleksei Iur'evich). I refer to the father as Iurii German, in keeping with more common practice.

2. Critics at Cannes recounted that, though they could not hear the soundtrack clearly, they could easily hear the thump of the cinema's folding chairs as the audience left. In Plakhov's ("Lekarstvo" 156) words, "It was not that *Khrustalev* missed out at Cannes; Cannes missed out at *Khrustalev*." Even Russia's brightest critics, such as Viktor Matizen and Iurii Gladil'shchikov, admitted utter confusion; D. Bykov ("German" 49) requested a libretto. For other comments, see Hoberman 48. Stephen Holden (B-4), reviewing the film for the *New York Times*, complained that the film was "virtually impossible to decipher. Its characters aren't properly identified, its politics not elucidated, its geography vague. . . . Everything that isn't white . . . is inky black." German ("Khrenanakhrena" 44) recounts a similar reaction to *Lapshin*, his earlier and most successful film, with 118 copies in initial distribution: "Elem Klimov and many other people started to scream that I was finished as a director. Andrei Smirnov announced I did not know how to set up a *mise-en-scène*. Rolan Bykov [a lead actor in *Trial*, German's previous work] declared he didn't understand anything whatsoever. At [the newspaper] *Izvestiia*, they collected an entire trunk full of readers' letters cursing me." For more thoughtful initial reactions to *Khrustalev* by leading critics, including Mikhail Iampol'skii, Evgenii Margolit, and Irina Shilova, see *Kinovedcheskie zapiski* 44 (1999): 5–36.

3. At various times in German's youth the family lived with Kheifits and Shvarts (German, "Kino" 133–35).

4. See Wood's (100) description of *Lapshin*, which, though written long before *Khrustalev*, is curiously prescient in every respect of sound technique and camera style of the later film:

Loosely episodic, the film is remarkable in its resistance to linear narrative: dialogue is often drowned out by senseless chatter or the clanging of buckets;

our view of important characters is frequently blocked by figures crossing the screen. In its cinematography, *Ivan Lapshin* consistently refuses to accept established priorities, as though every element of each shot must be allowed its meaning. The camera often enters the room behind characters' backs, like a guest, or at elbow level, like a curious child. There is no sense that the scenes are choreographed or pre-arranged, but rather a feeling that the camera, wide-eyed, is capturing what it can of a bewildering world.

The similarities, particularly in camera work, of *Lapshin* and *Khrustalev* (or, for that matter, the relative conventionality of *Trial* and *Twenty Days*) are not a function of the director of photography, because Valerii Fedosov was the cameraman for *Twenty Days* and for *Lapshin*. This pairing in German's work has been commented on in Berezovchuk; Aronson, "Po tu storonu kino"; and Iampol'skii, "Ischeznovenie" 21.

5. The stories told by returning sailors and pilots figured in a number of German's film episodes. See German, "Kino" 130 and "Razrushenie" 159, for example, for the biographical origins of the train scene in *Twenty Days*, in which a pilot (based on the German family friend Gennadii Diudiaev) recounts his valorous air fight ("He did this and I did that; he did *this* and I did *that*; he did this . . .") in a comically inarticulate fashion.

6. The lead character, Lokotkov, in Iurii German's novella was based on a senior lieutenant of the CheKa, Ivan Piatkin, a relatively well-known partisan figure. Aleksei German's cinematic Lokotkov was, by contrast, a rural policeman before the war, in part to accommodate the physical appearance of the actor Rolan Bykov (German, "Kino" 146). Aleksei German also incorporated elements of the partisan fighter Aleksandr Nikiforov, who had not been known to Iurii German at the time of his own writing.

7. See, for example, Iurii German's defense in *Leningradskaia Pravda*, July 6, 1946, of the writer Mikhail Zoshchenko during the furor surrounding the latter's 1946 story "Adventures of an Ape" ("Prikliucheniia obez'iany"). German's positive review of Zoshchenko's writing was singled out for criticism in the August 9, 1946, meeting of the Central Committee Orgburo session "On *Star* and *Leningrad*" (Russian State Archive of Socio-Political History [RGASPI] f.17, op. 117, d. 1032, ll. 46–67) and the subsequent Party resolution "On the Journals *Star* and *Leningrad*" (RGASPI f. 17, op. 116, d. 272, ll. 7–11), published in *Pravda*, August 21, 1946. See L. Karakhan, "Proiskhozhdenie" (Part 1) 96.

8. See German's account of the script development in "Eto ia vinovat" 55–56 and "'Vse nachinaetsia posle . . . '" 4–5. German ("Khren-nakhrena!") identifies Iurii Klenskii, the protagonist of *Khrustalev*, as part Iurii German and part family acquaintance, a military doctor who had spent time in the gulag. *Khrustalev* also draws upon childhood memories of his partner, Svetlana Karmalita, whose father was an established theater critic and had encountered political difficulties during the 1948 cosmopolitanism campaign (Hoberman 51).

9. *Seventh Satellite* (*Sed'moi sputnik*) is sometimes mistranslated as *Seventh Companion* or *Seventh Fellow-Traveler*. The Russian word for "satellite" (*sputnik*), in the sense here of a smaller astronomical body circling a larger planet, of course, has other connotations, but the film's primary reference is to astronomy (not traveling or Marxist sympathizers), as the protagonist Adamov's monologue reveals toward the end of the

film. Adamov identifies himself ideologically as a distantly orbiting satellite only barely and unwillingly pulled in to the gravitational field of the main planet, as the dominant Bolshevik ideology is coded in the film. Although Adamov's metaphor is open-ended, one might speculate that he has in mind Iapetus, the seventh (and farthest) satellite of Saturn. The mythological Iapetus, brother of Saturn and Titan, was the father of Prometheus, who defied the Olympians by bringing fire to humans. Prometheus in turn figures prominently in the Russian revolutionary tradition, and as a kind of proto-Bolshevik, symbol of the god-building potential of secular humanism. The repeated shots of Adamov carrying a large family clock (his only remaining household possession) recalls Saturn's association with time, perhaps because of the confusion between Cronos (sometimes spelled Cronus or Kronos, meaning "horned") and Chronos ("time"). German's codirector Aronov went on to shoot the adventure film *Green Chains* (*Zelenye tsepochki*; Lenfil'm, 1970), the family drama *Fifth Quarter* (*Piataia chetvert'*; Lenfil'm, 1972), the crime film *A Long, Long Affair* (*Dlinnoe, dlinnoe delo*; Lenfil'm, 1976), and the drama *Sail, Little Ship* (*Plyvi, korablik*; Lenfil'm, 1983).

10. "I really loved Grisha [Aronov]; he was a good, kind, smart person, but in terms of directing, it turned out, we were too different from one another. . . . In short, we agreed that the main director would be Grigorii Aronov, while I, as they say, would be his back-up" (German quoted in Lipkov, "Proverka" 204).

11. Nina Kosterina was fifteen in 1936, when she began keeping a diary that was to document the Stalinist purges from the perspective of a young woman from fifteen to twenty. Among the purge victims of whom she writes is her father, a member of the CP USSR. Her diary ends in 1941 as she herself joins the partisan movement against the Nazis. She was killed in partisan fighting. In some respects Kosterina occupies a place in Soviet culture analogous to Anne Frank. For an English translation, see Kosterina.

12. Nikiforov would infiltrate captured Soviet POWs in German camps and attempt to convince them to return to the Soviet side. According to his account, a number of them indeed returned, were rearmed, and fought bravely, earning war medals as a result of their courage in battle. At the war's end they were arrested. Nikiforov intervened on their behalf, on one occasion going directly to Andrei Zhdanov, who had directed the defense of Leningrad during the war and was newly appointed in 1946 to head Soviet cultural policy. Nikiforov himself was arrested as he left his meeting with Zhdanov and received a ten-year sentence (Fomin, *"Polka"* 115; Lipkov, "Proverka" 203). For Volodarskii's variant of the screenplay, see Volodarskii.

13. Together with Aleksei German she wrote an adaptation of Iurii German's novella *Greetings, Mariia Nikolaevna* for Semen Aranovich's *Torpedo Bombers* (*Torpedonostsy*; Lenfil'm, 1983) and cowrote, again with Aleksei German, the script for Ardak Amirkulov's drama *Death of Otrar* (*Gibel' Otrara*; Kazakhfil'm, 1991), as well as screenplays for German's own films *Khrustalev, the Car!* and *History of the Arkanar Massacre* (in production).

14. According to German ("Boius'" 10), Simonov, a member of the Central Committee, wrote a letter of support, subsequently signed by Kheifits and Kozintsev, to the Politburo.

15. See the January 13, 1972, Protocol, Goskino USSR archive, Moscow, f. 48, op. 5, d. 340: 1. For a detailed analysis of objections to the director's "representation of the

pathological moments of war" (by the chief editor of the Script Editorial Section, I. Ko-karev) and his "de-heroization of the great popular movement" (by associate director of Goskino Vladimir Baskakov et al.), including Lazarev's attempted suicide and Lokotkov's drinking at the film's conclusion, see Fomin, *"Polka"* 110–32. See also Lenfil'm director Kiselev's (in German, "Kino" 129–31) account of the cuts to the final submitted version of the film, many of which were later restored by German.

16. It is a small but significant historical detail that (as described in chapter 2), when the ASKIN film czar Ismail Tagi-zade flew with a delegation of six hundred So-viet film representatives to the 1991 Cannes International Film Festival, Boris Pavlenok was among the invited delegates (German, "Maska").

17. Smirnov, whose *Stories of Unknown Heroes* was reissued as the second vol-ume of his 1973 three-volume *Collected Works* (*Sobranie sochinenii*), was by no means a peripheral or quasi-dissident writer. It is reasonable that his works would have been known to the director, given his background. Fedor Poletaev, awarded a gold medal for valor in 1947 by the Italian government, was rehabilitated in the Soviet Union in large measure due to the efforts of Sergei Smirnov. See http://www.vor.ru/English/whims/whims_013.html.

18. See Captain N. Galay's memoirs, "The Partisan Forces" (153–71), in Liddell-Hart.

19. Kazanskii is best remembered for the fantasy film *Amphibian Man* (*Chelovek Amfibiia*; Lenfil'm, 1962), codirected with Vladimir Chebotarev. Several years after Kiselev's advocacy of *Operation "Happy New Year"* he was replaced by Viktor Blinov (Lipkov, "Proverka" 211).

20. Because of its delayed status (as with other delayed works of the Soviet pe-riod, such those of Muratova and Sokurov), *Trial* is even now difficult to integrate into the history of Soviet cinema. For an attempt to do so, using the trope of "trial" and "test," see Liderman, especially pp. 125–27.

21. German, for example, included a wicked parody of Pavlenok in *Twenty Days*. Advising German on his ideological responsibilities, Pavlenok had earlier recounted how, during the war, "photo-correspondents would come [to photograph us]; we would cover up any hole in our pants and we'd look terrific. That was just for photographs, whereas you have an entire film [to answer for]!" (quoted in Lipkov, "Proverka" 14). Solicitously heeding Pavlenok, German ("Aleksei German" 202) put this advice in the mouth of the film set's idiotic military consultant.

22. For Goskino's administrative comments on and required changes to *Twenty Days*, see Goskino USSR archive, f. 48, op. 4/2, d. 1115: 8–89. For German's amusing summary of Romanov's comments, see German, "Aleksei German" 207: "Change the appearance of the city of Tashkent. Change the sexual motifs. Take out A. Petrenko's monologue, etc., etc."

23. "I am a tyrant, a despot, a hooligan," German (quoted in Lipkov, "Proverka" 205) remarks in one interview; many such examples could be cited.

24. For an account of the complex publication history of Iurii German's work, as well as an invaluable analysis of the differences between the prose and the film, see Rifkin.

25. On Stenich (1898–1938), see Graffy, "Unshelving" 264 fn. 43.

26. On the August 12, 1952 (and onward) arrests and subsequent executions of the Jewish Anti-Fascist Committee, see Rubenstein and Naumov. The Doctors'

Plot, involving the arrest of leading medical figures, was one aspect of a larger power struggle at the very end of Stalin's life. Jews, often referred to by the euphemism "cosmopolitanism," were clearly "token foreigners" in this respect. Anti-Semitic in its discourse, the principal claim (see *Pravda,* January 13, 1953) was that nine Kremlin doctors had facilitated the 1948 death of Politburo member Andrei Zhdanov, as well as of other highly placed Soviet figures. Of these nine doctors, six were Jews. The official stance of suspicion (broadly assumed by the liberal intelligentsia to be staged) toward Jewish influence, particularly toward those in the medical profession (and most specifically in cardiology), led to scrutiny of leading medical institutes and hospitals for their ethnic profiles. This atmosphere of suspicion is the backdrop for Klenskii's clinic in late February 1953, six weeks after the *Pravda* article cited above. See Brent and Naumov.

27. All by itself, Aleksei Petrenko's ten-minute close-up monologue was filmed in a marathon twenty-six-hour working day (Lipkov, "Proverka" 214).

28. It was Averbakh who described to German the rape scene that eventually appeared in *Khrustalev.* Averbakh had worked as a medical intern in the prison camp system (German, "Khrena-nakhrena!").

29. Of course, to attribute German's work to the Leningrad school of cinema is akin to describing Aleksandr Blok as writing "in the spirit of" the Silver Age, when he himself *is* the Age. In one critic's useful overstatement, "German is the Columbus" (Pozdniakov 4). Other filmmakers often identified with Leningrad cinema include Semen Aranovich, Grigorii Aronov (with whom German codirected *Seventh Satellite*), Dinara Asanova, Vitalii Kanevskii, Lidiia Bobrova, and Valerii Ogorodnikov. For a useful discussion on cinema and Leningrad culture, see Dobrotvorskii and Sirivlia; see also Podoroga.

30. See, for example, German's ("Zhdu talantlivuiu smenu") own remark: "We [at Lenfil'm] are touched to a lesser extent than the central studios [presumably Mosfil'm and Gor'kii Film Studio] by the so-called *beau monde.* Not without grounds have the prizes, the festival bustle, the foreign expeditions given rise amongst filmmakers to the joke that 'not one millimeter of film will be shot on our native land.'"

31. The director under discussion in Dobrotvorskii's description was the Lenfil'm filmmaker Viktor Aristov, considered by some to be a "post-German" director. His films include the war film *Gunpowder* (*Porokh*; Lenfil'm, 1985), the drama *The First Hundred Years Are Hard* (*Trudno pervye sto let*; Lenfil'm, 1988), the thriller *Satan* (Lenfil'm, 1991), and (together with Iurii Mamin) *Rains in the Ocean* (*Dozhdi v okeane*; Lenfil'm, 1994). Aristov was assistant director to German for *Lapshin* and played secondary acting roles in Muratova's *Among the Grey Stones* and *Asthenic Syndrome.*

32. Among the many examinations of the Petersburg text, see, chronologically, Belinskii; Toporov, "O strukture"; Timenchik et al.; then Toporov, "Peterburg"; Lotman, "Simvolika Peterburga"; and Lotman, *Universe* 190–214. For a discussion of the Leningrad text in the context of Brodskii's work, see Reynolds. Concerning other geographic variants, see Lilly ("Conviviality," especially 429 fn. 11) for an overview on the Moscow text; Lilly, *Moscow and Petersburg*; Liusyi on the Crimean text; and Mednis for an overview of the phenomenon of such literary hypertexts. On the so-called Petersburg diaspora in Moscow, including (for a time) German himself, see Tkachenko.

33. Brodskii, Rein, and the poets Dmitrii Bobyshev and Anatolii Naiman, closely associated with Akhmatova in the early 1960s, were often referred to as "Akhmatova's orphans." See Anatolii Naiman and Anatoly Naiman.

34. A more comprehensive account of twentieth-century Leningrad culture (as distinct from Petersburg) would also mention the centrality of the Soviet-era Hermitage (with its deeply respected tradition of dedicated, and often impoverished, curators, archivists, and so forth), which had functioned as a kind of secular shrine for recluses and introverts. Sokurov intersects with both these worlds in his *Russian Ark*. See also Aliona van der Horst's five-part television series *Hermitage-niks: A Passion for the Hermitage* (*Passie voor de Hermitage*; First Run/Icarus, 2003), which explores the lives and worldviews of the Hermitage employees.

35. "Everything of mine has been banned. *Trial on the Road* was filmed in 1971. . . . It received the State Prize, but for fifteen years it was banned. *Lapshin* was banned for two and a half years. *Twenty Days* was banned for a year" (German, "Aleksei German" 201).

36. This primacy of poetry is not therefore shared by the poets themselves. After all, much Symbolist poetry orients itself according to tropes from music; for much Acmeist verse, it is often architecture that serves as the creative touchstone for thinking about art. The argument here concerns the poetic orientation of the Leningrad intelligentsia.

37. German's cameramen have included Iakov Sklianskii (*Trial*), Valerii Fedosov (*Twenty Days* and *Lapshin*), and Vladimir Il'in (*Khrustalev*). Of these, Fedosov (1941–90) is most closely associated with German's poetics. Sklianskii had emigrated to the United States (see his interview in Stone, "A First Glimpse") and his name therefore, even now, does not appear in the credits for *Trial*. Fedosov completed two of German's single-author films and would have shot *Khrustalev* were it not for his failing health. See Avrunin for analysis and interview fragments. Instead, Il'in, who had filmed Aranovich's *Torpedo Bombers*, based on German's and Karmalita's screenplay, was chosen.

38. Even German's descriptions of other filmmakers are cast in terms of their literary equivalents. "I don't like everything by Sokurov, but he works with the film itself in an interesting way," he comments. "He achieves the kinds of effects that [Velemir] Khlebnikov does in poetry" (German, "Khrena-nakhrena!" 44).

39. The film begins on the night of February 28 to March 1, when Stalin was thought to have had his final stroke. The entire action is played over three days. The script, published in the journal *Kinostsenarii* (April 1995 and May 1998) as well as German and Karmalita (511), indicates that the first scene opens on March 1, 1953; the last scenes are set in 1963. The examination of archival evidence undertaken by Brent and Naumov suggests that Stalin's final stroke occurred early in the morning of March 2. See also Medvedev.

40. Respectively, these lines in Russian are as follows: "mal'chishke malomu / Ne sladki kholoda" (*Sobranie* 2:193); "Da i menia bez vsiakikh povodov / Zagnali na cherdak; "I zhizn' nachnetsia nastaiashchaia, / I kryl'ia budut mne! . . . Poznal, poznal svoe mogushchestvo! . . . / Vot vskriknul . . . i lechu!" (2:194); and "Vse, vse po staromy, byvalomu, / Da tol'ko—bez menia!" (2:194). Cf. another of German's favorite stanzas, this by Pasternak, but on a similar theme: "No kto my i otuda / Kogda ot vsekh tekh let / Ostalis' peresudy / A nas na svete net" ("But who we are and where we're from / When

after all those years / The gossip's all that's left behind / And we—no longer here"). German ("Kino" 125) cites the verses in reference to Lapshin, but they are equally suited to the sensibility of *Twenty Days*, *Khrustalev*, or, for that matter, *Seventh Satellite*.

41. Blok's poetry is replete with examples; in the same, familiar 1912 poem ("Night, street, lamppost . . ."), for example: "you will die—you will start it all anew / And everything will repeat, as of old" ("umresh'—nachnesh' opiat' snachala / I povtoritsia vse, kak vstar' ").

42. German comments to Hoberman (49), "Gathering those cars cost me a year of my life. It was impossible to find them."

Doubles were routinely prepared so as to avoid such an incident as transpired during the Krestinskii trial, when the defendant deviated from the script prepared under torture and instead denounced his accusers (D. Bykov, "German" 49; German, "Izgoniaiushchii d'iavola" 124; Hoberman 50). Such doubles are described in Aleksandr Solzhenitsyn's *Arkhipelag GULag*.

Stalin regularly consulted with prominent imprisoned cardiologists, who were summoned from the gulag to read Stalin's cardiogram. See Hoberman (53) for information on Iakov Rapoport, one such imprisoned (and impetuously freed) Kremlin doctor.

43. An earlier, Soviet-era version of Rein's "Aunt Tania," in *Beregovaia polosa* (Moscow: Sovremennik, 1989), 4–7, omits this passage, presumably because of its explicit imperial nostalgia. It likewise omits the poem's epigraph by the émigré poet Vladislav Khodasevich (1886–1939).

44. On post-Soviet retro cinema, particularly those films based on familiar literary adaptations, see Karriker. On a comparison of German's *Khrustalev* to Mikhalkov's *Burnt by the Sun* as a kind of anti-Mikhalkov, see Plakhov, "Lekarstvo" 156. For an extended comparison of Mikhalkov's film to German's *Khrustalev*, see D. Bykov, "German"; Siladii 32–33.

45. The rape scene in *Khrustalev* also casts Russian prisoners among the other passengers of the champagne truck (German, "Khrena-nakhrena!").

46. Similar ideological inversions punctuate German's texts throughout. As Lapshin, Adashova, and others (in *Lapshin*) are singing together the second verse from the "Hymn of the Comintern," the stanza about imprisoned revolutionaries, predicts—on the eve of the Purges—a cry of support for the unjustly arrested: "Comrades in prison, behind cold walls, we are with you, we are with you, though you are not here in our ranks" (*Pesni* 5).

47. A McGuffin (sometimes MacGuffin) is a device that is itself insignificant or arbitrary but serves to catch the audience's interest and organize plot elements early in the narrative. "We have a name in the studio, and we call it the 'McGuffin,'" explains Hitchcock. "It is the mechanical element that usually crops up in any story. In crook stories, it is most always the necklace and in spy stories it is most always the papers." See http://www.macguffin.nl/Macguffin.html.

48. Elsewhere, in an oblique reference to Chekhov: "Any clanging, rustling, 'sound of a broken string,' a fallen cooking pot can be a thousand times [more] cinematically expressive than any music of any composer" (German, "Kino" 151).

49. Compare Ol'ga Shervud's (49) much later remark regarding *Khrustalev*: "such an unimaginable density of sight and sound that there is almost 'nothing to

discern' and 'nothing to hear.' In point of fact, it is practically 'silent cinema.'" Here, presumably, "silence" is that which is not heard, that which bears no informational load. After the Cannes premiere German redid the soundtrack, adding information in the boy narrator's introduction to orient the viewer. For details, see German, "Khrena-nakhrena!"

50. See Egorova's (269) comment on German's and others' move in the late 1970s and early 1980s away from composed music to "information codes" appropriate to (and integrated into) the historical setting of the times.

51. Cf. L. Karakhan ("Proiskhozhdenie," Part II: 83): "Whom should we follow? What is important? But everything is important. . . . Every person, every utterance, pronounced even by the narrator's voice, however minor or insignificant the role in the plot they may play, is important, full of meaning, full of life, fate, and in every fate—history."

52. The most exquisite cameo is the brief dialogue in *Twenty Days without War* between "Woman with Watch" (brilliantly played by Liia Akhedzhakova) and Lopatin concerning her husband's military watch. German's cameos bear a kinship resemblance to Muratova's delight in Gogolian cameo interruptions as an integral part of the narrative structure.

53. Abrau-Diurso, so named for its location between Lake Abrau and the Diurso River near Novorossiisk (Krasnodar region), is the site of Russia's most famous vineyards, including those that produced Sovetskoe Shampanskoe (Soviet Champagne). See http://www.abraudurso.ru/.

54. One version of history suggests that the newly installed guard Ivan Khrustalev, following Beria's orders, poisoned Stalin. One might speculate that German's choice of title, a reference to Beria's "loud, undisguisedly triumphant" command "Khrustalev, [bring] the car!" (Radzinsky 579), intentionally conveys another layer of meaning: "Khrustalev, [bring on] the machine!" (*mashinu*), so as to process history forward to the next stage. See Radzinsky 569–70, 574–579. See further the account by the dacha commandant's assistant, Pavel Lozgachev, who reports that Ivan Khrustalev (not Stalin) had given that night's order dismissing the staff: http://news.bbc.co.uk/1/hi/world/europe/2793501.stm.

55. Although German is an admirer of Muratova's work, he prefers her early cinema. See German, "Khrena-nakhrena!"

56. See Tat'iana Tolstaia's debate with Aleksandr Genis on the self-opening umbrella as historical fact and the adequacy of historical fact to the film's logic.

57. "I utterly do not want to do a film about the present, because I don't like it. I cannot make a film about characters whom I do not love. I must hate them and love them. I hate present-day Russia, but I do not love it" (German, "Izgoniaiushchii d'iavola" 129).

58. *Russia-Troika* (*Rus'-Troika*) was in fact the original working title of *Khrustalev*.

59. Cf. Ivan Varfolomeev, arrested in 1950, who confessed his participation in a plot led by Harry Truman, Pierre Dupont, and Omar Bradley to fire nuclear missiles from the U.S. Embassy in Moscow at the Kremlin. See Brent and Naumov.

60. See Plakhov's ("Lekarstvo" 156) comment that *Khrustalev*, following the second line of Gogol' and Dostoevskii, broke with "the pseudo-classical tradition, according to which it is necessary to speak about Russia in the language of Tolstoi."

61. As if in alphabetic enactment of that "five minutes' walk and fifty years ago," the camera meanders along the bookshelf to a volume by Lessing, then cuts to Lapshin's apartment, where the boy asks on the telephone for Klava Lesovaia.

62. In *Khrustalev* German is explicit in this regard. The narrator's voice-over informs the viewer that, after his father's brief return, the boy never saw him again, leaving provocatively unexplained Klenskii's transformation to vagrant king. See Shilova, "Karnaval" 7 for an effort to relate this technique to other films.

63. "The action is shot either through the eyes of the son, or through the eyes of the father, or through no one's eyes, or, perhaps, through our own eyes, which induces a sensation of dizziness" (Tolstaia 16).

64. German does not specify when Stalin dies, but the film suggests both that he died several days earlier and that he was murdered. "The fifth of March doesn't make any sense," German ("Khrena-nakhrena!" 44) has argued. "Articles on the 'Doctors' Plot' were running in every newspaper during those days. Why, from 1 March onwards, did those publications disappear? Who could have ordered it, if Stalin had been alive?"

65. See the extensive discussion of this and German's responses in Lipkov, "Proverka."

66. German ("Kino" 153) comments in characteristically laconic style, "For Lapshin to have survived 1937 is for me an impossibility."

67. Indeed, the film was released in only five copies; one of these was funded by Nikita Mikhalkov (German, "Trudno"; "Khrustalev" 2).

68. The exact shooting dates are December 22, 1992, to June 20, 1996 (German, "Izgoniaiushchii" 129).

69. I use the translation *Trial on the Road* for German's *Proverka na dorogakh* rather than the popular rendition used on IMDb.com and elsewhere (*Roadcheck* or *Checkpoint*), so as to avoid confusion with Aleksandr Rogozhkin's *Checkpoint* (*Blokpost*; CTV, 1998). The translation of the title as *Trial on the Road* is routinely used in cinema scholarship, including by Graffy, Wood, and Youngblood, cited here. Where the title *Checkpoint* appears here and elsewhere, it refers to Rogozhkin's film.

CHAPTER 8

1. Not for nothing does the gangster trio of *Dead Man's Bluff*, for example, meet to do business in a zoo amid displays of iguanas, snakes, and lizards, where a father and his little son feed a live mouse to a crocodile. In this universe it is not that the hero is incomprehensible, but that there is little beyond the reptile brain to understand. For a cogent objection to Balabanov's character as the subject of "post-ideological disillusionment," see McCausland 190.

2. On comparisons with Quentin Tarantino, see Abdullaeva 31; Romney, "Brat-Pack"; Shepotinnik in "*Brat/Zhmurki*" 8; Zel'venskii 11. On comparisons with David Lynch, see Clarke; Horton, "Lynch-Pin?"; and Romney, "Of Freaks and Men." On comparisons with Peckinpah, see Volobuev in Arkus, *Noveishaia* 1:155 .

3. Although the title invokes the 1961 two-act play by Samuel Beckett, bewildered scholars have already noted that the film seems to have little to do with the original other than a stance of grim mockery and a stylized portrayal of disenfranchised life.

4. See http://www.ctb.ru/.

5. The four films were Aleksei Balabanov's *Trofim*, Vladimir Khotinenko's *Road* (*Doroga*), Aleksandr Khvan's *Wedding March* (*Svadebnyi marsh*), and Dmitrii Meskhiev's *Exercize No. 5* (*Eksersiz No. 5*). The proposal for the compilation film was made at the First Forum of Young Cinema in Yalta in January 1994. Several major directors, elected by votes of the participants, were invited to shoot a twenty-minute film each for the centennial of cinema. Ivan Dykhovichnyi was elected but refused; Sergei Sel'ianov cowrote his contribution, *Trofim'*, with Balabanov; Valerii Todorovskii ceded his place to Meskhiev, with whom Todorovskii had cowritten in the past and who had come in as a close finalist in the Yalta voting; Khotinenko and Khvan accepted the commission. See Abdullaeva 40; D. Bykov, "Krushenie" 132.

6. The boy actors, Aleksei Dë (as Kolia) and Chingiz Tsyndendambaev (as Tolia), were in fact neither conjoined nor twins.

7. The most insightful reading of this film is contained in Stishova, "Chasti rechi."

8. See, for example, the block of articles entitled "Novyi geroi: Killer," *Seans* 16 (1997): 104–22, with contributions by Liubov' Arkus, Mikhail Brashinskii, Marina Drozdova, and Aleksandr Sekatskii. See also Lipovetskii's excellent analysis.

9. See Moskvina, "Peremirie" 152; Trofimenkov and Gracheva in separate contributions to *"Mne ne bol'no*: Kritiki o fil'me" 35. In addition to being the basis for Verdi's 1853 opera *La Traviata*, the novel also found a place in cinema, with at least eight screen adaptations, including André Calmettes and Henri Pouctal's 1910 silent film *La Dame aux Camélias* with Sarah Bernhardt, and George Cukor's 1936 *Camille* with Greta Garbo. Balabanov's version, starring Renata Litvinova, Russia's answer to Greta Garbo, is in some respects in dialogue with the latter adaptation. In Balabanov's film a kept woman, loved by a much younger, pure-hearted man, is dying of cancer rather than the traditional tuberculosis. As in Dumas and Verdi, their unlikely love is cut short by her death.

10. Balabanov ("Voprosy rezhisseru" 153) himself has commented that melodrama was a new kind of cinema for him, one he had not shot before, and he was interested in how it worked. In a much earlier interview with Tat'iana Pozniak in 1998 she asks, "What kind of cinema would you never shoot?" Balabanov's ("Aleksei Balabanov") answer: "Probably melodrama."

11. See, for example, Paul Rabinow's interview with Foucault in Foucault, *Space, Knowledge, and Power* 239–56.

12. Hay Market is located on St. Petersburg's Hay Square (Sennaia ploshchad'), known as Peace Square (Ploshchad' mira) from 1963 to 1991.

13. The 1932 jazz song's composer, Harry Warren (1893–1981), largely forgotten today, was a major Hollywood film composer of his era, credited with such hits as "I Only Have Eyes for You" (1934) and "Jeepers Creepers" (1938). See *Encyclopedia of Composers and Songwriters* at http://www.pbs.org/wnet/gperf/shows/songbook/multimedia/bio_warren.html.

14. Tommaso Campanella's 1602 *City of the Sun* is a fictional dialogue between the Grandmaster of the Knights Hospitallers, a military-religious order, and a Genoese sea captain, who tells the story of the utopian City of the Sun.

15. In both *Happy Days* and *Freaks* we can strongly sense Kuprin's hand, in particular from such short stories from his second, 1897 collection *Miniatures* (*Miniatiury*)

as "Natal'ia Davydovna," whose heroine leads a double life (schoolteacher by day, a nymphomaniac by night) or "A Terrible Moment" ("Strashnaia minuta"), the story of a married woman in inconstant control of sexual restraint.

16. Standard demographic literature tells us that a generational cohort is often taken to be between ten and twenty years (except for the generation whose youth was marked by World War II, typically a foreshortened generation). For a discussion of the literature, as well as a model of twentieth-century (U.S.-centered) generational breaks, see Schuman and Scott; for a longer ranger and more popular treatment, see the two volumes by Strauss and Howe. Anninskii, cited here, asks questions in the Russo-Soviet context, absent any scholarly methodology, similar to those posed in Schuman and Howe's much-quoted work.

17. Correspondingly, born in the 1930s, Anninskii's own generation—who would include, by way of orientation, such figures as the poets Evgenii Evtushenko (b. 1933) and Andrei Voznesenskii (b. 1933) and the directors Andrei Konchalovskii (b. 1937) and Larisa Shepit'ko (b. 1938)—came to youthful confirmation in the late Thaw period, when the poets' recitations filled football stadiums of listeners. It reached its finale, the second wave of professional prominence as culture's elder statesmen, in the *perestroika* period.

18. On the sense that Anninskii makes of his own generation, see his *Shestidesiat-niki i my*. See also Galina Belaia's memoire-essay ("Ia rodom iz shestidesiatykh. . .") at her seventieth birthday celebration (March 21, 2005) at the Department of History and Philosophy of the Russian State University for the Humanities (RGGU) (http://www.yavlinsky.ru/culture/index.phtml?id=2200).

19. The problems with Anninskii's model, therefore, have less to do with lethal flaws as with its greater applicability to those fields where the artist has greater control over the means of production. Soviet cinema, intensely subject to state administration at all stages of its existence, was thereby also more vulnerable to disruption. Hence the generational cluster in literature may have held together more tightly than in an industry in which an arrested work and its director—requiring a considerable budget, and then utterly dependent on state distribution and exhibition—are consigned to virtual oblivion. Anninskii's model, which is only roughly useful in cinema compared to its value in literary production, is inadvertently brilliant in helping us see more clearly the nonsynchronicity across cultural fields.

20. See, for example, http://brat2.film.ru/chat.asp.

21. Sergei Bodrov Jr. (1971–2002) died along with a film crew of twenty-seven on shooting location in the Kolka-Karmadon rock and ice slide of September 20, 2002. See http://www.cosis.net/abstracts/EGU04/02505/EGU04-J-02505–1.pdf. Bodrov's linkage to another youthful cult figure, Viktor Tsoi (1962–90), who also died tragically, predates Bodrov's death. Tsoi first emerged in 1982 at the Leningrad Rock Club as a talented singer and performer, soon the lead of the group Kino (Cinema), whose best-known albums during his lifetime were 45 (1982) and *Blood Group* (*Gruppa krovi*; 1987). He then starred as Moro in Rashid Nugmanov's *Needle* (*Igla*; Kazakhfil'm Studios, 1988), a cult film in the late *perestroika* period. His last collection, *Black Album* (*Chernyi al'bom*; 1990), includes his vocals from a tape left behind in the automobile crash that killed him on August 15, 1990.

22. In *Trofim* two feckless film employees, played by Balabanov and Aleksei German, cut Trofim out of the faux documentary footage. In the opening shot of *Brother* the film director is an arrogant fool. In *Freaks* the young director Putilov cravenly flees to the West and finds fame by passing off the pornographers' work as his own; in *War* John becomes famous for his documentary, which lands the Russian hero Ivan in prison. To this one might conditionally add the monologue of the cinephile Radlov (*Freaks*), who expounds to Putilov on cinema's capacity to "reveal truth to the common people," when Putilov's own pornography efforts are already invading Radlov's household and setting up the conditions for the family's destruction.

23. Tat'iana Pozniak comments, "The young Petersburg filmmaker Aleksei Balabanov has no relations whatsoever with the press as such, because he doesn't want any: he is concerned with other values" (quoted in Balabanov, "Aleksei Balabanov").

24. On race, for example, see http://brat2.film.ru/b&w.asp.

25. Cf. Romney ("Brat-Pack"):

> [Balabanov's] films can't easily be made to yield straightforward lessons either about morality or about the state of Russian society. *In person, Balabanov has a reputation for elusiveness,* baffling journalists with the assertions that he's a patriot and an Orthodox Christian and that "the future is Russian." He may be in deadly earnest, but that doesn't make him any less a corrosive provocateur—a patriot perhaps, but one who glories in a virulently subversive attitude. (Emphasis mine)

26. I do not contest other associative links. In the case of Liza's flagellation alone, for example, see Largier. Balabanov's work as a whole, however, draws deeply on a Gogolian and Dostoevskian—that is to say, in certain respects, Petersburg—tradition in ways that cannot, for want of space, be explored here.

27. Note in Kharms (57), for example, the compatibility of his 1936 "Story of the Fighting Men" with *Dead Man's Bluff*: "Aleksey Alekseyevich held Andrey Karlovich down in a crushing lock and, having smashed him in the mug, let him go. Andrey Karlovich, pale with fury, flung himself at Aleksey Alekseyevich and banged him in the teeth. Aleksey Alekseyevich, not expecting such a swift onslaught, collapsed on the floor, whereupon Andrei Karlovich sat astride him, pulled his set of dentures from his mouth."

28. Freud ("The Economic Problem" 161) speculates that masochism exists in three registers of behavior: primary masochism (the realm of physical pain and sexual arousal); female masochism, for Freud the most paradigmatic figure; and moral masochism (the torment of the ego by the super-ego). The figure of Liza in *Freaks*, for example, captures all three. The film makes clear that the target of scorn and mirth is reserved for the third, the liberal guilt of the film's two cultured families (and, by implication, his liberal film critics).

29. We can ascribe the mother's conversational slip, identifying St. Petersburg as "Leningrad," to her provincialism. In a different register, we could also see the mistake as a device that lengthens the cultural distance between Tula, still oriented toward known and stable things of the past, and St. Petersburg, a city that Tula does not yet know.

30. Biriulevo is a run-down, working-class suburb of Moscow, comparable in some respects to some areas of Chicago's industrialized landscape.

31. Is it too far a stretch to imagine such Hollywood representatives as the Motion Picture Association as the cultural arm of the U.S. government? Probably so, yet see, for example, the MPA website at http://www.mpaa.org/AboutUs.asp.

> Since its early days, the MPA, often referred to now as "a little State Department," has expanded to cover a wide range of foreign activities falling in the diplomatic, economic, and political arenas. The Motion Picture Association conducts these activities from its headquarters in Washington, D.C. and from offices in Los Angeles, California; Brussels; São Paulo; Singapore; and Toronto.

See A. Karakhan for the issue of political correctness. See also Julian Graffy's ("Brother") characterization of *Brother* as containing "casual contemporary Russian racism towards Jews, Chechens and other 'black-arsed' trans-Caucasians. In Danila, it illustrates the beginning of the backlash against total cultural Americanisation."

32. Я узнал, что у меня
Есть огромная семья–
И тропинка, и лесок,
В поле каждый колосок!

Речка, небо голубое–
Это все мое, родное!
Это Родина моя!
Всех люблю на свете я! (http://brat2.film.ru/phrases.asp)

CHAPTER 9

1. See, for example, Beissinger, in particular "Soviet Empire as 'Family Resemblance.'" For a sweeping critique of the misuse of the term, see Alexander Motyl's extirpative review of Niall Ferguson (*Empire* and *Colossus*), on the one hand, and Hardt and Negri (*Empire* and *Multitude*), on the other, in "Is Everything Empire?"

2. "Art has always been free of life," Shklovskii (39) insists in his 1923 *Knight's Move* (*Khod konia*), "and its flag has never reflected the color of the flag that flies over the city fortress."

3. Not evident here in Said's text is the fact that the quotation is a reference to Benita Parry's title, *Delusions and Discoveries: Studies on India in the British Imagination, 1880–1930*.

4. Said's textual references here include *Ulysses*, *À la recherche*, *Heart of Darkness*, and *To the Lighthouse*.

5. See in particular Griffin, "The Palingenetic Core" and "Notes." Griffin's best-known and most elaborate exposition in found in *The Nature of Fascism*, especially 26–55.

6. See Antliff, especially chapter 1; Griffin, *Modernism and Fascism*.

References

"VI s"ezd kinematografistov SSSR." *Iskusstvo kino* 8 (1990): 3–6.

Abdrashitov, Vadim. "A chto, proizoshla smena epokh?" Interview by Oleksii-Nestor Naumenko. *Iskusstvo kino* 9 (2007): 78–87.

———. "Kazhdyi raz my stoim na doroge, ni nachala, ni kontsa kotoroi ne vidno." Interview by Marina Pork. *Ekran* 4 (1995): 9–11.

———. "Mesto neuznavaemo: Uznavaema voina." Interview by Ella Korsunskaia. *Kinostsenarii* 5 (1997): 136–45.

———. "Pliumbum, ili Opasnaia igra." Interview by L. Vasil'eva. In *Fil'my rezhissera Vadima Abdrashitova*. Soveksportfil'm brochure, n.d. (approximately 1986).

Abdullaeva, Zara. "A s platformy govoriat: Eto gorod Leningrad . . ." *Iskusstvo kino* 3 (1996): 40–43.

———. *Kira Muratova: Iskusstvo kino*. Moscow: NLO, 2008.

Abramov, Fedor. *Dereviannye koni: Povesti i rasskazy*. Moscow: Sovremennik, 1978.

Aizlewood, Robin. "The Return of the 'Russian Idea' in Publications, 1988–91." *Slavonic and East European Review* 71.3 (July 1993): 490–99.

Alaniz, Jose. "Mythopoeia, 'Metahistory,' and Aleksandr Sokurov's *Sun* (*Solntse*), 2004." *Kinokultura* 10 (2005). http://www.kinokultura.com/reviews/R10–05soln tse.html.

"Aleksandr Nikolaevich Sokurov." Biographical summary. *Kinograf* 3 (1997): 41–43.

Anderson, Benedict. *Imagined Communities: Reflections on the Origin and Spread of Nationalism*. Revised edition. New York: Verso, 1991.

Andreeva, Ol'ga. "Iurii Arabov." Bibliography of Works by and about Iurii Arabov. *Kinograf* 11 (2002): 118–66.

Anemone, Anthony. "Moi drug Ivan Lapshin/My Friend Ivan Lapshin." In Beumers, ed., *The Cinema of Russia*. 202–11.

Anninskii, Lev. "Ar'ergardnyi boi: Iz tsikla 'Shestidesiatniki.'" *Sovetskii fil'm*, May 1990: 28–29.

————. "Khrustal'naia noch'." *Ekran i stsena* 42.510 (1999): 4.

————. *Shestidesiatniki i my.* Moscow: SK SSSR/Kinotsentr, 1991.

————. "The Sixties Generation, the Seventies Generation, the Eighties Generation . . . : Toward a Dialectic of Generations in Russian Literature." *Culture's Tapestry: On the Writing of Lev Anninskii,* edited by Nancy Condee and Vladimir Padunov. Special issue of *Soviet Studies in Literature* 27.4 (1991): 11–28. Reprinted from "Shestidesiatniki, semidesiatniki, vos'midesiatniki . . . K dialektike pokolenii v russkoi kul'ture." *Literaturnoe obozrenie* 4 (1991): 10–14.

Antliff, Mark. *Avant-Garde Fascism: The Mobilization of Myth, Art, and Culture in France, 1909–1939.* Durham, N.C.: Duke University Press, 2007.

Arabov, Iurii. *Solntse i drugie kinostsenarii.* St. Petersburg: Seans (Amfora), 2006.

————. "Stsenarist—eto naemnik." Interview by Irina Liubarskaia. *Iskusstvo kino* 4 (2005): 105–11.

Arkhangel'skii, Aleksandr. "Desnitsa i shuitsa N. S. Mikhalkova." *Iskusstvo kino* 3 (1995): 4–8.

Arkus, Liubov'. "German Aleksei." In Arkus, ed., *Noveishaia,* 1:250–53.

————. "15 Mai, 1986: Pervyi Plenum pravleniia Soiuza kinematografistov. Pervym sekretarem SK izbran Elem Klimov." In Arkus, ed., *Noveishaia,* 4:69–70.

————, ed. *Sokurov: Chast' rechi.* Saint Petersburg: Seans, 2006.

————. "Vopros ekspertam." *Kinoprotsess* 5 (1999): 29.

Arkus, Liubov', ed., *Noveishaia istoriia otechestvennogo kino 1986–2000.* 7 vols. St. Petersburg: Seans, 2001–04.

Arkus, Liubov', and Viktor Matizen. "25 dekabria 1986: Na zasedanii Politbiuro TsK KPSS predsedatelem Goskino SSSR vmesto Filippa Ermasha utverzhden Aleksandr Kamshalov." In Arkus, ed., *Noveishaia,* 4:156–59.

Arkus, Liubov', and Andrei Plakhov. "Mai, 17: Pri SK SSSR sozdana postoianno deistvuiushchaia Konfliktnaia komissiia po tvorcheskim voprosam. Predsedatelem komissii izbran Andrei Plakhov." In Arkus, ed., *Noveishaia,* 4:70–71.

Arkus, Liubov', and Dmitrii Savel'ev. "13 mai: V Kremlevskom dvortse s'ezdov otkryvaetsia Piatyi s'ezd Soiuza kinematografistov SSSR." In Arkus., ed., *Noveishaia,* 4:63–67.

Arkus, Liubov', and Dmitrii Savel'ev, eds. *Sokurov.* Saint Petersburg: Seans, 1994.

Arkus, Liubov', Vasilii Stepanov, and Konstantin Shavlovskii, eds. and comps. *Seans Guide: Rossiiskie fil'my 2006 goda.* St. Petersburg: Seans, 2006.

Armstrong, John A. *Nations before Nationalism.* Chapel Hill: University of North Carolina Press, 1982.

Arnason, Johann P. "Communism and Modernity." *Daedalus* 129.1 (Winter 2000): 61–90.

Aronson, Oleg. "Ekstsentrika priema i materiala: O fil'makh Kiry Muratovoi." In Aronson, *Metakino.* Moscow: Ad Marginem, 2003. 205–17.

————. "Giperdokument, ili Svidetel'stvo o zhizni: Lenin po Aleksandru Sokurovu." In Aronson, *Metakino.* Moscow: Ad Marginem, 2003. 173–83.

————. *Metakino.* Moscow: Ad Marginem, 2003.

————. "Mezhdu priemom i attraktsionom." *Iskusstvo kino* 9 (1997): 102–7.

————. "Po tu storonu kino: *Khrustalev, mashinu!* Alekseia Germana i problema 'sovetskogo.'" In Aronson, *Metakino.* Moscow: Ad Marginem, 2003. 218–27.

Attwood, Lynne, ed., *Red Women on the Silver Screen*. London 1993.

Avdeyeva, G. "The Anatomy of Power: The Moscow Premiere of Alexandr Sokurov's Film *Taurus*." *Russian Cultural Navigator* (2001). http://www.vor.ru/culture/cultarch162_eng.html.

Avrunin, Naum. "'Ia liubliu reshat' trudnye zadachi': O kinooperatore Valerii Fedosove." *Kinovedcheskie zapiski* 64 (2003): 97–108. http://www.kinozapiski.ru/article/126/.

Bagrov, Petr. "Ermler, Stalin, and Animation: On the Film *The Peasants* (1934)." *Kinokultura* 15 (January 2007). http://www.kinokultura.com/2007/15-bagrov.shtml#Video.

———. "Soviet Melodrama: A Historical Overview." Trans. Vladimir Padunov. *Kinokultura*, July 2007. http://www.kinokultura.com/index.html.

Balabanov, Aleksei. "Aleksei Balabanov." Interview with Tat'iana Pozniak. *Nevskoe vremia* 50.1692 (1998). http://www.dux.ru/enpp/newspapers/nevrem/arts/nevrem-1692-art-51.html.

———. "Voprosy rezhisseru." In Arkus et al., eds., *Seans Guide*, 153.

Barrera, Mario. *Race and Class in the Southwest: A Theory of Racial Inequality*. Notre Dame, Ind.: University of Notre Dame Press, 1980.

Barrett, Thomas M. "Southern Living (in Captivity): The Caucasus in Russian Popular Culture." *Journal of Popular Culture*. Special *Festschrift* in honor of Richard Stites. 31.4 (1998): 75–93.

Barton, Ruth. *Irish National Cinema*. New York: Routledge, 2004.

Basina, Nataliia. "Sootvetstvuiushchaia stat'ia." *Seans* 17–18 (1999): 48.

Baskakov, V., C. Drobashenko, and E. Efimov. *Sovetskoe kino 70-e gody: Osnovnye tendentsii razvitiia*. Moscow: Iskusstvo, 1984.

Batchan, Alexander. "Andrei Plakhov on the Work of the Conflicts Commission." *Wide Angle* 12.4 (1990): 76–80.

———. "Mad Russian." Interview with Viktor Demin. *Film Comment* 23.3 (1987): 48–51.

Bazin, André. "Bazin on Marker." Trans. David Kehr. *Film Comment* 34.4 (2003): 43–44.

———. "The Stalin Myth in Soviet Cinema." Trans. Georgia Gurrieri. *Film Criticism* 3.1 (1978): 17–26.

Beckett, Samuel. *"Endgame" and "Act without Pride."* Trans. Samuel Beckett. New York: Grove, 1994.

Beissinger, Mark R. "Demise of the Empire State: Identity, Legitimacy, and the Deconstruction of Soviet Politics." In Crawford Young, ed., *The Rising Tide of Cultural Pluralism: The Nation-State at Bay?* Madison: University of Wisconsin Press, 1993.

———. "The Persisting Ambiguity of Empire." *Post-Soviet Affairs* 11.2 (1995): 149–84.

———. "Soviet Empire as 'Family Resemblance.'" *Slavic Review* 65.2 (2006): 294–303.

Belinskii, V. G. *Sobranie sochinenii v trekh tomakh*. Ed. F. M. Golovenchenko. Vol. 2. Moscow: OGIZ, 1948. 763–91.

Belopol'skaia, Viktoriia. "*Mariia*." In Arkus and Savel'ev, eds., 143–46.

———. "V tverdom pereplete zhanra." *Seans* 9 (1994): 83.

Berdiaev, Nikolai. *Russkaia ideia*. Paris: YMCA Press, 1971.

Berezovchuk, Larisa. "Identifikatsiia vremeni." *Kinovedcheskie zapiski* 76 (2005): 178–212.

Berlin, Isaiah. *Vico and Herder: Two Studies in the History of Ideas*. New York: Viking, 1976.

Berry, Ellen E. "Grief and Simulation in Kira Muratova's *The Aesthenic Syndrome*." *Russian Review,* July 1988: 446–54.

Beumers, Birgit. *Burnt by the Sun.* KINOfile Film Companion 3. London: I. B. Tauris, 2000.

———. "Cinemarket, or the Russian Film Industry in 'Mission Impossible.'" *Europe-Asia Studies* 51.5 (1999): 871–96.

———. "The Mikhalkov Brothers' View of Russia." In Hutchings and Vernitski, eds., 135–52.

———. *Nikita Mikhalkov.* London: I. B. Tauris, 2005.

———. Review of Aleksandr Sokurov, *Russian Ark* (*Russkii kovcheg*). *Kinokultura* 15 (February 2003). http://www.kinokultura.com/reviews/Rark.html.

———, ed. *The Cinema of Russia and the Former Soviet Union.* New York: Wallflower Press, 2007.

———, ed. *Russia on Reels: The Russian Idea in Post-Soviet Cinema.* London: I. B. Taurus, 1999.

———. "To Moscow! To Moscow? The Russian Hero and the Loss of the Centre." In Beumers, ed., *Russia on Reels.* 76–91.

Bezrukova, Liudmila. "Takogo Lenina my eshche ne videli." *Trud* 3 (March 2001).

Blakesley, R. P. "Seas, Cities, and Dreams: The Paintings of Ivan Aivazovsky." *Slavonic and East European Review* 81.3 (2003): 548–49.

Blok, Aleksandr. *Sobranie sochinenii v vos'mi tomakh.* Vol. 2: *Stikhotvoreniia i poemy 1904–1908.* Moscow-Leningrad, GIKhL, 1960.

———. *Sobranie sochinenii v vos'mi tomakh.* Vol. 3: *Stikhotvoreniia i poemy 1907–1921.* Moscow-Leningrad, GIKhL, 1960.

———. *Zapisnye knizhki 1901–1920.* Leningrad: Gosudarstvennoe izdatel'stvo khudozhestvennoi literatury, 1930.

Bluntschli, J. K. *Allgemeine Staatslehre.* 6th ed. 1866. Cited in Michael Hughes, *Nationalism and Society: Germany 1800–1945.* New York: Edward Arnold, 1988. 17.

Bogemskii, Georgii. "*Ochi chernye* v Italii." *Kino* (Latvia) 3 (1987): 14–16.

Bogomolov, Iurii. "Killer—brat killera." *Iskusstvo kino* 10 (1997): 27–31.

———. "Kontsy v vodu—kompleksy naruzhu . . ." *Iskusstvo kino* 3 (1995): 13–18.

Bokshitskaia, Elena. "Pouchitel'naia istoriia studenta VGIKa, a vposledstvii kinorezhissera tret'ei kategorii Aleksandra Sokurova." Interview with Aleksandr Sokurov. *Iunost'* 2 (1987): 9–13.

Bollag, Brenda. "Klimov & Co." *Film Comment* 23.3 (1987): 40–43.

Bollag, Brenda, and Michel Ciment. "Entretien avec Kira Muratova." *Positif* 324 (1988): 8–12.

Bortin, Mary Ellen. "Soviet Cinema Promised Independence." *Boston Globe,* January 24, 1987.

Bossart, Alla. "Luna. Sobaka. Koshka. Ru." In Maliukova, comp., 81–88.

Bourke, Joanna. *Dismembering the Male: Men's Bodies, Britain, and the Great War.* Chicago: University of Chicago Press, 1996.

Bozhovich, Viktor. "Iz zhizni fantomov." *Iskusstvo kino* 7 (1992): 14–17.

———. *Kira Muratova: Tvorcheskii portret.* Moscow: Soiuzinformkino, 1988.

———, comp. *Pokaianie.* Moscow: Kinotsentr, 1988.

———. "Rentgenoskopiia dushi." *Iskusstvo kino* 9 (1987): 51–70.

Brandenberger, David. *National Bolshevism: Stalinist Mass Culture and the Formation of Modern Russian National Identity, 1931–1956*. Russian Research Studies Center 93. Cambridge, Mass.: Harvard University Press, 2002.

Brashinskii, Mikhail. "Vadim Abdrashitov." In Arkus, ed., *Noveishaia*, 1:30–31.

Brashinsky, Michael, and Andrew Horton, eds. *Russian Critics on the Cinema of Glasnost*. Cambridge, U.K.: Cambridge University Press, 1994.

"*Brat/Zhmurki*: Aleksei Balabanov." *Seans* 27/28 (2006): 4–8.

Brent, Jonathan, and Vladimir P. Naumov. *Stalin's Last Crime: The Plot against the Jewish Doctors, 1948–1953*. New York: Harper Perennial, 2004.

Breslauer, George. *Gorbachev and Yeltsin as Leaders*. Cambridge, U.K.: Cambridge University Press, 2002.

Brooks, Peter. *The Melodramatic Imagination: Balzac, Henry James, Melodrama, and the Mode of Excess*. New Haven, Conn.: Yale University Press, 1995.

Broude, Inna. *Takoe vot kino . . .: Russkie fil'my 1990-kh*. Tenafly, N.J.: Hermitage, 2001.

Brubaker, Rogers. *Nationalism Reframed: Nationhood and the National Question in the New Europe*. New York: Cambridge University Press, 1996.

Brudny, Yitzhak. *Reinventing Russia: Russian Nationalism and the Soviet State, 1953–1991*. Russian Research Studies Center 91. Cambridge, Mass.: Harvard University Press, 2000.

Bryden, Ronald. "The Roads to *Heartbreak House*." In Christopher Innes, ed., *The Cambridge Companion to George Bernard Shaw*. Cambridge, U.K.: Cambridge University Press, 1998. 180–94.

Buckler, Julie A. "Melodramatizing Russia: Nineteenth-Century Views from the West." In McReynolds and Neuberger, eds., 55–78.

Buttafava, Giovanni. "Aleksei German, or the Form of Courage." In Anna Lawton, ed., *The Red Screen: Politics, Society, Art in Soviet Cinema*. New York: Routledge, 1992. 275–82.

Buzychkin, Vadim. "Arkhitektura: Ekzamen na chestnost'." *Moskovskie novosti* 8 (March 1987): 12.

Bykov, Dmitrii. "German versus Mikhalkov." *Iskusstvo kino* 6 (2000): 47–55.

———. "Kira Muratova: Chto-to drugoe." *Literaturnaia gazeta*, December 16, 1992.

———. "Kira Muratova: Ia ne koshka i ne Gospod' Bog." *Stolitsa* 20 (1994): 48.

———. "Kira Muratova nauchila Vysotskogo khripet'." *Profil'* 9 (March 11, 1997).

———. "Krushenie poezda." *Iskusstvo kino* 5 (1996): 132–37.

———. "Toska Il'i Averbakha." *Kinovedcheskie zapiski* 69 (2005): 133–38.

Bykov, Rolan. "Plus Sixty." *Moscow News* 29 (1988): 15.

Bykovsky, Yegor, and Vladimir Orlov. "Soviet Power Is No More." *Moscow News*, October 29, 1993.

Carleheden, Mikael. *Second Modernity: Jürgen Habermas and the Social Theoretical Discourse of Modernity*. Gothenburg, Sweden: Daidalos, 1996.

Certeau, Michel de. "Walking in the City." In *The Practice of Everyday Life*. Berkeley: University of California Press, 2002. 91–110.

Chaadaev, Petr. "Philosophical Letters." In James M. Edie, James P. Scanlan, and Mary-Barbara Zeldin, eds., *Russian Philosophy*. Vol. 1: *The Beginnings of Russian Philosophy; The Slavophiles; The Westernizers*. Knoxville: University of Tennessee Press, 1976. 106–54.

Chekhov, A. P. *Bezotsovshchina*. In *A. P. Chekhov: Polnoe sobranie sochinenii i pisem v tridtsati tomakh*. Ed. N. F. Bel'chikov. Moscow: Nauka, 1978. 11: 4–180. Commentary 393–402.

Chernetsky, Vitaly. "Postcolonialism, Russia and Ukriane." In *Empire, Union, Center, Satellite: The Place of Post-Colonial Theory in Slavic/Central and Eastern European/(Post-)Soviet Studies*, edited by Jonathan Brooks Platt. Special issue of *Ulbandus* 7 (2003): 32–62.

Chernetsky, Vitaly, Nancy Condee, Harsha Ram, and Gayatri Spivak. "Are We Postcolonial? Post-Soviet Space." *PMLA* 120.3 (2006): 819–36.

Cherniavsky, Michael. "'Holy Russia': A Study in the History of an Idea." *American Historical Review* 63.3 (1958): 617–37.

———. *Tsar and People: Studies in Russian Myths*. 2nd edition. New York: Random House, 1969.

Chernov, Sergei. "Novyi glava sovetskogo kino." *Novoe russkoe slovo*, January 30, 1987.

Christie, Ian. "The Cinema." In Graffy and Hosking, eds., 43–77.

———. "Grandmother's Russia." *Sight and Sound* (October 2008): 40–41.

———. "Klimov: *Perestroika* in Person." *Sight and Sound* 56 (1987): 156.

———. "Russkii kovcheg/Russian Ark." In Birgit Beumers, ed., *The Cinema of Russia*. 242–51.

Chuprinin, Sergei. "Drugaia proza." *Literaturnaia gazeta*, February 8, 1989.

Clarke, Roger. "Film: Freaks and Film-makers." *The Independent* (London), August 20, 1999.

Clermont, Pierre. *Le communisme à contre-modernité*. Paris: Universitaires de Vincennes, 1993.

Cohen, Stephen F. "Scholarly Missions: Sovietology as a Vocation." In *Rethinking the Soviet Experience: Politics and History Since 1917*. New York: Oxford University Press, 1985. 3–37.

Cohen, Stephen F., and Katrina vanden Heuvel, eds. *Voices of Glasnost: Interviews with Gorbachev's Reformers*. New York: Norton, 1989.

Colley, Linda. *Britons: Forging the Nation, 1707–1837*. New Haven, Conn.: Yale University Press, 1992.

Compagnon, Antoine. *Les cinq paradoxes de la modernité*. Paris: Seuil, 1990.

Condee, Nancy. "The Dream of Well-Being." *Sight and Sound* 7.12 (December 1997): 18–21.

———. "From Emigration to E-migration: Contemporaneity and the Former Second World." In Terry Smith, Okwui Enwezor, and Nancy Condee, eds., *Antinomies of Art and Culture: Modernity, Postmodernity, Contemporaneity*. Durham, N.C.: Duke University Press, 2008. 235–249.

———. "No Glory, No Majesty, No Honor: The Russian Idea and Inverse Value." In Beumers, ed., *Russia on Reels*. 25–33.

———. "Sokurov's Chechnia: Aleksandr Sokurov's *Aleksandra* (2007)." Review of Aleksandr Sokurov's *Aleksandra*. *Kinokultura* 18 (October 2007). http://www.kinokultura.com/2007/18r-alexandra.shtml.

Condee, Nancy, and Vladimir Padunov. "The Frontiers of Soviet Culture: Reaching the Limits?" *Harriman Institute Forum* 1.5 (1988): 1–8.

———. "*Makulakul'tura*: Reprocessing Culture." *October* 57 (Summer 1991): 79–103.

———. "Pair-A-Dice Lost: The Socialist Gamble, Market Determinism, and Compulsory Postmodernism." *Postcommunism: Rethinking the Second World*. Special issue of *New Formations* 22 (Spring 1994): 72–94.

———. "Perestroika Suicide: Not by *Bred* Alone." *New Left Review* 189 (September–October 1991): 67–89.

Dadamian, Gennadii. *Sotsial'no-ekonomicheskie problemy teatral'nogo iskusstva*. Moscow: Iskusstvo, 1982.

Dal', Vladimir. *Tolkovyi slovar' zhivogo velikorusskago iazyka v chetyrekh tomakh*. Vol. 2. Reprint of 3rd edition. 1905. Moscow: Progress, Universe, 1994.

Dällenbach Lucien, *Le Récit spéculaire. Essais sur la mise en abyme*. Paris: Seuil, 1977.

Dawisha, Karen, and Bruce Parrott, eds. *The End of Empire? The Transformation of the USSR in Comparative Perspective*. Armonk, N.Y.: M. E. Sharpe, 1997.

Deutsch, K. W. *Nationalism and Social Communication: An Inquiry into the Foundations of Nationalism*. 2nd ed. Cambridge, Mass.: MIT Press, 1966.

D'iachenko, Andrei. "Prizraki angliiskogo moderna." In Arkus and Savel'ev, eds., 107–8.

Dobrotvorskaia, Karina. "Pliaska smerti: *Skorbnoe beschuvstvie* i estetika moderna." In Arkus and Savel'ev, eds., 103–6.

———. "Povorot." *Seans* 11 (1995): 7.

Dobrotvorskii, Sergei. "Gorod i dom." In *Sergei Dobrotvorskii: Kino na oshchup'*. St. Petersburg: Seans, 2001. 189–96.

———. "Proverka na dorogakh istorii." *Sovetskii fil'm* 6 (1986): 7–9.

———. "Uznik zamka K." *Seans* 9 (1994): 82.

Dobrotvorskii, S., and N. Sirivlia. "Mednyi vsadnik 'Lenfil'ma.'" *Iskusstvo kino* 3 (1996): 22–28.

Dolin, Anton. "À la guerre kak na voine." *Iskusstvo kino* 7 (2002): 26–29.

———. "Kira Muratova: Obozhaiu klounadu." *Gazeta.ru* 128 (June 28, 2002).

Dondurei, Daniil. "Artistic Culture." In Dmitri N. Shalin, ed., *Russian Culture at the Crossroads: Paradoxes of Postcommunist Consciousness*. Boulder, Colo.: Westview Press, 1996. 259–78.

———. "Kinodelo: Na puti k rynku." In A. G. Dubrovin and M. E. Zak, eds., *Rossiiskoe kino: Paradoksy obnovleniia*. Moscow: Materik, 1995. 126–40.

———. "Mestobliustiteli." Discussion with Larisa Maliukova. In Maliukova, comp., 3–9.

———, ed. *Otechestvennyi kinematograf: Strategiia vyzhivaniia*. Moscow: Dubl'-D, 1991.

———. "Posle imperii: Kinorynok po-russki." *Iskusstvo kino* 11 (1993): 3–9.

———. "Rynok vmesto sobesa." *Iskusstvo kino* 10 (1996): 28–37.

———. "The State of the National Cinema." Speech at the Third Congress of the Russian Filmmakers' Union (December 22–23, 1997). Trans. Birgit Beumers. In Beumers, ed., *Russia on Reels*. 46–50.

———. "V storonu prodiuserskoi modeli." *Iskusstvo kino* 4 (1995): 52–53.

Dondurei, Daniil, and Sergei Solov'ev. Excerpts of comments on the reform of the film distribution system from *Izvestiia. Current Digest of the Soviet Press* 42.31 (1990): 3, 14–15.

Dondureyi, Daniil, and Natalia Venger. *Russian Film Industry 2001–2006*. Moscow: STS, 2006.

Donets, L. "Tantsy vo vremia chumy." *Iskusstvo kino* 5 (1998): 52–55.

Dostoevskii, Fedor. *Polnoe sobranie sochinenii v tridtsati tomakh.* Ed. V. G. Bazanov. Vol. 26–27. Leningrad: Nauka, 1984.

Doyle, Michael. *Empires.* Ithaca, N.Y.: Cornell University Press, 1986.

Drozdova, Marina. "Modnik." *Iskusstvo kino* 12 (1994): 35–37.

Drubek-Meyer, Natascha. "An Ark for a Pair of Media: Sokurov's *Russian Ark.*" *Artmargins* 5 (May 2003). http://www.artmargins.com/content/cineview/meyer.html.

Dugin, Aleksandr. *Proekt "Evraziia."* Moscow: EKSMO, 2004.

Dunlop, John B. *The Rise of Russia and the Fall of the Soviet Empire.* Princeton, N.J.: Princeton University Press, 1995.

———. "Soviet Film under Gorbachev." Meeting Report: Kennan Institute for Advanced Studies. May 6, 1987.

Dymshits, N., and A. Troshin, eds. and comps. *Iz proshlogo v budushchee: Proverka na dorogakh.* Moscow: VGIK, 1990.

Edensor, Tim. *National Identity, Popular Culture, and Everyday Life.* London: Berg, 2002.

Egorova, Tatiana. *Soviet Film Music: An Historical Survey.* Trans. Tatiana A. Ganf and Natalia A. Egunova. Amsterdam: Harwood, 1997.

El'iashev, D., and O. Lapshin. "Ia, ty, on, ona—vmeste tselaia strana (korotkie zametki ob odnom davnem kinovpechatlenii)." Unpublished manuscript.

Elsaesser, Thomas. "Tales of Sound and Fury: Observations on the Family Melodrama." In Barry Keith Grant, ed., *Film Genre Reader II.* Austin: University of Texas Press, 1995. 350–80.

Ely, Christopher. *This Meager Landscape: Landscape and National Identity in Imperial Russia.* DeKalb: Northern Illinois University Press, 2002.

Engelstein, Laura. Review of Aleksandr Etkind, *Khlyst: Sekty, literatura i revoliutsiia. Slavic Review* 58.2 (1999): 482–83.

Eremenko, I. N., and Iu. D. Novikov. *Rossiia i Chechnia (1990–1997): Dokumenty svidetel'stvuiut.* Moscow: RAU-Universitet, 1997.

Erofeev, Viktor. "Krushenie gumanizma N. 2." *Moskovskie novosti* 51 (December 22, 1991).

———. "Proshchanie s gumanizmom." *Iskusstvo kino* 9 (1997): 94–96.

Eshelman, Raoul. "Sokurov's *Russian Ark* and the End of Postmodernism." *Artmargins,* July 30, 2003. http://www.artmargins.com/content/cineview/eshelman.html.

Etkind, Aleksandr. "Bremia britogo cheloveka, ili Vnutrenniaia kolonizatsiia Rossii." *Ab Imperio* 1 (2002): 265–98.

Evreinoff, Nicolas. *Histoire du théâtre russe.* Paris: Éditions du Chêne, 1947.

Evreinov, N. "Vziatie Zimnego dvortsa." *Krasnyi militsioner* 14 (1920): 4–5.

Faraday, George. *The Revolt of the Filmmakers: The Struggle for Autonomy and the Fall of the Soviet Film Industry.* University Park: Pennsylvania State University Press, 2000.

Figes, Orlando. *Natasha's Dance: A Cultural History of Russia.* New York: Henry Holt, 2003.

Filippov, Sergei. "Kino s kommunisticheskim litsom." *Ogonek* 10 (March 1991): 30–31.

Finn, P. "Zametki pessimista: K semidesiatiletiiu Il'i Averbakha." *Iskusstvo kino* 9 (2004): 137–57.

Fisher, William. "Gorbachev's Cinema." *Sight and Sound,* Autumn 1987: 238–43.

Fishman, Boris. "Its Freedoms No Longer New, Russian Cinema Matures." *New York Times,* October 23, 2003.

Fitzpatrick, Sheila. "Ascribing Class: The Construction of Social Identity in Soviet Russia." In Sheila Fitzpatrick, ed., *Stalinism: New Directions.* New York: Routledge, 2000. 20–46.

———. *The Commissariat of Enlightenment: Soviet Organization of Education and the Arts under Lunacharsky.* Cambridge, U.K.: Cambridge University Press, 1970.

Fitzpatrick, Sheila, and Yuri Slekine, eds. *In the Shadow of Revolution: Life Stories of Russian Women from 1917 to the Second World War.* Princeton, N.J.: Princeton University Press, 2000.

Fix, Sergei. "Video Piracy Reaches into U.S. Studios." *We/My,* September 16–19, 1993: 14.

Fomin, Valerii. *Kino i vlast'. Sovetskoe kino: 1965–1985 gody. Dokumenty. Svidetel'stva. Razmyshleniia.* Moscow: Materik, 1996.

———. *"Polka": Dokumenty. Svidetel'stva. Kommentarii.* Moscow: NIIK, 1992.

Foucault, Michel. "Space, Knowledge, and Power." Interview with Paul Rabinow. Trans. Christian Hubert. In Paul Rabinow, ed., *The Foucault Reader.* New York: Pantheon, 1984. 239–56.

Franklin, Anna. "Torrents of Spring." *Screen International,* May 30, 1997: 13–14.

Franklin, Simon, and Emma Widdis, eds. *National Identity in Russian Culture: An Introduction.* Cambridge, U.K.: Cambridge University Press, 2004.

Freud, Sigmund. "Beyond the Pleasure Principle." 1920. In James Strachey, trans. and ed., *The Standard Edition of the Complete Psychological Works of Sigmund Freud.* London: Hogarth, 1961. 18:7–64.

———. "Civilization and Its Discontents." 1930. In James Strachey, trans. and ed., *The Standard Edition of the Complete Psychological Works of Sigmund Freud.* London: Hogarth, 1961. 21:57–146.

———. "The Economic Problem of Masochism." 1924. In James Strachey, trans. and ed., *The Standard Edition of the Complete Psychological Works of Sigmund Freud.* London: Hogarth, 1961. 19:157–70.

Friedrich, Carl, J., Michael Curtis, and Benjamin R. Barber. *Totalitarianism in Perspective: Three Views.* New York: Praeger, 1969.

Frodon, J. M. "Kira Muratova: L'oeuvre mutilée." *Le point* 818 (May 23, 1988): 72

Furikov, L. "Ne do zhiru . . ." *Kinomekhanik* 4 (1996).

Galichenko, Nicholas. *Glasnost—Soviet Cinema Responds.* Ed. Robert Allington. Austin: University of Texas Press, 1991.

Gambrell, Jamey. "Notes on the Underground." *Art in America,* November 1988: 131.

———. "Perestroika Shock." *Art in America,* November 1988: 124–35.

———. "Whither the Artists Union?" *Art in America,* November 1988: 132.

Gans, Herbert J. "Symbolic Ethnicity: The Future of Ethnic Groups and Cultures in America." *Ethnic and Racial Studies* 2 (January 1979): 1–20.

Garrard, John, and Carol Garrard. *Inside the Soviet Writers' Union.* New York: Free Press, 1990.

Garros, Véronique, Natalia Korenevskaya, and Thomas Lahusen, eds. *Intimacy and Terror: Soviet Diaries of the 1930s.* Trans. Carol A. Flath. New York: New Press, 1995.

Gellner, Ernest. "Adam's Navel: 'Primordialists' *versus* 'Modernists.'" In Mortimer and Fine, eds., 31–35.

―――. *Nations and Nationalism*. Oxford: Blackwell, 1990.

―――. "Return of a Native." *Political Quarterly* 67.1 (1996): 4–13.

―――. *Thought and Change*. London: Weidenfeld & Nicholson, 1964.

Gerasimov, Il'ia. "Rossiiskaia imperiia Nikity Mikhalkova." *Ab imperio* 1 (2000). http://abimperio.net/scgi-bin/aishow.pl?state=index_eng&idlang=1.

German, Aleksei. "Aleksei German: 'Ia mechtal o chetvertoi kategorii . . .'" Interview with L. Zakrzhevskaia. In Fomin, *Kino i vlast'*, 199–208.

―――. "Boius' sniat' plokhoe kino." Interview with Iuliia Kantor. *Izvestiia*, July 19, 2003.

―――. "Eto ia vinovat pered frantsuzami, a ne oni peredo mnoi." Interview with El'ga Lyndina. *Iskusstvo kino* 8 (1994): 55–58.

―――. "Iz rechi Alekseia Germana pered pokazom fil'ma *Khrustalev, mashinu!* v Rossii. 27 avgusta 1999 goda, Sankt-Peterburg, kinoteatr Avrora." *Kinoprotsess* 5 (1999): 25.

―――. "Izgoniaiushchii d'iavola." Interview with Serge Toubiana, Charles Tesson, and Guy Séligmann. Introductory remarks by Nina Zarkhi. *Iskusstvo kino* 6 (1999): 120–29.

―――. "Kino proizrastaet iz poezii." Conversation with T. Iensen. *Voprosy literatury* 12 (1986): 124–57.

―――. "Khrena-nakhrena!" Interview with Oleg Sul'kin. *Novoe russkoe slovo*, October 2, 1998.

―――. "Maska, ia tebia znaiu?" *Moskovskie novosti*, no. 19 (May 12, 1991): 14.

―――. "Pochemu ia ne snimaiu kino posle 1985 goda." Interview with Natal'ia Riurikova. *Literaturnaia gazeta*, May 1, 1991.

―――. "Postizhenie dobra (O Konstantine Simonove)." In *Ekran 88*. Moscow: Iskusstvo, 1988. 140–43.

―――. "Razrushenie mifov." Interview with and commentary by El'ga Lyndina. *Teatr* 10 (1987): 153–67.

―――. "Trudno byt' Germanom." Interview with Natal'ia Kilesso. *Moskovskii komsomolets*, October 19, 1999.

―――. "'Vse nachinaetsia posle . . .': Monolog rezhissera." *Kinostsenarii* 4 (1995): 3–6.

―――. "Zhdu talantlivuiu smenu." *Sovetskaia kul'tura*, January 8, 1987.

German, Aleksei, and Svetlana Karmalita. *Chto skazal tabachnik s Tabachnoi ulitsy i drugie kinostsenarii*. St. Petersburg: Seans, 2006.

Gersova, L., comp. "Kira Muratova otvechaet zriteliam." *Kinovedcheskie zapiski* 13 (1992): 157–68.

Gertsen, A. I. "Du développement des idées révolutionnaires en Russie." In *Sobranie sochinenii v 30-i tomakh*. Ed. V.P. Volgin. Moscow: Izdatel'stvo Akademii nauk SSSR, 1956. 7:412–33.

Getmanchuk, A. "Kira Muratova: Pravda vsegda shokiruet." *Komsomol'skaia Pravda* 127 (June 2, 1990).

Gillespie, David A. "Textual Abuse: The (Mis) Treatment of the Body in Russian Literature." *Australian Slavonic and East European Studies*. 12.2 (1988): 1–14.

Ginsberg, Robert. *The Aesthetic of Ruins*. Amsterdam: Rodopi, 2004.

Ginzburg, Carlo. "Morelli, Freud, and Sherlock Holmes: Clues and Scientific Method." *History Journal Workshop* 9 (Spring 1980): 5–36.

Gladil'shchikov, Iurii. "Novye vremena." *Literaturnaia gazeta*, June 13, 1990.

———. "Priglashenie k diskusii: Amerika Rossii podarila parokhod." *Literaturnaia gazeta*, April 4, 1990.

———. "Tak kto zdes' Khrustalev?" *Itogi*, May 26, 1998.

———. "Uzh polnoch' blizitsia . . ." *Stengazeta*, September 7, 2007. http://www.sten gazeta.net/article.html?article=3691.

Gladil'shchikov, Iurii, Lev Rubinshtein, and Nikita Sokolov. "Moshchi i nemoshchi." *Itogi*, March 27, 2001.

Gleason, Abbott. *Totalitarianism: The Inner History of the Cold War.* New York: Oxford University Press, 1995.

Gledhill, Christine, ed. *Home Is Where the Heart Is: Studies in Melodrama and the Woman's Film.* London: BFI, 1987.

———. "The Melodramatic Field: An Investigation." In Gledhill, ed., 5–43.

Goble, Paul. "Russia and Its Neighbors." *Foreign Policy* 90 (1993): 79–88.

Golutva, Aleksandr. "Goskino ne podarok, no bez nego eshche khuzhe." Interview by Viktor Matizen. *Novoe russkoe slovo*, February 20–21, 1999: 26.

Gordon, Michael R. "Russia's New Court Sculptor: Only the Colossal." *New York Times*, January 25, 1997.

Graffy, Julian. "Brother." *Sight and Sound* 10.5 (May 2000): 44. http://www.bfi.org.uk/ sightandsound/review/322.

———. "The Literary Press." In Graffy and Hosking, eds., 107–57.

———. "Recent Soviet Cinema: Salvaged Films, Salvaged Careers." *Slovo* 1 (1988): 40–47.

———. "Unshelving Stalin: After the Period of Stagnation." In Richard Taylor and Derek Spring, eds., *Stalinism and Soviet Cinema.* New York: Routledge, 1993. 212–27.

Graffy, Julian, and Geoffrey A. Hosking, eds. *Culture and the Media in the USSR Today.* Houndsmills, U.K.: Macmillan/SSEES, 1989.

Graham, Seth. "*Chernukha* and Russian Film." *Studies in Slavic Cultures* 1 (2000): 9–27.

Gramsci, Antonio. *The Modern Prince and Other Writings.* New York: International Publishers, 1957.

Grashchenkova, Irina. "Parad Planet." http://mega.km.ru/cinema/encyclop.

Gray, Rosalind. *Russian Genre Painting in the Nineteenth Century.* Oxford: Oxford University Press, 2000.

Greenfeld, Liah. *Nationalism: Five Roads to Modernity.* Cambridge, Mass.: Harvard University Press, 1992.

———. "Transcending the Nation's Worth." *Daedalus* 122.3 (1993): 47–62.

Greenleaf, Monika. *Pushkin and Romantic Fashion: Fragment, Elegy, Orient, Irony.* Stanford: Stanford University Press, 1994.

Greenleaf, Monica, and Stephen Moeller-Sally, eds. *Russian Subjects: Empire, Nation, and the Culture of the Golden Age.* Evanston, Ill.: Northwestern University Press, 1998.

Griffin, Roger. *Modernism and Fascism: The Sense of a Beginning under Mussolini and Hitler.* London: Palgrave Macmillan, 2007.

———. *The Nature of Fascism.* London: Routledge, 1993.

———. "Notes towards the Definition of Fascist Culture: The Prospects for Synergy between Marxist and Liberal Heuristics." *Renaissance and Modern Studies* 42 (Autumn 2001): 95–115.

————. "The Palingenetic Core of Fascist Nationalism." In Alessandro Campi, ed., *Che cos'è il fascismo? Interpretazioni e prospettive di ricerche.* Rome: Ideazione editrice, 2003. 97–122.

Grimstead, David. "Melodrama as Echo of the Historically Voiceless." In Tamara K. Hareven, ed., *Anonymous Americans: Explorations in Nineteenth-Century Social History.* Englewood Cliffs, N.J.: Prentice Hall, 1971. 80–98.

Grois (Groys), Boris. *Utopiia i obmen.* Moscow: Znak, 1993.

Guseinov, Gusan. "Chto takoe novorusskii steb? K teorii eskhrofemizma: Mezhdu ser'ezno-smeshnym i strashno-smeshnym." Paper presented at Two Centuries of Russian Humor and Satire. University of Nottingham, July 20–23, 2000.

Gusiatinskii, Evgenii. "Brat zhil, brat zhiv, brat budet zhit'." *Iskusstvo kino* 3 (2001): 30–33.

Gvozdev, Leonid. "Khrustalev, iz mashiny!" *Moskovskaia Pravda,* April 27, 2000.

Habermas, Jurgen. *The Postnational Constellation: Political Essays.* Trans. Max Pensky. Cambridge, Mass.: MIT Press, 2001.

Hall, John A. "Nationalisms: Classified and Explained." *Daedalus* 122.3 (1993): 1–28.

Hardy, Forsyth. "Russians on the Cinema." *Scotsman,* August 15, 1987.

Harris, Jonathan. "The Public Politics of Aleksandr Nikolaevich Yakovlev, 1983–89." Carl Beck Papers in Russian and East European Studies No. 901. Pittsburgh: University of Pittsburgh, 1990.

————. *Subverting the System: Gorbachev's Reform of the Party's Apparat, 1986–91.* Lanham, Md.: Rowman & Littlefield, 2005.

Harte, Tim. "A Visit to the Museum: Aleksandr Sokurov's *Russian Ark* and the Framing of the Eternal." *Slavic Review* 64.1 (2005): 43–58.

Hechter, Michael. *Internal Colonialism: The Celtic Fringe in British National Development, 1536–1966.* Berkeley: University of California Press, 1975.

Heilman, Robert. *Tragedy and Melodrama: Versions of Experience.* Seattle: University of Washington Press, 1968.

Hellbeck, Jochen. "Fashioning the Stalinist Soul: The Diary of Stepan Podlubnyi, 1931–9." In Sheila Fitzpatrick, ed., *Stalinism: New Directions.* New York: Routledge, 2000. 77–116.

Herder, J. G. *Ideen zur Philosophie der Geschichte der Menschheit: Mit Kants Rezensionen der "Ideen" und seiner Abhandlung Idee zu einer allgemeinen Geschichte in weltbürgerlicher Absicht.* Berlin: Deutsche Bibliotek, 1914.

Hift, Fred. "Soviet Video Pirates Run Amok." *Christian Science Monitor,* August 8, 1991.

Hill, John. "British Film Policy." In Albert Moran, ed., *Film Policy: International, National and Regional Perspectives.* London: Routledge, 1996. 101–13.

————. "The Issue of National Cinema and British Film Production." In Duncan Petrie, ed., *New Questions of British Cinema.* London: British Film Institute, 1992. 10–21.

Hingley, Ronald. *Russian Writers and Soviet Society, 1917–1978.* New York: Random House, 1979.

Hirschman, A. O. *Exit, Voice and Loyalty: Responses to Decline in Firms, Organizations, and States.* Cambridge, Mass.: Harvard University Press, 1970.

Hoberman, J. "Alexei Guerman among the Long Shadows." *Film Comment* 35.1 (1999): 48–53.

Hobsbawm, E. J. *Nations and Nationalism Since 1780: Programme, Myth, Reality.* Cambridge, U.K.: Cambridge University Press, 1990.

Hoffmann, David L., and Yanni Kotsonis, eds. *Russian Modernity: Politics, Knowledge, Practices.* New York: St. Martin's, 2000.

Hokanson, Katya. "Literary Imperialism, *Narodnost'* and Pushkin's Invention of the Caucasus." *Russian Review* 53.3 (1994): 226–352.

———. "Pushkin's Captive Crimea: Imperialism in *The Fountain of Bakhchisarai.*" In Greenleaf and Moeller-Sally, eds., 123–48.

Holden, Stephen. "The Weather Is Bad, but Life Is Worse." Review of *Khrustalev, the Car! New York Times,* September 28, 1998.

Holdsworth, Nick. "Video Piracy Plagues Russia." uk.news.yahoo.com, July 8, 2003.

Holson, Laura M., and Steven Lee Meyers. "The Russians Are Filming! The Russians Are Filming!" *New York Times,* July 16, 2006.

Horton, Andrew James. "Lynch-Pin? The Imagery of Aleksei Balabanov." *Kinoeye* (*Central Europe Review*) 2.18 (2000). http://www.ce-review.org/00/18/kinoeye18_horton.html.

———. "*War,* What Is It Good for?" Review of Aleksei Balabanov's *War. Kinoeye* (*Central Europe Review*) 2.2 (2002). http://www.kinoeye.org/02/18/horton18_no3.php.

Horton, Andrew, and Michael Brashinsky. *The Zero Hour: Glasnost and Soviet Cinema in Transition.* Princeton, N.J.: Princeton University Press, 1992.

Hosking, Geoffrey Alan. *Empire and Nation in Russian History.* The Fourteenth Charles Edmondson Historical Lectures (February 3–4, 1992, Baylor University). Waco, Tex.: Markham Press Fund, 1993.

———. "The Freudian Frontier." Review of Susan Layton, *Russian Literature and Empire: The Conquest of the Caucasus from Pushkin to Tolstoy. Times Literary Supplement,* March 10, 1995.

———. *Russia: People and Empire, 1552–1917.* Cambridge, Mass.: Harvard University Press, 1997.

Hroch, Miroslav. *Social Preconditions of National Revival in Europe.* Cambridge, U.K.: Cambridge University Press, 1985.

Hutchings, Stephen, and Anat Vernitski, eds. *Russian and Soviet Film Adaptations of Literature, 1900–2001: Screening the Word.* London: Routledge Curzon, 2005.

Iampolski, Mikhail. "Representation-Mimicry-Death: The Latest Films of Alexander Sokurov." In Beumers, ed., *Russia on Reels.* 127–43.

———. "Truth in the Flesh." *Film Studies* 1 (Spring 1999): 70–72.

Iampol'skii, Mikhail. "Diskurs i povestvovanie." *Kinostsenarii* 6 (1989): 175–88.

———. "Ischeznovenie kak forma sushchestvovaniia." *Kinovedcheskie zapiski* 44 (1999): 21–27.

———. "Istina tela." In Arkus and Savel'ev, eds., 165–67.

———. "Kovcheg, plyvushchii iz proshlogo." In Arkus and Savel'ev, eds., 109–15.

———. "Smert' v kino." In Arkus and Savel'ev, eds., 273–78.

Ignatova, Polina. "Culture Ministry Set to Revive National Filmmaking." *Gazeta.ru,* July 5, 2002.

Ionescu, Ghita. *The Breakup of the Soviet Empire in Eastern Europe.* Baltimore: Penguin, 1967.

Isaacs, Harold R. *Idols of the Tribe: Group Identity and Political Change.* Cambridge, Mass.: Harvard University Press, 1975.

Iskander, Fazil'. *Sandro iz Chegema.* Moscow: Moskovskii rabochii, 1989.

Iufit, A. Z., ed. *Russkii sovetskii teatr 1917–1921*. Leningrad: Iskusstvo, 1968.

Iurizditskii, Sergei. "Mne zhizn' interesna sama po sebe." Conversation with Anastasiia Leshchenko. *Kinovedcheskie zapiski* 67 (2004): 327–38. http://www.kinoza piski.ru/article/52/.

Iutkevich, S. I., ed. *Kinoslovar'*. Moscow: Sovietskaia Entsiklopediia, 1986.

Jackson, John Brinckerhoff. "The Necessity for Ruins." In *The Necessity for Ruins, and Other Topics*. Amherst: University of Massachusetts Press, 1980. 89–102.

Jameson, Fredric. *The Geopolitical Aesthetic: Cinema and Space in the World System*. Bloomington: Indiana University Press/BFI, 1992.

———. "History and Elegy in Sokurov." *Critical Inquiry* 33.1 (2006): 1–12.

———. "Of Islands and Trenches: Neutralization and the Production of Utopian Discourse." In *The Ideologies of Theory: Essays 1971–1986*. Vol. 2: *The Syntax of History*. Vol. 49 of the series Theory and History of Literature. Ed. Wlad Godzich and Jochen Schulte-Sasse. Minneapolis: University of Minnesota Press, 1988.

———. *The Political Unconscious: Narrative as a Socially Symbolic Act*. Ithaca, N.Y.: Cornell University Press, 1981.

Johnson, Vida T. "The Search for a New Russia in an 'Era of Few Films.'" *Russian Review* 56.2 (1997): 281–85.

Jones, Wendy S. *Consensual Fictions: Women, Liberalism, and the English Novel*. Toronto: University of Toronto Press, 2005.

Kaganovsky, Lilya. "Bodily Remains: The Positive Hero in Stalinist Fiction." Ph.D. diss., University of California, Berkeley, 2000.

———. *How the Soviet Man Was Unmade*. Pittsburgh: University of Pittsburgh Press, 2008.

Kappeler, Andreas. "The Ambiguities of Russification." *Kritika* 5.2 (2004): 291–97.

———. *Russland als Vielvölkerreich: Entstehung, Geschichte, Zerfall*. Munich: C. H. Beck, 1992.

Kapralov, Georgii. "Chto kormit kinostudiiu." *Pravda*, February 14, 1986.

Karakhan, Aleksei. "Politkorrektnost' ili muzhitskaia pravda?" *Iskusstvo kino* 7 (2002): 33–35.

Karakhan, Lev. "Cinema without Controls: Nostalgia for the State." Paper presented at the American Association for the Advancement of Slavic Studies, Boston, Mass, November 1996.

———. "Jobless Prophets: Glasnost and the *Auteurs*." In Michael Brashinsky and Andrew Horton, eds., *Russian Critics on the Cinema of Glasnost*. New York: Cambridge University Press, 1994. 30–34.

———. "Proiskhozhdenie" (Part I). *Iskusstvo kino* 1 (1987): 83–97.

———. "Proiskhozhdenie" (Part II). *Iskusstvo kino* 2 (1987): 75–94.

Kariuk, Gennadii. "Ona nauchila menia snimat'." Interview by Pavel Sirkes. *Iskusstvo kino* 2 (1995): 104–6.

Karlinsky, Simon. *Anton Chekhov's Life and Thought*. Trans. Michael Heim and Simon Karlinsky. Berkeley: University of California Press, 1978.

Karriker, Alexandra Heidi. "Retro Cinema and New Vistas: Sochi's Kinotavr in 1996." *Russian Review* 56.2 (1997): 291–93.

Kataev, V. B. *Proza Chekhova: Problemy interpretatsii*. Moscow: Izdatel'stvo Moskovskogo universiteta, 1979.

Kaufmann, Eric. "Naturalizing the Nation: The Rise of Naturalistic Nationalism in the United States and Canada." *Comparative Studies in Society and History* 40.4 (1998): 666–95.

Kedourie, Elie. *Nationalism.* London: Hutchinson, 1966.

Kelly, Catriona. *Comrade Pavlik: The Rise and Fall of a Soviet Boy Hero.* London: Granta, 2005.

Kemp, Stuart. "Russia Gaining in Cinema Share." *Hollywood Reporter,* September 23, 2003.

Kennedy, Harlan. "Soviet Spring." *Film Comment* 23.3 (1987): 33–36.

Kennedy, Janet. "Pride and Prejudice: Serge Diaghilev, the *Ballet Russes* and the French Public." In Michelle Facos and Sharon L. Hirsh, eds., *Art, Culture, and National Identity in Fin-de-Siècle Europe.* New York: Cambridge University Press, 2003. 90–118.

Kharitonov, Mark. "Zachem Kafka?" *Iskusstvo kino* 12 (1994): 32–35.

Kharms, Daniil. *Incidences.* Ed. and trans. Neil Cornwell. London: Serpent's Tail, 1993.

Khodasevich, Vladislav. "Tam ili zdes'?" *Dni* 804 (September 25, 1925). Reprinted in Vladislav Khodasevich, *Sobranie sochinenii.* Ed. John Malmstad and Robert Hughes. Ann Arbor: Ardis, 1990. 2:368.

Khokhriakova, Svetlana. "Kira Muratova: Ia zdorovyi organizm s optimisticheskim ustroistvom." *Kul'tura,* September 11, 1997.

———. "Moshenniki, starushki, primadonny i dama s sobachkoi." *Novoe russkoe slovo,* July 2–3, 2003.

"Khrustalev, 'Kristall-Palas'!" *SK novosti* 3 (2000): 2.

Kichin, Valerii. "Nika, Sestra Oskara." *Novoe russkoe slovo,* January 2–3, 1993.

Kishkovsky, Sophia. "A Theater Boom Is Born in Russian Film Industry." *New York Times,* September 10, 1998.

Klein, Andy. "Movie Association Wants to Crack Down on Piracy in CIS." *We/My,* January 25–February 7, 1993: 14.

Kliamkin, I. M., and V. V. Lapkin. "Russkii vopros v Rossii." Part 1. *Polis* 5.80 (1995): 78–90.

Kliuchevskii, V. O. *Sochineniia.* Vol. 1 of 8. Moscow: Gosudarstvennoe izdatel'stvo politicheskoi literatury, 1956.

Knight, Nathaniel. "Ethnicity, Nationality and the Masses: *Narodnost'* and Modernity in Imperial Russia." In Hoffmann and Kotsonis, eds., 41–64.

Knox-Voina, Jane. "'Everything Will Be OK': A New Trend in Russian Film." *Russian Review* 56.2 (1997): 286–90.

Koch, H. W. "1933: The Legality of Hitler's Rise to Power." In H. W. Koch, ed., *Aspects of the Third Reich.* New York: Palgrave Macmillan, 1986. 39–61.

Kohn, Hans. *The Idea of Nationalism.* 2nd ed. New York: Collier Macmillan, 1967.

Kolstoe, Paul. *Russians in the Former Soviet Republics.* Bloomington: Indiana University Press, 1995.

Korobov, Vladimir. "So Many Books, yet So Few; or, The New Publishing Crisis." Trans. Marian Schwartz. *Russian Social Science Review* 38.1 (1997): 82–89.

Kosterina, Nina. *The Diary of Nina Kosterina.* Trans. Mirra Ginsburg. New York: Crown, 1968.

Kotkin, Stephen. *Magnetic Mountain: Stalinism as a Civilization.* Los Angeles: University of California Press, 1995.

Kovalov, Oleg. "My v odinokom golose cheloveka." In Arkus and Savel'ev, eds., *Sokurov*. 7–13.

———. "Rossiia, kotoruiu my pridumali." *Seans* 17/18 (1999): 202–9.

Kozlov, Vladimir. *Mass Uprisings in the USSR: Protest and Rebellion in the Post-Stalin Years*. Trans. Elaine McClarnand MacKinnon. Armonk, N.Y.: M. E. Sharpe, 2002.

"Kritiki o fil'me." Short comments by Russian critics on Abdrashitov's *Play for a Passenger*. *Seans* 11 (1995): 4–5.

"Kritiki o fil'me." Short comments by Russian critics on Abdrashitov's *Time of the Dancer*. *Seans* 16 (1997): 98–99.

Kriukova, A. "Davali by snimat' fil'my." *Nezavisimaia gazeta*, May 5, 1994.

Kudriavtsev, Sergei. *Svoe kino*. Moscow: Dubl'-D, 1998.

———. "Ukrotitel'nitsa faktury." In *Svoe kino*. Moscow: Dom Khanzhonkova, 1998. 289–95.

Kujundzic, Dragan. "After 'After': The *Arkive* Fever of Alexander Sokurov." *Artmargins*, May 5, 2003. http://www.artmargins.com/content/cineview/kujundzic.html.

Kulish, Aleksandr. "Dos'e prem'ery: *Utomlennye solntsem*." *Chital'nyi zal* 1 (1995): 109. Reprinted from "Konets igry," *Nezavisimaia gazeta*, November 9, 1994.

Kundera, Milan. *The Unbearable Lightness of Being*. Trans. Michael Henry Heim. New York: HarperPerennial, 1991.

Laitin, David D. *Identity in Formation: The Russian-Speaking Populations in the Near Abroad*. Ithaca, N.Y.: Cornell University Press, 1998.

Lake, David A. "The Rise, Fall, and Future of the Russian Empire." In Dawisha and Parrott, eds., 30–62.

Lang, Robert. "Tragedy, Melodrama, and the 'Moral Occult.'" In Robert Lang, *American Film Melodrama: Griffith, Vidor, Minnelli*. Princeton, N.J.: Princeton University Press, 1989. 14–21.

Largier, Niklaus. *In Praise of the Whip: A Cultural History of Arousal*. New York: Zone, 2007.

Larsen, Susan. "Encoding Difference: Figuring Gender and Ethnicity in Kira Muratova's *A Change of Fate*." In Nancy Condee, ed., *Soviet Hieroglyphics: Russian Visual Culture in Late 20c. Russia*. Bloomington: Indiana University Press/BFI, 1995. 113–29.

———. "In Search of an Audience: Russian Cinema of Reconciliation." In Adele Barker, ed., *Consuming Russia: Popular Culture, Sex, and Society since Gorbachev*. Durham, N.C.: Duke University Press, 1999. 192–216.

———. "*Korotkie vstrechi* [*Brief Encounters*]." In Birgit Beumers, ed., *The Cinema of Russia*. 116–25.

———. "National Identity, Cultural Authority, and the Post-Soviet 'Blockbuster': Nikita Mikhalkov and Aleksei Balabanov." *Slavic Review* 62.3 (2003): 491–511.

Lash, Scott. *A Different Modernity: A Different Rationality*. London: Blackwell, 1999.

Laurent, Nathalie. "La 'Transparence' à l' épreuve: L'example du VGIK." *L'Autre Europe* 14 (1987): 81–84.

Lawton, Anna. *Kinoglasnost: Soviet Cinema in Our Time*. Cambridge, U.K.: Cambridge University Press, 1992.

———. "Soviet Cinema Today." In *Thirtieth International Film Festival Catalogue*, March 25–April 5, 1987: 33–34.

Layton, Susan. *Russian Literature and Empire: The Conquest of the Caucasus from Pushkin to Tolstoy.* Cambridge, U.K.: Cambridge University Press, 1994.

Lebedev, A. K., and G. K. Burova, eds. *I. E. Repin i V. V. Stasov. Perepiska.* 3 vols. Vol. 1. Moscow: Iskusstvo, 1948–50.

Leighton, Lauren G. *Russian Romanticism: Two Essays.* The Hague: Mouton, 1975.

Lekan, Thomas. *Imagining the Nation in Nature.* Cambridge, Mass.: Harvard University Press, 2004.

Lenin, V. I. *The Development of Capitalism in Russia: The Process of the Formation of a Home Market for Large-Scale Industry.* Moscow: Foreign Languages Publishing House, 1956.

Leont'ev, Konstantin. *Analiz, stil' i veranie: O romanakh gr. L. N. Tolstogo.* Brown Slavic Reprints 3. Providence, R.I.: Brown University Press, 1965.

Lermontov, Mikhail. *Sochineniia v dvukh tomakh.* Vol. 1. Moscow: Khudozhestvennaia literatura, 1970.

Lewin, Moshe. *Political Undercurrents in Soviet Economic Debates: From Bukharin to the Modern Reformers.* London: Pluto Press, 1975.

Liddell-Hart, B. H., ed. *The Red Army.* New York: Harcourt Brace, 1956.

Liderman, Iuliia. *Motivy "proverki" i "ispytaniia" v postsovetskoi kul'ture.* Introduction by Evgenii Margolit. Soviet and Post-Soviet Politics and Society Series. Andreas Umland, series editor. Stuttgart: Ibidem, 2005.

Lieven, Dominic. *Empire: The Russian Empire and Its Rivals.* New Haven, Conn.: Yale University Press, 2000.

———. "The Russian Empire and the Soviet Union as Imperial Polities." *Journal of Contemporary History* 30 (1995): 607–36.

Lilly, Ian K. "Conviviality in the Pre-Revolutionary 'Moscow Text' of Russian Culture." *Russian Review* 63.3 (2004): 427–48.

Lilly, Ian K., ed. *Moscow and Petersburg: The City in Russian Culture.* Astra Press: Nottingham, 2002.

Lincoln, W. Bruce. *Nicholas I: Emperor and Autocrat of All the Russias.* Bloomington: Indiana University Press, 1978.

Lipkov, Aleksandr. *German, syn Germana.* Moscow: Kinotsentr, 1988.

———. *Nikita Mikhalkov.* Moscow: Soiuz kinematografistov SSSR, 1981.

———. "Proverka . . . na dorogakh." *Novyi mir* 2 (1987): 202–25.

Lipovetskii, Mark. "Vsekh liubliu na svete ia!" *Iskusstvo kino* 11 (2000): 55–59.

Listov, Viktor. "Khoronili Stalina bez Stalina." *Kinovedcheskie zapiski* 44 (1999): 8–10.

Litvinova, Renata. "Boites' svoikh zhelanii—oni sbyvaiutsia." Interview with Igor' Mantsov. *Iskusstvo kino* 8 (1994): 10–14.

———. "Monologi medsestry." *Kinotsenarii* 5 (1994): 112–33.

Liusyi, A. P. *Krymskii tekst v russkoi literature.* St. Petersburg: Aleteiia, 2003.

Lopate, Phillip. "In Search of the Centaur: The Essay-Film." In Charles Warren, ed., *Beyond Document: Essays on Non-fiction Film.* Middletown, Conn.: Wesleyan University Press, 1998. 243–70.

Lotman, Iurii. "Poetika bytovogo povedeniia v russkoi kul'ture XVIII veka." *Trudy po znakovym sistemam* 8 (1977): 65–89.

———. "Simvolika Peterburga i problemy semiotiki goroda." In *Semiotika goroda i gorodskoi kul'tury: Peterburg. Tartu.* Special issue of *Trudy po znakovym sistemam* 18

(1984) in the series *Uchenye zapiski tartuskogo gos. Universiteta*, Issue . 664 (1984). Tartu: Tartuskii gosudarstvennyi universitet, 1984. 30–45.

Lotman, Yuri M. *Universe of the Mind: A Semiotic Theory of Culture.* Trans. Ann Shukman. Introduction by Umberto Eco. New York: I. B. Tauris, 1990.

Lovell, Stephen. *The Russian Reading Revolution: Print Culture in the Soviet and Post-Soviet Eras.* New York: St. Martin's, 2000.

Lunacharskii, Anatolii. "O frantsuzskoi drame." In Aleksandr Deich, ed., *A. V. Lunacharskii o teatre i dramaturgii: Izbrannye stat'i.* Vol. 2: *Zapadnoevropeiskii teatr.* Moscow: Iskusstvo, 1958. 255–60.

Lynch, Allen C. *How Russia Is Not Ruled: Reflections of Russian Political Development.* Cambridge, U.K.: Cambridge University Press, 2005.

MacCormick, Neil. "Does a Nation Need a State?" In Mortimer and Fine, eds., 125–37.

MacDonald, Gina. *Jane Austen on Screen.* Cambridge, U.K.: Cambridge University Press, 2003.

Maliukova, Larisa, comp. *90-e: Kino, kotoroe my poteriali.* Moscow: Zebra E, 2007.

Mann, Michael. "Nation-States in Europe and Other Continents: Diversifying, Developing, Not Dying." *Daedalus* 122.3 (1993): 115–40.

Manonni, Octave. "Je sais bien, mais quand-même . . ." In Slavoj Žižek, ed., *Jacques Lacan: Critical Evaluations in Cultural Theory.* Vol. 1: *Psychoanalytic Theory and Practice.* New York: Routledge, 2003. 125–44.

Mantsov, I. "Kollektivnoe telo kak romanticheskii geroi-liubovnik." *Iskusstvo kino* 8 (1994): 7–9.

Margolit, Evgenii. "Golyi nerv nereal'nosti." Russart.com, http://russart.com/?cid=2428.

———. "'Ia okom stal gliadet' boleznenno-otverstym . . .'" *Kinovedcheskie zapiski* 44 (1999): 17–20.

———. "Melodrama v sovetskom kino." In Liubov' Arkus, ed., *Noveishaia istoriia otechestvennogo kino: 1986–2000.* Vol. 6: *Kino i kontekst: 1992–1996.* St. Petersburg: Seans, 2004. 227–237.

Markov, Semen. "Kinoperestroika." *Novoe russkoe slovo*, September 26, 1987.

———. "Zriteli golosuiut nogami." *Novoe russkoe slovo*, June 5, 1987.

Markwick, Roger D. *Rewriting History in Soviet Russia: The Politics of Revisionist Historiography, 1956–1974.* New York: Palgrave, 2001.

Martin, Terry. *The Affirmative Action Empire: Nations and Nationalism in the Soviet Union, 1923–1939.* Ithaca, N.Y.: Cornell University Press, 2001.

———. "An Affirmative Action Empire: The Soviet Union as the Highest Form of Imperialism." In Suny and Martin, eds., 67–90.

———. "Modernization or Neo-traditionalism? Ascribed Nationality and Soviet Primordialism." In Hoffmann and Kotsonis, eds., 161–82.

Maslova, Lidiia. "Shest' siuzhetov v poiskakh smysla." *Iskusstvo kino* 2 (1998): 24–33.

Maternovsky, Denis. "Movie Stars Take Over the Subway." *Moscow Times*, December 29, 2003.

———. "U.S. Giant Joins the Battle of the Multiplexes." *Moscow Times*, September 23, 2003.

Matich, Olga, and Michael Heim, eds. *The Third Wave: Russian Literature in Emigration.* Ann Arbor, Mich.: Ardis, 1984.

Matizen, Viktor. "*Khrustalev, mashinu!*, nevedomyi shedevr." *Kino Park*, August 1998: 20–21.

——. "Steb kak fenomen kul'tury." *Iskusstvo kino* 9 (1993): 59–62.

Mau, Vladimir, and Irian Starodubrovskaya. *The Challenge of Revolution: Contemporary Russia in Historical Perspective.* Oxford: Oxford University Press, 2001.

Mayall, James. *Nationalism and International Society.* Cambridge, U.K.: Cambridge University Press, 1990.

McCausland, Gerald. "The Post-Soviet Conditions: Cultural Reconfigurations of Russian Identity." Ph.D. diss., University of Pittsburgh, 2006.

McDaniel, Tim. *The Agony of the Russian Idea.* Princeton, N.J.: Princeton University Press, 1996.

Mcnab, Geoffrey. "Aleksandr Sokurov's New Film Is an Upbeat Character Study of the Japanese Emperor Hirohito." *Sight and Sound* 15.9 (2005): 12–14.

McReynolds, Louise, and Joan Neuberger, eds. *Imitations of Life: Two Centuries of Melodrama in Russia.* Durham, N.C.: Duke University Press, 2002.

McReynolds, Louise, and Joan Neuberger. Introduction to McReynolds and Neuberger, eds., 1–24.

Mednis, N. E. *Russkie literaturnye sverkhteksty.* Novosibirsk: Novosibirskii gosudarstvennyi pedagogicheskii universitet, 2003.

Zhores Medvedev, Zhores. "Zagadka smerti Stalina." *Voprosy istorii* 1 (2000): 83–91.

Menashe, Louis. "Moscow Believes in Tears: The Problems (and Promise?) of Russian Cinema in the Transition Period." *Cineaste* 26.3 (2001): 10–17.

Mikhalkov, Nikita. "The Function of a National Cinema." Speech at the Fourth (Extraordinary) Congress of the Filmmakers' Union (May 29–30, 1998). Trans. Birgit Beumers. In Beumers, ed., 50–53.

——. "Ia sdelal kartinu dlia sta millionov inostrantsev, zhivushchikh v moei strane . . ." Interview with Liubov' Arkus. *Seans* 17–18 (1999): 18–19.

——. "Mne khotelos' ikh zashchitit' . . ." Conversation with El'ga Lyndina. *Ekran* 1 (1995): 1, 4–9.

——. "Rezhisser ne dolzhen dolgo nakhodit'sia pod obaianiem svoei kartiny: Eto opasno." *Iskusstvo kino* 3 (1995): 9–13.

——. "Tak konchaiutsia smutnye vremena." Interview with Valerii Kichin. *Novoe russkoe slovo*, July 21, 1998.

Mindadze, Aleksandr. *Vremia tantsora: Kinopovesti.* Moscow: Izdatel'stvo AST-LTD, 1997.

Minogue, Kenneth, and Beryl Williams. "Ethnic Conflict in the Soviet Union: The Revenge of Particularism." In Motyl, ed., 225–42.

Mitcham, S. W., Jr. *Why Hitler: The Genesis of the Nazi Reich.* Westport, Conn.: Praeger, 1996.

Mitchell, David T., and Sharon T. Snyder. *Narrative Prosthesis: Disability and the Dependencies of Discourse.* Ann Arbor: University of Michigan Press, 2000.

Mitrokhin, Nikolai. *Russkaia partiia: Dvizhenie russkikh natsionalistov v SSSR 1953–1985 gody.* Moscow: Novoe literaturnoe obozrenie, 2003.

"*Mne ne bol'no*: Kritiki o fil'me." *Seans* 29/30 (2006): 33–35.

Monroe, Robin. "Californian Brings Muscovites the Big Screen." *Moscow Times*, July 10, 2003.

Morozova, N. "Kira Muratova: Fikus—eto rastenie. I ne bolee togo." *Sovetskaia molodezh*, October 24, 1990.

Mortimer, Edward, with Robert Fine, eds. *People, Nation and State: The Meaning of Ethnicity and Nationalism*. London: I. B. Tauris, 1999.

Moskvina, Tat'iana. "Chelovek—gora." *Kul't lichnostei*, June–August 2002: 53–59.

———. "La Grande Illusion." In Beumers, ed., *Russia on Reels*. 91–104.

———. "Peremirie." In Arkus et al., eds., *Seans Guide*, 149–52. Reprinted from *Seans* 29/30 (2006): 36.

———. "Pro Ivana i Dzhona." *Iskusstvo kino* 7 (2002): 20–25.

———. "Russkaia mysl' v kitaiskikh stepiakh." In Maliukova, comp., 51–55.

Motyl, Alexander J. "Building Bridges and Changing Landmarks: Theory and Concepts in the Soviet Nationalities." In Motyl, ed., 255–70.

———. "Is Everything Empire? Is Empire Everything?" *Comparative Politics*, January 2006: 229–49.

———, ed. *Thinking Theoretically about Soviet Nationalities: History and Comparison in the Study of the USSR*. New York: Columbia University Press, 1992.

Mulvey, Laura. "Notes on Sirk and Melodrama." In Gledhill, ed., 75–79.

Monroe, Robin. "Californian Brings Muscovites the Big Screen." *Moscow Times*, 10 July 2003: 7.

Muratova, Kira. "Iskusstvo—eto utekha, otrada i opium." *Iskusstvo kino* 7 (1992): 13.

———. "Iskusstvo rodilos' iz zapretov, styda i strakha." Interview by Pavel Sirkes. *Iskusstvo kino* 2 (1995): 90–98.

———. "Mne vsegda khotelos' sdelat' tikhiii, skromnyi, normal'nyi fil'm . . ." Interview by Jane Knox-Voina and Vladimir Voina. *Iskusstvo kino* 11 (1997): 59–63.

Naiman, Anatolii. *Rasskazy o Anne Akhmatovoi*. 2nd ed. Moscow: Vagrius, 1999.

Naiman, Anatoly. *Remembering Anna Akhmatova*. Trans. Wendy Rosslyn. New York: Henry Holt, 1993.

Naiman, Eric. "On Soviet Subjects and the Scholars Who Make Them." *Russian Review* 60 (July 2001): 307–15.

Nairn, Tom. *After Britain: New Labour and the Return of Scotland*. London: Granta, 2000.

———. *The Break-up of Britain: Crisis and Neo-Nationalism*. 3rd ed. London: Common Ground, 2003.

Nepomnyashchy, Catharine Theimer. "Perestroika and the Soviet Creative Unions." In John O. Norman, ed., *New Perspectives on Russian and Soviet Artistic Culture*. London: St. Martin's, 1994. 131–51.

Neuberger, Joan. "Between Public and Private: Revolution and Melodrama in Nikita Mikhalkov's *Slave of Love*." In McReynolds and Neuberger, eds., 259–82.

Nicholson, Alex. "Pirate Peddlers Feel the Pinch." *Moscow Times*, July 17, 2003.

Nikolaevich, Sergei. "Nikita Mikhalkov: Dela semeinye." *Domovoi* 10 (1995): 45–60

Nivat, Georges, ed. *Odna ili dve russkikh literatury?* Lausanne, Switzerland: Éditions L'Age d'Homme, 1981.

Ogurtsov Sergei. "Vozhd' umiraet, no telo zhivet." *Vechernyi klub*, August 25, 2000.

Osnovnye napravleniia perestroiki sovetskogo kinematografa. Moscow. Typed, photocopied manuscript, December 1986.

Ozouf, Mona. *Festivals and the French Revolution*. Trans. Alan Sheridan. Cambridge, Mass.: Harvard University Press, 1991.

Pagden, Anthony. *Lords of All the World: Ideologies of Empire in Spain, Britain, and France, c. 1500–c. 1800.* New Haven, Conn.: Yale University Press, 1995.

Panofsky, Erwin. "Style and Medium in the Motion Pictures." 1934. In Gerald Mast and Marshall Cohen, eds., *Film Theory and Criticism.* 2nd ed. New York: Oxford University Press, 1979. 151–69.

Parrott, Bruce. "Analyzing the Transformation of the Soviet Union in Comparative Perspective." In *The End of Empire? The Transformation of the USSR in Comparative Perspective.* Ed. Dawisha and Parrott. 3–29.

Parry, Benita. *Delusions and Discoveries: Studies on India in the British Imagination, 1880–1930.* London: Allen Lane, 1972.

Parthé, Kathleen F. *Russian Village Prose: The Radiant Past.* Princeton, N.J.: Princeton University Press, 1992.

Passek, Jean-Loup, ed. *Le cinéma russe.* Paris: L'Equerre, 1981.

Pavlyshyn, Marko. "Ukrainian Literature and the Erotics of Postcolonialism: Some Modest Propositions." *Harvard Ukrainian Studies* 17.1–2 (1993): 110–26.

Pelevin, Viktor. *Omon Ra: Fantastika.* Moscow: Tekst, 1992.

Pesni. Leningrad: Muzgiz (Leningradskoe otdelenie), 1937.

Peterson, Nadya L. *Subversive Imaginations: Fantastic Prose and the End of Soviet Literature, 1970s–1990s.* Boulder, Colo.: Westview, 1997.

Petrie, Duncan, ed. *Screening Europe: Image and Identity in Contemporary European Cinema.* London: British Film Institute, 1992. 73–76.

Petrovskaja, Katja. "And He Saw: It Was Good." Roundtable on Alexander Sokurov's film *Russian Ark. Artmargins,* July 30, 2003. http://www.artmargins.com/content/cineview/roundtable.html.

Piatyi s"ezd kinematografistov SSSR, 13–15 maia 1986 goda: Stenograficheskii otchet. Moscow: Soiuz kinematografistov SSSR (Vsesoiuznoe biuro propagandy kinoiskusstva), 1987.

Picker, Henry, comp. *Hitlers Tischgespräche im Führerhauptquartier: Entstehung, Struktur, Folgen des Nationalsozialismus.* Berlin: Propyläen Auflage, 2003.

Pipes, Richard. "Introduction: The Nationality Problem." In Zev Katz, Rosemarie Rogers, and Frederic Harned, eds., *Handbook of Major Soviet Nationalities.* New York: Free Press, 1975. 1–4.

———. "Is Russia Still an Enemy?" *Foreign Affairs* 76.5 (1997): 65–78.

Plakhov, Andrei. "Une brève histoire des cinémas russes et soviétiques." In *Cinémas d'Europe du Nord: De Fritz Lang à Lars von Trier.* Ed. Lucy Lean, trans. Seth Graham and Guillaume Villeneuve. Paris: Arte Éditions, 1988. 195–231.

———. "Dva goda zhizni." *Sovetskii ekran* 10 (1988): 10.

———. "Kira Muratova: Vpolne marginal'naia maniia velichiia." In *Vsego 33: Zvezdy mirovoi kinorezhissury.* Vinnitsa: Akvilon, 1999. 201–12.

———. "Lekarstvo ot nostal'gii." In Maliukova, comp., 154–58.

———. "Mne nuzhna lozhka degtia." *Kommersant,* Nobvember 4, 1998.

———. "Soviet Cinema into the 90s." *Sight and Sound* 58 (Spring 1989): 82–83.

———. "Vtoroe rozhdenie." *Moskovskie novosti* 8 (February 22, 1987).

Plakhova, Elena. "Muratova i Madonna." *Iskusstvo kino* 9 (1997): 96–98.

Podoroga, V. "Molokh i Khrustalev: Materialy k noveishei istorii 'Peterburgskogo teksta.'" *Iskusstvo kino* 6 (2000): 56–71.

Polnoe sobranie zakonov Rossiiskoi Imperii s 1649 goda, Vol. 4. St. Petersburg: n.p., 1885.

Popov, Dmitrii. "Bog umer." *Iskusstvo kino* 3 (1990): 37–41.

"Portret: Aleksei Balabanov." Interviews with Balabanov, Viktor Sukhorukov, et al. *Seans* 17/18 (1999): 217–27.

Pozdniakov, Aleksandr. "Karknul voron: 'Nevermore.'" *Ekran i stsena* 42.510 (1999): 4.

Prigov, Dmitrii. *Texts of Our Lives/Teksty nashei zhizni*. Ed. and intro. Valentina Polukhina. Essays in Poetics 5. Series eds. Joe Andrew and Robert Reid. Keele, U.K.: Keele University, 1995.

Prizel, Ilya. *National Identity and Foreign Policy: Nationalism and Leadership in Poland, Russia, and Ukraine*. Cambridge, U.K.: Cambridge University Press, 1998.

Prokhorov, Alexander. "Soviet Family Melodrama of the 1940s and 1950s: From *Wait for Me* to *The Cranes Are Flying*." In McReynolds and Neuberger, eds., 208–31.

Prokhorova, Elena. "Svoi sredi chuzhikh, chuzhoi sredi svoikh/At Home among Strangers, A Stranger at Home." In Birgit Beumers, ed., *The Cinema of Russia*. 168–78.

Prokof'eva, Elena. *Koroleva ekrana: Istoriia Very Kholodnoi*. Moscow: Izdatel'skii dom IGS, 2001.

Pushkin, Aleksandr. *Sobranie sochinenii v desiati tomakh*. Vol. 10: Letters 1831–1837. Ed. V. Volina. Moscow: Khudozhestvennaia literatura, 1978.

"Putin Urges Government to Crack Down on Piracy." *Moscow Times*, November 4, 2003.

Quayson, Ato. "Looking Awry: Tropes of Disability in Post-Colonial Writing." In Rod Mengham, ed., *An Introduction to Contemporary Fiction*. Cambridge, U.K.: Polity Press, 1999. 53–98.

Radzinsky, Edvard. *Stalin: The First In-depth Biography, Based on New Documents from Russia's Secret Archives*. New York: Anchor, 1997.

Raeff, Marc. *Russia Abroad: A Cultural History of the Russian Emigration, 1919–1939*. New York: Oxford University Press, 1990.

Rakitina, K. Bibliography of works by and about Aleksandr Sokurov. *Kinograf* 3 (1997): 44–71.

Ram, Harsha. *The Imperial Sublime: A Russian Poetics of Empire*. Madison: University of Wisconsin Press, 2003.

Razguliaeva, Mariia. "Zheleznyi German." *Vecherniaia Moskva*, July 21, 2003.

Razlogov, Kirill. "Mezhdu Rossiei i zapadom." In V. P. Shestakov, comp., *Rossiia i zapad: Dialog ili stolknovenie kul'tur (sbornik statei)*. Moscow: Ministerstvo kul'tury Rossiiskoi federatsii (Rossiiskii institut kul'turologii), 2000. 33–54

Razzakov, F. *Nikita Mikhalkov: Chuzhoi sredi svoikh*. Moscow: Eksmo, 2005.

Rein, Evgenii. "Niania Tania." In *Temnota zerkal: Stikhotvoreniia i poemy*. Moscow: Sovetskii pisatel', 1990. 113–17.

Renan, Ernest. "Qu'est-ce qu'une nation?" In *Ernest Renan et l'Allemagne*. Ed. Émile Buré. New York: Brentano's, 1945.

Reports and commentary on the Fifth USSR Film Workers' Congress. *Current Digest of the Soviet Press* 38.20 (1986): 1–8, 20.

Reynolds, Andrew. "Returning the Ticket: Joseph Brodsky's 'August' and the End of the Petersburg Text?" *Slavic Review* 64.2 (2005): 307–32.

Rezanov, G., and T. Khoroshilova. "Ismail Tagi-zade, chelovek, kotoryi mozhet kupit' sovetskoe kino." *Komsomol'skaia Pravda*, September 28, 1991.

Riasanovsky, Nicholas. *Nicholas I and Official Nationality*. Berkeley: University of California Press, 1959.

Richardson, Paul. "Film Flam." *Russian Life*, July–August 2007: 7.

Richters, Katja. "The Moscow Patriarchate in Estonia: Russian versus International Concerns." *Problems of Post-Communism*. January–February 2008: 3–11.

Rifkin, Benjamin. *Semiotics of Narration in Film and Prose: Case Studies of "Scarecrow" and "My Friend Ivan Lapshin."* Russian and East European Studies in Aesthetics and the Philosophy of Culture Series, vol. 2. Willis H. Truitt, general editor. New York: Peter Lang, 1994.

Robinson, David. "Films That Came in from the Cold." *The Times*, December 1, 1986.

Rogger, Hans. *National Consciousness in Eighteenth-Century Russia*. Cambridge, Mass.: Harvard University Press, 1960.

Romm, Mikhail. "Kinematograf v riadu iskusstv." *Iskusstvo kino* 12 (2001): 56–63.

Romney, Jonathan. "Brat-Pack." *New Statesman*, April 10, 2000. http://www.newstatesman.com/200004100043.

———. "Of Freaks and Men." *Sight and Sound* 10.5 (2000): 53. http://www.bfi.org.uk/sightandsound/review/464/.

Rosecrance, Richard. *The Rise of the Trading State: Commerce and Conquest in the Modern World*. New York: Basic Books, 1986.

Rosenholm, Arja and Sari Autio-Sarasmo, eds. *Understanding Russian Nature: Representations, Values and Concepts*. Helsinki: Kikimora, 2005.

Rtishcheva, Natal'ia. "Dos'e prem'ery: *Utomlennye solntsem*." *Chital'nyi zal* 1 (1995): 108.

Rubanova, Irina. Unpublished manuscript.

Rubenstein, Joshua, and Valdimir P. Naumov, eds. *Stalin's Secret Pogrom: The Postwar Inquisition of the Jewish Anti-Fascist Committee*. Trans. Laura Esther Wolfson. New Haven, Conn.: Yale University Press, 2005.

Rudnev, Oleg. "Kakoe kino nam propishet doktor Tagi-zade?" *Izvestiia*, May 6, 1991.

Rudnitskii, Konstantin. "O chem? Vo imia chego?" *Sovetskii ekran* 1 (1975): 2.

Rudnitsky, Konstantin. *Russian and Soviet Theatre: Tradition and the Avant-Garde*. London: Thames and Hudson, 1988.

Rywkin, Michael. "The Russia-Wide Soviet Federated Socialist Republic (RSFSR): Privileged or Under-Privileged?" In Edward Allworth, ed., *Ethnic Russia in the USSR: The Dilemma of Dominance*. New York: Pergamon, 1980. 179–87.

Sabrodin, Vladimir, and Karin Messlinger, eds. *Amazonen der Avantgarde im Film*. Berlin: Die Kinemathek, 1999.

Said, Edward. *Culture and Imperialism*. London: Chatto and Windus, 1993.

———. *Orientalism*. New York: Vintage, 1978.

Sales, Roger. *Jane Austen and Representations of Regency England*. New York: Routledge, 1994.

Sandler, A. M., ed. *Nikita Mikhalkov: Sbornik*. Moscow: Iskusstvo, 1989.

Savel'ev, Dmitrii. "Krugi razzhalovannogo." In Arkus and Savel'ev, eds., 59–62.

———. "Out of Ideology: The Post-Soviet Melodrama." Trans. Vladimir Padunov. *Kinokultura*, July 2007. http://www.kinokultura.com/index.html.

Scanlan, James P., ed. *Russian Thought after Communism: The Recovery of a Philosophical Heritage*. Armonk, N.Y.: M. E. Sharpe, 1994.

Schmemann, Serge. "Some Soviet Films Belie the Old Political Stereotype." *New York Times*, October 24, 1982.

———. "Winds of Change Stir Soviet Film." *New York Times*, October 12, 1986.

Schmid, Ulrich. "The Empire Strikes Back: Sokurov Takes Revenge on de Custine." *Artmargins*, July 30, 2003. http://www.artmargins.com/content/cineview/roundtable.html.

Schuman, Howard, and Jacqueline Scott. "Generations and Collective Memories." *American Psychological Review* 54 (1989): 359–81.

Seckler, Dawn (unsigned). "Brother 2." http://www.rusfilm.pitt.edu/2001/brat.html.

Segida, Miroslava. "72 Lenina i 172 Dzhigarkhaniana." *Novoe russkoe slovo*, September 20–21, 1997.

———. "Segida-info." *Iskusstvo kino* 4 (1996): 73–76.

Segida, Miroslava, and Sergei Zemlianukhin, comps. *Domashniaia sinemateka: Otechestvennoe kino, 1918–1996*. Moscow: Dubl'-D, 1996.

———. *Fil'my Rossii: Igrovoe kino/TV/video (1992–2003)*. Moscow: Dubl'-D, 2004.

Serebrennikov, Kirill. "*Solntse*: Portret fil'ma." *Seans* 25–26 (2005): 151.

Seton-Watson, Hugh. *Nations and States: An Inquiry into the Origins of Nations and the Politics of Nationalism*. Boulder, Colo.: Westview Press, 1977.

———. *The Russian Empire, 1801–1917*. Oxford: Oxford University Press, 1967.

Shafarevich, Igor'. *Rusofobiia*. Moscow: Eksmo, 2005.

Schama, Simon. *Landscape and Memory*. New York: Knopf, 1995.

Shatina, Z. G., and V. N. Antropov, comps. *Khudozhestvennye fil'my: Katalog literaturnykh ekranizatsii (900 imen)*. Moscow: Golden Bi, 2005.

Shaw, Bernard. *Bernard Shaw's Plays*. Ed. Warren S. Smith. Norton Critical Edition. New York: Norton, 1970.

———. *The Bodley Head Bernard Shaw: Collected Plays with Their Prefaces*. Ed. Dan H. Laurence. 7 vols. London: Max Reinhardt, The Bodley Head, 1970–74.

Shchigolev, Andrei. "Dezha viu, ili kuda privodiat mechty." *Iskusstvo kino* 3 (2001): 33–35.

Shemiakin, A. "Akvariumnye ryby etogo mira." *Iskusstvo kino* 9 (1993): 105–10.

Shepotinnik, Petr. "Nostal'giia ne otmeniaetsia." *Seans* 9 (1994): 20.

Shervud, Ol'ga. "Trudno byt' Germanom." *Itogi*, June 24, 2003.

Shilova, Irina. "Karnaval, ne znaiushchii raia." *Kinovedcheskie zapiski* 44 (1999): 6–8.

———. "O melodrame." *Voprosy kinoiskusstva* 17 (1976): 112–35.

———. "P'esa 'dlia passazhira' i . . . kritikov." *Chital'nyi zal* 1 (1995): 113–16.

———. "Posle posmotra." In *Rezonans*. Moscow: Soiuzinformkino, 1988.

———. "Renata Litvinova: Actress and Persona." *Kinokultura* 19 (January 2008). http://www.kinokultura.com/2008/19-shilova.shtml.

———. "V poiskakh utrachennoi liubvi." *Kinotsenarii* 2 (1989): 186–87.

Shiverskaia, Natal'ia. "Zhivye liudi—eto ochen' opasno." *Vremia*, June 6, 2001.

Shklovskii, Viktor. *Khod konia: Sbornik statei*. Moscow: Gelikov, 1923.

Shmarina, L. "Shlagbaumy na dorogakh." In *Iz proshlogo v budushchee: Proverka na dorogakh. Ob istorizme kino*. Moscow: VNIIK, 1990.

Shpagin, Aleksandr. "Averbakh." http://mega.km.ru/cinema/encyclop.asp?TopicNumber=5746

Shteppa, K. F. *Russian Historians and the Soviet State*. New Brunswick, N.J.: Rutgers University Press, 1962.

Shvarts, Evgenii. *P'esy.* Ed. K. M. Uspenskaia. Leningrad: Sovetskii pisatel', 1982.

Siladi, Akosh (Szilàgyi, Akos). "Sto let smerti." *Kinovedcheskie zapiski* 44 (1999): 28–36.

Simmons, Ernest J. *Chekhov: A Biography.* Boston: Little, Brown, 1962.

Singer, Ben. *Melodrama and Modernity: Early Sensational Cinema and Its Contexts.* New York: Columbia University Press, 2001.

Sinyavsky, Andrei. *Soviet Civilization: A Cultural History.* Trans. Joanne Turnbull with Nikolai Formozov. New York: Arcade, 1990.

Sirivlia, N. "'Temnye sily nas zlobno gnetut.'" *Iskusstvo kino* 11 (1991): 38–46.

Sirkes, P. "Kira Muratova: Iskusstvo rodilos' iz zapretov, styda i strakha." *Iskusstvo kino* 2 (1995): 90–98.

Slezkine, Yuri. "The USSR as a Communal Apartment, or How a Socialist State Promoted Ethnic Particularism." *Slavic Review* 53.2 (1994): 414–52.

Slobin, Greta. "The 'Homecoming' of the First Wave Diaspora and Its Cultural Legacy." *Slavic Review* 60.3 (2001): 513–29.

Smirnov, Igor'. "Totalitarnaia kul'tura, ili mazokhism." In *Psikhodiakhronologika: psikhistoriia russkoi literatury ot romantizma do nashikh dnei.* Moscow: Novoe literaturnoe obozrenie, 1994. 231–314.

Smirnov, Sergei. *Rasskazy o neizvestnykh geroiakh.* Moscow: Molodaia gvardiia, 1964.

Smith, Anthony D. *The Ethnic Origins of Nations.* Oxford: Basil Blackwell, 1986.

———. "The Nation: Real or Imagined?" In Mortimer and Fine, eds., 36–42.

———. *Theories of Nationalism.* New York: Holms and Meier, 1983.

Smith, Graham. *The Post-Soviet States: Mapping the Politics of Transition.* New York: Oxford University Press, 1999.

Smith, Tony. *The Pattern of Imperialism: The United States, Great Britain, and the Late-Industrializing World Since 1815.* New York: Cambridge University Press, 1981.

Sokurov, Aleksandr. "Avtory o svoei rabote." In *Skorbnoe beschuvstvie.* Restored DVD version. Krupnyi plan, 2005.

———. "Death, the Banal Leveller (on Tarkovsky)." *Film Studies* 1 (Spring 1999): 64–69.

———. "Glavnym iskusstvom po-prezhnemu ostaetsia literatura . . ." *Kinovedcheskie zapiski* 23 (1994): 65–75.

———. "In One Breath: The Making of *Russian Ark*." Interview on DVD copy of *Russian Ark.* 2002.

———. "An Interview with Aleksandr Sokurov." Interview by Jeremy Szaniawski. *Critical Quarterly* 33.1 (2006): 13–27.

———. "Izobrazhenie i montazh." Interview by Dmitrii Savel'ev. *Iskusstvo kino* 12 (1997): 110–23.

———. "*Molokh*: Interview with Alexander Sokurov." Interview on DVD copy of *Molokh.* 1999.

———. "Nastoiashchee iskusstvo predlagaet uzkii krug." Interview by Dmitrii Savel'ev. *Iskusstvo kino* 4 (2005): 95–104.

———. "The Solitary Voice: An Interview with Aleksandr Sokurov." Interview by Edwin Carels. *Film Studies* 1 (Spring 1999): 73–77.

———. "Teni zvuka." Television interview for TV-6 Moscow with Petr Shepotinnik, Asia Kolodizhner, and Liubov' Arkus. *Iskusstvo kino* 12 (1994): 13–17.

———. "*Tiutchev.*" In Arkus, ed., 452–55.

————. "Tvorcheskii alfavit." *Kinograf* 3 (1997): 72–94.

Solchanyk, Roman. "Russia, Ukraine, and the Imperial Legacy." *Post-Soviet Affairs* 9.4 (1993): 337–65.

"*Solntse*: Portret fil'ma." *Seans* 25–26 (2005): 142–90.

Solov'ev, Vladimir. "Russkaia ideia." Trans. G. A. Rachinskii. In *Sobranie sochinenii*. 14 vols. Brussels: Zhizn' s bogom, 1969. 11:91–117.

Sontag, Susan. *Illness as Metaphor*. New York: Vintage, 1979.

Spector, Michael. "Moscow on the Make." *New York Times Magazine,* June 1, 1997. http://www.michaelspecter.com/times/1997/1997_06_01_mag_moscow.html.

Spravochnik "Kinofestivali Rossii." A publication of the Guild of Film Directors of Russia. Moscow: Kinogil'diia, 2003.

Stalin, J. V. "Marxism and the National Question." In *Works*. 13 vols. Moscow: Foreign Language Publishing House, 1954. 2:300–81.

Stishova, Elena. "Chasti rechi." *Iskusstvo kino* 6 (2002): 47–50.

————. "Konets sezona." *Iskusstvo kino* 12 (1991): 83–86.

————. "Vyshli my vse iz naroda." *Iskusstvo kino* 8 (2003): 23–27.

Stites, Richard. "The Misanthrope, the Orphan, and the Magpie: Imported Melodrama in the Twilight of Serfdom." In McReynolds and Neuberger, eds., 25–54.

————. *Serfdom, Society, and the Arts in Imperial Russia: The Pleasure and the Power*. New Haven, Conn.: Yale University Press, 2005.

Stone, Judy. "A First Glimpse at Banned Soviet Movies." Review of the 1987 San Francisco International Film Festival. *Datebook,* March 29, 1987.

————. "Soviet Director Bids Farewell to Censorship." *San Francisco Chronicle*, October 11, 1987.

Strauss, William, and Neil Howe. *The Fourth Turning*. New York: Broadway, 1997.

Strauss, William, and Neil Howe. *Generations: The History of America's Future, 1584 to 2069*. New York: William Morrow, 1991.

Sul'kin, Oleg. "Khrustalev, *Niku!" Novoe russkoe slovo,* April 28, 2000.

————. "Renata Litvinova obozhaet dukhi 'Krasnaia Moskva': Portret russkoi divy na fone skuchnykh voprosov." Essay on and interview with Renata Litvinova. *Novoe russkoe slovo,* September 16, 1997.

————. "*Vremia tantsora* prishlo v Ameriku." Article and interview with Vadim Abdrashitov. *Novoe russkoe slovo,* October 22, 1997.

[Sul'kin, Oleg]. "'Gorbushku' mogila ispravit?" *Novoe russkoe slovo,* December 23–24, 2000.

Suminova, T. N. *Nikita Mikhalkov: Fil'mograficheskii i bibliograficheskii ukazatel'*. Moscow: Studiia "TRITE," Russkii Arkhiv, 1995.

Suny, Ronald Grigor. "Ambiguous Categories: States, Empires and Nations." *Post-Soviet Affairs* 11.2 (1995): 185–96.

————. "The Empire Strikes Out! Imperial Russia, 'National' Identity, and Theories of Empire." In Suny and Martin, eds., 23–66.

————. "History." In *Encyclopedia of Nationalism*. Vol. 1: *Fundamental Themes*. Ed. Alexander J. Motyl. San Diego: Academic Press, 2001. 335–58.

————. *Revenge of the Past: Nationalism, Revolution, and the Collapse of the Soviet Union*. Stanford: Stanford University Press, 1993.

Suny, Ronald Grigor, and Terry Martin, eds. *A State of Nations: Empire and Nation-Making in the Age of Lenin and Stalin*. Oxford: Oxford University Press, 2001.

Surkova, Ol'ga. "K voprosu o 'iasnoi idee.'" *Iskusstvo kino* 5 (1998): 66–67.

Sutotskaya, Eleonora. "And the Loser Is . . . Russian Cinema." *Russian Life*, August 1995: 12–13.

Synessios, Natasha. *Mirror*. KINOfiles Film Companion 6. London: I. B. Tauris, 2001.

Szporluk, Roman. "After Empire: What?" *Daedalus* 123.3 (1994): 21–39.

———. "The Russian Question and Imperial Overextension." In Dawisha and Parrott, eds., 65–93.

Taagepera, Rein. "Size and Duration of Empires: Systematics of Size." *Social Science Research* 7 (1978): 108–27.

Taroshchina, S. "Mstia moia strashna." *Literaturnaia gazeta*, February 15, 1995.

Taruskin, Richard. *Defining Russia Musically: Historical and Hermeneutical Essays*. Princeton, N.J.: Princeton University Press, 1997.

Taubman, Jane A. "The Cinema of Kira Muratova." *Russian Review* 52 (1993): 367–81.

———. *Kira Muratova*. KINOfiles Filmmakers' Companions 4. London: I. B. Tauris, 2005.

Taylor, Richard. *October*. London: British Film Institute, 2002.

Taylor, Richard, and Ian Christie. *The Film Factory: Russian and Soviet Cinema in Documents 1896–1939*. New York: Routledge, 1994.

Telingater, Helena. "Film Exposition Short on Classics." *We/My*, March 8–21, 1993: 13.

Thompson, Ewa M. *Imperial Knowledge: Russian Literature and Colonialism*. Westport, Conn.: Greenwood Press, 2000.

Tillett, Lowell. *The Great Friendship: Soviet Historians on the Non-Russian Nationalities*. Chapel Hill: University of North Carolina Press, 1969.

Timenchik, R. D., V. N. Toporov, and T. V. Tsiv'ian. "Sny Bloka i 'Peterburgskii tekst' nachala XX veka." In Z. G. Mints, ed., *Tezisy I Vsesoiuznoi (III) konferentsii "Tvorchestvo A. A. Bloka i russkaia kul'tura XX veka."* Tartu: Tartuskii gosudarstvennyi universitet, 1975. 129–35.

Tirdatova, Evgeniia. "V ritme tango." *Ekran i stsena* 33–34 (1994): 4.

Tishkov, Valerii. *Obshchestvo v vooruzhennom konflikte (etnografiia chechenskoi voiny)*. Moscow: Nauka, 2001.

Tishkov, Valery, and Martha Brill Olcott. "From Ethnos to Demos: The Quest for Russia's Identity." In Anders Åslund and Martha Brill Olcott, eds., *Russia after Communism*. Washington, D.C.: Brookings Institution Press, 1999. 61–90.

Tkachenko, Inna, with commentary by Pavel Lobkov. "Iz Peterburga—v Moskvu, v Moskvu!" *Iskusstvo kino* 4 (1999): 84–95.

Tolstaia, Tat'iana. "Globus glazami dvukhmernoi bloshki." *Novoe russkoe slovo*, November 9, 1999.

Tolz, Vera. "Conflicting 'Homeland Myths' and Nation-State Building in Postcommunist Russia." *Slavic Review* 57 (Summer 1998): 267–94.

———. *Russia: Inventing the Nation*. New York: Oxford University Press, 2001.

Toporov, V. N. "O strukture romana Dostoevskogo v sviazi s arkhaicheskimi skhemami mifologicheskogo myshleniia." In Jan van der Eng and Mojmír Grygar, eds., *Structure of Texts and Semiotics of Culture*. Slavistic Printings and Reprintings 294. The Hague: Mouton, 1973. 225–302.

———. "Peterburg i peterburgskii tekst russkoi literatury." In *Semiotika goroda i gorodskoi kul'tury: Peterburg. Tartu.* Special issue of *Trudy po znakovym sistemam* 18 (1984) in the series *Uchenye zapiski tartuskogo gos. Universiteta,* Vyp. 664 (1984). Tartu: Tartuskii gosudarstvennyi universitet, 1984. 4–29.

Totaro, Donato. "Staring into the Soul: Aleksandr Sokurov's *Povinnost'*." *Central European Review* 2.3 (2000). http://www.ce-review.org/00/3/kinoeye3_totaro.html.

Trofimenkov, Mikhail. "Nigde i vsegda: *Dni zatmeniia*." In Arkus and Savel'ev, eds., 129–30.

———. "Origin of the Species: Post-Soviet Melodrama." Trans. Gerald McCausland. *Kinokultura,* July 2007. http://www.kinokultura.com/index.html.

———. "Ostanovilsia poezd." *Seans* 11 (1995): 6.

Troost, Linda, and Sayre Greenfield, eds. *Jane Austen in Hollywood.* Lexington: University of Kentucky Press, 2001.

Tsyrkun, Nina. "Kira Muratova: 'A mne naplevat', chto vam naplevat', chto mne naplevat'.'" *Novoe russkoe slovo,* July 6–7, 2002.

Tuminez, Astrid. *Russian Nationalism Since 1856: Ideology and the Making of Foreign Policy.* New York: Rowman & Littlefield, 2000.

Turovskaia, Maiia. "Na korable Kapitana Shotovera." *Sovetskaia kul'tura,* August 4, 1987.

———. "*Sonata dlia Gitlera*." In Arkus and Savel'ev, eds., 147–48.

Ulbandus. Special issue on "Empire, Union, Center, Satellite: The Place of Post-Colonial theory in Slavic/Central and Eastern European/(Post-) Soviet Studies." Ed. Jonathan Brooks Platt. 7 (2003)

Ustiian, Gennadii. "Rokovoe vlechenie." *Seans* 17/18 (1999): 49.

"V poiskakh molodogo." Proceedings of Young Filmmakers' Meeting (April 23, 1996). *Iskusstvo kino* 7 (1996): 24–33.

Vail', Petr. "'Trudno byt' bogom,' skazal tabachnik s Tabachnoi ulitsy." *Iskusstvo kino* 8 (2000): 4–20.

Valentino, Russell Scott. "Adapting the Landscape: Oblomov's Vision in Film." In Hutchings and Vernitski, eds. 153–63.

Vasil'eva, Zhanna. "Chrevo kita: O fil'me Alekseia Germana *Khrustalev, mashinu!*" *Kul'tura* 36.7196 (1999).

———. "Leonid Mozgovoi: Idti ot sebia—no kak mozhno dal'she." Interview with actor Leonid Mozgovoi. *Literaturnaia gazeta,* March 28, 2001.

Venzher, Natal'ia. "Ekonomika vyzhivaniia zastavliaet kinoteatry zabyt' o prokate." *Lium'er ekspress* 0 (February 1995): 18–19.

———. ". . . Vyderzhivaiut tol'ko samye stoikie." *Literaturnaia gazeta,* May 26, 1993.

Venzher, N., D. Dondurei, and V. Dubitskaia, "Kinematograf v Rossii: problemy vyzhivaniia." In N. Venzher and G. Reisner, comps., *Kino. TV. Partnery '93.* Moscow: Dubl'-D, MAI, 1993. 7–60.

Vershbow, Alexander. "Piracy against Progress." *Moscow Times,* November 25, 2003.

Verdery, Katherine. "Whither 'Nation' and 'Nationalism'?" *Daedalus* 122.3 (1993): 37–46.

[Veselaia, Elena]. "Novaia metla." *Moskovskie novosti* 85 (December 10–17, 1995).

Vicinus, Martha. "Helpless and Unfriended: Nineteenth-Century Domestic Melodrama." *New Literary History* 13 (1981): 127–43.

Volodarskii, E. *Proverka na dorogakh. Kinostsenarii* 3 (1995): 4–37.

von Geldern, James. *Bolshevik Festivals 1917–1920*. Berkeley: University of California Press, 1993.

Von Szeliski, John J. "Lunacharsky and the Rescue of Soviet Theatre." Special International Theatre Issue. *Educational Theatre Journal* 18.4 (1966): 412–20.

Walsh, Nick Paton. "Russian Cinema Holds Out for a New Type of Hero." *The Guardian*, September 29, 2002.

Wells, H. G. "The Dreamer in the Kremlin." *New York Times*. December 5, 1920. http://query.nytimes.com/gst/abstract.html?res=9B04E5DE1F30E433A25756C0A9649D946195D6CF.

Werth, Paul. "Georgian Autocephaly and the Ethnic Fragmentation of Orthodoxy." *Acta Slavica Japonica* 23 (2006): 74–100.

Whitney, Craig. "Yeltsin Appears in Public to Honor a Hero of the Past." *New York Times*, October 24, 1993.

Whittaker, Cynthia. *The Origins of Modern Russian Education: An Intellectual Biography of Count Sergei Uvarov, 1786–1855*. DeKalb: North Illinois University Press, 1984.

"Who's Who in Soviet Film Industry." *Variety*, July 5–11, 1989.

Williams, Raymond. *Keywords*. London: Fontana, 1976.

Woll, Josephine. *Real Images: Soviet Cinema and the Thaw*. London: I. B. Taurus, 2000.

Wood, Tony. "Time Unfrozen: The Films of Aleksei German." *New Left Review* 7 (January–February 2001): 99–107.

Young, Deborah. "The Name of the Game Is Capitalism." *Variety*, July 8, 1991.

———. "Soviet Filmers Abolish States' Censor System." *Variety*, October 1, 1986.

Youngblood, Denise. *Russian War Films: On the Cinema Front, 1914–2005*. Lawrence: University Press of Kansas, 2007.

Zel'venskii, S. "Gde ia ne budu nikogda." *Seans* 27/28 (2006): 9–11.

Zernatto, Guido. "Nation: The History of a Word." *Review of Politics* 6.3 (1944). 351–66.

Zimmer, Oliver, and Eric Kaufmann. "In Search of the Authentic Nation: Landscape and National Identity in Canada and Switzerland." *Nations and Nationalism* 4.4 (1998): 483–510.

Ziukov, B. B., ed. *Vera Kholodnaia: K 100-letiiu so dnia rozhdeniia*. Moscow: Iskusstvo, 1995.

Zorin, Andrei. "Kruche, kruche, kruche . . . Istoriia pobedy: Chernukha v kul'ture poslednikh let." *Znamia* 10 (1992): 198–204.

Zorkaia, Neia. "Aleksei German." Issue 1 in the Series *Predstavliaem molodykh*. Moscow: Soiuzinformkino, 1978.

Index